An Introduction to

Music and Art

in the Western World

An Introduction to

Music and Art

in the Western World

Tenth Edition

Milo Wold
Linfield College, Emeritus

Gary Martin
University of Oregon

James Miller
University of Oregon

Edmund Cykler

Brown & Benchmark
PUBLISHERS

Madison   Dubuque, IA   Guilford, CT   Chicago   Toronto London
Caracas   Mexico City   Buenos Aires   Madrid   Bogota Sydney

Book Team

Publisher *Rosemary Bradley*
Developmental Editor *Deborah Daniel Reinbold*
Production Editor *Kristine Queck*
Proofreading Coordinator *Carrie Barker*
Designer *Kristyn Kalnes*
Art Editor *Miriam Hoffman*
Photo Editor *Rose Deluhery*
Permissions Coordinator *Lu Ann Wilson*
Production Manager *Beth Kundert*
Production/Costing Manager *Sherry Padden*
Marketing Manager *Kirk Moen*
Copywriter *Jennifer Smith*

Basal Text *10.5/12.5 Garamond*
Display Type *GillSans*
Typesetting System *Macintosh/QuarkXPress*
Paper Stock *50# Courtland Matte*

President and Chief Executive Officer *Thomas E. Doran*
Vice President of Production and Business Development *Vickie Putman*
Vice President of Sales and Marketing *Bob McLaughlin*
Director of Marketing *John Finn*

 A Times Mirror Company

Cover design by *Anna Manhart*

Cover image: Judith Leyster, *Self Portrait,* c. 1630. Oil on canvas, 29 3/8 × 25 5/8. © 1995 Board of Trustees, National Gallery of Art, Washington, Gift of Mr. and Mrs. Robert Woods Bliss (detail). Photo by Lorene Emerson.

New art for this edition rendered by A & R Editions, Inc., includes examples 2.1, 2.2, 6.2, 6.4, 8.3a, and text art on pages 20 and 259.

Copyedited by *Michelle Campbell;* proofread by *Sarah Greer Bush*

Contents

‥‥◄●◉●►‥‥

Preface *xi*
Key to Pronunciation *xiii*

‥‥◄●◉●►‥‥

Chapter **1**

The Arts and Society 1

Pronunciation Guide *1*
Study Objectives *1*
Sociocultural Aspects of the Arts **1**
The Functions of the Arts **4**
Art Periods **5**
A Laboratory of Experience **6**
Summary *8*
Suggested Readings *8*

‥‥◄●◉●►‥‥

Chapter **2**

The Organization of the Elements of the Visual Arts and Music 9

Pronunciation Guide *9*
Study Objectives *9*
The Aesthetic Response **10**
Elements and Materials of the Visual Arts **12**
  Medium 12
  Line 12
  Space 13
  Color 14
  Principles of Organization 15
  Expressive Content in Visual Art 17
  Style 17

|| **A CLOSER LOOK:** Raphael, *Sistine Madonna* 18
Elements and Materials of Music **19**
  Rhythm 19
  Pitch 22
  Melody 23
  Texture 24
  Harmony 27
  Dynamics 27
  Tone Color 28
  Formal Organization 29
  Expressive Content in Music 29

    || **A CLOSER LOOK:** Mozart, *Eine kleine Nachtmusik* 30
A Suggested Analogy **31**
Summary *32*
Suggested Readings *32*

‥‥◄●◉●►‥‥

Chapter **3**

The Greeks and Their Predecessors (Antiquity–100 B.C.) 33

Chronology *33*
Pronunciation Guide *34*
Study Objectives *34*
Paleolithic Period **34**
  Egypt 36
  Crete and the Aegean 42
  Greece 43
Architecture **46**
    || **A CLOSER LOOK:** Parthenon 48
Sculpture **50**
Painting **56**

Music 58
Summary 60
Suggested Readings 61

Chapter **4**

The Roman Empire and the Early Christians (100 B.C.–A.D. 500) 62

Chronology 62
Pronunciation Guide 63
Study Objectives 63
Roman Architecture 65
Roman Sculpture 69
Roman Music 73
Early Christian Art 74
Early Christian Music 77
Summary 79
Suggested Readings 79

Chapter **5**

The Medieval Period—Romanesque (500–1100) 80

Chronology 80
Pronunciation Guide 80
Study Objectives 81
The Medieval Period: General Characteristics 81
The Church and Medieval Art 85
The Romanesque Period 88
  Architecture 88
  Sculpture 91
  Painting 92
  Music 94
Summary 99
Suggested Readings 101

Chapter **6**

The Medieval Period—Gothic (1100–1400) 102

Chronology 102
Pronunciation Guide 102
Study Objectives 103
Architecture 106
  || A CLOSER LOOK: Reims Cathedral 109
Stained Glass 113
Sculpture 115
Painting 117
Music 119
  || A CLOSER LOOK: Machaut, *Messe de Notre Dame* (Kyrie) 122
Summary 126
Suggested Readings 127

Chapter **7**

The Renaissance (1400–1600) 128

Chronology 128
Pronunciation Guide 129
Study Objectives 130
Painting 135
  Fra Angelico 135
  Botticelli 136
    || A CLOSER LOOK: Botticelli, *Adoration of the Magi* 137
  Leonardo da Vinci 138
  Michelangelo 140
  Titian 142
  Raphael 142
  Albrecht Dürer 143
  Mathias Grünewald 143
  Pieter Brueghel 145
Sculpture 145
  Donatello 145
  Michelangelo 147

Properzia dé Rossi   148
Tilman Riemenschneider   148

Architecture   149

Music   153
Sacred Music   154
Josquin Desprez 155
Palestrina 156
Music of the Protestant Church 156
Secular Music   157

|| A CLOSER LOOK: Bennet, *Thyrsis? Sleepest Thou?*   159

Mannerism—A Transition in Art and Music   163

Summary   164
Suggested Readings   166

...◗◉◖...

Chapter **8**

The Baroque and Rococo Periods (1600–1775)   167

Chronology   167
Pronunciation Guide   169
Study Objectives   170
The Spirit of the Baroque   170
Painting   175
Tintoretto   175
Rembrandt   176

|| A CLOSER LOOK: Rembrandt, *The Night Watch*   177

Rubens   180
Velásquez   181
Peeters   182
Pozzo   182

Sculpture   182
Architecture   186
Music   194
Vocal Music   196
Monteverdi 197
Gabrieli 198
Schütz 198

Instrumental Music   199
Homophonic Texture—Instrumental 199
Corelli 201
Vivaldi 201
Polyphonic Texture—Instrumental 204
Bach 204

|| A CLOSER LOOK: Bach, *Cantata No. 4*   207

Handel   209

The Rococo Period   211
Painting   213
Watteau   214
Boucher   214
Sculpture   215
Architecture   216
Music   217

Summary   217
Suggested Readings   220

...◗◉◖...

Chapter **9**

The Classic Period (1750–1800)   221

Chronology   221
Pronunciation Guide   222
Study Objectives   222
Neoclassicism in the Visual Arts   222
Painting   223
David 223
Charpentier 224
Ingres 224
Benjamin West 224
Sculpture   225

Classicism in Music   225
Haydn   229

|| A CLOSER LOOK: Haydn, *Symphony no. 101 in D*   230

Mozart   233

Summary   238
Suggested Readings   239

Chapter **10**

The Romantic Period (1800–1900) 240

Chronology 240
Pronunciation Guide 242
Study Objectives 242
Romanticism 242
Painting 245
  Géricault 246
  Delacroix 246
  Benoist 247
  Goya 248
  Turner 248

  || A CLOSER LOOK: Turner, *Rain, Steam, and Speed: The Great Western Railway* 249

  Corot 250
Architecture 250
Music 251
  Beethoven 254

  || A CLOSER LOOK: Beethoven, *Symphony no. 3 in E-flat Major* 255

  Schubert 257

  || A CLOSER LOOK: Schubert, *Erlkönig* 258

  Fanny Mendelssohn-Hensel, Felix Mendelssohn, Frédéric Chopin, Robert Schumann, Clara Schumann 262
  Brahms, Mahler, Verdi, Puccini 264
Summary 266
Suggested Readings 268

Chapter **11**

Nineteenth-Century Realism and Nationalism (1840–1900) 269

Pronunciation Guide 269
Study Objectives 269

Visual Realism 270
  Courbet 270
  Daumier 271
  Eakins 271
  Thompson 272
  Homer 272
Realism in Music 272
  Berlioz 273

  || A CLOSER LOOK: Berlioz, *Symphonie fantastique* 273

  Wagner 277
  Liszt, Richard Strauss 278
Nineteenth-Century Nationalism 280
  Smetana 281
  The Russian Five 282
  Tchaikovsky, Mussorgsky 283
Summary 284
Suggested Readings 285

Chapter **12**

Impressionism and Post-Impressionism (1860–1900) 286

Chronology 286
Pronunciation Guide 286
Study Objectives 287
Impressionism 287
Post-Impressionism 288
Painting 288
  Manet 289
  Monet 289
  Morisot 290
  Renoir 290
  Cassatt 291

  || A CLOSER LOOK: Cassatt, *The Bath* 291

  Gauguin 292
  Seurat 292
  Cézanne 292
  van Gogh 293

Sculpture 294
Degas 294
Rodin 295
Music 295
Debussy 295
Ravel 298
Boulanger 298
Summary 298
Suggested Readings 299

···••◉•◉•◉···

C h a p t e r **13**

Modernism in the Arts to 1945 (1900–1945) 300

Chronology 300
Pronunciation Guide 301
Study Objectives 302
Painting 304
Expressionism 305
Matisse 305
Klimt 305
Rouault 306
Kandinsky 306
Kollwitz 306
Cubism 307
Picasso 307

| | A CLOSER LOOK: Picasso, *Guernica* 308

Goncharova 310
Mondrian, Klee 310
Surrealism 310
Dali 311
Blume 311
Miró 312
Chagall 312
Rivera 312
Hayden 314
O'Keeffe 315
Sculpture 315
Barlach 316
Lehmbruck 316
Moore 316
Brancusi 317
Hoffman 319

Arp 319
Giacometti 319
Kinetic Art 320
Calder 320
Architecture 321
Wright 323
Gropius 326
Morgan 326
Music 327
Schoenberg 328
Berg 329
Webern 330
Vaughan Williams 331
Stravinsky 331
Bartók 332
Ives 334
Gershwin 334
Popular Music 334

| | A CLOSER LOOK: Ives, *The Unanswered Question* 335

Summary 338
Suggested Readings 339

···••◉•◉•◉···

C h a p t e r **14**

The Arts Today (1945 to the Present) 340

Chronology 340
Pronunciation Guide 341
Study Objectives 341
Painting 344
Léger 344
Lawrence 344
Bearden 346
Abstract Expressionism 346
Pollock 346
de Kooning 347
Rothko 347
Pop Art 347
Rauschenberg 348
Warhol 349
Indiana 349

Lichtenstein 349
Oldenburg 349
Johns 349
Op Art 350
Agam 352
Riley 352
Photo-Realism 353
Kinetic Art 353
Sculpture 353
Smith 354
Hepworth 355
de Saint Phalle 355
Marisol 356

Smithson 356
Christo 356
Catlett 358
Bourgeois 358
Architecture 359
Music 367
Popular Music 367
Music in the Concert Hall 370
Summary 377
Suggested Readings 378

Glossary 379
General Readings 388
Index 391

Preface

⋯⋯━●━▶⋯⋯

This book explores the traditions of music, painting, sculpture, and architecture of the Western world. It is not intended to be a complete history of the fine arts or music. It is an introduction to many individual works from important art periods, dating from the Greeks and their predecessors to the present time. We attempt to show how the arts reflect the sociocultural conditions of their time and place, how media are used, and how they give form to style. The authors hope this book will guide readers in distinguishing beauty in the great variety of musical sounds of the world and in the artistic, decorative, and utilitarian objects of all cultures.

A book shares some characteristics with museums or concerts in that some works are given greater prominence than others. Equally, museums and concerts by their very nature exclude certain works and consciously focus on others. Historically, one or more of the arts may have been dominant during particular periods. As a consequence, the treatment of the arts is not identical in each chapter.

Many representative works of music and art from each period have been selected for this text. However, additional examples of each should be sought out for further study and enjoyment. Readers are urged to supplement the text's illustrations of painting, sculpture, and architecture with prints or postcards available from most bookstores. Perhaps even more important, since a book cannot include sounds of musical performance, readers should find complementary listening experiences using the abundant CDs and cassettes available today. Listening is an essential part of the study of music. (To aid in the understanding of the music, graphic representations of some compositions are included as well.)

Each chapter provides a survey of a major stylistic period, identifying and discussing some major art works. In this edition, new sections titled "A Closer Look" have been added throughout the book to explore selected works of art and music in more depth. We hope that these sections will not only provide detailed information about specific works, but show how much can be discovered about any piece of art or music.

Greater attention is given, in this edition, to the artistic contributions of minorities and women. These groups have been significantly involved in the arts throughout history, though their recognition has been slow in coming. We have attempted to give some examples and to encourage further exploration.

The art of our own century is constantly evolving and we have again revised and updated chapters 13 and 14 to reflect this. Other changes include the replacement and improvement of several colorplates and black and white photos.

Each chapter includes a pronunciation guide, study objectives, terms in boldface, a summary, and suggested readings. All of the historical chapters, from chapter 3 onward, begin with a timeline or chronology of people and events. As terms that may be new to the reader are introduced in the text, they are printed in boldface, and a brief definition is included. These terms are also included in a comprehensive glossary at the end of the book.

Throughout history spellings of proper names change. A Russian composer's name originally written in the Cyrillic alphabet, for instance, allows for a variety of transliterations. This is but one example of the problems of spelling encountered in writing about the arts. The authors have attempted to use currently accepted English spellings.

Acknowledgments

We are deeply indebted to our many colleagues and friends who have given their time and knowledge to assist in various ways. A special word of appreciation is due to those colleagues in numerous colleges and universities who have used the material in their classrooms and have offered constructive criticism and suggestions.

Reviewers

Nelle Agee
Dr. David Alexander
Nancy Andrew
Antone J. Aquino
Thomas Atwater
N. Kay Ault
LaMar Barrus
H. Kenneth Benjamin
W. M. Brown
Leland Chou
Paul Christianson
Dee M. Connett
Jamie L. Connors
William Ellis
Eloy Fominaya

Dudley E. Foster, Jr.
Gerhard W. Franzmann
Bluma K. Greenberg
D. E. Hill
Lawrence Horn
James S. Horner
Marion B. Howe
James A. Jarrell
Wallace N. Johnson
Dale A. Jorgenson
A. D. Macklin
Helen Trotter Midkiff
Shirley M. Mihok
Lois Muyskens
Dr. Fran M. Page

Ronald W. Phillips
James W. Rogers
Joseph Sabatella
Andrea H. Savage
Orville H. Schanz
Dan M. Schultz
JoAnn M. Soloski
Michael Sparks
Willametta Spencer
Donald Walpole
Frederick W. Westphal
Robert A. Whisnant
Warren W. Whitney
Jan Helmut Wubbena
Louis A. Zona

Key to Pronunciation

Vowels

ay = a in rate
a = a in rat
ah = a in rah
aw = aw in raw
e = e in red
ee = e in be
i = i in rid
ih = i in ride
o = o in rot
oh = o in rote
oo = oo in root
ow = ow in now
oy = oy in toy
u = u in rut
yoo = u in mute
ü = German ü
oe = German oe

Consonants

B, D, F, H, K, L, M, N, P, R, T, V, W, Z as in English
g = g in go
s = s in so
ch = ch in check
sh = sh in shut
zh = z in azure
th = th in thin
kh = ch in Scottish loch

The breve mark (˘) over a vowel denotes a nasal sound; i.e., a = ă as in bang, ŏ = o in song.
The acute (´) mark designates the accented syllable when there is a stress accent.

Chapter 1

·····➤◉◄·····

The Arts and Society

Pronunciation Guide

Bach (Bakh)
Beethoven (Bay´-toh-ven)
Boucher (Boo-shay)
Dali (Dah-lee)
Debussy (Deh-byoo-see)

Esterházy (Es´-ter-hah-zee)
Goya (Goy´-yah)
Handel (Han´dle)
Haydn (High-dn)
Mozart (Moh´-tsahrt)

Picasso (Pee-kah´-soh)
Vinci, Leonardo da
(Veen´-chee, Lay-oh-nahr´-
doh dah)
Wagner (Vahg´-ner)

Study Objectives

1. Explore how the arts are the result of the dominant sociocultural climate of particular periods.
2. Learn to understand the arts through study and direct experience.

The goal of this book is to provide a useful understanding of the meaning of the arts within an historical context. It has three basic aims: (1) to develop a breadth of knowledge about the cultural patterns of the Western world; (2) to develop insight into the nature of art and music; and (3) to develop techniques of critical analysis for appreciating and understanding works of art. This is in no sense a history of visual art or a history of music. Instead, we introduce the various kinds and periods of art with the hope that the reader will be encouraged to explore them further. A study of the arts can ultimately provide a means of broadening our understanding of the heritage of the past and the values of the present.

SOCIOCULTURAL ASPECTS OF THE ARTS

Art, in any age, is the expression of the characteristic attitudes of the people of that age toward important aspects of life. More often than not, the social class that holds economic, political, or religious power imposes its likes and

1

dislikes on the rest of society. Consequently, religious and social patterns have often determined the nature and function of music and art. For example, when the Church was the principal social institution in Europe, the task confronting artists was the expression of religious sentiments in harmony with the prevailing doctrine. Bach's *Passion According to St. Matthew* was written for the Lutheran church at Leipzig in the early eighteenth century. This great work is much more than a sincere expression of Bach's own spiritual devotion. It is the musical reflection of a literal acceptance of the doctrines and spiritual beliefs of the Lutheran church.

Similarly, court life provides an illustration of the social fabric as a determining force in the function of art. In periods when courtly activity was prevalent, the artist's role was to mirror the cultivated etiquette of essentially social activities. Boucher's delicately molded nudes in playful poses represent the sensual spirit of the French Rococo court; *Eine kleine Nachtmusik,* a serenade by Mozart, is charming, graceful music for the social gatherings of Viennese court life.

The period immediately following World War II illustrated the strong effect of economics on the arts. There was tremendous buying power in the hands of youth, thanks to a growing economy and the advertising success of the mass media. As a result, commercial and popular images emerged as a vital force in art, especially in the United States. Popular culture may even influence the works of other artists. The widely acclaimed *Mass* by Leonard Bernstein, for example, incorporates a number of elements from the rock music of the fifties and sixties.

In addition to the influence of the dominant group of the time, the arts are affected by their inheritance from the past. Each cultural pattern leaves its mark on the following generation, and the artistic characteristics of any age are influenced in some degree by earlier traditions and forms. As we shall see, each period embodies a particular set of aesthetic goals that set it apart from the preceding age. We refer to the artistic features of a particular period, place, or individual as a **style.** Consequently, style is that combination of characteristics that makes works of art recognizable as manifestations of a period, person, genre, time, and place. Furthermore, the style of one art can influence another: the Impressionist poets and painters of the late nineteenth century had a profound influence on the composer Debussy, whose music was thus also called "Impressionist."

In order to understand the sociocultural conditions from which art develops, we must look on history as something more than a mere chronicle of past events. We must also examine the social, political, economic, religious, and artistic environment out of which grew painting, sculpture, architecture, and music. History thus leaves its imprint on the role that art plays in an epoch and on the very character of art itself.

As the patterns in economic, political, spiritual, and intellectual life change, so does the art. The art of ancient Greece, for example, is very different from that of the Gothic period. An investigation of the dominant attitudes toward important aspects of life in these two periods reveals differences also found in their art. The study of social and intellectual life will enhance our understanding of the character and quality of the art in each period we survey.

Conversely, an intimate knowledge of art provides clues to intellectual and social life. The music that Bach wrote for Lutheran congregations during the early eighteenth century is very different from that which Haydn wrote for the court of Prince Esterházy only fifty years later. Their music reflected different attitudes toward religion and other institutions, yet both men were great creative artists. Both were following closely the patterns of their own age and composed for patrons who made specific demands upon them. No one will deny that the paintings of Boucher for the court of Louis XV are very different from those of Picasso in the twentieth century, for each in his own way represented the culture of his time. Boucher portrayed charmingly flirtatious images of the art of love, whereas Picasso, expressing the impulses of the scientific age, employed analytical Cubism to convey its spirit.

Particular events or crises have elicited creative responses from artists and musicians. Picasso's *Guernica* (see fig. 13.2), painted in reaction to the mass bombing during the Spanish civil war of 1937, and Penderecki's *Threnody for the Victims of Hiroshima,* a musical response to that holocaust, are two such works in the twentieth century. These two works deepen our understanding of historical events.

The artist's personality, of course, maintains its unique identity within a certain style and period. All artists leave the imprint of their personalities on their art, yet they have much in common with their contemporaries. Leonardo da Vinci helped make the Renaissance a great artistic age, and his paintings and drawings, in turn, were made great by the humanism set in motion during the Gothic period and eventually flowered in the Renaissance. Bach and Handel lived at the same time. Although their personalities and their music were very different, they both expressed characteristics of the Baroque. The paintings of Rivera and Dali were certainly not alike, yet the work of each represented an aspect of contemporary life that we can all recognize. In the post–World War II era, the music of the Beatles came to embody the ideals of the protest movement, but their music still was rooted in the traditional harmonies and rhythms of blues and early rock. Even iconoclasts have their roots firmly set in the traditions of their own time.

An understanding of art, therefore, involves not only the artwork itself but the forces brought to bear on the artist, such as location, religion, political climate, and economic status. We see this particularly in our own day, as the emergence of developing countries, cultural exchange programs, and the instant availability of art through the media have brought about the cross-fertilization of ideas on a global scale. Artists and composers whose indigenous cultures are non-Western are creating works in Western idioms, and Western artists likewise incorporate non-Western elements in their works. By understanding the social underpinnings of art, we achieve a better understanding of the cultural heritage of Western civilization and can better appreciate its contribution to what it means to be human. Such understanding, after all, is the basis for studying **humanism.**

THE FUNCTIONS OF THE ARTS

To gain insight into works of art, you must become familiar with their functions. What were they used for and for whom were they created? Obviously, a church is built for religious purposes but for what kind of religion? A Gothic cathedral serves a different purpose than does a Protestant church, and an Islamic temple is different from a Jewish synagogue.

Architecture is a dynamic art. During its lifetime a building often undergoes considerable change. It may be redecorated, used for a different purpose, or remodeled to meet the needs of new functions. In some instances, a building may be damaged by fire, war, or some disaster and then restored in the style of the current period.

A painting may serve many purposes. It may be used for religious education; it may satisfy the ego of some wealthy merchant who commissioned it; or it may be propaganda against the horrors of war, as are certain works of the nineteenth and twentieth centuries. Similarly, sculpture may commemorate a historic event or symbolize the function of a building. Under certain conditions, artists create artworks without practical objectives but as deep and abiding expressions of human feeling. But even then, the artist has certain well-defined aims influenced by such things as personality, patronage, and epoch.

Music is also a functional art. There is music for war, worship, dancing, love, comedy, and a host of other purposes. In the case of the visual arts, function can usually be determined by subject matter. Instrumental music, being abstract, relies on form, melody, harmony, rhythm, and expressive quality to achieve its purpose; in some compositions, the function is implied by means of announced programs or stories. The function of vocal or dramatic music is determined in large measure by the meaning of the text itself.

Not all art has high purpose. There is a great wealth of art, especially music and painting, that aims to amuse and to provide a pleasant diversion from life's everyday events. Popular music, salon music, illustrations, caricatures, and cartoons are by their very nature diversionary. Although their purpose cannot be denied, much of this art is by nature ephemeral and does not achieve lasting value.

The function of any art is inseparably connected with the social, economic, political, and religious patterns of its age. For example, in the Romanesque and the Gothic periods religious art was in great demand because the Church was the one all-powerful institution. As the power of the Church declined, art for religious purposes diminished in quantity. In the Romantic period of the early nineteenth century there was a new concern for such problems as social injustice, the exploitation of labor, and the struggle for democratic idealism. Consequently, artists provided works of art that highlighted these issues and served both as propaganda for social reforms and as documents of faith in democratic ideals. An important function of Nationalist art was to unite minority peoples into social, cultural, and political units.

ART PERIODS

For the sake of convenience, our survey will be divided into the large and broadly defined periods customarily applied to the arts. In each of these, the dominant trends in religion, economics, and society will briefly set the stage for the discussion of visual art and music. The various arts will not receive equal emphasis in each period, for certain arts better embody the values of a particular style than do others. For example, while painting was indeed important in the time of the Greeks, it will not be as important to our study as sculpture. Likewise, architecture was of primary importance in the Gothic, and painting was considered the major art in the Renaissance.

It is impossible to divide history into periods of time with exact dates as boundaries. It is equally difficult to mark off one period of art from another. History is a process of change that becomes clearer as time progresses. While one period of art reaches its zenith, another is being born, the result of normal cultural growth and change. While Gothic ideals were gradually waning, for example, Renaissance humanism was emerging, and during the late Renaissance the seeds of the Baroque were being germinated. The process of stylistic change moves slowly, and characteristics of one artistic period often overlap those of another.

Terms such as *Gothic, Renaissance, Baroque,* and *Rococo* customarily designate artistic style periods. The dates used to designate each period are used only to indicate the span of time in which we can say, with some degree of certainty, a particular style was dominant. The following periods and dates are those we shall use:

The Greeks and Their Predecessors (Antiquity–100 B.C.)
The Roman Empire and the Early Christians (100 B.C.–A.D. 500)

The Medieval Period—Romanesque (500–1100)
The Medieval Period—Gothic (1100–1400)
The Renaissance Period (1400–1600)
The Baroque and the Rococo Periods (1600–1775)
The Classic Period (1750–1800)
The Romantic Period (1800–1900)
Nineteenth-Century Realism and Nationalism (1840–1900)
Impressionism and Post-Impressionism (1860–1900)
Modernism in the Arts to 1945 (1900–1945)
The Arts Today (1945 to the Present)

A LABORATORY OF EXPERIENCE

Developing insight into the nature of art and music will involve much more than biographical studies of great composers, painters, and sculptors or the recognition of their works by title, although these are certainly important. Only an intimate acquaintance with art through seeing and hearing allows it to become a part of personal experience. What does the eye see and the ear hear? What constitutes an aesthetic experience in terms of art? These are important questions, for real insight comes only by perceiving the forms and sounds the artists create. One must become an observer and a hearer as well, spending hours in the laboratory of the art museum and concert hall or the equivalent time acquainting oneself with art reproductions and recordings.

Reproductions of painting and sculpture should not remain in bound volumes but should take their place on the walls of the home, where they become a part of everyday experience. Even better would be a few originals by little-known artists, chosen with discrimination and taste. With architecture, you can study the various styles and examples in your community. Similarly, you should listen to musical works again and again until you recognize the details easily. The themes and texture of a musical work should be so indelibly impressed upon the memory that they are not forgotten readily. What is experienced will, in turn, become more meaningful in the light of historical background and the personal history of the artist.

Another aspect of artistic insight is the ability to analyze the materials of art and to understand how they are organized. Such organization, as we have seen, is dependent on the cultural context and on the stylistic conventions of the period. Just as the artist uses the methods of synthesis in creating, so one must learn to synthesize and be able to account for what one sees and hears in terms of larger cultural and stylistic forces. The aesthetic experience reaches full bloom by absorbing into one's own experience all the aspects of an artwork: function, material, form, cultural milieu, and the artist's personality.

Art centers of Europe

What techniques can be employed in an effort to bring about this synthesis? What practical tools for seeing and hearing can be utilized in the laboratory of experience? These questions lead to the third aim of this book: to develop techniques of analysis as a means to general understanding and critical judgment. This process begins in the next chapter.

Summary

The history of the human race is much more than a chronicle of political, economic, and military successes and failures. The record of intellectual, spiritual, economic, and political life has been documented in the artistic activities of every period. A study of the arts in relation to the life and times that produced them helps us to develop a more profound understanding of human behavior in the past and some understanding of the present. The purpose of this book is to correlate the arts with cultural history in order to develop insight into the cultural patterns of the Western world. This can be accomplished through the study of specific works of art and music that represent the important trends and styles of artistic activity in the major periods of Western civilization.

Suggested Readings

In addition to the specific sources that follow, the general readings on pages 388 and 389 contain valuable information about the topic of this chapter.

Cornwell, Terri Lynn. *Democracy and the Arts: The Role of Participation*. New York: Praeger Pub. Co., 1990.
Elsen, Albert E. *Purposes of Art*. 4th ed. New York: Holt, Rinehart & Winston, 1981.
Kaplan, Max. *The Arts: A Social Perspective*. Rutherford, NJ: Fairleigh Dickinson University Press, 1990.
Langer, Susanne K. *Problems of Art*. New York: Scribner, 1977.
Raynor, Henry. *A Social History of Music from the Middle Ages to Beethoven*. New York: Schocken Books, 1972.
Raynor, Henry. *Music and Society Since 1815*. London: Barrie and Jenkins, 1976.
Read, Herbert E. *The Meaning of Art*. 2d ed. London: Faber and Faber, 1984.

Chapter 2

···⏤◉⏤···

The Organization of the Elements of the Visual Arts and Music

Pronunciation Guide

Bartók (Bahr´-tok)
Berlioz (Bayr-lee-ohz)
Delacroix (De-lah-krwah)
Duccio (Doo-choh)
Duchamp (Dü-chăh)
Dufay, Guillaume (Dü-fah-ee, Gwee-ohm)

Giorgione (Johr-joh´-nay)
Penderecki (Pen-der-et´-skee)
Praetorius (Pray-tor´-ee-us)
Raphael (Rahf´-ah-el)
Rembrandt (Rem´-brant)
Schubert (Shoo´-bert)

Stockhausen (Shtock´-how-zen)
Strauss (Shtrows)
Stravinsky (Strah-vin´-skee)
van Gogh (van Gokh)

Study Objectives

1. Understand the nature of the aesthetic experience.
2. Develop techniques for analyzing the elements of art and music as they appear in specific works.

In the study of the arts, it is important to examine the elements that artists employ and manipulate in the creation of their works. Artists use raw materials such as stone, paint, or sound, and create from these materials new forms according to principles of design for an expressive end.

Every work of art has some special characteristic of content or form that distinguishes it from that which is *not* art. For some people form can often be an end in itself. There is pleasure and delight in the sheer magic of technical perfection, and pleasure in such elements as rhythm and melodic movement in music, or the interplay of shape and color.

Art deals with the whole spectrum of human experience, and artists interpret and express experiences in distinctive ways. These can range from the fantastic to the realistic and from the beautiful and sublime to the ugly. While the arts naturally vary in their characteristic subject matter, they share some common objectives: the interpretation of human experience and the reflection of a particular culture and time.

A work of art thus presents, through many different physical means, its creator's interpretation of life. A shape, color, melody, or chord are only a few of the means by which this is accomplished. By selecting and transforming materials, artists can intensify our sensations and thus impress upon us a multitude of responses. The success of a work of art—be it painting, sculpture, or music—can be measured by the extent to which our senses perceive and respond to the experience the artist seeks to evoke.

THE AESTHETIC RESPONSE

Aesthetic experiences deal primarily with human feelings. There are some people who look upon the experience of art merely as pleasurable sensation. For others, the response to art is more complex. In both cases, the creative artist arouses specific emotions or feelings, and these are a key part of the aesthetic experience. In music, such emotive states are stimulated by tonal and rhythmic patterns. Because of music's inherent abstraction, the response to music varies greatly with individuals. Time and place, moreover, can vary each individual response. In painting and sculpture, representational forms, as well as pure formal patterns, awaken feelings. Architecture depends upon form, size, proportion, and function to evoke the aesthetic response.

According to Stephen Pepper's *Principles of Art Appreciation,* there are four ways of producing emotions through art.

Colorplate 49 follows p. 258.

1. Artists can use direct stimulation, such as the excitement of a march or the lilting pattern of a dance tune. In painting, this kind of stimulation occurs through the use of colors and agitated lines. In *Liberty Leading the People* by Delacroix (colorplate 49), the forward diagonal movement from left to right and the atmosphere of somber colors against the smoke-filled background intensify our own feelings about the subject.
2. Types and symbols that through common usage are charged with emotional meaning can also stimulate emotion. For example, the broken sword, the dying horse, and the dead child in Picasso's *Guernica* (see fig. 13.2) all suggest the terror and carnage that were a part of the artist's message. This type of stimulation does not usually apply to music unless it has a text that suggests these symbols. Except for a few obviously imitative sounds, instrumental music cannot be so clearly associated with specific symbols. Even in abstract music,

however, rhythmic or melodic patterns can be symbols of emotion. An obvious example of this is the rhythmic motive at the opening of Beethoven's fifth symphony, which, by tradition, suggests Fate knocking.

3. Feeling can also be aroused by representation of emotional behavior in a work of art. In Goya's *The Third of May* (colorplate 52) the look of terror on the face of the highlighted prisoner, the witnesses' shielding of their eyes from the execution, the clenched fists and gestures of disbelief of other prisoners, together with the shadowy bodies of fallen prisoners, provide an emotional climax to the painting that has already been suggested by line and color. Berlioz does this musically in the first movement of the *Symphonie fantastique,* in which the fragmentary and vague harmonies are contrasted with the lyric and intense melody of the "beloved" to call forth a feeling of reverie and passion. He even suggests these states of emotional response by the title "Reveries and Passions."

Colorplate 52 follows p. 258.

4. Artists can also evoke emotional responses by providing evidence of their own feelings. In Beethoven's third symphony (*Eroica*), the dynamic power and majesty of the music can be readily associated with the composer's idea of heroism. In the visual arts, Vincent van Gogh is noted for paintings that reveal his feelings, such as *The Starry Night* (colorplate 72). Bold, swirling strokes and heavy, contrasting colors give a kind of elemental strength to the painting that reflects the artist's feelings.

Colorplate 72 follows p. 290.

Aesthetic responses can be awakened in other, more subtle ways. Artists do not rely on any one of these means to the exclusion of the others. Furthermore, artists depend on repeated viewing or listening for the various facets of an artwork to be fully appreciated. Beethoven's *Eroica*, for example, becomes meaningful aesthetically only as the listener becomes better acquainted with its musical language. Understanding, therefore, comes in part because of the listener's personal effort. The greater the mastery of the musical language, the greater the understanding and the greater the listener's aesthetic response.

Virtually all relevant information can help conscientious and sympathetic observers enlarge and heighten their aesthetic responses to any art object—visual or aural. It is important to understand that the appreciation of art takes effort. An artwork does not exist through the efforts of the creative artist alone. The completed communication depends on the efforts of both creator and observer. It is never passive and can be made real only through active participation.

In the creative process, artists must constantly make judgments regarding the content and organization of the artwork. Some judgments may be logical, justifiable on a rational basis. Others are intuitively felt on a deeply personal level and lend themselves much less readily to logical argument. Artists arrange materials to heighten interest, to awaken emotional states, and to relate the parts to the whole.

The listener or viewer employs a mode of judgment very similar to the creative process. These judgments are sometimes logical and rational but are intuitive and personal as well. It is sometimes difficult to convince people to rely on their intuitive conclusions about artworks. However, intuitive responses, when based on informed appreciation, may be credible and valid.

ELEMENTS AND MATERIALS OF THE VISUAL ARTS

There is no general agreement about what the essential components of the visual arts are. Some people include only line, shape, and color. Others would add volume, texture, and direction. In this book, we will speak of medium, line, space, and color as the four elements of the visual arts. These artistic elements must have some physical form, and the way they are manipulated and relate to one another within the work of art may be referred to as its formal organization.

Medium

The word **medium** refers to the artist's physical materials, such as stone, wood, metal, paper, cloth, paint, glass, and plastic, whose properties influence how the other elements will be organized. In painting, the physical properties of such materials as oil and watercolor determine the technique and provide the artist with a discipline that is reflected in the expressive qualities of the artwork.

Line

One of the most common elements used by all artists to create form is line. Painters sometimes use line to delineate forms. They more often imply line where none is present by juxtaposing two colors. The boundary between the colors is perceived as a line. Sculptors create line by defining form. Even the architect's organization of space results in the lines of a building. There are many different manifestations of line. Lines may be curved, with a smooth-flowing rhythm; or they may be straight, with sharp, dynamic angles. Lines may be clearly defined or vague and diffused; they may be simple and direct; or they may show great detail and ornamentation. The quality of line may be delicate and refined; or it may be broad, showing great strength and solidity.

By the use of line, artists can create geometric shapes, such as spheres, triangles, and squares. Shapes created by line may be representational or nonrepresentational (abstract). They may also be two-dimensional or three-dimensional, and in the case of some twentieth-century art, they may suggest a fourth dimension, imaginatively adding the illusion of action to three-dimensional forms. Color, texture, and intensity of line also affect quality.

Line also has expressive significance. Horizontal lines suggest repose and stability (colorplate 1). A sense of strength is shown by vertical lines (colorplate 2). Diagonal lines reflect tension and action (colorplate 3). Long curves express relaxation and a sense of calm, while short, quick curves are often used to express dynamic agitation. Whatever the line qualities may be, each artist uses line in conformity with his or her personality, philosophy, and stylistic period.

Colorplates 1, 2, and 3 follow p. 18.

Space

Space is the three-dimensional volume that can be experienced physically in sculpture and architecture but only suggested in painting. The architect deals with the organization of space, as does the landscape architect and city planner (fig. 2.1). For example, space may appear restricted by being enclosed within heavy walls with few windows. In contrast, it can be expanded by letting one room flow into another, eliminating doors and using large amounts of glass, as in much modern architecture. The landscape architect can contract space by restricting portions of the garden with borders and hedges, or expand the sense of spatial volume by providing easy access to all areas, both physically and visually. In painting, space is an illusion of the third dimension.

Medieval paintings reveal a different understanding of space and perspective than do more recent works of art. For example, Duccio's *Christ Entering Jerusalem* (colorplate 4) presents three groups of people on shallow shelves of space at the very front of the picture plane. Rows of people are placed like flat images laid one upon another. The architectural fragments only minimally employ **linear perspective,** which uses lines that imply a vanishing point. Unlike the aerial photograph of Versailles (fig. 2.1), Duccio's painting has no **aerial perspective,** that is to say, there is little effect of atmospheric conditions on the color and detail of distant objects within the painting.

Colorplate 4 follows p. 18.

Very different techniques are employed in more modern paintings. Looking through an opening into a landscape without end gives the observer a sensation of infinite space. In Ruisdael's *Wheatfields* (colorplate 5), this is accomplished by the relationship of size and position, lack of detail in the distance, overlapping of shapes, and receding color intensity. Raphael's *School of Athens* (colorplate 6) demonstrates a more controlled, three-dimensional spatial character by following rules of linear perspective. Groups of figures are organized so the central figures of Plato and Aristotle are framed by the rounded arch in the background. In contrast, three-dimensional space may be denied by a flat plane on which figures and objects are placed so as to

Colorplates 5 and 6 follow p. 18.

Figure 2.1 An aerial view of Versailles. The palace is in the center with the *Parterres du Nord* on the left and the *Parterres du Midi* on the right. In the foreground are the water gardens and the *Fountaine de Latone.* (Courtesy French Government Tourist Office)

*Colorplate 9
follows p. 50.*

have relationships on only two dimensions (colorplate 9). Most visual art suggests space that seems either to expand or to contract. Vertical and horizontal space is contracting if the eye is drawn inward; it is expanding if objects or scenes are suggested to exist outside the boundaries of the artwork.

Color

The element of color can be understood best by examining its three constituents: hue, saturation (sometimes called intensity), and value. The property of reflected light that allows persons to distinguish a color is called **hue.** The names we give to colors (violet, green, red) are also called hues. There are three **primary colors**—red, blue, and yellow. If any two of these colors are combined, the resultant colors are known as secondary colors. Blue and yellow create green; red and blue, violet; red and yellow, orange. Differing combinations of the primaries can, of course, create the infinite variants of the entire spectrum. An examination of the light traveling through a prism cast on a surface will confirm this fact.

Saturation refers to the relative purity or vividness of a color with respect to its appearance in the spectrum. The reddest red separated by a prism would be described as possessing a high saturation level. If a small amount of blue were added to it, the hue would still be recognizable as red, although a keen eye might detect that small amount of blue.

In addition to hue and saturation, all colors have black and white present to some degree, which is referred to as **value.** The more white present, the higher the value of the color. Conversely, the more black present, the lower the value of the color. In their natural, refracted states, some colors (such as yellow) have higher values than others (such as blue). The value of any color can be changed by the addition of black or white.

In painting, there are two types of color organization: monochromatic and polychromatic. **Monochromaticism** means the colors are derived mainly from one color, with different values and a unity of hues. **Polychromaticism** results from many contrasting colors. In addition to contributing to the reality of form, color has a great number of other functions. It can define form and line, and create eye movement by cleverly shifting the emphasis from one color mass to another. It can add to the sense of motion by expanding or contracting space, with dark colors for contraction and lighter colors for expansion.

Color also contributes to the emotional or expressive quality of a work. For example, high intensities or bright colors evoke a sense of excitement, while low intensities and somber colors suggest serenity, calmness, or mystery. In art, color is often used to symbolize ideas, such as purple for royalty, blue for faith, and white for purity. There are a host of other symbolic ideas and objects that have color associations.

Principles of Organization

Form is the arrangement of materials and elements into a recognizable pattern that conveys the function and meaning of an artwork. While there is an endless variety of artistic possibilities in material, subject matter, and function, there are only several principles of organization by which artists are guided: (1) unity, (2) variety, (3) balance, and (4) focus. All works of art have these principles present to some degree, but the importance of individual principles will vary from work to work.

Each work of art must have enough variety to interest the observer and enough unity to avoid chaos. In other words, every artist seeks enough coherence to achieve unity in the work, and at the same time, enough variety to combat monotony. Unity and variety are by no means independent of one another, and they are not always equally present. Certain art epochs reveal strong tendencies toward the dominating use of one or the other of these principles.

Repetition and contrast are important methods of achieving unity and variety. A painting may achieve unity by repeating colors, patterns, and lines. Raphael's *School of Athens* (colorplate 6) uses the repeated diminishing arch form as an element of repetition at the same time as it emphasizes linear perspective. Repetition is enhanced by the decorative patterns on the floor and in the first arch. The human forms are painted in greatly contrasting poses. Achieving unity and variety is one of the most technically demanding accomplishments required of the artist, for it consists of a skillful handling of one motive with the ever-present danger of monotony. A painter may use many variants of a single color as did Rembrandt. Likewise, the artist may use only one motive of line in varying patterns, sizes, and positions.

Colorplate 7 follows p. 18.

Balance in the visual arts may be achieved in many ways. Symmetry is the basis for the balance in Grant Wood's *American Gothic* (colorplate 2), Raphael's *School of Athens* (colorplate 6), or his *Sistine Madonna* (colorplate 7). Balance without symmetry is evident in *Wheatfields* by Ruisdael (colorplate 5) and Giorgione's *Sleeping Venus* (colorplate 1). Painters may use shapes, implied masses, and blocks of light and dark to achieve balance.

In the visual arts, the principle of focus is expressed in the point or points of emphasis in the painting. In the *School of Athens* (colorplate 6), the perspective, the implied lines in the groupings of people, and the framing in the arch all lead to the two central characters, which are the primary point of focus. Paintings frequently have multiple points of focus. The two faces in *American Gothic* (colorplate 2) exemplify the principle of multiple focus. In Duchamp's *Nude Descending a Staircase, No. 2* (colorplate 3), there is no central focus but, rather, a general sense of movement from upper left to lower right.

The term **form** has several meanings in art. The first meaning refers to the way all the elements of an artwork are organized into an expressive whole. This organization may draw attention toward a focal point, creating closed form, or it may lead the observer out and beyond the immediate scope of the artwork, creating open form. Form may have balance of mass and void, or it may be unbalanced and asymmetrical.

Another meaning, plastic form, is used to designate the shape or mass of an object. Many objects approximate forms such as the sphere, cone, cylinder, or square. The sculptor molds materials into these shapes. The architect encloses space within the confines of these primary forms. The painter creates the illusion of plastic forms with line and color. The differences between these two definitions must be kept in mind: form is a method of organizing the total picture; plastic form designates shapes or masses.

Not all of the foregoing concepts apply to the visual arts in the same degree. For example, color is usually less important in sculpture than in painting, whereas the physical character of material is more important in sculpture and architecture than in painting. It must also be remembered that all the elements add to the total character of the artwork.

Expressive Content in Visual Art

Artworks have expressive content that results from the elements themselves and from organization, function, and the artist's creativity. This is an intangible but very real quality of art, for expressive content is the heart of what the artist wishes to convey. Whether the work is a character study in painting, a heroic group in sculpture, or a private dwelling, the respective goal of each artist is to make the character real, to evoke a sense of heroism, or to give the building the warmth and intimacy of a home. The success of the work of art is in direct proportion to the artist's achievement of these aims. The creative artist possesses the intuitive power to sense relationships and the technique to organize materials so that a work of art communicates some message or experience. In the final analysis, the only really important aspect of art is its success in conveying its expressive content; all else is but a means to that end.

Style

The various ways artists employ the elements and the principles of organization determine artistic styles. Artists who are subjected to similar cultural forces might organize the elements in much the same manner—subject, of course, to the function of the artwork, as well as to the individual differences and personalities of the artists. There are cases in which an artist continues in a style that was prevalent in a bygone era and refuses to conform to the present culture. Sometimes, however, great artists are forward-looking and provide the connecting link between one artistic age and another. They have the intuition and the courage to recognize that times are changing, that new forces are at work. A Leonardo da Vinci or a Beethoven, then, becomes a prophet of a new era. In such cases, an analysis of the elements will reveal nonconformity to the accepted contemporary style and will show some stylistic characteristics that foreshadow the succeeding period. Leonardo's *Mona Lisa* displays many of the characteristics of Renaissance painting, but it also exhibits some of the qualities later identified with the Baroque. The same is true of Beethoven. He was trained in the classicism of eighteenth-century music, yet his later works fulfill many of the demands of Romanticism. He, thus, became the prophet of the new Romantic spirit in music. Some twentieth-century artists, such as Picasso and Stravinsky, revealed in their works a variety of styles as they kept pace with the extremely rapid cultural changes of their times.

Raphael, *Sistine Madonna*

A useful analysis of Raphael's *Sistine Madonna* (colorplate 7) will include an examination of its elements, organization, and function. The function of this work is religious. The main subjects are the Madonna and the baby Jesus, flanked by St. Sixtus and St. Barbara. To assure that the identity of the subjects is clear, the artist surrounded the head of each figure with a faint halo, all except the two little angels below, whose wings identify them as heavenly. There is nothing else to identify the figures as being holy. They look like mere humans—real people Raphael knew and chose to use as models.

Line

Line is a prominent element in this work. The lines are very sharp, clearly defining the various forms, separating them from the background. They are also primarily curved, suggesting a smooth-flowing, vertical motion. Unity is achieved by a rhythm of similar linear motives and variety by a contrast of visual pauses among these motives.

Space

The figures in the painting are partially enclosed by the drapery. The background, made up of barely discernable cherub faces, is quite flat and does not suggest any substantial sense of perspective. The figures, however, are so molded as to seem real in a plastic sense, giving a three-dimensional effect. In addition, they seem to project forward, a projection implied by the gesture and look of the two figures on either side of the Madonna and the protruding knee of the Madonna. This spatial quality is also implied by the emergence of the major figure from the sea of cherubic faces.

Color

The painting is polychromatic. There is a rich color harmony achieved through contrast, especially among the reds and blues. Repetition and contrast of color provide both unity and variety.

Medium

The *Sistine Madonna* is painted in oil on canvas in such a manner that the brushstrokes are blended together and are not visible.

Formal Organization

The lines of the figures draw the eye inward toward the figure of the Madonna and Child. All motion is directed toward this group, providing the painting with a dynamic quality. The gaze of the figure on the left, the vertical line of the figure on the right, the upward look of the cherubs, even the drapery above, bring the eye toward the focal point; the form is thus closed. The form is also balanced, for the figures on the two sides create a balance around the vertical axis of the central group. Here again the drapery emphasizes the perfect balance of form. The organization of this painting is one of independent parts. No figure is merged with another; each is complete in itself and could be removed without destroying the reality of any other—but not, however, without destroying the formal balance of the whole.

In summary, this is an oil painting of a religious subject in which line plays an important part. It has closed form with little depth, and it is polychromatic. It uses all the basic principles of organization, with repetition and contrast dominating. The reality of the human form is perhaps the strongest impression one gets. The expression of religious feeling is poetic, beautiful, but not overwhelmingly powerful. In its subject matter, costuming, use of color, and formal pose, Raphael's painting is a good example of Renaissance art and is typical of the religious artworks of that period. The synthesis of all elements, both objective and subjective, results in a broader understanding of the artwork and a keener insight into its meaning. If, for example, a work of the Romantic period had been analyzed, we would have found a very different subject, different use of the elements, and a different function.

Colorplate 1 Giorgione, *Sleeping Venus,* 1508–1510. Oil on canvas, 43 × 69 in. Staatliche Kunstammlungen, Dresden, Germany. (Erich Lessing/Art Resource, NY) *(See p. 13, 16)*

Colorplate 2 Grant Wood, *American Gothic,* 1930. Oil on beaverboard, 30 × 25 in. (Friends of American Art Collection, 1930.934. Photograph © 1994 The Art Institute of Chicago, All Rights Reserved) *(See p. 13, 16)*

Colorplate 3 Marcel Duchamp, *Nude Descending a Staircase,* No. 2, 1912. Oil on canvas, 58 × 35 in. Philadelphia Museum of Art: Louise and Walter Arensberg Collection. *(See p. 13, 16)*

Colorplate 4   Duccio di Buoninsegna, *Christ Entering Jerusalem* from the *Maestà altar,* 1309–1311. Tempera on wood, 39 × 22 in. (Scala/Art Resource, NY) *(See p. 13)*

Colorplate 5 Jacob van Ruisdael, *Wheatfields,* 1670. Oil on canvas, 51 1/4 × 39 3/8 in. The Metropolitan Museum of Art, NY. Bequest of Benjamin Altman, 1913, 14.40.623. *(See p. 13, 16)*

Colorplate 6   Raphael, *School of Athens,* 1510–1511. Fresco, c. 26 × 18 ft. Stanza della Segnatura, Vatican, Rome. (Scala/Art Resource, NY) *(See p. 13, 16, 50, 142)*

Colorplate 7 Raphael, *Sistine Madonna*, 1513. Oil on canvas, 8 ft. 8 in. × 6 ft. 5 in. Gemäldegalerie, Staatliche Kunstammlungen, Dresden, Germany. (Erich Lessing/Art Resource, NY) *(See p. 16, 18, 135, 143)*

ELEMENTS AND MATERIALS OF MUSIC

Music is the most abstract of all the arts and exists in its fullest sense only through the medium of performance. It moves in time with constantly changing rhythms and pitches. Consequently, music requires repeated hearings if we are to appreciate the full impact of its message. When we listen, there are elements and processes that can be studied in making an expressive and stylistic analysis. In this book, there are numerous examples in musical notation. However, since few can look at a piece of notated music and recreate mentally exactly what the notation indicates, it is important to listen to all the examples in the book.

Some of the principles of organization found in the visual arts are also important in music. The problem of achieving unity and variety is similar. In general, composers solve their problems in much the same manner as do painters, sculptors, and architects. A composer may use only one simple theme and build variations on that theme by playing it backwards, upside down, in fragments, or in various rhythmic and harmonic permutations. The same harmonic formula may be varied by use of a higher register or different instruments. The use of **dynamics** and emphasis is another way both unity and variety can be achieved.

As in the visual arts, there is no consensus about the essential components in music. In this book, we examine rhythm, pitch, melody, texture, harmony, dynamics, and tone color to see how composers organize them to create musical works.

Rhythm

The element of music which deals with time and its division is called **rhythm.** When a composer creates a composition, all of the time for all of the instruments and voices which perform the work must be notated in the **score.** This information in the score is transmitted to the performers by symbols that are referred to as notes (for the sounds), and **rests** (for the silences). Listeners and performers sometimes forget that silence is an important ingredient in music.

The notes and rests, or sounds and silences, can be examined together. The symbols shown in example 2.1 account for either sound or silence and are listed from the longer durations to the shorter.

Example 2.1   Basic rhythmic notation

NOTES   RESTS

○   Whole   ▬

♩ (half)   Half   ▬

♩   Quarter   ξ

♪   Eighth   γ

♬   Sixteenth   ǵ

One can continue adding flags to the notes and rests to create ever shorter relative durations. The relations among these symbols is constant, but the speed with which they follow one another may vary from one composition to another. There are two ways to extend the duration of notes. These are the tie (♩ ♩), which can unite consecutive notes, and the dot (♪), which increases the duration of the preceding note or rest by one half its value. For an illustration of notation in printed music see example 2.2.

The apparent speed with which notes move in a composition is referred to as **tempo.** Fast tempos or rapidly recurring patterns give a feeling of excitement, while slow tempos tend to suggest repose. Sometimes in a musical score a note followed by a number (♩ = 60) appears at the upper left corner of the first page. This information tells the performer that there should be sixty quarter notes per minute in this work. Musicians sometimes refer to these notes as beats; there are then sixty beats per minute.

Most Western music is organized into regularly recurring groupings. These units are called **measures,** and the measures indicate the groupings in a particular **meter.** The measures are separated from each other by **bars,** vertical lines going from top to bottom across the score. At the beginning of the printed music, a symbol (often two numbers that look like a fraction but are not) tells the performer what the recurring groupings are to be. This symbol is called the **meter signature.** The numbers in the meter signature each have a different meaning: The lower number always describes a kind of note (4 meaning "quarter" or 8 meaning "eighth," and so forth). The

Example 2.2 Musical notation: Prelude no. 8 by J. S. Bach

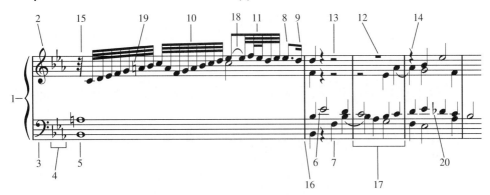

1. Grand Staff
2. Treble Clef Sign
3. Bass Clef Sign
4. Key Signature
5. Whole Note
6. Half Note
7. Quarter Note
8. Dotted Eighth Note
9. Sixteenth Note
10. Thirty-Second Note

11. Sixty-Fourth Note
12. Whole Rest
13. Half Rest
14. Quarter Rest
15. Thirty-Second Rest
16. Bar Line
17. Measure
18. Tie
19. Natural Sign
20. Flat Sign

upper number tells the performer or listener how many of those notes, or their equivalents, are included in any given measure in that meter.

Some meters that most of us are familiar with are 3/4, which is associated with waltzes or minuets, and 2/4 or 6/8, often associated with marches. There are usually strong and weak beats in measures. In 3/4 meter, there is a strong beat followed by two lesser beats: *oom*-pah-pah. In marches, strong beats typically alternate with weaker beats: *left*-right, *left*-right. Other common symbols indicating meter are: C (for common), with four quarter notes per measure, and C (sometimes called "cut time"), with two quarter notes per measure. Another way of emphasizing a note or chord is by accenting it. Several common symbols indicating an accent in printed music are >, ^, and . These are placed above the notes that receive emphasis.

In some periods of Western music, composers have used mostly symmetrical meters. In other periods, composers have made great use of asymmetrical meters (5/8 or 11/8, for example). Some meters, such as those of a march, are very simple, regular, and strongly marked. More complex rhythms are often so subtly marked that the patterns are hardly noticeable. Not only can a particular meter be asymmetrical, but different metric schemes can be mixed together in a composition, as in example 2.3.

The Organization of the Elements of the Visual Arts and Music   21

Example 2.3   "Dance #1" from *Six Dances in Bulgarian Rhythm* by Bartók

One further complication can arise from these metric groupings. One expects to find two pulses in each measure of a march, left-right, left-right. So how does one account for some marches in 6/8 meter? It is fairly easy to see the connection between 2/4 and the march, but a six-beat meter requires explaining. If the top number can be divided by three, the result of that division most often tells the performer how many beats are in a measure of that music. These meters are called compound meters. So, some marches are in compound meter (6/8); they consist of two beats per measure, each beat comprising three eighth notes. Some are in simple meter (2/4). However, it is possible to have measures with six beats in them as well. Usually, such music will be at a much slower tempo than the true compound meters.

Recognizable note groupings or patterns that are readily identifiable are often referred to as **motives.** These may have a special rhythmic character. Larger groupings, akin to language groupings such as phrases or sentences, are commonly called **phrases.**

On occasion, composers wish to heighten or reduce intensity in music. This can be achieved by changing the tempo. Acceleration of tempo is commonly indicated in the score by the Italian abbreviation *accel.,* and a slackening of tempo is frequently shown by *rit.* or *ritard.*

Pitch

Pitch is traditionally described as "high" or "low." Actually, it is the frequency of vibrations of the sounding body (a string, a membrane, a column of air, or an electronic modulator, among others) that determines the pitch of a **tone.** Tones generated by a great number of vibrations are said to be higher than those of fewer vibrations. While the human ear can hear a very large range of vibration frequencies, music up to the advent of electronic synthesizers in the mid-twentieth century traditionally used only those tones between approximately eight vibrations per second and twenty thousand vibrations per second. Moreover, only a very limited number of sounds or tones from among the infinite number possible are actually used.

The keyboard of the piano, with its eighty-eight tones a half step apart from each other, has the approximate range of the pitch materials used in Western music for over one thousand years.

Melody

Melody is a series of single tones sounded successively and organized rhythmically to express a musical idea. It can be either sung or played. It may be simple, without ornamentation, or it may be elaborate, with much ornamentation. It may be smooth-flowing and lyric in quality, with only small skips or pitch **intervals** between successive tones, or very angular, with many large pitch intervals. In extended melodies, there might be a combination of both. Example 2.4 shows a melody that is simple, without ornamentation, as well as smooth and lyric.

Example 2.4   "London Bridge"—Traditional

Example 2.5 shows a melody with elaborate ornamentation.

Example 2.5   Aria, "Every Valley" from *Messiah* by George Frideric Handel *Copyright © 1940 by Hawkes & Son (London) Ltd. Renewed 1967. Reprinted by permission of Boosey & Hawkes, Inc.*

Whereas the melody in example 2.4 proceeds with notes close to each other in a step-wise fashion **(conjunct motion),** example 2.6 is a melody with many large pitch intervals or leaps **(disjunct motion),** as is often characteristic of instrumental works.

Example 2.6 *Don Juan* (first theme) by Richard Strauss

Texture

In the history of Western music, melody has been used in three different textures: (1) as a single unaccompanied line, called **monophony;** (2) as a combination of melodic lines, called **polyphony;** and (3) as a single line with chordal harmonic accompaniment, called **homophony.** Each of these is an example of **texture** in music. The chants of the Roman Catholic Church (ex. 2.7), known as Gregorian chant, are illustrative of monophonic texture:

Example 2.7 *In adventu Domini,* Hymnus—Gregorian chant

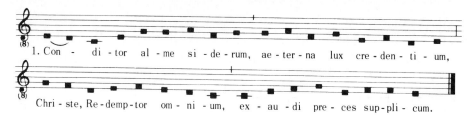

Polyphony is a musical texture in which two or more melodic lines are sounded simultaneously. The simplest example of such a texture is that of the **round** or **canon,** in which the same melody is heard in two or more voice parts begun one after the other. Example 2.8 is a canon in three voices. The second and third voices sing the same melody as does the first voice, but each enters two measures later than the preceding one. Canons were first written to be sung, but composers later also wrote instrumental canons. Because of their vocal origin, each melodic line continued to be called a **voice.**

Example 2.8 *Viva la musica,* canon in three voices by Michael Praetorius

Example 2.8 *Continued*

In example 2.9, Guillaume Dufay took the Gregorian chant melody of example 2.7 and composed two additional lines of melody to create a polyphonic texture. He also changed its rhythmic structure and gave it a metric organization of three pulses. At the same time, he altered the melodic line of the original chant to fit the polyphonic texture; this line is the top voice in the example.

Example 2.9 *Conditor alme siderum* by Guillaume Dufay

Example 2.9 *Continued*

The third type of texture, homophony, is characterized by a single melody supported by a vertical harmonic accompaniment. Example 2.10, like many traditional and popular songs, is an example of homophony.

Example 2.10 "Jeanie with the Light Brown Hair" by Stephen Foster

Harmony

While melody is a series of single tones sounded successively, **harmony** is a group of simultaneously sounded tones (a **chord**) of two or more pitches. Harmony may result from the weaving together of melodic lines, from vertical chords, or from a combination of both. Various systems of harmonic organization have been used in Western music. These have been commonly referred to as modality, tonality, and atonality. **Modality** is a type of harmony based on the use of the eight church modes, scales in common usage during the Middle Ages. Each mode gave rise to a slightly different harmonic organization, since each modal scale was different in structure and had certain unique extramusical associations.

Whereas modal harmony predominated in the vocal writing of the polyphonic masters of the fifteenth and sixteenth centuries, tonal harmony (tonality) increasingly displaced it in the seventeenth century and became the controlling practice of the eighteenth and nineteenth centuries. **Tonality** is a harmonic-melodic system in which the vertical structure of chords and the melodic movement of tones are organized around a central tone, called the **tonic,** to which both the harmony and the melody gravitate. This tone is derived exclusively from the **major** and **minor** scales. Since all major and minor scale patterns gravitate toward a home or tonic tone, tonality is the unified system for all such scales.

Both modality and tonality employ **consonance** and **dissonance.** Consonance gives a feeling of repose, while dissonance gives a feeling of tension. **Atonality,** however, combines tones harmonically without the use of the traditional tonal centers of either modality or tonality. Judged on the basis of either modality or tonality, atonal music strikes the listener as completely dissonant. Atonal music, however, uses combinations of pitches as ends in themselves rather than as means to an end, as in the modal or tonal systems of harmony. Twelve-tone, or **dodecaphonic,** music is often described as atonal. Other harmonic practices less structured than twelve-tone music achieve atonality through the use of experimental devices such as tone **clusters,** chance or **aleatoric** combinations, and electronically produced sounds. Atonal and twelve-tone music belong to the musical developments of the twentieth century.

Dynamics

Dynamics in music are gradations in sound volume. Dynamics became an increasingly important factor in music as the desire for intensity of expression grew in the eighteenth and, particularly, in the nineteenth and twentieth centuries. Composers found dynamic variation a vital tool for intensifying emotional expression and gave explicit directions about its use in their compositions. While there can be no specific indication of dynamic level, composers usually mark their works with the traditional p for the Italian word *piano,* meaning soft, and f for the Italian word *forte,* meaning loud. Multiple use of p or f signals the degree of loudness or softness the composer intends, from *pppp* to *ffff.*

Tone Color

Tone color (also known as **timbre**) is the specific quality of sound produced by an instrument, voice, or any sound-generating device in musical performance. Physically, tone color results from the presence or absence, as well as the intensification, of certain overtones in the sound as heard by the human ear. The tone color of an instrument depends on the method of producing the sound and on the material and construction of the instrument. Three main instrument families traditionally have been recognized based on the method of sound production: (1) strings, (2) winds, and (3) percussion. The sounds may blend together into a single sonority, or they may retain their individual qualities even when played or sung together. The tonal quality of the human voice is determined principally by the anatomy of the singer—whether soprano, alto, tenor, or bass—as well as by the way the singer uses his or her voice.

In the twentieth century, a whole new range of tone colors has been introduced into music through the employment of electronic devices. True electronic music is generated by an electronic tone generator. Electronic media are also used for the manipulation of recorded sounds through the use of tape recorders, amplification or resonating devices, and filters. An example of such a composition is *Gesang der Jünglinge* by Stockhausen (see page 371).

Traditional instruments can also be used to produce varied tonal effects. Glissandos, bowing on the untuned portion of the strings behind the bridges of stringed instruments, and plucking the strings of the piano with fingers (or plectra) are only a few of the techniques in use today. New tonal effects are also obtained by adding devices to traditional instruments. Beyond this, composers have called for a great number of sounds generated by what have traditionally been considered nonmusical instruments or devices such as typewriters, wind machines, automobile horns, and shattering of glass. In their search for new tonal colors and combinations of sounds, composers have often combined many of these devices. They are also blending these new sounds with those of traditional instruments.

Formal Organization

Musical form is the manner in which such components as melody, harmony, rhythm, and tone color are organized. While there are many variants, there are only two elementary types of formal organization, a fact that indicates the simplicity of all artistic forms. One type of formal organization is theme and variation; the other is repetition and contrast. Obviously, both of these devices can be employed with very brief musical ideas or motives. They can each be applied to melody, harmony, rhythm, tone color, or any combination of these. Moreover, these two means of organization can be either independently pursued or combined.

Extended formal design leads to such forms as dance, rondo, song form, theme and variation, sonata, and so forth. In large compositions, such as symphonies, operas, or masses, a number of separate movements, usually of different formal designs, are combined for a unified common purpose or expression.

Expressive Content in Music

The expressive content of music is strongly related to the human feelings it awakens in the listener. Most people respond to music primarily through the emotions, and aesthetic experiences can be described in terms of those emotions. Sometimes the feelings coalesce into a mood that is common to a section or an entire piece, but sometimes they are varied and transient.

Expressive content is also determined in part by our response to the various components of the music. As composers present and manipulate rhythms, melodies, harmonies, and textures, listeners may perceive these events and respond in purely musical ways. The response, for example, to a vigorous rhythm or a "catchy" melody is partly musical, not just emotional.

Another part of the human response to music relates to the perception of form or structure, created through repetition, contrast, and mutation. The balance among them is critical. Ill-advised repetitions, for example, can create tedium and unrestrained contrast can be perceived as chaos.

Occasionally, the listener's response to music is representational. A particular rhythmic pattern, for example, may remind one of a galloping horse, as in the piano accompaniment to Schubert's *Erlkönig* (see ex. 10.2). In *Threnody in Memory of the Victims of Hiroshima* by Penderecki (see ex. 14.1) the varying intensities of the sound clusters intensify the feeling of lament for the victims. For some listeners, the sounds may even trigger the imagination so strongly that they experience vicariously some aspects of that tragedy. For the most part, however, music is frequently abstract and not easily connected to specific visual or representational content. The expressive content, in other words, can be purely musical, conveyed by sound alone.

A Closer Look

Mozart, *Eine kleine Nachtmusik*

Various components of music can be observed in the first movement of Mozart's *Eine kleine Nachtmusik,* which literally means *A Little Night Music.* The entire work, in four movements, is written for a four-part string orchestra and constitutes what is known as a classical **sonata.** Without going into a detailed analysis of the first movement, let us observe how the composer has organized the components of music.

Rhythm

The music moves in a very lively four-beat meter that is absolutely constant and regular. While the overall rhythmic organization gives a distinct feeling of balance, Mozart presents and manipulates numerous rhythmic patterns of differing lengths. Constant variations of the larger patterns are achieved by repetitions of the smaller patterns in various combinations, and short rhythmic phrases are often balanced by larger ones, or vice versa. This constant asymmetry posed against the feeling of complete balance lends rhythmic vitality to the movement.

Melody and Texture

The principal melody is heard almost exclusively in the upper part, played by the first violins. There are many instances of ornamentation—trills, very rapidly repeated notes, and scale patterns—and the movement is basically homophonic in texture, with the three lower parts supporting the first violins. Mozart wrote so skillfully for those instruments not playing the melody, however, that one is rarely conscious of a subordinate accompaniment. There are even passages—often transitional ones—in which the lower parts become independent of the main melody; such passages are brief examples of polyphony within the essentially homophonic movement.

Harmony

The harmony is purely tonal. The first part of the movement, which is repeated, presents two groups of thematic material. The first is in the key of G major and the second in the closely related key of D major. A short passage ends the G major section and forms a bridge, or link, to the key of D major. The process of moving from one key to another is called **modulation;** the bridge leading to the establishment of the new key of D major includes an example. The two keys at first arouse a feeling of contrast and unrest, but by the end of the movement, the harmonic feeling is one of repose rather than tension.

Dynamics and Expressive Content

Mozart made considerable use of dynamic contrasts, but the overall effect is one of conscious reserve rather than dynamic exaggeration. The contrasts, combined with the melodic material, tend to suggest coquettishness rather than deep emotional feeling.

Tone Color

There is no attempt to develop any tonal color beyond that of the normal string quality. Mozart naturally exploited a responsive and expressive string quality by employing the most comfortable and typical range for each of the stringed instruments.

Formal Organization

The movement is a simple sonata-allegro form. The basic organization is statement, repetition, contrast, and return. Following this plan requires the listener to be aware of the melodic motives and how Mozart repeats and varies them. Subtle variations within the repetitions lend interest to the work, which, nevertheless, appears straightforward and simple in its outward presentation.

A SUGGESTED ANALOGY

Acknowledging that sociocultural forces affect all the arts, it may be useful to draw analogies among them, although exact comparisons cannot be made. We can, however, make the following tentative correlations between the elements of the visual arts and music.

Visual line has its counterpart in melody and rhythm. The spatial element is suggested in music both by gradation of volume and the distribution of pitches among the parts. Visual form is closely allied to aural form, for the same principles of design are used in both. Unity of organization has no direct counterpart in music, but the sense of unity is suggested by the clarity of melody and harmonic texture, by the consistence of rhythm, and by the repetition of a theme or idea. Visual color has a direct analogy in tone color of instruments played both separately and in combination. The raw materials of visual art (pigment, canvas, stone, glass, and so forth) are also analogous to the raw materials of music (sounds produced by instruments and voices).

A comparative analysis, for example, of a symphony and a work of sculpture, both from the year 1800, will not reveal conformity in every element. If, however, the two works grew out of much the same social condition, they may show strong similarities of expressive content. Careful study will show, for example, a relationship between the Gregorian chant and the Romanesque cathedral and similarly how a Bach fugue and a Rembrandt painting both arose out of the spirit of the Baroque and conformed to patterns of organization typical of the period. In the twentieth century, Op Art and electronic music are both closely related to physics. One produces optical effects of illusion through color and line manipulation; the other evokes aural sensations by electronic manipulation of sounds. For persons who can see and hear the objective elements in these works, for those who can relate them to the cultural scene, the resultant aesthetic experience will be unforgettably real.

The two examples of art just analyzed, the *Sistine Madonna* and *Eine kleine Nachtmusik,* are representative of their historical periods. Other historical periods have their own styles that we will try to differentiate, recognize, and understand. An increased awareness of the elements of art and their place within the social milieu will also help us understand our own cultural heritage.

Summary

All artists, whether visual or musical, are concerned with principles of design. There are two basic principles of design—repetition and contrast, and theme and variation. All creative artists use these principles to achieve enough variety to stimulate interest and enough unity to avoid chaos. The components of the visual arts include medium, line, space, and color; artists manipulate and arrange these according to their principles of organization. Raphael's *Sistine Madonna* was presented as an example of how artists use the elements to communicate an expressive message in keeping with the style and functions of Renaissance art.

The components of music include rhythm, pitch, melody, texture, harmony, dynamics, and tone color. After a discussion of these musical components, a movement by Mozart was analyzed to demonstrate how composers achieve their expressive ends by shaping the basic materials according to the principles of musical organization.

Suggested Readings

In addition to the specific sources that follow, the general readings on pages 388 and 389 contain valuable information about the topic of this chapter.

Arnheim, Rudolph. *Art and Visual Perception*. 2d ed. Berkeley: University of California Press, 1974.

Cooper, Grosvenor. *Learning to Listen: A Handbook for Music*. Chicago: University of Chicago Press, 1962.

Copland, Aaron. *What to Listen for in Music*. Rev. ed. New York: Mentor Books, 1989.

Dondis, Donis A. *A Primer of Visual Literacy*. Cambridge, MA: MIT Press, 1973.

Haas, Karl. *Inside Music: How to Understand, Listen to and Enjoy Good Music*. New York: Doubleday, 1984.

Kreitler, Hans, and Shulamith Kreitler. *Psychology of the Arts*. Durham, NC: Duke University Press, 1972.

Myers, Leonard B. *Emotion and Meaning in Music*. Chicago: University of Chicago Press, 1961.

Taylor, Joshua C. *Learning to Look: A Handbook for the Visual Arts*. 2d ed. Chicago: University of Chicago Press, 1981.

Chapter 3

···◆●►···

The Greeks and Their Predecessors
(Antiquity–100 B.C.)

Chronology

Visual Arts	Music	Historical Figures and Events
•Venus of Willendorf (c. 20,000–18,000 B.C.)		
•Lascaux cave paintings (c. 14,000–10,000 B.C.)		
		•Cycladic period (c. 3000–1200 B.C.)
•Step Pyramid of Saqqara (c. 2750 B.C.)		
		•Egyptian Fourth Dynasty (2575–2465 B.C.)
•Mycerinus and His Queen (c. 2500 B.C.)		
•Great Sphinx at Giza (c. 2500 B.C.)		
•Acrobats and Bull (c. 1500 B.C.)		
	•Pythagoras (c. 582–c. 500 B.C.)	
	•(Greek modal scales)	
		•Aeschylus (525–456 B.C.)
		•Sophocles (496–406 B.C.)
•Phidias (490–432 B.C.)		•Persian Wars (c. 490 B.C.)
		•Socrates (470–390 B.C.)
		•Plato (427–347 B.C.)
		•Athens at War with Sparta (c. 404 B.C.)
		•Aristotle (384–322 B.C.)
•Praxiteles (390–330 B.C.)		
•Lysippus (c. 360–c. 316 B.C.)		
		•Hellenistic period (c. 325–100 B.C.)

Aphrodite (Ahf-roh-dy´-tee)
Apollo (Ah-pol´-loh)
Aristotle (Ah´-ris-tot-tul)
Athena (Ah-thee´-nah)
Cycladic (Sih-cla´-dic)
Dionysus (Dih-oh-nih´-sus)
Hermes (Hur´-meez)
Lysippus (Lih-sip´-pus)

Mycenaean (My-su-nee´-un)
Mercury (Mur´-kyu-ree)
Nike of Samothrace (Ny´-kee
of Sah´-moh-thrays)
Parthenon (Pahr´-the-non)
Pergamum (Pur´-gah-mum)
Pericles (Peh´-rik-lees)
Phidias (Fi´-dee-us)

Plato (Play´-toh)
Praxiteles (Prax-ih´-ta-lees)
Prometheus (Proh-mee´-thee-
us)
Pythagoras (Pi-thag´-oh-rus)
Venus de Medici (Vee´-nus
day May´-dee-chee)

Study Objectives

1. Survey artistic activity prior to the Greeks.
2. Appreciate the major features of Greek architecture, sculpture, and music.
3. Understand the intellectual concepts revealed in Greek life and art.

PALEOLITHIC PERIOD

Art objects and artifacts are important sources of information about civilizations prior to written history. The number of artworks lost because of their impermanence can only be imagined, since many were created using organic materials subject to destruction by fire, flood, and decay. By comparison, objects created from metals or stone are more likely to survive the ravages of time and nature. They too, however, are susceptible to deterioration and may bring to our eyes a decidedly different appearance than they possessed originally. Among the earliest objects that have survived are stone figures archaeologists have given the generic title of *Venus,* such as the *Venus of Willendorf* (fig. 3.1), a small stone figure found in Austria, dating from roughly 20,000 B.C. (Upper Paleolithic era). It is a symbolic sculpture most probably designed to represent and call forth human fertility. In many early civilizations, people associated fecundity with the female rather than the male and chose to represent females in their ceremonial images. The reduction of detail and the exaggeration of aspects of the human form in the *Venus of Willendorf* lend this ancient work a striking similarity to much twentieth-century sculpture, in which a realistic representation of form is likewise not the artist's primary goal.

Because of their artistic quality, state of preservation, and antiquity, the paintings in the Lascaux caves near Montignac, France, are among the most important art discoveries of the twentieth century (colorplate 8). According

*Colorplate 8
follows p. 50.*

Figure 3.1 *Venus of Willendorf,*
c. 20,000 B.C. Limestone, 4 1/2 in. high.
Natural History Museum, Vienna

to one widely accepted story, the paintings were discovered in 1941 by children playing in a field. Deep within those caves, early artists had painted human and animal figures and weapons, using mixtures of red and yellow ochre—natural colors found in iron ore. In spite of the fragile nature of the materials used in these paintings, the images have survived. In places, the walls are nearly covered with stylized figures representing animals that inhabited western Europe 15,000 years ago. It is one thing to represent an animal with proportional accuracy, but quite another to express its nature and movement. These unnamed artists captured the essence of the animals, using expressive lines and subtle colors.

Because most of the record of the people of the Paleolithic period has been destroyed by natural as well as human forces, we will never know with certainty the purposes of their art objects. They may have been used in religious rituals related to some aspect of the hunt; they may express recognition of a common spirit among living things; or they may be a first effort to express ideas or events in a symbolic manner approaching written language. We can only attempt to explain the artistic efforts of civilizations that existed many millennia ago. Nevertheless, we can safely conjecture that both the *Venus of Willendorf* and the cave paintings of

The Greeks and Their Predecessors (Antiquity–100 B.C.)　　35

Figure 3.2 Step Pyramid of Saqqara, c. 2750 B.C. Limestone, 200 ft. high. (Hirmer Fotoarchiv, Munich)

Lascaux were objects associated with early religion. One thing *is* known: in those early millennia, art played an important role in life.

Egypt

Fifteen thousand years later, Egyptian culture began to emerge. For more than four thousand years—from c. 5000 B.C. to c. 1000 B.C.—Egypt was the site of an extraordinary evolution of the visual arts. As in the Paleolithic period, religious belief seems to have been the primary impetus for Egyptian artists. In early dynasties, Egyptians worshiped a huge array of gods and goddesses represented in art by both human and animal figures. Also central to Egyptian religion was a deep concern for life after death, with elaborately decorated tombs to provide a permanent residence for the deceased. After their death, Egyptian kings became permanent figures in the panoply of gods. Even during their lifetimes, they began the construction of lavish tombs with statuary and paintings for their remains. When they died, these tombs were filled with the art treasures, food, and household goods valued by the newly deified King-God.

Pyramids are lasting images associated with Egyptian architecture and have long been considered masterpieces of ancient art. The Step Pyramid of Saqqara is the oldest of these grand monuments. This two-hundred-foot high pyramid was the most visibly dramatic feature of a funerary complex of structures in honor of King Zoser (fig. 3.2). Imhotep, the earliest architect known by name, built this structure of dressed stone about the year 2750 B.C. It rises in six steps to its pinnacle. (The simpler and better-known geometric pyramidal shape evolved later.) The construction of these monuments required the moving, shaping, and elevation of thousands of massive blocks of stone, some weighing over one hundred tons. In addition, the interior engineering and decoration were carried out with great care and imagination. One of the most complete collections of artifacts found inside pyramids is in the Louvre museum; these artifacts are Fourth Dynasty (2575–2465 B.C.) objects entombed in the famous pyramids of Giza. (I. M. Pei has designed pyramidal structures for his recent addition to the Louvre, thereby bringing some fundamental structural images from ancient Egypt to this important museum, as well as intimating something of its holdings.)

With the pyramids, the second lasting image associated with Egyptian civilization is the Great Sphinx at Giza (fig. 3.3). This sphinx reflects the facial features of King Khafre atop a lion's body. Other sphinxes exhibit an enormous variety of animal/human combinations. In keeping with early Egyptian aesthetics, these grand sculptures often combined the faces of deified kings and bodies of magnificent animals to reflect the power of the monarch. However, much of the meaning of these pictorial images was not understood for centuries. Egyptology (the systematic study of early Egyptian civilization) began only in the late eighteenth century, when Napoleon made an expedition to Egypt in 1798. The French subsequently explored the temples at Luxor and Karnak (fig. 3.4), two sites three hundred miles southeast of Cairo. These temples, and several others, may be of greater architectural importance to Western art than are the more famous pyramids. The Greeks most certainly copied the **post-and-lintel** construction of the Egyptians in which two or more vertical columns support a horizontal beam (see fig. 4.1). They may also have developed their stone capitals in response to some seen in Egypt. The several kinds of capitals in Egyptian temple construction served an ornamental as well as structural purpose. Some had the appearance of a single, open flower; others looked like a papyrus bud, a lotus, or a bundle of palm leaves. The columns were grouped for support, and they provided shade in the scorching desert. They were often carved with incised pictorial images collectively presenting a narrative, as in the temple of Amon at Karnak. It was a French Egyptologist, Jean François Champollion, who deciphered the entire Egyptian alphabet, making the interpretation of these images possible. The term *hieroglyphics* was introduced to refer to the symbolic writing system of the Egyptians.

The obelisk is yet another architectural form derived from the Egyptians. It is a slender, tapered square shaft surmounted by a pyramid. Those found in Egypt were often covered with decorative writing and images and were commemorative structures with characteristics of both sculpture and architecture. The Washington Monument in the United States' capital is clearly derived from an obelisk.

Figure 3.3   Great Sphinx at Giza, c. 2500 B.C. Sandstone, 65 × 240 ft. (Foto Marburg/Art Resource, NY)

A feature of many Egyptian art objects is their grand scale: pyramids reaching four hundred feet in height, a fifty-six-foot statue of Ramses II, the Temple of Amon (the largest of all Egyptian temples, it covers an area one thousand feet by three hundred feet). Much tomb painting contains pictures of delicacy and refinement. Birds and vegetation may be painted with a high degree of realism adjacent to hieroglyphics that are abstracted symbols of familiar objects. Despite Egypt's favorable, dry climate, only a few examples of Egyptian painting on wood survive. Relief or incised representations on smooth surfaces (flat or curved) are more abundant. The Egyptians developed their own conventions of presenting figures in space and in motion using stylized, frozen gestures and postures. Their treatment of perspective, accomplished largely by overlapping figures, may appear naive and arbitrary to twentieth-century eyes.

Figure 3.4 Temple at Karnak, Egypt, XIX Dynasty, c. thirteenth century B.C. Sandstone. (Foto Marburg/Art Resource, NY)

Figure 3.5 *Pair Statue of Mycerinus and His Queen,* Dynasty IV, c. 2599–1571 B.C. Basalt, 4 ft. 8 in. high. Harvard MFA Expedition, Courtesy, Museum of Fine Arts, Boston

The sculpture depicting Mycerinus and His Queen (fig. 3.5) enhanced these rulers' power and status and likely aided in their deification. The figures are nearly life-size and are in a rigid, formal pose with an emphasis on stasis and solidity. The three-dimensionality of the figures was obtained by imposing frontal and side views of the figures on two facets of a block of stone and carving away the material extraneous to the two views. The method has similarities with relief sculpture. One can readily see that the base and back of the sculpture retain the evidence of the original rectangular stone block. As is common in Egyptian sculpture, the bodies of these figures are generalizations of the human figure rather than exact likenesses of the king and queen. The faces are the primary sources of individuality, and even they are generalized to some degree. Like much Egyptian art, this statue conveys a feeling of serenity and monumentality.

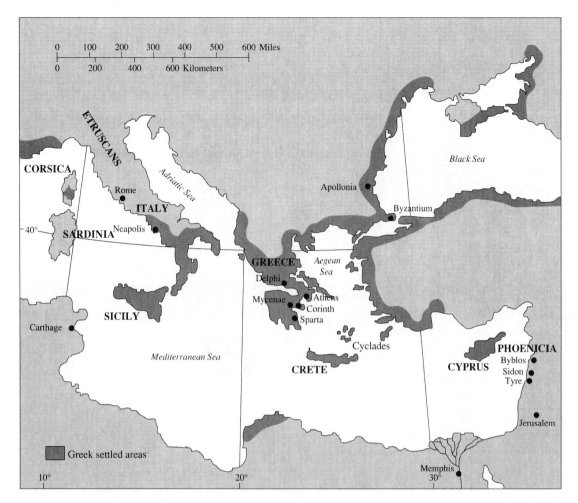

Map of the Mediterranean in the Classic era

Since no notated Egyptian music exists, much less is known about music than about the other arts. There is, however, written evidence of music in Egyptian culture, including choral groups in the service of Egyptian kings. There are also visual representations of musicians performing on instruments. *Feast at the Home of Nakht* (colorplate 9) is a painted panel depicting three figures in Egyptian attire playing rudimentary stringed and wind instruments. The instrument on the right, a type of harp, is similar to later instruments we know of from Greece and Africa. The faces in profile, the almond-shaped eyes, and the general gracefulness of line are characteristic of Egyptian figure painting. Surrounding the figures is a decorative band of recurring shapes, and varied colors and textures.

Colorplate 9 follows p. 50.

The Greeks and Their Predecessors (Antiquity–100 B.C.)   41

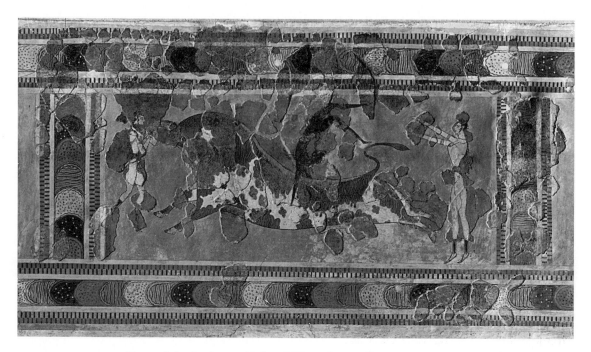

Figure 3.6 *Acrobats and Bull,* c. 1500 B.C. Fresco, 32 in. high. Crete, Heraklion Museum. (Nimatallah/Art Resource, NY)

Crete and the Aegean

Because of its strategic location in the Mediterranean Sea, the island of Crete, the site of Minoan culture, was a dynamic force in ancient history. Its civilization is almost as old as that of Egypt, but its artistic connection to Greece is much stronger. Our knowledge of Minoan art is based primarily on the ruins of their palaces and wall paintings. The **fresco,** or wall painting on wet plaster, from Knossos, *Acrobats and Bull* (fig. 3.6), features a stylized bull ridden by an acrobat, with two female figures in attendance. The fresco technique here gives the wall surface and the bull a varied coloration. However, the most striking artistic effect is the illusion of motion conveyed by the elegant, attenuated lines describing the bull's form. The artist's freedom in rendering this subject naturally is more akin to the style of the cave paintings of Lascaux than to the monumental sculptures of Egypt.

The civilization of Crete influenced much of the adjacent Aegean region, including the island group immediately to the north, called the Cyclades. The artists of the Cycladic period (c. 3000 B.C.–1200 B.C.) created the oldest life-size female statues in existence. Various smaller marble statuettes of human female figures associated with burial rituals remain as well. The appearance of these slender, more realistic figures is strikingly modern when compared with the rotundity of the Venus of Willendorf (see fig. 3.1). Another civilization that developed from earlier Minoan culture was the Mycenaean, which flourished c. 1500 B.C. on the lower peninsula of Greece. In addition to important architectural remains, especially fortresses and palaces, there are examples of Mycenaean gold and silver masks, assorted utensils, and weapons.

Greece

The Western world has always looked upon ancient Greece as the cradle of its cultural development. Consequently, it is appropriate for an extended study of art epochs to begin with its art. We begin with a brief survey of the major periods recognized by scholars of Greek culture.

The Archaic Age of Greek art, extending from about 1000 B.C. to 800 B.C., is the age in which an indigenous Greek art was slowly developing. The second period, often called the Lyric Age and extending from 800 B.C. to the sixth century B.C., is noted for its expressiveness and realism. This was the great age of lyric poetry, from which the period takes its name. The Golden Age, or the Age of Pericles, which flourished in the fifth century B.C. and extended into the fourth century B.C., is considered the high point of Greek culture. During this era, there occurred such a development in drama, architecture, sculpture, and music that the age is still looked upon as the source from which our own culture emerged. The Hellenistic period of Greek culture dates from about 325 B.C. to 100 B.C. and is viewed as a period of decadent Greek art. The following discussions of art and music will concentrate on the Golden Age and its major forms and styles.

The end of the lengthy Persian wars in 480 B.C. precipitated a flood of artistic energy resulting in the Golden Age of Greek art. The spoils of war provided the necessary wealth for artistic patronage, and the stability of a world at peace gave artists the confidence and incentive for renewed creative output. After all, the gods must have approved of their actions to have given the Greeks victory over the Persians. In homage to their gods, the Greeks undertook a great program of public building in which architecture, sculpture, pottery, painting, literature, drama, and music played important roles. When Pericles came to power about 460 B.C., he embarked on a program designed to make Athens the cultural and artistic center of Greece. The core of the program was the construction of a group of buildings on the Acropolis (colorplate 10), of which the Parthenon (fig. 3.7) was the largest and most nearly perfect. With such a fertile ground for artistic activity, it is not surprising that Athens attracted the finest scholars and artists from the entire Greek world. This was the age of Plato, Aristotle, Pythagoras, and Praxiteles, to mention but a few. With the finest minds in the empire centered in one city of about 100,000 inhabitants, Athens held the position of the cultural capital of the Western world.

Colorplate 10 follows p. 50.

Figure 3.7 Greek architecture, model of the Parthenon, Athens, c. 440 B.C. Restored model. Metropolitan Museum of Art, NY, purchase 1890, Levi Hale Willard Bequest

Recognizing that art reflects the attitudes of a people toward important aspects of life, this study of Greek art begins by examining the religion, philosophy, and society of the Athenians. By Athenian society, we do not mean all of the people living in Athens. Slavery was an accepted institution, and the peasants were not much better off. Foreigners could live there and transact business but could not hold office or take part in public affairs. It was the freeborn citizens who constituted Athenian society and were patrons of the arts. The dominant attitude of this group can be summed up as one of "worldliness." The Greeks were concerned mainly with problems of human life, of life in this world, with all that this implies. To live beautifully and happily was the aim of Athenians, and they believed that man was the measure of all things. The Greek temperament sought to master the world by knowing it and reducing it to logical explanations.

The Greeks did not harbor the fear and awe of the supernatural found in other early cultures. Life after death held little interest for them, for Greek religion did not confront, as did the Egyptians and later, Christians, the mystery of death and suffering. The Greek gods and goddesses dwelt in eternal bloom. A Greek tombstone makes no allusions to the darkness of the grave and offers no hope of a glorious resurrection. It shows the commemorated person in some delightful image of the life once lived—a lady selecting a pearl from a basket, a young man stripped for a foot race with his favorite dog beside him. The Greeks did not look upon death with faith in the future, but neither did they dwell upon it with morbid regret. Sorrow for the departed was dignified by the restrained and simple grace with which their memory was portrayed in the marble **relief sculpture,** a sculpture in which three-dimensional forms are carved from a flat background, on the tombstone.

The Greek gods were merely humans endowed with a greater physical beauty and a little more wisdom than ordinary mortals. When the Greeks strove toward the heights of the gods, they sought to rival them for their greater power, not for their moral perfection. The gods themselves were anthropomorphic; that is, they were represented as humans—ideal humans, for the Greeks saw in their gods an idealized likeness of themselves. A different god was worshipped for every aspect of nature and human activity. Zeus was the king of the gods. He ruled from Mount Olympus over such gods as Apollo, the sun god; Mercury, the patron god of commerce and trade; Aphrodite, the goddess of love and beauty; and Athena, the patron goddess of Athens. Besides these, there was a host of lesser gods and goddesses. Greek citizens did not rely on any one god for their spiritual needs, for no god was infallible. Gods could even be outwitted on occasion, as they were by the mortal Prometheus when he stole fire from them. Despite their anthropomorphism, the Greeks were a very religious people, building temples and celebrating festivals in honor of the gods. A daily visit to the temple was a part of each day's routine.

Greek thinkers began to refuse to accept the blind will of their gods as an explanation of the universe. They pursued knowledge, finding order and recurrent patterns in all spheres of intellectual activity. It was the basic structure of the universe that they were seeking, and to them geometry and numbers described it. They brought reason to the fore, using numbers as symbols of the cosmic force they believed was operating throughout the universe. This mathematical reasoning dominated much of their lives, including their art and music. The Greeks began to push earlier superstitions and magic aside in favor of logic and reason.

It is not difficult to find the results of this philosophy in Greek art. It was life that fascinated Greek artists, and this life was glorified in terms of physical perfection. A perfect body was the incarnation of the perfect mind. What was perfect was both beautiful and good. Their art demonstrates again and again the ideal of physical perfection through which the Greeks expressed eternal love, youth, and play. The deep-rooted belief that the gods were ideal humans was responsible for the emphasis on human form in sculpture—an emphasis that gave rise to the concept of the ideal body in art. Interested primarily in the human being, they naturally thought that they should study the effects of art, especially music, on people. This was advocated by such philosophers as Plato and Aristotle.

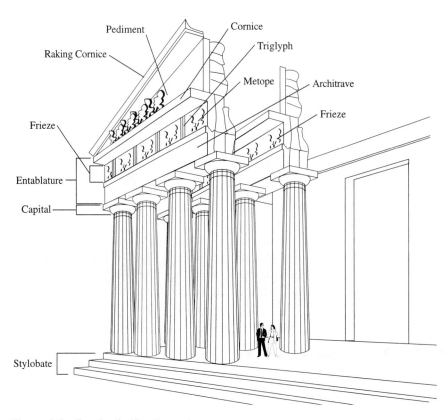

Figure 3.8 Facade of a Greek temple

Because the Greeks were so strongly committed to rational explanation, it is natural that their art should consciously reflect proportions with mathematical precision. All Greek art, architecture, and sculpture, as well as music, is permeated with this element of mathematical exactness. On the other hand, space was represented with some difficulty in Greek vase painting. Space was intangible, without a convincing reality and was, therefore, a challenge to the decorators of vases.

ARCHITECTURE

The main features of Greek temple architecture are shown in the accompanying illustrations (figs. 3.7, 3.8 and 3.9). The columns, without which a covering roof would be impossible, rest on a platform called a **stylobate.** Each **column** has a **capital,** an ornate or simple top to the column. Above the capitals and below the roof is the horizontal **entablature,** which may have unadorned, as well as highly decorated spaces. The elements of the entablature are the **cornice,** frieze, and the **architrave.**

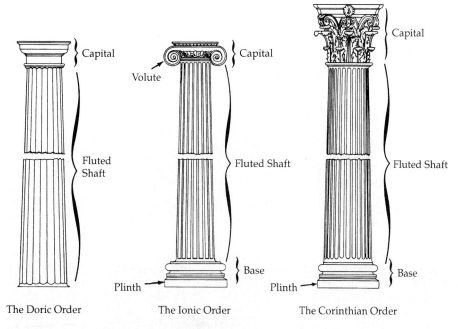

Volute

Plinth

Plinth

The Doric Order   The Ionic Order   The Corinthian Order

Figure 3.9 The three orders of Greek columns

One of the most important parts of the Greek temple, resting above the entablature, is the **pediment,** the triangular space at the front and back of the building extending from the cornice to the roof line. The pediment was frequently reserved for significant sculpture or bas-relief images.

All Greek architects employed post and lintel construction (see fig. 4.1). Since it was so readily available, stone was the usual building material, but because of its brittle quality it had limitations. The distance between columns was determined by the tensile strength of the horizontal beam. In the case of stone, the distance could not be great because the weight of the stone would cause it to break. Consequently, wide buildings had to have many columns with comparatively little distance between them. Similarly, tall buildings were impractical because of the weight that would be placed on the columns. Nevertheless, the limitations of the material were appropriate to the designs of the time. It was only when Christianity prevailed in Europe, and when architects began to use different methods and materials, that religious architecture began to point toward the heavens.

In Greek architecture, several major styles governed the form of columns and other elements. There were three styles, or **orders:** Doric, Ionic, and Corinthian (fig. 3.9), each originally associated with a specific region of Greece. The sturdy **Doric** order, associated with mainland Greece, was the simplest. The fluted columns rested without a base on the stylobate, and were surmounted by a plain capital. The **Ionic** order, associated with Ionia, was very slender and graceful, rested on a pedestal, and was surmounted by a voluted capital. The **Corinthian** order, used widely in the luxury-loving city of Corinth, had a very ornate design, with a slender, fluted column resting on a decorated base and a richly ornamented capital, adorned with acanthus leaves.

A Closer Look

Parthenon

The Parthenon is one of the most famous buildings of the ancient world and one of the supreme examples of Doric architecture. It is a temple dedicated to the goddess Athena, after whom the city of Athens was named.

During an annual festival honoring Athena, a magnificent procession led to the **Acropolis,** the hill on which the Parthenon is situated. Processions and the rituals of popular worship took place in the area surrounding the temple, which was designed to be viewed from outside rather than from within. Inside, priests conducted ceremonies before a thirty-seven foot statue of the goddess (fig. 3.10). Unfortunately, the statue no longer exists. Our knowledge of it comes from written descriptions and from smaller replicas.

The construction of the Parthenon began under Pericles in 447 B.C. and, except for its famous sculptures, was finished in 438 B.C. Iktinos and Callicrates, the architects of the Parthenon, employed rational elements of proportion and the subtle adjustment of shapes and lines to evoke lightness and harmony. Much of the harmony of the building stems from their careful use of mathematical proportions, especially the ratio 9:4. That is the ratio of several elements: the length to the width of the building, the width to the height without pediment, and the width of each column to the distance between columns, axis to axis.

The Parthenon rests on a stone foundation (stylobate) of three steps. It has two **colonnades** or rows across the front and back, and one row of columns on each side. Inside these rows of columns is the **cella,** the main chamber of the temple. A large portion of the cella was walled off and used as a public treasury.

Figure 3.10 *Statue of Athena,* original, c. 435 B.C. Restored model. Courtesy of the Royal Ontario Museum, Toronto

The temple's Doric columns are carefully crafted to avoid straight lines. Each column swells slightly at the middle and narrows imperceptibly toward its top **(entasis).** The columns thus have a lightness that is not found in columns of uniform

Figure 3.11 Equestrian Group from the Parthenon, north frieze, c. 442–439 B.C. Marble, 3 ft. 5 3/4 in. high. Athens, Greece. (Hirmer Fotoarchiv, Munich)

thickness. Although the measurements of the building were calculated and executed with precision, the columns are not perfectly spaced and tilt slightly inward. The stylobate upon which the temple rests curves slightly upward at the ends, apparently to give the temple an image of lightness. The technical perfection of the building is remarkable, as the blocks of marble and the drums of the column are joined and adjusted without cement.

Another striking innovation of the Parthenon was the **frieze,** a low relief sculpture placed above the columns, or at the top of an exterior wall. The frieze became a standard feature of subsequent Grecian temples. For this project, Phidias created sculpture superior in quality and quantity to that of any other Grecian temple. The artist conveys a sense of action through the repeated angular lines of the horses' legs and of the multilayered figures (fig. 3.11).

The exterior frieze of the Parthenon consists of alternating **metopes** and **triglyphs** above the columns. The ninety-two scenes in the metopes portray mythical battles. The triglyphs are simpler decorative panels. A second interior frieze is found around the top of the wall of the cella. Here, Phidias decided to represent the

glory of Athenian democracy, and created a frieze that portrayed the people of Athens parading toward the center of the east facade.

The sculpture of the west pediment illustrates the contest between Athena and Poseidon for the patronage of Athens, and that of the east pediment represents the birth of Athena. The east pediment also displayed *The Three Fates* (fig. 3.12), representing the goddesses present at every birth. This is a serene and realistic piece, with lifelike bodies beneath flowing robes.

Unfortunately, little of the sculpture of the pediments survives in place. In 1799, Lord Elgin, the British Ambassador to Turkey, obtained permission from the occupying Turks to take most of the remaining sculptures of the east frieze from Greece to England. In 1816, the sculptures were purchased by the British Museum, where they are currently housed, and are now referred to as the Elgin Marbles.

The Parthenon integrated in a single building several ideas of supreme importance in Greek culture. It united religious life with intellectual aims; it reconciled the physical body with spiritual life; and it demonstrated that the substance of art was a part of everyday existence. The Classical style of the Parthenon reemerged with force in the Renaissance

Figure 3.12 *The Three Fates,* Parthenon, from Athens, c. 440 B.C. Marble, over life-size. London, England. Copyright British Museum

and in the Neoclassical period [see figs. 7.7, 8.6, 8.11, colorplate 6 (following p. 18), and colorplate 44 (following p. 226)]. Its impact may be observed in civic, academic, ecclesiastical, and domestic architecture from the eighteenth century onward in the United States—specifically in the Greek Revival movement that gave many American college campuses their most important buildings.

SCULPTURE

The deep-rooted belief that the gods could be approached and worshipped through an image in stone brought forth the highest talents of Greek sculptors. Although Greek sculpture was motivated mainly by religion, artists also created monumental sculpture in honor of national achievements and favorite personalities, scholars, athletes, and other distinguished citizens.

Of all the visual arts, sculpture was one of the best suited to the expression of Greek thought, for it embodied the central philosophy of the Greeks—that humans were the measure of all things. The most significant life experiences were those that could be grasped directly by the senses and the mind. To be convincingly real, therefore, an object must have convincing form. Sculpture was perfectly suited to such a purpose.

Sculpture not only existed as an art by and for itself; it was also incorporated into the architectural design of the temples. A frieze was placed in

Colorplate 8 Detail of cave painting at Lascaux: bison, c. 15,000 B.C. Lascaux Caves, Perigord, Dordogne, France. (Douglas Mazonowicz/Art Resource, NY) (See p. 34)

Colorplate 9 Detail of musicians from *Feast at the Home of Nakht*, painted west wall, Tomb of Nakht, Thebes, Egypt. XVIII dynasty. c. 1360 B.C. The Metropolitan Museum of Art, NY. 15.5.19d *(See p. 14, 41)*

Colorplate 10 View of Acropolis and Athens. (Vanni/Art Resource, NY) (See p. 43)

Colorplate 11 Giovanni Paolo Panini, *The Interior of the Pantheon, Rome,* c. 1740. Oil on canvas, 50 1/2 × 39 in. Samuel H. Kress Collection, © 1994 Board of Trustees, National Gallery of Art, Washington, D.C. *(See p. 66, 223)*

Colorplate 12 Interior of San Vitale, c. A.D. 547. Marble and mosaics. Ravenna, Italy. (Scala/Art Resource, NY) *(See p. 76)*

Colorplate 13   *Empress Theodora and Retinue*, c. A.D. 547. Mosaic. San Vitale, Ravenna, Italy. (Scala/Art Resource, NY) *(See p. 76)*

Figure 3.13 *Porch of the Maidens—Erechtheum,* 421 B.C. Marble, figures ca. 8 ft. high. Acropolis, Athens, Greece. (Foto Marburg/Art Resource, NY)

many panels on the exterior, as well as on the interior walls of the temple. Color was an accessory to carvings in all parts of the building, as some re-maining patches of pigment indicate. The effect must have been very differ-ent from the monotonous whiteness that we usually associate with Greek art. Because their temples were dedicated to the gods, the Greeks adorned every available space in the pediment and metopes with figures represent-ing the gods and their activities. In addition, sculptures of the gods and goddesses were placed in prominent sections or rooms of the building.

There is one notable example in which sculpture became part of the structural plan of a temple, as well as a decorative element—the *Erechtheum* (fig. 3.13), with its famous *Porch of the Maidens.* The carved figures carry the weight of the temple's entablature with such ease that we are completely unaware of the downward thrust of several tons of stone on

Figure 3.14 Praxiteles, *Hermes with the Infant Dionysus,* c. 340 B.C. Marble copy of probable bronze original, 7 ft. 1 in. high. Olympia Archeological Museum, Athens, Greece.

their heads. The figures stand gracefully, delicately balanced with one foot behind the other. Each of the bodies carries its burden with the same grace and vitality found in the columns of the Parthenon.

Greek sculptors expressed their society's worldly concerns through a naturalistic, lifelike depiction of the human body. Since the gods were like humans, their statues had to be realistic: the forms were molded in perfect accord with the proportions of the human body. Even though the statues were executed in stone, one has the feeling that there is flesh and blood beneath the surface. Apart from the sculptures from the Parthenon, much of our acquaintance with Greek sculpture derives from Roman copies of Greek works.

Praxiteles was one of the foremost artists of the Golden Age. The statue of *Hermes with the Infant Dionysus* (fig. 3.14) is thought by many scholars to be the only example of this great master's works. Made of marble, it represents the god Hermes carrying Dionysus on his left arm. The child is reaching for some object, probably a bunch of grapes that Hermes might have held in his missing right hand. Grapes and wine are often associated iconographically with Dionysus. The form is very delicately molded, as if the skin were stretched over the inner body. It is in closed form. There is nothing outside the work itself necessary to its understanding. All action and direction are centered toward the middle of the statue: the reaching of the child, the direction of the look—even the object, missing as it is, was without doubt in the center of the work.

Despite the realism of their works, the Greeks did not model their sculpted bodies after real people. They created an ideal human form from their own imagination—an ideal which could only be associated with the gods. For this reason, their sculptures seem to lack personality and individuality. These are qualities reserved for humans, who possess faults and imperfections of both body and character. The statues of the gods, like the figure of Hermes, represent the highest ideal of both mind and body; consequently, no mere mortals could serve as models.

Another great sculptor of the fourth century was Lysippus. The *Aphrodite (Venus de Medici)* (fig. 3.15) is representative of the style of this master and is quite typical of Greek classicism. The emphasis is on the human form, a posed figure that is static, with no movement. It shows classical proportions of the body, with perfect balance. Its form is closed; there is no interest or suggestion of anything outside of the figure—it is complete in itself. The weight of the body is placed on the left foot, with the right foot slightly behind it, in opposition for the sake of balance. There is little emotion expressed; the figure is serene, refined, and very real but hardly alive.

The Athenians were defeated by the Spartans in 404 B.C., influencing the dissolution of Athenian democracy. Because the Spartans—and later Alexander the Great—were conquerors, Greek culture was spread over all of Asia Minor. The Hellenic world became a world of international merchants, industrialists, and warriors. Individualism and personal wealth supplanted civic duty and religious devotion. The calm reason and idealism of the Golden Age faded. In its place arose a taste for garish emotionalism, the exotic, the vulgar, and the dramatic. The temple at Pergamum in Asia Minor (Turkey) shows how the Greek style had changed from the days of the Parthenon. *The Altar of Zeus* at Pergamum, built about 175 B.C. (fig. 3.16), has been reconstructed from archaeological records. It was freestanding, not attached to the temple proper. It stood on a high platform approached by an impressive flight of steps. The sculpted figures, which dominate the altar, represent the struggle among gods and humans. Deeply carved figures with wild movement enhance the feeling of violence and agony of the battle. Gone is the restraint of the earlier Greeks. Space, movement, and emotion replace the reasoned balance of the Parthenon.

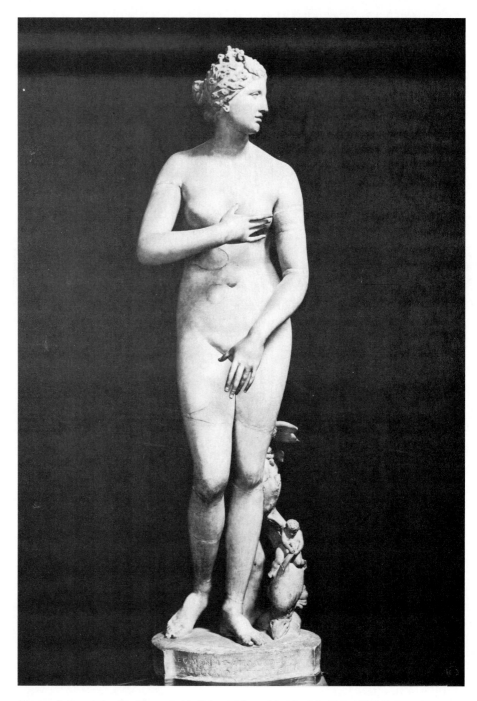

Figure 3.15 *Aphrodite (Venus de Medici)*, c. 200 B.C. Marble, 5 ft. high. Uffizi Gallery, Florence, Italy. (Alinari/Art Resource, NY)

Figure 3.16 *The Altar of Zeus,* from Pergamum, Turkey. West front, c. 175 B.C. Marble. Pergamum Museum, Berlin, Germany. (Bildarchiv Foto Marburg/Art Resource, NY)

Perhaps the finest example of Hellenistic sculpture is *Nike of Samothrace* (fig. 3.17), often called *Winged Victory.* The figure of Victory is shown as if at the moment of alighting on the prow of a ship. The spreading wings and the forward movement of the body that causes the drapery to move in the wind give the work a feeling of vibrant life, motion, and space. Greek art had undergone a great change from the Golden Age and was to be further integrated with non-Grecian cultural ideals under the influence of the Romans in the first century B.C.

In 1506, a statue of Laocoön and his two sons (fig. 3.18) was found in the ruins of the house of the Emperor Titus in Rome. This sculpture records the strangulation of Laocoön and his sons by serpents sent by the goddess Athena. Greek legend recounts the displeasure Laocoön evoked in Athena when he resisted bringing the famed Trojan horse into the city of Troy. This work has been attributed to three sculptors—Agesander, Athenodorus, and Polydorus of Rhodes—whose technical skills are immediately evident in the complex interaction of the figures. Useful comparisons could be made between this work and any of the other sculptures of the Greeks, but the most striking contrasts are evident between it and the *Porch of the Maidens—Erechtheum* (see fig. 3.13). The dynamic lines of the Laocoön release the energy of the subject, whereas the static rigidity of the latter reflects the quality of stone.

Figure 3.17 *Nike of Samothrace (Winged Victory),* c. 200–190 B.C. Marble, 8 ft. high. Louvre, Paris. (© Reunion des Musées Nationaux)

PAINTING

A few examples of Greek painting exist in such typical ancient forms as **murals,** or wall paintings, and panels. The primary sources for information about Greek painting, however, are the many elegant vases that have survived. Although the making of pottery is usually considered one of the minor arts, these vases reflect an extraordinary level of artistic ability, rife with creative expression. The vases show scenes of gods, warriors, heroic events, and myths of endless variety, as well as scenes from everyday life. The vase paintings cannot be dismissed as mere repetitive decorations.

Figure 3.18 *Laocoön and His Two Sons,* first or second century A.D. Marble, 7 ft. high. Vatican Museum, Rome, Italy. (Photo Vatican Museums)

They demonstrate sophisticated techniques in design and painting and an expression of creative individuality that lift them beyond the mundane decorations of ordinary painted vases.

In the Greek vase (fig. 3.19), the unknown artist painted an **oinochoe,** one of the principal Greek vase shapes, with a rather typical early Greek scene of human and animal forms. The **lyra,** played by the central figure, was a common stringed instrument used by the early Greeks. It had a sound box usually made of tortoise shell, and the player plucked the strings

Figure 3.19 Greek vase, red oinochoe with lyra player, listener, and dog, 490–480 B.C. The Metropolitan Museum of Art, NY. Rogers Fund, 1992

with a plectrum. The whole of the picture is framed by two bands of designs frequently found in Greek decorations.

MUSIC

The word *music* is of Greek origin, but there is no way of knowing exactly what Greek music sounded like. All the information we have about Greek music comes through the writings of philosophers and scholars, depictions of instruments in Greek art works, and a few dozen fragments of stone and papyrus inscribed with musical notation. Two of these fragments, *A Hymn to the Sun* and *Skolion of Seikilos,* have been reconstructed by musicologists and made available on recordings, but such recreations can be only informed conjecture.

Greek music most often combined poetry, music, and dancing—with poetry usually the ruler, music the accompaniment, and dancing the rhythmical expression of the poetic text. As in architecture and sculpture, music frequently had close associations with religion and was used as communication between the Greeks and their gods. There were also important civic celebrations—including agricultural and military celebrations, as well as such life-cycle events as weddings and funerals—in which music played a required role. Whatever the context in which it was used, Greek music must have sounded very different from what we are accustomed to hearing, for it was based on a very different organization of the basic materials of sound. This music was nearly always monophonic and vocal, although there were also some purely instrumental pieces. Rhythm was determined by the poetic meter of the text, and the melodic line rose and fell with the inflections of speech. Since the music was monophonic, there was no harmony in the modern sense. Instruments, such as the lyra and the **aulos** (a wind instrument), were used but not harmonically. In vocal performances, they probably imitated the voice; in dance and ceremonial music, instruments played in unison. Music was very important in Greek drama and was probably sung by a number of voices. Our word *chorus,* in fact, comes from the Greek term for the all-male group that sang and danced in classical plays by Sophocles, Aeschylus, and other dramatists.

Despite this music's lack of similarity to our own, we owe a great deal to it. Their concern for proportion and mathematical precision led the Greeks to develop the first systematic studies of musical sound. Pythagoras, a Greek mathematician, is credited with discovering the mathematical ratios of the fundamental pitch intervals: the octave, fourth, and fifth were considered consonances, or "perfect," and all others were dissonances, or "imperfect." His conclusions were based on careful observations of the lengths and vibrations of strings.

Critical to an understanding of Greek music is the doctrine of **ethos.** The Greeks believed that certain scales, or as they were called, modes, possessed moral and ethical values in terms of the emotional responses they produced in listeners. Music had a very definite influence on character and, according to Greek writers, could influence the will in at least three ways: music could spur to action; it could lead to the strengthening of the whole being, just as it could undermine mental and spiritual balance; and it could suspend completely the normal willpower, rendering people unconscious of their acts. This doctrine explains the important role music played in the Greeks' system of education and government. Plato, in the *Republic* and the

Laws, assigns a vital role to the type of music that could be used in education. Similar ideas about modes were to be important for the next 1500 years. We still hold to these basic theories, although we no longer assume this power for scales but to certain combinations of melody, rhythm, harmony, and tone color. Modern science is demonstrating that the values ascribed to music by the Greeks do exist in some measure. Physicians are turning to music as a therapeutic agent in relieving pain, lessening fatigue, and preserving mental health. Modern industrialists recognize the value of music in industry as a means of combating fatigue and encouraging greater production. The modern science of acoustics is founded on these scientific inquiries into the nature of sound.

Summary

The Greeks developed a set of intellectual and emotional concepts that, in their freedom from superstition and intolerance, have never been surpassed. They produced an expressive and lasting art because of a high degree of realism and imagination. Greek citizens exemplified such real devotion to the principles of truth and beauty and such freedom of intellectual processes that they have become a desirable prototype for all time.

The education of Greek citizens made them aware that what we call culture was an essential part of living, not something to be extraneously sought after once the material demands of life had been satisfied. It has been said that every free citizen in Athens could play the aulos and take part in the chorus at the drama. The visual beauties of the Parthenon and other temples were matters of ordinary experience to those people. No wonder creative art flourished as it did and reached the heights of excellence that have seldom been surpassed.

Greek architecture and sculpture showed an almost perfect mathematical balance. Their art was, for the most part, calm and ordered, with clarity of line and restrained movement. Only in the Hellenistic era is violent motion and emotion expressed.

Because the economic and material foundation of Greek life declined, their society collapsed. The artistic glory that lived with Plato and Aristotle faded into an era of sensuality and sentimentality. The Greeks fell victim to their Roman conquerors, but the art of the Golden Age remains as a symbol of a culture that has hardly been equaled for its devotion to truth and beauty.

Suggested Readings

In addition to the specific sources that follow, the general readings on pages 388 and 389 contain valuable information about the topic of this chapter.

Groenewegen Frankfort, H. A., and Bernard Ashmole. *Art of the Ancient World*. Englewood Cliffs, NJ: Prentice-Hall, 1984.

Lawrence, A. W. *Greek Architecture*. The Pelican History of Art Series. New York: Penguin Books, 1984.

Pollitt, J. J. *Art and Experience in Classical Greece*. New York: Cambridge University Press, 1972.

Pollitt, J. J. *Art in the Hellenistic Ages*. New York: Cambridge University Press, 1986.

Spencer, Harold, ed. *Readings in Art History*. Vol. 1, *Ancient Egypt through the Middle Ages*. 3d ed. New York: Scribner, 1982.

Thomson, James. *Music through the Renaissance*. 2d ed. Dubuque, IA: Wm. C. Brown Publishers, 1984.

Woodford, Susan. *The Parthenon*. New York: Cambridge University Press, 1981.

Chapter 4

---✦◉✦---

The Roman Empire and the Early Christians

(100 B.C.–A.D. 500)

Chronology

Visual Arts	Music	Historical Figures and Events
		•Mythical "founding" of Rome 753 B.C.
		•Carthage destroyed (146 B.C.)
		•Marcus Tullius Cicero (106–43 B.C.)
		•Julius Caesar (100–44 B.C.)
		•Publius Virgil (70–19 B.C.)
		•Vitruvius (c. 50–10 B.C.) *De Architectura (On Architecture)*
		•Virgil's *Aeneid* (c. 25 B.C.)
		•Birth of Christ (c. 4 B.C.)
		•Crucifixion of Christ (A.D. c. 29)
•Colosseum built (A.D. 74–80)		•Publius Hadrian (A.D. 76–138)
• *Pont du Gard* (first century A.D.)		
•Pantheon built (A.D. 120)		
•Marcus Aurelius (A.D. 121–180)		
•Meditations (A.D. c. 174)		
		•Constantine I—The Great (A.D. c. 274–337)
		•Edict of Milan (A.D. 313)
		•First Council of Nicaea (A.D. 325)
		•Constantinople established as capital of the Roman Empire (A.D. 330)
•Old St. Peter's Basilica (A.D. 333–390)		
		•St. Ambrose (A.D. 340–397)
		•St. Jerome (A.D. c. 340–420) Latin translation of the Bible
		•St. Augustine (A.D. 354–430)
		•St. John Chrysostom (A.D. c. 374–407) Leader of the Eastern Church
		•Fall of Rome (A.D. 410)
		•City of God (A.D. 413–426)
		•Boethius (c. A.D. 480–524)
•Hagia Sophia (A.D. 532–537)		
•Church of San Vitale (A.D. c. 547)		

Pronunciation Guide

Ara Pacis (Ah´-rah Pah´-chis)   Pantheon (Pan´-thi-ohn)   San Vitale (Sahn Vee-tah´-lay)
Constantine (Kahn´-stan-teen)   *Pont du Gard* (Pont dü Gar)   Sophia (Soh-fee´-ah)
Etruscan (Et-rus´-kan)

Study Objectives

1. Learn how the Romans succeeded the Greeks in their artistic activities.
2. Learn about the contributions of the early Christians in art and music.

The rise and fall of Roman civilization, as well as the rise of the Christian church and its spread throughout Europe, are of primary importance to the understanding of the cultural development of the long and mystical period called the Middle Ages or Medieval period.

Rome first rose to a position of importance about 400 B.C. A small society of landowners and farmers, the Romans became aware of their strength by suppressing the Etruscans, whose territory embraced contemporary Tuscany, and extended south to Rome and north to Mantua. The Romans gradually came to think of themselves as a people with a destiny to fulfill—a mission to bring law and order to all peoples by conquering the whole then-known world. One of their first successes was the destruction of their economic rival, Carthage, in 146 B.C. With their armies, the Romans spread their political and economic control further. One by one, the Grecian city-states fell under the Roman yoke.

The influence of Greek culture was spread throughout the Western world by the Roman conquerors. The Romans recognized the greatness of Hellenic culture, and they sought to acquire the glories of Greek art by possessing its creators, as well as the works themselves. When they conquered Greek cities, they stripped the temples and public buildings of their statues. There are records of Roman generals returning with enormous quantities of art objects, which then found their way into Roman homes. When this supply was exhausted, the Romans began importing artists to make copies of captured art and to create works in the Grecian style. Scholars, artists, and artisans were brought to Rome as slaves and given the task of supplying an ever-increasing demand for Hellenic art. The imperial city of Rome was also immeasurably enriched by the public works engineered by Roman masters and executed by Greek slaves. These buildings' designs derived stylistically from the Greeks but also showed the influence of the Etruscans. Local materials also were important in the appearance of these buildings. Some slaves, who gained their freedom through the generosity of their masters, became teachers of Roman youth, thus enriching the cultural and intellectual life of the Italian city.

The Roman Empire and the Early Christians (100 B.C.–A.D. 500)   63

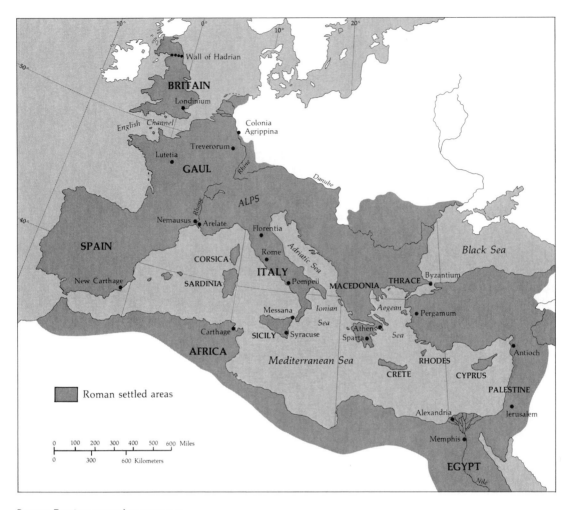

Roman Empire: second century A.D.

Roman religion was akin to that of the Greeks, but the Romans placed greater faith in the strength of their armies than in their gods. Like the Greeks, they also were "worldly." They had only a vague concern for life after death and put little credence in any idea of immortality. Religion centered on the home, with special household gods for each family activity. Consequently, worship was carried on in the home more than in the temple. Not content to borrow only art from the Greeks, they borrowed gods as well.

The Romans were also systematizers, excelling in architecture, engineering, and law. A number of architectural treatises were written, most no longer extant, recording the Romans' principles of design. One of them, *De Architectura (On Architecture)*, by the first century architect, Vitruvius, relies heavily on Greek ideas, but it documents many of the design considerations of his contemporaries as well. This work, available in English today, was an important influence on Renaissance artists. The Romans left monuments of civil construction that have been admired ever since. They crisscrossed Europe with a system of military roads, many of which still exist. They built aqueducts for bringing water into cities from long distances, and they engineered drainage systems that brought thousands of acres of swamplands into agricultural production. These activities were all closely allied with the Romans' self-styled destiny as empire builders.

Roman law has been the basis of all subsequent legal systems of Western civilization. The Romans could never have subjected other peoples had they not perfected a practical system of law and justice. Their law, according to Cicero, was based on the standards of justice determined not by divine revelation, but by common citizens using good sense. As Roman laws were put into practice and legal procedures were standardized, the law was codified and systematized by what we might call "legal engineering."

ROMAN ARCHITECTURE

The architectural needs of the Romans were very different from those of the Greeks. Public arenas, forums, and baths were more important than temples. The Romans required public buildings where thousands could be accommodated as spectators at public games and entertainments. Large buildings spanning acres of space created new problems for architects and engineers. The Greek type of post-and-lintel construction was incapable, as we have seen, of spanning large areas of space. The Romans, who excelled in architectural innovation, solved this problem by using the **arched vault** of the Etruscans (fig. 4.1). By crossing two such arches, they produced the **barrel vault,** a semicylindrical vault joined by two parallel walls, and the **groined vault,** created by the intersection of two barrel vaults, which is capable of spanning large volumes of space, both horizontally and vertically. This technique gave rise to the **dome,** a hemispherical vault supported by columns or walls, which is now recognized as a symbol of authority because of its extensive use by the Romans in public buildings. Other problems were solved by the development of stronger concrete.

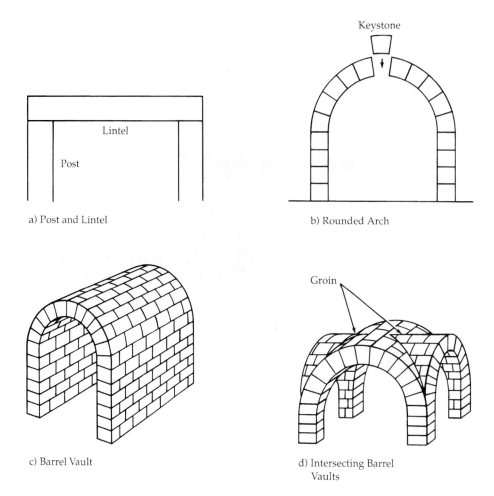

Figure 4.1 Methods of construction in Roman architecture

The temple known as the *Pantheon* (fig. 4.2), a building for all the gods, is an excellent example of the adaptation of Greek design to Roman use. The **portico,** or porch, is of Greek design, with Corinthian columns supporting a rather too tall pediment compared to that of the Parthenon. The main part of the edifice is a huge, oval-shaped structure capped by a dome. Because columns were not necessary to support the roof in this vaulted building, there was a great, open hall capable of accommodating huge crowds (see colorplate 11). The Pantheon, unlike the Greek temple, was to be viewed from within, and the interior is, therefore,

Colorplate 11 follows p. 50.

Figure 4.2 Pantheon, c. A.D. 117–125. 110 × 110 ft. Rome, Italy. (Scala/Art Resource, NY)

much more impressive than the exterior. It is as high as it is wide (110 × 110 ft.), giving a sense of expanding space that is enhanced even more by the light streaming in through a circular opening in the hemispheric dome. Seven semicircular niches in the interior walls contained statues of Roman gods. It is clear that the Pantheon was a temple to hold a congregation (like our churches, synagogues, and mosques) rather than merely a sanctuary for a Greek god. While the Pantheon is one of the best-designed examples of Roman religious building, it—like the others—lacked the balance and poise of those built by the Greeks. Although the Greek orders were used for the columns, the ornaments were crude in comparison with those of the Greeks and were not perfectly integrated into the architectural plan. Examination of extant architectural monuments suggests that the Romans were not natural artists but buyers and borrowers whose copies were often less expressive than the originals.

Figure 4.3 Colosseum, A.D. 72–80. Travertine, tufa, brick, and marble, c. 615 × 510 ft. Rome, Italy. (© Sue Klemens/Uniphoto Picture Agency)

A monument to the Roman desire for space and pleasure is the Colosseum (fig. 4.3), the great open-air arena used for games and gladiatorial combats. It is one of the most remarkable structures of its age because of its size and utility. It was constructed on the principle of the round arch. With arches placed side by side in tiers, it was possible to construct a building four stories high. This vast, oval structure was about 600 feet long, with a seating capacity close to 45,000. Underneath the seats were countless rooms for attendants, cages for wild animals, and even small shops. It was also built in such a manner that the floor of the arena could be flooded. On these occasions audiences could enjoy the sight of naval battles fought before their very eyes. There was little decoration on the Colosseum, for the plain, rhythmic flow of columns and arches provided sufficient eye appeal. The whole edifice reflects the efficiency of Roman engineering in solving spatial and structural problems. Today, in a decayed condition, the Colosseum is an important tourist attraction.

A truly utilitarian application of the Roman arch can be seen in the *Pont du Gard* at Nîmes, France (fig. 4.4). This aqueduct was built in the first century A.D. as part of a system designed to bring water to Nîmes, a town that was first a Greek settlement, and later a Roman outpost. Crossing the river Gard in a three-tiered span about 900 feet long and 180 feet high, the *Pont du Gard* is evidence of the Romans' concern for controlling the vast reaches of the Empire with technologically advanced public works.

Figure 4.4 *Pont du Gard,* first century B.C. 854 ft. long × 162 ft. high. Nîmes, France. (Foto Marburg/Art Resource, NY)

The Roman house (fig. 4.5) suggests a concern for personal magnificence and spatial control. Because much of the owner's personal business and worship was carried on in the home, it was natural to spend large sums of money on domestic housing. The lavishly built houses contained many of the conveniences we think of as modern, such as central heating, running water, and sanitation. Their plans usually included a central court surrounded by a columned structure in the Greek fashion and elaborate rooms for dining and entertaining. Large parcels of land were reserved for gardens, walks, and pools. The size and opulence of villas was directly proportional to the wealth or political power enjoyed by the owners. This is confirmed by the writings of their contemporaries and excavations of archeological sites. A sincere appreciation of the finer values of life then as now, however, did not always coexist with wealth and power.

ROMAN SCULPTURE

Art in Rome was not confined to the temples but was in great demand for private use. An elaborate industry developed to make copies of Greek statues and other objects of art brought to Rome as war booty. This was done

The Roman Empire and the Early Christians (100 B.C.–A.D. 500)   69

Figure 4.5 House of the Vettii, A.D. 65. Pompeii, Italy. (Courtesy University Prints)

in part by enslaved artists. To expedite the copying process, the Romans devised a method of casting in which a mold made from the original was used to create plaster copies. This innovation made it possible to make as many copies as desired. It was not, however, the restrained sculpture from the Parthenon that was copied; more often it was art from the first century B.C., when Greek art had become more lavish and sensual.

Not all Roman art, however, was imitative of Greek models. The Romans excelled in portrait sculpture for a very good reason. In order to honor their soldiers, prominent citizens, and merchants, they created sculptural likenesses of them for prominent places in public buildings, as well as homes. Moreover, it was not unusual for wealthy people to commission a number of statues of themselves while still living so that a realistic likeness would be available after death (fig 4.6). Some even went so far as to have their own tombs constructed and decorated with reliefs showing their heroic deeds.

Figure 4.6 *Augustus of Prima Porta,* c. 20 B.C. Marble, 6 ft. 8 in. high. Vatican Museum, Rome, Italy. (Alinari/Art Resource, NY)

Figure 4.7 Roman bust, first century B.C. Marble, 14 in. high. The Metropolitan Museum of Art, NY. Rogers Fund, 1912, 12.233

The "ideal form" of the Greeks did not interest the Romans in the slightest; rather, their heroes were portrayed as they actually lived and walked among the people. In order to meet the demands for this kind of sculpture, artists often created a number of generic torsos of various kinds—for soldiers, politicians, and other important citizens. When a certain kind of statue was needed, it was necessary only to model the face, which was then placed on an appropriate torso. The marble bust of an unidentified Roman (fig. 4.7), with its bald head, wrinkled brow, and set jaw, reflects the Roman concern for realistic portrayal. Likewise, the full-length portrait of *Augustus*

Figure 4.8 Panel from *Ara Pacis Frieze* (Altar of Peace), c. 10 B.C. Marble, c. 5 ft. 3 in. × 5 ft. 8 in. Rome, Italy. (Alinari/Art Resource, NY)

of Prima Porta (fig. 4.6) presents the Emperor in an oratorical, youthful pose. This is an idealized male figure, derived from an earlier Greek statue.

Another lasting innovation of Roman sculptors was the perspective created in groups of figures carved in relief. By making distant figures smaller and placing them behind foreground figures, artists created an illusion of space. A famous example is the *Ara Pacis Frieze* (fig. 4.8), in which there is a distinction between foreground and background. The foreground figures are in high relief, giving them the appearance of approaching the viewer. The effect is heightened because the artist turned the feet of these figures outward and beyond the flat surface of the marble slab. Furthermore, the background figures are shown in profile, while the others have their faces turned toward the observer, adding to the impression of depth.

ROMAN MUSIC

What is known about Roman music is based on contemporaneous visual art and written documents. Vitruvius, mentioned earlier, devoted a substantial section of his treatise on architecture to musical acoustics and included a description of the building of organs, then known as the *hydraulis*. Cicero recommended the study of music to those who wished to become orators.

Later, Boethius, a Roman of the early Christian era, included music with geometry, arithmetic, and astronomy in the Quadrivium, the four essential areas of knowledge. (Music had already been given an important position in the liberal arts in the first century B.C.) He thought of musicians as comprising three categories: performers, creators, and critics or theorists. The last received his highest esteem. Boethius's treatise included a reasoned theoretical description of music, not only of importance to his contemporaries, but to theorists of the Middle Ages as well.

Music had practical applications in Roman society. It accompanied processionals, was an essential part of theatrical entertainments, and, much like at our football games, was a part of gladiatorial spectacles as well. Considering the extent of their musical life, it is unfortunate they had no system of notation, denying us the possibility of even approximating the sounds of their music.

EARLY CHRISTIAN ART

During its early days, Christianity had little place for visual art of any kind. It had no architecture except the catacombs of Rome, which originally were burial places. It had no wealth, for most of its early converts were from the lower and middle classes, and art cannot thrive without wealth. Artistic expression had been the prerogative and luxury of the Roman citizen; consequently, the less privileged had little or no artistic experience. Another more fundamental reason for the lack of art was its association with everything pagan and corrupt—and Roman. Because Christianity was in direct opposition to the existing religious and social structure, anything that formed an integral part of that structure was an abomination, as was Roman society itself. It was only after upper-class Romans became converted and after the authorities ceased to persecute the Christians that a new art began to flourish.

Christian art revolved around the teaching of its various doctrines, as well as the rituals of worship. Ritual, theology, and symbolism were borrowed freely from the Jews and the Greeks. The part played by Judaism is well known. Needless to say, the Old Testament is Hebraic, and certain portions of present-day Christian rituals and services evolved from Jewish practice. The influence of Judaic culture came also through its literature, especially the Old Testament stories and psalms. Because Jews abided by the Mosaic Law that forbade images, there was very little representational art.

The religious practices of the Greeks, notably Baptism and the Eucharist, also contributed to the Christian ritual. The Eucharist, which became the Lord's Supper of the Christian faith, derived from similar ceremonial meals celebrated by both Jews and Greeks. The cross itself became, symbolically, the floor plan for the Christian church. The predecessor of the cruciform church, the **basilica,** a rectangular hall flanked by aisles, was derived

Figure 4.9 Greek (left) and Latin (right) crosses— Sandgren

from the form of Greek temples of worship. Most churches in Italy used the design of the Roman cross, in which the upright is longer than the crossarm. Those in the East and in Greece used the Greek cross, in which the arm is equal in length to the upright (fig. 4.9). The floor plan for the basilica of *Old St. Peter's* (fig. 4.10) preceded the more elaborate plan for Hagia Sophia (fig. 4.11) by some 200 years.

In A.D. 313, the Roman Emperor Constantine signed the Edict of Milan, legalizing Christianity throughout the Roman Empire. Because the center of Roman power was shifting toward the East, Constantine moved his capital to Byzantium, which was later called Constantinople and is now called Istanbul (the capital of Turkey). It was amid these surroundings and under these circumstances that the arts of western Asia came to play a more important role in Christian art, especially architecture and painting.

The style of art and architecture we now call "Byzantine" resulted from Near Eastern artistic conventions influencing the demands and ideals of the new religion. After the Church became well organized and accepted, its more wealthy converts desired churches built in a more elaborate fashion. The eastern preferences for brilliant colors, complex patterns, and sensuous expression aroused the spirit of mystic exaltation and emotion inherent in a religion that held out the promise of immortality. Hagia Sophia (fig. 4.11), located in Istanbul, is the prototype of the influence of the eastern temperament on Christian art. The floor plan was in the form of the Greek cross, with a huge dome centered over the entire square formed by the cross. Like the Roman Pantheon, Hagia Sophia was most impressive from the interior. The marble walls were richly decorated with multi-colored, representational **mosaics** of tile against a background of gold leaf. Light, let in by a row of windows set in the base of the dome, played on the jewel-like colors of the

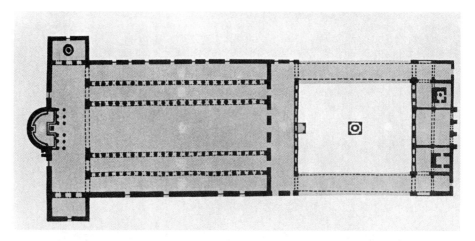

Figure 4.10 Floor plan of the basilica of *Old St. Peter's*. Rome. (Figure adapted from *Gardner's Art Through the Ages,* Fifth Edition by Horst de la Croix, copyright © 1970 by Harcourt Brace & Company, reproduced by permission of the publisher.)

interior like the rays of sun on a brilliant diamond. In addition, the sacred relics, altars, crosses, and statues were ornamented with precious stones set in backgrounds of richly carved gold and silver.

All of these treasures were destroyed or whitewashed over during the subsequent centuries of Turkish and Arabic rule. Most of the mosaics were covered by patterns associated with Islam though some have been restored. The present-day spires and minarets were added by Moslem artists and have no Christian significance. In recent years, the Turkish government has allowed the layers of later decoration to be removed, showing portions of the original Byzantine art.

Another superb example of the Byzantine style is the church of San Vitale in Ravenna, Italy (colorplate 12). It was modeled after Hagia Sophia and was richly decorated with colorful mosaics. A sense of great height is intensified by rows of windows at every level, flooding the interior with light.

Colorplate 12 follows p. 50.

Mosaics were one of the predominant Byzantine art forms. They consist of small colored bits of tile and glass commonly used to form geometric patterns or natural figures. Their beauty was enhanced by the introduction of controlled light. *Empress Theodora and Retinue* (colorplate 13) is a typical example of this kind of art. Decorative patterns and rich textures are represented in what may appear to be a rather intractable medium. Only subtle movement is expressed and that especially in the attenuated fingers of the figures. Space is more implied than represented in the composition.

Colorplate 13 follows p. 50.

Figure 4.11 Anthemius of Tralles and Isodorus of Miletos, *Hagia Sophia,* A.D. 532–537, minarets added c. 453. Istanbul (Constantinople), Turkey. (Hirmer Fotoarchiv Munich)

EARLY CHRISTIAN MUSIC

The earliest Christians, as we have seen, had little opportunity to develop art. This applied equally to music. Early Christian history gives only a vague notion of the use of music, partly because of the inadequate system of notation that made preservation almost impossible. It is known that the Jewish psalms were incorporated into the Christian liturgy. In fact, these chants probably served as their greatest source of musical material. The psalms were sung—as they were by the Jews—monophonically and unaccompanied by instruments. The Gospels, the letters of the Apostle Paul, and the book of Revelation refer to the singing of psalms and hymns. Psalms were sung by a single person, or they could be performed responsorially. In responsorial singing, a leader or cantor alternates with the others assembled for worship. In yet a third form, antiphonal psalmody, two equal-sized groups alternate in the singing of verses. All of these styles had antecedents in Jewish worship and are still practiced in many churches and synagogues today. The text was of primary importance in each of these musical expressions, but that did not preclude the possibility of elaboration in performance. The florid ornaments of the Christian chants are most likely taken from contemporaneous vocal styles of the eastern Mediterranean and Near East, including Jewish and Arab chants. They are analogous to the brilliant colors and designs of Byzantine architecture.

The melodic lines of early Christian music spanned a narrow range and emphasized the words at the expense of the music. It was monodic and had no harmony. It was also vocal, for instruments were associated with pagan rites. In Rome, the early Christians were a clandestine group, meeting secretly in the catacombs and always in fear of detection. That they had any music is a wonder, but its power was evident even in the earliest days. Like the Greeks, they saw in music a tremendous force for shaping one's moral life and a means of coming into mystical contact with God.

As Christianity grew, there were many who came into the Church knowing the popular songs. Believing these songs to be evil influences, the Church made every effort to purge this popular music from the service. Music existed for one purpose only, to serve God. It could not exist for its own sake as an expressive art form. It is not surprising, then, to find little change in the scope of music during these early times. As an expressive art, music received no encouragement. On the contrary, music for pleasure was a sin, to be dealt with by the Church authorities. It was only after Christianity became the Roman state religion that music, as well as other arts, became an integral part of the ritual and a moving force in the development and spread of Christianity.

Secular music and instrumental music are not described by the early church founders and leaders. Their contemporaries, secular Romans, did write about instruments and their uses. It must be assumed that the only people among the Christians capable of writing were the clergy, and they had no reason to document practices with which they were in disagreement.

Summary

The Romans were the empire builders of western Europe from about 100 B.C. to A.D. 300. They were mainly concerned with increasing their power and controlling large geographic areas politically and economically. As a result, they became master politicians, lawmakers, and engineers. Their artistic activity revealed this ambition. Their greatest achievements were in the areas of architecture and engineering. With the invention of the arch and vault, they constructed impressive arenas, baths, and public buildings, and they spanned great areas with aqueducts, bridges, and roads.

The Romans admired and copied the Grecian style of sculpture and decoration, especially that of the Hellenic period. However, they made notable contributions in portraiture, sculpting their important citizens, generals, and heroes. There was very little artistic activity that did not serve a functional and practical purpose for the pleasure and glory of the Empire.

The earliest Christian art did not constitute a style in itself. There is little record of early Christian art until Constantine moved the capital of Christianity to Byzantium. Byzantine architecture reflects both Roman-Greek and Near Eastern influences. The multi-colored mosaic decorations demonstrate the Eastern love of stylized patterns of brightly contrasted color. The churches contained great, domed spaces with mosaic decoration. Music in the early Christian church was confined to vocal chants that were most likely borrowed from the Jewish liturgy. We know little about this music because we have no examples of notation and few historical records.

Suggested Readings

In addition to the specific sources that follow, the general readings on pages 388 and 389 contain much valuable information about the topic of this chapter.

Spencer, Harold, ed. "Readings in Art History." Vol. 1, *Ancient Egypt through the Middle Ages.* 3d ed. New York: Scribner, 1983.

Wheeler, Mortimer. *Roman Art and Architecture.* New York: Thames Hudson, 1965.

Chapter 5

⸭⸺◉⸺⸭

The Medieval Period—Romanesque
(500–1100)

Chronology

Visual Arts	Music	Historical Figures and Events
• Boethius (c. 480–524) • Hagia Sophia, Constantinople (532–537)		
	• Gregorian chant (c. 540–1100) • Pope Gregory (c. 540–604)	
		• Rise of the Monasteries (A.D. c. 650) • Charlemagne (742–814) • Second Council of Nicaea (787) • Feudalism established (c. 900) • Cluny Abbey founded (910) • Otto the Great (912–973)
• Baptistry, Cathedral and Tower, Pisa (1052–1272)	• Guido of Arezzo (c. 997–1050)	
		• The Norman Conquest (1066)
• The Bayeux Tapestry (c. 1088) • Notre Dame la Grande, Poitiers, France (late 11th century) • San Ambrogio, Milan (late 11th century) • St. Trophime portal, Arles, France (c. 1105) • La Madeleine tympanum, Vézelay (c. 1130)		

Pronunciation Guide

Agnus Dei (Ahn´-yoos Day´-ee)
Ambrogio (Ahm-broh´-joh)
Aquinas (Ah-kwih´-nahs)
Charlemagne (Shar-lah-mayn)
La Madeleine (Lah Mah-de-layn)
Credo (Kray´-doh)

Kyrie eleison (Ki´-ree-ay ay-lay´-ee-son)
Gloria in excelsis (Gloh´-ree-ah in eks-chel´-sis)
Guido of Arezzo (Gwee-doh of Ah-ret-soh)
Ite, missa est (Ee´-te, mee´-sah est)

Nicaea (Nai-see´-ah)
Notre Dame la Grande (Noh-trah Dahm´ lah Grahnd´)
Pisa (Pee´-zah)
Poitiers (Pwah-tyay)
Sanctus (Sahnk´-toos)
St. Trophime (San Troh-feem)
Vézelay (Vay-ze-lay)

1. Learn about Romanesque art as the mirror of the religious beliefs and practices of the Church, the dominant medieval patron of the arts.
2. Understand the symbolism in Church architecture.

THE MEDIEVAL PERIOD: GENERAL CHARACTERISTICS

The span of history known as the medieval period or the Middle Ages extends, roughly, from the year 500 to about 1400. This rather lengthy period is commonly divided into two important subperiods, the Romanesque (500–1100) and the Gothic (1100–1400). The medieval period fascinates us not only because of its civilization, but also because of our ties to the institutions and people of that age. Any study of the Middle Ages would include such personalities as St. Thomas Aquinas, St. Francis, and Dante. Many of our economic and religious institutions date back to medieval days, when the middle class emerged from the ranks of the medieval city burghers and the merchant class. Labor unions, in fact, have their origin in the guild systems of the thirteenth century. It was also at this time that the Christian church became an organized institution and came to dominate many aspects of European life. The universities of today owe many of their traditions to their medieval counterparts; in fact, a few European universities have had a continuous existence since the medieval period.

The Middle Ages saw many changes in the conditions on which music and the visual arts depended for their existence and growth. A study of the basic features of social, religious, economic, and political life is necessary for an understanding of the artistic aims and practices of this fascinating age.

The artistic developments in the medieval period spring from the basic attitudes of the Church, for the Church was almost the sole patron of the arts and was to remain so for many centuries. All activities of life were connected inseparably with the supreme and new ecclesiastical power, which in its first thousand years was to give an entirely new face to all of Europe. A philosophy of otherworldliness, in contrast to the worldly attitude of the Greeks and Romans, was the guiding principle of the Church. The doctrine of salvation formed the core of Christianity, and around this doctrine the early rituals and institutions were built. Medieval Christianity did not offer a promise of material well-being. On the contrary, it taught that this life was dirty and sordid—to be endured, not enjoyed. Life in the Middle Ages was full of human suffering, which helped the Christians concentrate on religion and on the hope of salvation.

Poverty was a virtue because it was less likely that people would be tempted by evil if they had little of this world's goods. The idea that a rich person had as much chance of going to heaven as a camel had of going through a needle's eye was more than an epigram. If admonition was not enough, there was always the prospect of hell to consider. The medieval church emphasized the idea of the Devil, who was always on hand to waylay the faithful. He was especially active whenever there were pleasurable pursuits at hand. All avenues of pleasure were, therefore, closely guarded, and many faithful became hermits in the wilderness to avoid the Devil's persuasive temptations.

One result of this attitude was the rise of the monastic movement. Groups of devout worshipers joined in communal enterprises in which they lived, worked, and worshiped together. The organization of monastic buildings and their relationships were designed to accommodate this life of work and worship. As the plan of Cluny Abbey (France) illustrates, a monastery was in a sense a small city, with worship spaces of various sizes, infirmary, bakery, farm, stables, and living quarters (figs. 5.1, 5.2). To a large degree, the general plan of monasteries was similar throughout the Christian world.

The monks, as monastic residents were called, took vows of poverty, obedience, industry, and chastity. In this environment, one could contemplate God and bring the soul into harmony with the spirit of the Church. One labored not because labor was a healthy and happy occupation or because it would help others. The virtue of labor was that it reduced the fires of passion within one's soul. The monasteries provided a safe refuge for those who felt the need for spiritual protection.

While the monks spent most of their time in prayer and manual labor, they also found time to pursue intellectual activities. In fact, learning during much of the medieval period was centered largely in the monasteries. It was in such an environment that the major early scholars wrote the treatises that were to give them recognition.

Because it was pagan, Greek culture was generally condemned by Christian scholars. The works of Plato and Aristotle were banned until the time of St. Thomas Aquinas, in the thirteenth century, and then they were approved only through the interpretation of Aquinas. Doctrines that differed in any way from those laid down by the Church were considered heretical. The punishment for such beliefs often was burning at the stake or, at best, some form of torture that would drive out the evil spirits. If the guilty were spared, it was because of repentance and some form of penance. The Church was an elaborate organization designed to safeguard the faithful from evil.

Another medieval institution that left its imprint on art was feudalism, which reached its zenith about the twelfth century and provided a certain amount of protection and economic stability for the lower classes of society. It also enabled the nobility to exploit the helpless for economic and military purposes. Secular wealth was concentrated in the hands of the feudal lords,

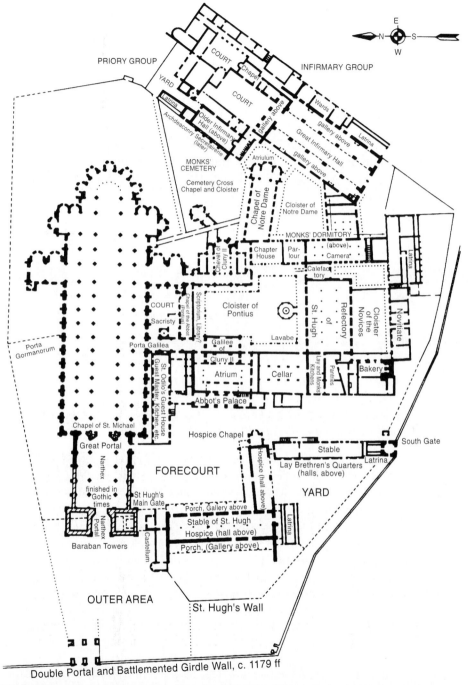

Figure 5.1 Plan of Cluny Abbey, founded A.D. 910. (From Kenneth John Conant, "Medieval Academy Excavations at Cluny, IX: Systematic Dimensions in the Buildings," *Speculum* 38(1963), p. 13, plate. Reprinted by permission of The Medieval Academy of America, Cambridge, MA.)

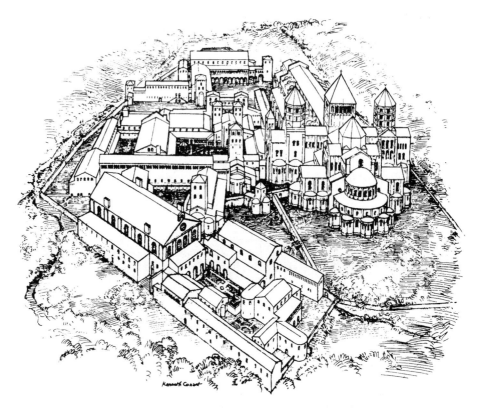

Figure 5.2 Aerial view of Cluny Abbey. (From Kenneth John Conant, *Cluny: Les églises et la maison du chef d'ordre*. The Medieval Academy of America, Publication No. 77. Cambridge, Mass.: The Medieval Academy of America, 1968. Reprinted by permission.)

who enjoyed complete sovereignty in their own domain. Among the artistic monuments of feudalism were the massive castles that graced the mountain slopes of medieval Europe. They served much the same purpose as the monasteries in that they provided safety from the hostile forces of neighboring nobles, as well as from wandering bands of highwaymen.

Because feudal lords held power by the grace of the Church, it is not surprising to find the Church closely allied to the feudal system. Many of the more powerful lords were also bishops or archbishops who enjoyed a double concentration of wealth and power. The Church and civil authority were, for all practical purposes, one and the same. The nobles often supplied the wealth, while the monks planned and directed the construction and decoration of the churches. The Church and feudalism together were a fortress of economic and political power based on agrarian and spiritual control. The Church emerged as the guardian of the land, as well as the custodian of salvation. To protect its power, it even suggested that people should be content with the station of life into which they were born. As the

Church expanded its ecclesiastical, civil, and economic authority, it became the supreme power of medieval Europe.

THE CHURCH AND MEDIEVAL ART

Because the Church was the supreme power, art had to have a religious function. This was true in almost every genre of medieval art and music. Religious architecture was one of two predominant types of construction, the other being the building of castles and fortresses. Where people lived was of little consequence, for the comforts of life were considered evil.

Illiteracy was almost universal, except among the monks, so biblical stories were most easily taught through the visual arts. Painting, stained glass, and sculpture served as tools of religious education. As sole patron of the arts, the Church could control most aspects of painting and sculpture. In 787, the Second Council of Nicaea established a set of rules for artistic representation of religious subjects that was to be binding upon artists for almost 500 years:

> The substance of religious scenes is not left to the initiative of the artists; it derives from the principles laid down by the Catholic Church and religious tradition. . . . His [sic] art alone belongs to the painter, its organization and arrangement belong to the clergy.

This was a very logical rule, for the Church, not the individual, was the guardian of the sacred truth on which the safety of society and the salvation of the soul depended. Nobody thought of artists as divinely inspired or more knowledgeable than the Church leaders. It was thus appropriate that artists were given exact specifications as to what they could represent.

Having been given subject matter and theme, the artist was bound further by strict conventions governing how sacred subjects were to be depicted. Jesus on the cross had to be shown with his mother on the right and St. John on the left. The soldier pierced the left side of Jesus. His halo contained a cross as the mark of divinity, whereas the saints had halos without a cross. Only God, Jesus, the angels, and the apostles could be shown with bare feet. It would be heresy, therefore, to depict the Virgin or the saints without coverings on their feet. These conventions were intended to help the observer identify religious figures. Thus, St. Peter was given a short beard, and St. Paul was always bald, with a long beard. There were numerous other conventions that may seem to us to infringe on artistic liberty or imagination.

The structure of cathedrals and monastic churches was also subject to conventions of style and decoration determined not by artistic taste but by theology. The usual floor plan was that of a Latin cross, itself a symbol of salvation in the Church. The Christian **liturgy,** the formal service of worship, determined many of the stylistic practices of the builders. The **chancel,** for example, was designed to separate the clergy from the congregation, as traditional rituals required. The chancel provided a place for the altar, where the service was held, as well as a place for the choir to be seated (see fig. 5.3).

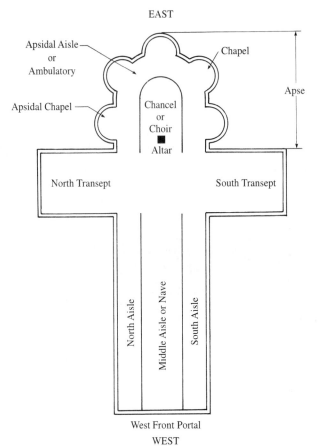

EAST

Apsidal Aisle
or
Ambulatory

Chapel

Apse

Apsidal Chapel

Chancel
or
Choir

■
Altar

North Transept

South Transept

North Aisle

Middle Aisle or Nave

South Aisle

West Front Portal

WEST

Figure 5.3 Floor plan of a medieval church—Beplat.

Because it was traditional for the priests and the congregation to face east (that is, the Holy Land), churches were usually oriented with the altar to the east and the main portal to the west. The symbolism of the Holy Trinity was used at every convenient opportunity. Wherever possible, the number three was in evidence—in triple arches, triple portals, and even triple meter in music.

Reverence for holy relics, such as a portion of a holy person's body, was also responsible for architectural detail. Relics were believed to perform miracles for those who paid homage to them, and great crowds of pilgrims would often be attracted to a church because of some special holy relic housed within its walls. To accommodate the many worshipers and pilgrims and to provide altar space for numerous clerics who were required to say daily Mass, small chapels were constructed along the **ambulatory,** the passageway around the **apse,** a semicircular part of the church that projects from its axis (fig. 5.3). There are other features of design arising from religious doctrine

Figure 5.4 Baptistry, cathedral, and tower, 1053–1272. Pisa, Italy. (Alinari/Art Resource, NY)

or practice. Even though most details of design were functional, they impressed upon the faithful an unquestioning faith in salvation by the cross.

Large-scale planning often resulted in a complex of structures around a church. This was especially true in the Italian Romanesque. At Pisa (fig. 5.4), the cathedral (center) is flanked by the baptistry (foreground) and the famous Leaning Tower, which contains the *carillon* (large, tuned hanging bells played from a keyboard).

Music also served a religious function during the medieval period, providing personal communication with God. As with painting and architecture, the Church exercised rigid control over the types and character of music, keeping it simple, unpretentious, and vocal. The liturgical service determined the music's formal structure as well as the subject matter and the text.

THE ROMANESQUE PERIOD

For the purpose of this study, the Romanesque period spans the years 500 to 1100. The Byzantine style of the early Church remained influential through the formative years of this period, although it was modified by Roman practices and ideas. As events of history moved toward the year 1000, other artistic styles were incorporated in the Romanesque. These styles include the Carolingian, during the reign of Charlemagne, and the Ottoman, with influences from the Ottoman Empire. The term *Romanesque* refers to the artistic style influenced by the Romans, a style marked by its stark simplicity and its use of the rounded arch. Because the Roman Empire left its imprint on all of Europe during the early medieval age, the term describes the entire period.

Although the Romanesque style dominated from about 500 to 1100, it was not until about the tenth century that there appeared a well-developed body of creative art in the Western church. With the gradual reestablishment of law and order after years of barbarian invasions, Europe—which had seen so much of the art and civilization of the Greek and Roman world disappear—was given a foundation for a new and vital civilization. Vital to this renewed spirit was the building of roads in northern Europe, which fostered a gradual growth of trade and commerce. Monastic society and feudalism combined to reclaim the land and to establish a fairly stable, agrarian society. These developments helped to provide economic stability for a new flourishing of artistic expression.

The Church, now well organized, reeducated its people in mind, manners, and morals. This reeducation provided moral and spiritual motivation for a new civilization and created new contexts for art forms to develop. Because wealth and social organization were centered largely in the monastic establishments of the Church, it was natural that the architecture, sculpture, painting, literature, and music of the Romanesque should reflect the culture of the cloister.

Architecture

Romanesque architects and builders, most of them monks or friars, adapted the stone arch of the Romans in much the same manner as had their Byzantine predecessors. They made arches of great solidity and strength, capable

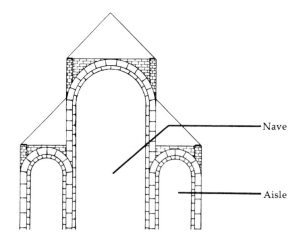

Nave

Aisle

Figure 5.5 Cross section of Romanesque church—Beplat.

of bearing tremendous weight (fig. 5.5). The necessity for fireproof buildings led to the use of heavy stone roofs. To support this great weight, exceedingly thick walls with few windows were used. Heavily vaulted ceilings and massive walls reflected the severe asceticism of the monastic builders. The impressive distances and gloomy spaces suggested a spirit of quiet renunciation of the world. There is none of the brilliant color and sensuous expression of Byzantine churches. In the dim twilight of Romanesque aisles, one could feel the very presence of God.

The exterior of Notre Dame la Grande at Poitiers in France (fig. 5.6), built in the eleventh century, is a fine example of the Romanesque spirit in architecture. The triple arches of the facade suggest the symbolism of the Trinity. Close examination reveals that the two outer arches are not the same height. This is often the case with Romanesque arches, for the churches were not always planned as organic units of perfect symmetry and balance, nor built during one sustained period. The upward thrust of the towers does not give the structure a feeling of height, for the towers are too low for the rest of the building. The total height is about the same as the width. The lines do not seem to flow smoothly from one part to another; on the contrary, there is an abruptness of line that detracts from eye appeal. There is balance among arches and towers, but its effect is minimized by a lack of precision. The church was obviously not planned as a thing of sensuous beauty for the eye but as a retreat in which people could find the presence of God.

The interior of San Ambrogio at Milan (fig. 5.7) demonstrates the treatment of the rounded arch. The large central aisle, or **nave,** is built up of a series of **bays,** which are areas between the heavy **piers.** A system of rounded arches forms the vault for each bay so that the appearance is one of great, hollow spaces surmounted by a massive ceiling. There is little light from windows, and there are innumerable dark recesses with no illumination

Figure 5.6 Notre Dame la Grande, eleventh century. Poitiers, France. (Hirmer Fotoarchiv)

except that furnished by burning tapers. Altogether, this is a forbidding atmosphere; a cloistered feeling pervades the total enclosed space.

A comparison of these two buildings or any other Romanesque churches with an example from Greek civilization, such as the Parthenon (fig. 3.7) reveals great differences. The Greek building is open, resting gracefully on the earth, suggesting a sense of peace and repose. This was a temple that served the needs of the Greeks as they came to worship and then went their way without fear of the wrath of the gods. It was a functional house of the gods but also gave great delight to the aesthetic sense of Greek citizens. Romanesque buildings, on the other hand, are heavy and dark. They shut out the light of the

Figure 5.7 Interior of San Ambrogio, eleventh and twelfth century. Milan, Italy. (Foto Marburg/Art Resource, NY)

world around, physically and symbolically. They were places where medieval men and women could come to contemplate God and find a haven from the harsh realities of life. They were functional buildings intended for large group meetings but with a design and purpose unlike that of the Greek temple. Each in its way reflects the philosophy and beliefs of those who worshiped.

Sculpture

Because sculpture and painting were representational arts, they were expected to deal with religious subjects in a purely functional way, serving a didactic purpose. According to Pope Gregory, who lived around A.D. 600, painting and sculpture were supposed to teach: "What the literate learn by reading, the uneducated learn by looking at pictures." Sculpture was functional in another manner as well. All Romanesque sculpture was subordinated to architecture and was almost always conceived as an architectural decoration, as well as an educational object.

Just as the Romanesque churches themselves were architecturally simple, today the sculpture seems archaic. The monks decorated the facades of their churches with sculpture representing biblical scenes. These reminded all who entered the portals that the source of salvation lay within. The figures portrayed on the facades of the cathedrals were often emaciated, elongated, and seemingly more like skeletons covered with fabric than living forms.

This distortion of human form was motivated by two beliefs. First, medieval people denied the importance of this life, so any human representation need not be realistic. Unlike Greek sculpture, with its delicate, lifelike forms, this sculpture distorted reality to teach a spiritual concept. Second, there was collaboration between sculptor and architect. The figures formed a part of the architectural plan and often helped to support the thrust of arches and columns. Because it was general practice to add carvings after columns had been placed in position, sculptural forms were often dictated by the structural design: tall, thin statues fit into the niches between columns. However, there seems to have been little conflict, for the limitations of design only emphasized the basic forms for which Romanesque faith called.

The portal of St. Trophime at Arles in the south of France (fig. 5.8) shows how sculptured figures were brought into the total design as an integral part of the building. Note the stylized rows of elongated figures stretching across the tops of the columns, as well as the large statues between columns. These figures of the apostles are not realistic. The bodies are flat. The viewer is hardly aware of plastic form. The heads of the figures are greatly enlarged, but they do seem to blend into the massiveness of the total structure. When viewed from directly below, the heads appear more rounded.

The **tympanum,** the area above the doorway and below an arch, of *La Madeleine* at Vézelay, France (fig. 5.9), is one of the most famous examples of Romanesque architectural sculpture. The subject, the Pentecostal scene, shows Christ bestowing his spirit upon the apostles by means of rays coming from his fingertips. The body of Christ is exceedingly unrealistic. It appears in a very awkward position and gives the impression of a fabric-covered frame of bones. Close examination of the other figures reveals the same absence of realism. The sculptured figures of the tympanum were symbols of a faith that denied earthly pleasures but promised eternal salvation to all who accepted its doctrines.

Painting

While painting played no role in the churches of the first few hundred years of the Church, it became more important in Christian art during the Middle Ages. It remained purely functional, however, and served the same

Figure 5.8 Portal of St. Trophime, c.1105. Arles, France. (Bridgeman Art Library)

educational purpose as sculpture. There are very few original examples of Romanesque paintings because they were usually painted on wood: either fire or normal decay destroyed most of them.

The crucifixion was a popular subject because its role in salvation was the focal point of the Church's doctrine. In the *Crucifixion* from Santa Maria del Antiqua (colorplate 14), as in the sculpture of the period, there is a denial of the flesh. The figures are not realistic, and as in earlier mosaics, there is no sense of space. There is classical balance, with the figure of Christ on the cross as the focal point. The human form has been elongated both to

Colorplate 14 follows p. 114.

Figure 5.9 Tympanum of La Madeleine (*Christ Sending Forth the Apostles*), c. 1130. Vézelay, France. (Bridgeman Art Library)

deny the reality of the flesh and to suggest Christ's agony and suffering. This was a painting less likely to please the aesthetic sense than to impress upon the beholders the Christian significance of the cross.

Music

As the medieval church exerted its influence, the nature and role of music underwent significant changes. Under the patronage of a fairly well-organized Church, music was ordered according to the liturgy and in keeping with a simple, ascetic faith. Because instruments were commonly used for secular purposes, they were at first banned so that worshipers might not be diverted from their spiritual aim. In addition, the use of instruments by the pagan Greeks and Romans militated against their use as a Christian musical medium. Vocal sound was predominant in the music of the religious service; it had to be simple and unpretentious in its expression of religious sentiment.

In general, medieval Christian music took its forms and liturgical order from the Byzantine (or Eastern) church and the Jewish temple. The Byzantines contributed the use of the hymn tune. More importantly, however, many melodies stemmed directly from the highly ornamented Jewish and Near Eastern chants. The theoretical basis for music—including the modal system—was acquired from the Greeks. However, only the names of the modes were taken from the Greeks; these modes did not indicate the same Greek tonal relationships.

Several styles of **chant**, early monophonic vocal music, were developed in the Western church in keeping with the variety of liturgical practices and languages. In Spain, for example, the chant was known as Mozarabic and in northern Europe as Gallican. The chant used in Rome came to be called **Gregorian chant** because of the encouragement and leadership of Pope Gregory (540–604), during whose tenure these chants were gathered and codified. Gregorian chants, which eventually became the predominant music of all branches of the Western church, flourished from the fifth to the eighth century, but their composition continued until the twelfth century. However, we know the names of none of the composers of these melodies; like folk songs, they have an anonymity that tends to give them a traditional and timeless character. We do know, though, the names of some of the important music scholars and theorists of the Medieval period. Guido of Arezzo, probably the most famous, contributed much to the development of notation and singing style of Gregorian chant.

The function of chant was to express faith in God in keeping with the otherworldly spirit of the age. All chants shared four important characteristics: (1) they were based on the church modes; (2) their rhythms were derived from Latin texts; (3) they were monophonic; and (4) their composers were unknown. Their musical forms consisted of settings of the various texts of the service. As an organized body of well-regulated religious practices emerged, one of the important developments was that portion of the central liturgical service of the Church, called the **Mass.** Eleven pieces of music were normally needed for the sung portion of the Mass. These were divided into two sections. The **Ordinary,** consisting of the Kyrie, Gloria, Credo, Sanctus, Agnus Dei, and Ite, missa est, was constant and used the same texts for every service. The second section, the **Proper** (parts of which are spoken), changed texts from service to service according to the needs of the

Church calendar. The sung portions consisted of the Introit, Gradual, Alleluia, Offertory, and Communion (ex. 5.1).

Example 5.1 Sung and recited parts of the Mass

Sung		Recited	
Proper	*Ordinary*	*Proper*	*Ordinary*
1. Introit			
	2. Kyrie		
	3. Gloria		
		4. Collects, Prayers, etc.	
		5. Epistle	
6. Gradual			
7. Alleluia or Tract (in Lent) with Sequence.			
		8. Gospel	
	9. Credo		
10. Offertory			
			11. Prayers
		12. Secret	
		13. Preface	
	14. Sanctus and Benedictus		
			15. Canon
			16. Pater Noster
	17. Agnus Dei		
18. Communion			
		19. Post Communion	
	20. Ite, missa est or Benediction		

Gregorian chants were based on a series of tone patterns known as church or ecclesiastical modes. Each of the **modes** required a different arrangement of the seven tones of the octave system (the notes represented by the white keys of the piano keyboard). The octaves D-d **(Dorian),** E-e **(Phrygian),** F-f **(Lydian),** and G-g, **(Mixolydian)** became the basis of the eight church modes (see ex. 5.2). Each mode had its own **dominant** and **final,** which served as the axes around which the other tones moved. For

Example 5.2 The eight church modes

the medieval church, as in ancient Greece, each modal scale had particular emotional significance. The melodies or chants constructed on these modal scales assumed these attributed characteristics.

The music in the Romanesque period was written in **neumes** on a four-line staff, as in the following Kyrie from the Ordinary of the Mass (ex. 5.3). This notation was developed by Guido in the eleventh century and used in chant manuscripts until the twentieth century. Example 5.4 is the same chant on a five-line staff, written in modern notation. This Kyrie is highly melismatic with many notes to a single syllable; the long, florid melodic passages, which are sung to the final vowel *e* of the words Kyrie and Christe, are typical of such chants. In medieval times, words were often added to these **melismas,** and the first words often gave the name to the chant. Examples 5.3 and 5.4 became known as the *Kyrie fons bonitatis* (Kyrie of the fountain of goodness), since these words began the added text that was placed under the notes of the long, decorative melisma. Later Church edicts forbade the use of verbal additions, but the chants often retained the name even though the text disappeared from use.

The Medieval Period—Romanesque (500–1100)   97

Example 5.3 *Kyrie fons bonitatis,* neumatic notation [tenth century]

Example 5.4 *Kyrie fons bonitatis,* modern notation

The Kyrie text is in three parts, a form that became traditional in the Mass. The text of the Kyrie is Greek and represents one of the oldest parts of the Mass. "Kyrie eleison" (God have mercy) is repeated three times, followed by "Christe eleison" (Christ have mercy), also repeated three times. "Kyrie eleison" then returns, twice in an altered version of the opening setting and finally in another, slightly longer version. Both of these versions, however, retain the final half of the opening Kyrie melody.

The chant is in the Phrygian mode, the mode in which the tone *e* (called the final) comes not only at the **cadence,** or point of rest in the melody, but also at the end of each of the three sections. The note *c* is the dominant tone of this mode and provides a center for the musical climaxes of the chant. The three repetitions of each phrase demonstrate the symbolism of the number three in the art of the Church. The musical structure of A (first Kyrie), B (Christe), and A (final Kyrie) is another example of the symbolic use of the number three. In addition to its religious symbolism, this three-part formal structure is satisfying aesthetically. The familiar pattern of statement-digression-restatement, or statement-tension-repose, appears often in Western music through the twentieth century.

Gregorian chant was used for the sung portions of the Proper and Ordinary of the Mass. In addition, there were many chant settings of hymns, parts of **Office Hours** of the Church, and other special texts. The chants varied in style: from intonations, in which the same tone was used to set long prose passages, such as the psalms; to simple settings of a single tone for each syllable of the text; to very elaborate chants, in which single syllables were prolonged by melismas. This music, like Romanesque architecture, is simple and straightforward. It is a fitting complement to the stark beauty of the architecture and sculpture. In the medieval period, the three arts combined to lift the devout into a spiritual exultation completely detached from everyday existence.

Summary

During the medieval period, which includes both the Romanesque and the Gothic periods, the Church was the primary patron of the arts. Moreover, because the Church held considerable power, it was able to dictate the function, subjects, and style of most art and music. A philosophy emphasizing spiritual life dominated religion and the arts. Almost all the clergy were members of monastic orders that functioned as havens from worldly temptation. We are indebted to the monastic orders for the preservation of Greek and Roman classical learning, although they often disagreed with its content. They were also the principal architects of nonsecular and secular buildings.

All art and education was under the guidance of the clergy; consequently, religious doctrine dictated the rules by which religious personages and subjects were represented. The same was true for music. The development of musical composition and the performance of sacred music were the province of the monastic clergy.

Feudalism was another institution that left its mark on medieval civilization. It gave some stability and economic protection to the lower classes and consolidated the wealth and strength of the nobility. There was usually a close relationship between the feudal lords and the Church, for the lords ruled their domains only with the blessing of the Church.

Romanesque builders used the Roman arch and vault, with massive walls as the principal method of construction, resulting in dark interiors. There was little sense of classic design. Churches were planned not for their beauty but as havens for the faithful.

The main function of sculpture and painting was religious education. Figures were usually distorted, almost to the point of denying the reality of the flesh; this was in keeping with the Church's denial of the world. Religious symbolism played a great part in all the arts—in architectural plans, in the details of sculptured and painted figures, and even in music.

Music was ordered to the specifications of the liturgy and in keeping with an ascetic faith. The Gregorian chant, based on ecclesiastical modes or scales, emerged as the most widely used music in the Western church. The liturgical texts dictated the choice of modes, formal organization, and style. The chants were set in varied styles from simple and syllabic to highly melismatic. The music of the chants was monophonic, a fitting reflection in sound of the simplicity of Romanesque architecture, sculpture, and painting.

The arts of the Romanesque are faithful expressions of the early medieval spirit. The monastic simplicity of life was expressed in unsophisticated facades, in ascetic-appearing sculpture, and in the monodic melodies of the Gregorian chant. As the Christian church fastened its hold on every facet of spiritual life, it also controlled the artistic expression of that faith. As time progressed, though, the feeling of otherworldliness became less powerful. New cultural and intellectual ideas spread throughout Europe after the Crusades. New economic forces cast a different light on the social, political, and religious patterns of life. The result was the age of the Gothic—still infused with the medieval spirit but tempered with an intellectualism and humanism that was to reach its full fruition in the Renaissance.

Suggested Readings

In addition to the specific sources that follow, the general readings on pages 388 and 389 contain valuable information about the topic of this chapter.

Ferguson, G. *Signs and Symbols in Christian Art.* New York: Oxford University Press, 1966.

Hoppin, Richard H. *Medieval Music.* New York: W. W. Norton, 1978.

Shaver-Crandell, Anne. *The Middle Ages.* Cambridge: Cambridge University Press, 1982.

Thomson, James. *Music through the Renaissance.* Dubuque, IA: Wm. C. Brown Publishers, 1984.

Zarnecki, George. *Art of the Medieval World: Architecture, Sculpture, Painting, the Sacred Arts.* New York: Abrams, 1976.

Zarnecki, George. *Romanesque.* New York: Universe Books, 1989.

Chapter 6

•••——◉•——•••

The Medieval Period—Gothic
(1100–1400)

Chronology

Visual Arts	Music	Historical Figures and Events
•Abbot Suger (1081–1151)		
		•The Crusades (late 11th to late 13th centuries)
	•Abbess Hildegard von Bingen (1098–1197)	
	•Bernart de Ventadorn (fl. 1150–1180)	
	•Perotin (c. 1150–c. 1240)	
•Notre Dame Cathedral of Paris (1163)	•Organum (c. 1182)	
•Wells Cathedral (c. 1190)		
	•Trouvères, troubadours, and minnesingers (c. 1200)	
		•Roger Bacon (1214–1294)
		•Magna Carta (1215)
•Salisbury Cathedral (c. 1220)		
•Amiens Cathedral (c. 1225)		•St. Thomas Aquinas (1225–1274)
•Reims Cathedral (c. 1225–1299)		
•Chartres Cathedral rebuilt (c. 1240)		•Dante Alighieri (1265–1321)
•Giotto (1266–1337)	•Guillaume de Machaut (c. 1300–1377)	•Francesco Petrarch (1304–1374)
		•Papacy in Avignon (1305)
		•Giovanni Boccaccio (1313–1375)
		•Geoffrey Chaucer (1340–1400)
		•Black Death (c. 1348)

Pronunciation Guide

Amiens (Ah-meeăh)
Chartres (Shahr-tr)
Cimabue (Chee-mah-boo´-ay)
Giotto (Joht´-toh)

Machaut (Mah-shoh)
Or la truix (Ohr lah troo-ee)
Perotin (Pay-roh-tăh)
Pisano (Pee-sah´-noh)

Reims (Răs)
Rouen (Roo-ăh)
Siena (See-en´-ah)

Study Objectives

1. Study how humanism and secularism found their way into the arts.
2. Learn about the Gothic arch, the skeletal frame that made great height and enormous window space possible in architecture.
3. Understand how polyphonic music became an artistic form in which interwoven melodies and rhythmic elements produced a skillful interplay.

The spiritual attitude that dominated the Romanesque age was not as strong and sure during the Gothic. In the earlier period, people believed that the world was a God-inspired mystery that could be expressed in simple, direct art. In the Renaissance that followed the Middle Ages, people believed, as did the Greeks, in cultivating rationalism and humanism. Between these two periods came the Gothic, in which there was a gradual movement toward humanism, which focused on the accomplishments of humankind, replacing the earlier spiritual or mystical emphasis. In place of blind faith, there arose an intellectualism and a religious skepticism that eventually caused the separation of Church and State. The artistic consequence was a body of creative art that was intellectually ordered and demonstrated secular influences but still fundamentally expressed the religious fervor of the age.

This change to a more secular age came about through the subtle influences of a variety of trends and events. When the year 1000 passed into history without the predicted end of the world, people began to think in terms of a more pleasurable life. Salvation through the remission of sins was still paramount in their thinking, but they reduced it to a formula. They organized theological doctrines into a scientific system of philosophy called *scholasticism*. It argued that while religious dogma was unquestionable and infallible, it could be explained and clarified by means of logic and reason. Spiritual life and salvation were thus subject to academic scrutiny.

Scholasticism was the product of the medieval university, which had evolved from the earlier monastic schools. The medieval curriculum was divided into the so-called quadrivium and trivium. The *quadrivium* included arithmetic, geometry, astronomy, and music—all under the heading of "Mathematics." The *trivium* included rhetoric, grammar, and logic. These subjects were looked upon as systematic studies, influenced by the idea of order. Like religion, architecture, painting, sculpture, and music were reduced to strict rules and formulas. The same protocol that bound the Romanesque painter applied to the Gothic. In addition, architecture was subjected to an elaborate plan of religious symbolism, and even music was ordered according to strict rules: the fact that music was listed as "Mathematics" is evidence of the influence of scholasticism. Consequently, there was less individual creative imagination in the arts than we normally attribute to such endeavors. It is not until the Renaissance that artworks begin to reveal the individuality of their creators and to express human emotions more explicitly.

While scholastic philosophy systematized salvation, it did not bring forth the deep and abiding faith that many believed it would. Worship tended toward an empty formalism, with the letter of the doctrine superseding the spirit of Christianity. Men like Dante were conscious of the inconsistency that existed between the Christian ideal and Christian practice. Many of the clergy were corrupt; some of them actually practicing piracy when not reading their services. High positions in the papal state were openly obtained by a process of barter and trade. The Church was losing its moral and political power, as well as its spiritual significance. At one time, three different popes were engaged in the shocking spectacle of trying to excommunicate each other. Even in the face of such conduct, scholasticism gave tacit approval by holding that the sacraments were still valid even if the clergy administering them were immoral.

This decline of spiritual values gave rise to skepticism regarding spiritual authority and law. It cannot be said that the Church lost its hold, but certainly, the faithful were less concerned with the self-denial of earlier years and more interested in their own happiness and well-being. The arts, in turn, responded with a more humanistic expression.

Another factor that weakened the focus on the afterlife was the Crusades. These pilgrimages to wrest the Holy Land from the Moslems were unsuccessful in their main objective, but they did open up new vistas in social and cultural thought. Material wealth through trade, love of a full life, and a sense of high adventure were but a few of the results. More important, the Crusaders came into contact with Near Eastern civilizations. They tasted luxury and experienced a culture and social code that contrasted sharply with the customs of their own land and with the spiritual concepts in which they had been trained. Upon their return, the Crusaders copied social customs and forms of entertainment they had come to know in the East.

Moreover, those returning from pilgrimages showed signs of becoming more intellectually and economically independent. Their new experiences, as well as scholasticism, made them skeptical of the religious doctrine that threatened the punishment of hell for every pleasurable impulse. The spiritual and temporal power of the Church, its authority to save or damn, its teaching of hell, its doctrine of an avenging God—all these awed and frightened medieval people. They loved Mary, admired Jesus, and feared God.

The love for Mary was perhaps both cause and effect in the development of the ideals of "courtly love." These ideals were rather rigidly defined, written as a set of rules, then articulated practically in the poetry written and sung by the *troubadours* and *trouvères*. Among these poets were women as well as men. Their rigorously formal poetry celebrated the beauty and virtue of anonymous women, whose descriptions easily might be confused with the Blessed Virgin. Mary, characterized as lovely and sympathetic, was a humanizing influence and became an object of great affection.

Closely allied with the Crusades was the development of towns and the building of a more adequate system of roads, especially in northern Europe. Romanesque art was mainly monastic, but the Gothic cathedral of the twelfth to fourteenth centuries was the creation of the towns and bishops. With the growth of commerce and industry and a corresponding growth of towns, the bishops, bourgeoisie, and guilds grew steadily more wealthy. The towns enthusiastically built churches partly to express their faith and partly to surpass rival towns in magnificence. Thus, a spiritual fervor lasted in spite of a growing secularization and criticism of the clergy. As a product of communal effort, the Gothic cathedral was placed on the public square, surrounded by the homes of its builders and paid for by public subscription. It became the religious, civic, and social center of community life. It functioned as church, picture gallery, concert hall, theater, library, and school—truly a multipurpose artwork.

The influence of Gothic culture on art is revealed in its subjects, forms, and symbols. In fact, the Gothic cathedral was a veritable compendium of symbols. The floor plan of the building is in the shape of a cross. The light flowing through the stained-glass windows symbolized Christ as the light of the world, and a central nave and two side aisles represented the Holy Trinity. Externally, three portals correspond to the three main aisles of the church. These portals were often filled with sculpture that was both representational and symbolic. Above the central portal the four Evangelists were represented: a man for St. Matthew, a lion for St. Mark, an ox for St. Luke, and an eagle for St. John. The combination of the symbolic and representational art objects included in Gothic art became a visual history of, and metaphor for, the people of God.

The same tradition of symbolism prevails in painted art and in music, especially music with texts. Numbers had specific religious references: 1 for God, 2 for the dual nature of Christ, 3 for the Holy Trinity, 4 for the gospels, 5 for the wounds of Christ, 6 for the days of creation, 7 for the deadly sins and the joys of Mary, and so forth. Of course, these are not the only symbolic meanings for these numbers. Colors, plants and flowers, animals, and various fabricated objects were also frequently invested with symbolic meaning. Light, one of the most pervasive consequences of Gothic architecture, symbolized the person of Jesus, who declared, "I am the light of the world."

The Gothic artist found beauty in the human spirit, not in the physical body. The emotional tone became one of warmth and mystic longing. Gothic artists recreated the adventure and excitement of their age with towering spires, dynamic decoration, and complicated sinews of masonry. Gothic artists sought to integrate religious emotion with the reality of life by putting side by side the noble and the ignoble, the real and the mystic. In the spirit of their age, Gothic artists strove to rise above the coarseness of this life and project the observer into the beauties of heaven.

ARCHITECTURE

The Gothic cathedral, with its spires rising majestically over the towns of northern Europe, is a physical counterpart to the spiritual urge for rising above the earthly. The Gothic style came into being in France. Ecclesiastic architecture in Italy had been dominated too much by the Byzantine-Romanesque for Italian builders to be leaders in the new movement. In fact, the term *Gothic* was used by the Italians of the Renaissance and later Classicists as a description for a style they thought vulgar and associated with the barbaric Goths. It was only after the Gothic was well established in France, Germany, and England that southern Europe responded at all, and then only mildly.

The rounded arch of the Romanesque was quite inelastic because the height of the arch could not be more than half of its width. This limitation hampered the Gothic builders, who sought in their buildings to reach great heights. Their ingenuity and experimentation created the pointed arch (fig. 6.1), which made possible the vaulting of large spaces and extreme heights. One of the main problems was coping with the lateral or outward thrust of the arch. Heavy walls served this purpose for the Romanesque arch. The pointed arch made the problem even more acute, for the higher the structure, the more lateral thrust there was to be neutralized. Gothic builders solved this problem with a series of supporting arches and **flying buttresses,** half arches (figs. 6.1, 6.2) that transferred outward thrust to piers outside the walls. The building was so delicately balanced by this system of bracing that theoretically it would collapse if any one of the supporting arches were removed. The ideal location of Notre Dame of Paris (fig. 6.2) next to the river allows the viewer a rare perspective on a complete buttressing system.

In contrast with the massive columns and thick walls of the Romanesque, the architecture of Gothic churches—with pointed arches, pinnacles, slender piers, and decorative ornamentation—introduced light into

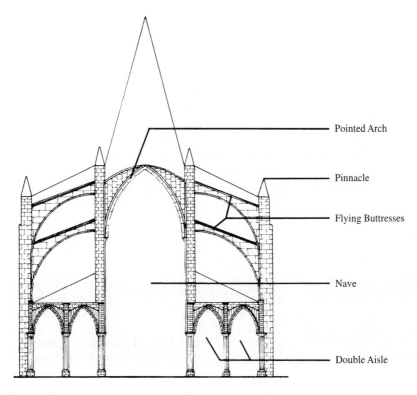

Pointed Arch

Pinnacle

Flying Buttresses

Nave

Double Aisle

Figure 6.1 Cross section of a Gothic church—Beplat.

the already expanding sense of spaciousness. Gothic cathedrals give the impression of energy forcing its way upward. Horizontal lines are permitted to exert some influence but are broken by the predominating upward thrust. The feeling of weight is defeated at every turn.

The sense of vertical space is even more impressive in the interior of these cathedrals. The eye of the observer is drawn upward by piers which become more slender and light as they progress higher and higher. Their outlines may become diffused by distance and ornamentation. Ribs of masonry frame multi-colored stained-glass windows that capture the sunlight, diffusing its rays into all colors of the spectrum. The amount of space, both vertical and horizontal, was limited in many instances only by the wealth and ingenuity of the builders.

Unfortunately, the architects who developed this style are largely unknown. Despite their anonymity, they were among the most innovative practitioners of architecture of all time. One person whose influence upon Gothic architecture exceeded that of any other was Abbot Suger. Although

Figure 6.2 Notre Dame, 1163–1235. Paris, France. (Hirmer Verlag, Munich)

he was born into a family of modest means, his educational opportunities placed him in contact with French royalty. Later, this connection allowed his creative imagination to be wedded to his political and diplomatic skills. His opportunities for influence were enhanced in 1122 when he was elected Abbot of St. Denis. In 1124, he developed his plans for rebuilding the church of the Abbey, located some six miles north of Paris. He took advantage of the then-current veneration of relics as a means of financing his construction projects. His role, subsequently, was something of a cross between an architect and a contractor. He wrote extensively, and philosophically, about his ideas concerning light and beauty in the service of the Church. For Suger, light was an apt metaphor for God's revelation. Although he was not the inventor of stained glass, Suger encouraged its use and employed it simultaneously to convey biblical representations and to flood the church interior with colored light. His writings on the spiritual and mystical significance of buildings was of great importance in the dissemination of the Gothic spirit in architecture.

A Closer Look

Reims Cathedral

Among the Gothic cathedrals of France, four are generally acknowledged to be outstanding: Reims, Chartres, Notre Dame of Paris, and Amiens. Each of these cathedrals is notable for several features: Chartres, for example, is known above all for its stained glass and sculpture, Amiens for the soaring height of its nave, Notre Dame of Paris for the balance and harmony of its west front, and Reims for its successful integration of architectural and sculptural forms, as well as for its historical, cultural, and political importance to France.

Reims has always held a special place in the hearts of the French. The first church to occupy the site of the present cathedral was completed in time for the baptism and coronation of King Clovis in the fifth century. There has been a church at the site continuously for approximately 1500 years. For centuries the Bishops of Reims held immense political, as well as spiritual power, and it was in this cathedral that virtually all French monarchs were crowned. In 1429, knowing of its role in authenticating royal appointments, Joan of Arc brought King Charles VII to Reims where he was to be crowned. Other monarchs, including Louis XIV, Louis XV, and Louis XVI, sought divine confirmation for their authority by being crowned there as well. The cathedral is still considered the ecclesiastical capital of France.

A new cathedral replaced the former church in the early ninth century. Subsequent modifications of that "Carolingian" cathedral took place in 976, 1152, and 1170. After a disastrous fire in 1210, the Bishop of Reims, Alberic de Humbert, committed himself to building a new, great cathedral. The building included stylistic features from the cathedrals at Chartres and Soisson, but the architectural style and construction techniques were incorporated into a unique design.

Three aspects of Reims Cathedral deserve attention: the west front, the statuary, and the interior use of height and light. Each of these features, among many others, contributes significantly to the beauty of the design, and the integration of interior and exterior features is one of the cathedral's great strengths.

West Front

Like almost all Gothic cathedrals, the main entrance to Reims Cathedral is from the west. Its west front (or **facade**) is considered one of the supreme monuments of the Middle Ages (fig. 6.3). In comparison with the Romanesque Notre Dame la Grande at Poitiers (see fig. 5.6), which sits heavily on its massive foundations, the cathedral at

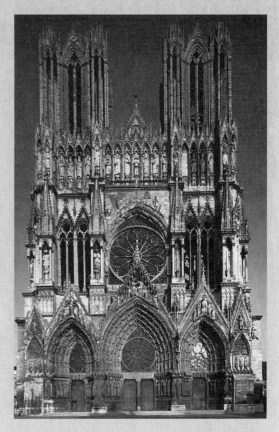

Figure 6.3 West facade of Reims Cathedral, begun 1211. Reims, France. (Hirmer Verlag, Munich)

Reims reaches upward toward the heavens with its lighter mass and greater height. Some consider the Reims facade the apogee of French Gothic ornament.

The west front consists of four important visual levels: the portals, the rose window, the Gallery of Kings, and the towers. The ground (or portal) level comprises three magnificent portals (large doors), each laden with sculpture and incorporating a tympanum filled with tracery windows.

At eye level, and below the curved arches of each portal, are rows of statuary representing biblical figures and saints. In their more realistic depiction of the human figures, these statues illustrate an important stylistic change in medieval sculpture. Unlike other cathedrals, within each of the portals are stained-glass windows. In the central portal, directly below the great rose window, is a smaller rose window. The pointed arches of the portal doorways and the great rose window represent the best in traditional Gothic style. In the gable immediately above each portal are clusters of statuary that depict important events of Christian sacred history: the left portal depicts the Crucifixion of Christ, the right portal presents the Last Judgment, and the central portal features the Crowning of the Virgin.

The second visual level is dominated by the rose window (colorplate 15, following p. 114), with its mammoth petals. This rose window, nearly forty feet across and containing thirty-four sections, is considered one of the most beautiful designs of the Middle Ages. Designed by Bernard de Soissons, it is certainly one of the masterpieces of architectural decoration. Unlike those of Chartres or Amiens, the Reims rose window is placed beneath an arch that relieves its starkness and ties it both architecturally and visually to the lower level.

On the third level, above the rose window, is the unique Gallery of Kings. The individual statues are on average about fifteen feet tall, but appear smaller due to their distance from the ground.

Above the Gallery of Kings are two matching towers, simply and elegantly proportioned. The unusual perforated stonework enhances their seeming lightness.

Statuary

Many of the best stone workshops in Gothic France were found in Reims, and this may have influenced the architects in choosing to create such elaborate sculpture for this cathedral. Reims contains more sculpture than any other cathedral—from 2300 to 5000 pieces, depending upon the method of reckoning.

The splendid west front alone has the statues of saints at ground level, the three cluster scenes at the top of the portals, and the Gallery of Kings. In addition, each of the portals has five string courses of sculpture moving up the curved surface of the portal arches, representing people and events from biblical and Christian history. These superb statues were all completed between 1250 and 1260.

Gothic sculpture, in its depiction of human beings, was more lifelike than its Romanesque predecessors. The sculpture of Reims was created in the new tradition, bringing human vitality and contemporary dress to many of the figures. A charming example can be found in the marked physicality and individuality of the smiling angel in the left portal of the west front (fig. 6.4). Elsewhere, a gruesome yet realistic statue depicts St. Nicaise holding his head in his hands; he was, according to legend, martyred by beheading.

Interior

The interiors of Gothic cathedrals are known above all else for their soaring heights. As architects

Figure 6.4 *Smiling Angel,* central portal, Reims Cathedral. Reims, France. (Hirmer Verlag, Munich)

sought to reach ever higher, the pressure on the walls became overpowering, requiring the development of flying buttresses to distribute the weight of walls and roofs. Though of lesser height than Beauvais or Amiens, the cathedral at Reims needed a double tier of flying buttresses on its exterior.

The interior of the cathedral is dominated by its nave, which was designed to lead the eyes of worshipers heavenward. One is immediately impressed by the interior height (123 feet), by the pointed arches crowning the nave and the bays that lead into the side aisles, and by the columns that reach up to the curves of the main arches. The relative narrowness of the nave (44 feet) increases the dramatic effect.

One of the architectural innovations at Reims was the treatment of the **clerestory,** a part of the church above the aisles where the windows and lancets have a single tracery design. It is here also that bar tracery was first used to strengthen the window space. These developments allowed the use of significantly more glass in the walls, permitting light to filter through the double rose window of the west front and the other stained glass in the clerestory windows.

Devotional statues, tapestries, organ cases, and other objects ornament the interior of the cathedral today: some are the creations of outstanding artists of the twentieth century. Nevertheless, the primary artistic impact of this Gothic monument is its architectural integration of building, sculpture, and glass.

···◄◉►···

Figure 6.5 Salisbury Cathedral, begun 1220. Salisbury, England. (© A. F. Kersting)

The English Gothic evolved from its French counterpart and falls into three major style periods: Early English (a rather plain style), Decorated (with a more ornate use of carving), and Perpendicular (a style that emphasizes long vertical lines, perpendicular to the horizontal). The cathedral at Salisbury, England (fig. 6.5) is in the Early English style. Set in the center of a spacious park, its spire over the main transept (added over a century after the construction of the main body of the cathedral) gives an upward thrust to the whole. All lines lead upward, creating a momentum that stops only at the top of the spire.

Each Gothic cathedral or chapel had its own personality. That of Wells Cathedral is in part determined by its scissor arches, which were added to the interior out of engineering necessity about one hundred years after the completion of the main body of the cathedral (fig. 6.6). In another example,

Figure 6.6 Interior of Wells Cathedral, begun c. 1190. Wells, England. (© A. F. Kersting)

the intricate stonework of the fan vaulting, together with the tall tracery in the windows (Perpendicular Gothic), creates the special personality of King's College Chapel (colorplate 16).

Each cathedral expressed the communal faith of its builders, who often vied with each other to create buildings of surpassing beauty and magnificence. Each, however, followed the same fundamental plan and technique of construction. During the nineteenth century a strong Neo-Gothic movement emerged, especially in England. However, few of these structures sprang from the same purposes as had those of the Gothic age.

Colorplate 16 follows p. 114.

STAINED GLASS

Some of the most remarkable artistic efforts in the Gothic era are its stained-glass windows. These windows served many purposes: they admitted the much-needed light that was almost absent in the Romanesque; they were magnificent decorations that gave the interior a warm atmosphere; and they were also a means of instruction, serving as illuminated paintings for religious education. More and more the windows took the place of walls, for they occupied all the free space between the piers supporting the arches.

Stained glass was a craft that developed from the stylized mosaics of the Byzantine and Romanesque. The glass painter assembled bits of colored, translucent glass into a window panel, defining a subject with the sharp lines of contrasting glass. The lines of the figures were always strongly marked and the draperies clearly indicated. Because line and color had to be so sharply divided, it was very difficult to achieve much expressive detail. The element of depth was nearly nonexistent. As in Romanesque sculpture, the figures remained out of proportion and distorted. Little movement is suggested, and often there is a juxtaposition of forms with little relationship among the figures.

In works of stained glass, the communal spirit of the Gothic was expressed by including the trademarks of the donors. Many windows were the gifts of local guilds or wealthy patrons. The trademark or crest set into memorial windows records the personal or collective egos of the donors. Crests were usually placed in a prominent position in each window, often just below the central figure of the panel.

Colorplate 17 follows p. 114.

A window from Chartres Cathedral depicting the *Death of the Virgin* (colorplate 17) shows the technique of this remarkable craft. With all its brilliant polychromatic coloring, the representation is stiff and unreal. (In 1993, the entire "Life of the Virgin" series at Chartres was cleaned to restore it to its original colors.) The figures are stylized and expressionless, and they show no perspective in the manner in which they are grouped around the deathbed. The donor (in this instance, the shoemakers' guild) is memorialized by the figure of a cobbler at his bench.

The east windows of King's College Chapel (colorplate 16) serve the same instructive purpose. Their organization is, however, very different. The lancet windows at Chartres, though related to one another, are independent compositions separated by heavy stonework; the effect is one of light piercing the wall at several distinct locations. The modified lancet windows at King's College, on the other hand, are immediately adjacent to one another, giving the appearance of an entire wall flooded with light. The eighteen windows depict six sets of interrelated biblical scenes. The stonework of the screen supporting the windows runs virtually from the floor to the ceiling in one direct line, epitomizing the style of the English Perpendicular Gothic.

The architecture and stained glass of the Gothic were a complete expression of the people's faith. The spirit of scholasticism was deeply ingrained in the logic of their building technique—a technique in which the thrust and counterthrust were so calculated that the whole edifice stood as a

Colorplate 14 Anonymous, *Crucifixion,* c. 800. Tempera on wood panel. Santa Maria del Antiqua, Rome, Italy. (Scala/Art Resource, NY) *(See p. 93)*

Colorplate 15 Rose window. Stained glass. Reims Cathedral, Reims, France. © Caisse
National des monuments historiques et des sites/Agence Photographique/SPADEM.
(See p. 110)

Colorplate 16 Fan vaulting and east window, 1515. King's College Chapel, Cambridge, England. (© A. F. Kersting) *(See p. 113, 114)*

Colorplate 17 *Death of a Virgin,* c. 1200. Stained glass. Chartres Cathedral, Chartres, France. (Art Resource, NY) *(See p. 114)*

Colorplate 18 Central panel by Simone Martini, wing panels by Lippo Memmi, *The Annunciation,* 1333. Tempera on wood, 8 ft. 8 in. × 10 ft. Siena Cathedral. (Scala/Art Resource, NY) *(See p. 118)*

Colorplate 19 Giotto di Bondone, *Lamentation of Christ,* 1303–1306. Fresco, 7 ft. 7 in. × 7 ft. 9 in. Scrovegni Chapel, Padua, Italy. (Scala/Art Resource, NY) *(See p. 118)*

pattern of sinews and ribs, each supporting the other. This system, combined with the rich coloring of the stained glass and the physical reaching for the heavens, attests to the harmonious appeal of the Gothic. It was an appeal to the mind, eye, and spirit.

SCULPTURE

The elements of sculpture were treated essentially the same in the Gothic as they had been in the Romanesque. There was, however, an added predilection for expressive feeling and naturalism that was lacking in monastic Romanesque art. Figures were no longer merely symbols. They were people of character who served as reminders of moral truth. The saints came to have more natural countenances and personalities that suggested their individual characters, and they seemed more alive and real.

Naturalism was not confined to human personality but also was present in the decorative details carved on the moldings and capitals of the pillars. Realistic vines and flowers were often used to break up the smooth surface and to give energy to an otherwise static bit of stone. Nature in perspective was still unknown, but Gothic artists were aware they were living in an organic world in constant flux.

As it was during the Romanesque, sculpture was an integral part of architecture. In many structures, every portal, niche, and space not occupied by stained glass carried a message in stone. The influence of scholasticism made Gothic artists conscious of minutiae, both artistic and theological. Every movement and detail was made a symbol of faith that conformed to religious doctrine. Stories from the Old and New Testaments and scenes from the lives of the saints were depicted as sermons in stone. In addition, the influence of the cult of the Virgin Mary was pervasive. Almost every cathedral had a special statue of the Virgin prominently displayed. In fact, the Virgin became so popular that the artistic portrayal of Jesus was largely replaced by that of his Mother.

Unlike their Romanesque predecessors, Gothic sculptors created their figures independently of the columns, placing them upon pillars or in niches in the structure. This innovation made it possible to achieve effects of movement and space that were unknown earlier. Movement and plasticity were also enhanced by the Gothic treatment of drapery. Instead of large, ornamental scrolls that seemed only to symbolize form, Gothic drapery was deeply carved, permitting light and shade to suggest depth and movement.

The elongation of the body, which has the tendency to endow it with lightness and immateriality, was still used with striking success. Sculptured figures seemed to grow from their bases. Elongation also tended to conventionalize bodily form. While there was often real personality revealed in

Figure 6.7 *Apostles, Portal of Le Beau Dieu,* 1225, Amiens Cathedral. Amiens, France.

facial features and in the position of the body, no real individuality could be achieved through the form itself. Gothic sculptors gave little attention to gender-related characteristics. The madonnas and female saints show very slight physical indications of gender. Breasts, for example, are usually very small and are often set too high on the chest.

The sculpture of the cathedral at Amiens reveals the Gothic spirit in stone. The figures of the Apostles from the central portal (fig. 6.7) are set apart from the wall and are covered with a Gothic canopy to integrate them with the architecture. While the bodies lack individuality, the position of the hands and turning of the heads make them seem more alive and real. The full folds of drapery, which fall gracefully about the forms, suggest plasticity and refinement.

In Italy, neither the sculptors nor the architects of the Gothic period were influenced by the style of the northern Europeans. However, the wave

Figure 6.8 Giovanni Pisano, *Annunciation, Nativity, and Shepherds* from pulpit at Siena Cathedral, Italy, 1260. Marble, c. 34 × 40 in. Pistoia, Italy. (Foto Marburg/Art Resource, NY)

of humanism was influential in the thirteenth century even in Italy. The *Annunciation, Nativity, and Shepherds* from the pulpit at Siena Cathedral (fig. 6.8) is an example of Italian medieval sculpture with such humanistic influence. The artist, Giovanni Pisano (1265–1314), created an animated stone surface upon which the deeply carved figures reflect the excitement of the occasion. Individually, the figures possess a naturalism and their gestures a vigor that anticipates the Renaissance and even the Baroque, yet in true Gothic style, Pisano shows no perspective. He crowds the three stories into one scene.

PAINTING

During the Gothic period, the art of painting, except for the illumination of manuscripts, was a minor art in the north. It remained for the Italians of the thirteenth and fourteenth centuries to raise painting to an importance equal with that of sculpture. The famous wall paintings in the Arena Chapel at Padua served the same didactic purpose as stained-glass windows, but did not transmit the spiritual essence of light as did stained glass.

Like architecture and sculpture, Gothic painting adhered to the canons of medieval theology. Symbols were arranged according to the traditional manner of biblical storytelling, and the protagonists were presented according to theological specifications. The differences between the painting of Italy and that of northern Europe lay in the areas of naturalism and human emotion.

Colorplate 18
follows p. 114.

The Annunciation of the Siena Cathedral altar (colorplate 18) by Simone Martini (1284–1344) is a case in point. Medieval symbolism is abundantly present. The Archangel Gabriel holds the olive branch as a symbol of peace. The vase of lilies, symbols of virginity, stands between the two figures. Over the central scene stand the three Gothic arches with a dove, the symbol of the Holy Ghost, at the point of the central arch. The natural arrangement and the feeling for emotion elevate this painting into the realm of the spiritual. The Virgin shrinks back with a look of awe as the angel Gabriel raises his hand in preparation for speaking. Expression is real, even if the forms themselves are not plastic in a physical sense. The denial of the flesh is still apparent, and the vase and the lilies are more convincingly real than the human forms. Each figure, each item, is separate and self-contained, reflecting the spiritual implications of the story. Line is clearly defined, and the postures of the central figures reveal the influence of the new humanism.

The most famous painter of the Gothic age is the Italian, Giotto (c. 1266–1337). Art historians look upon this Florentine master's work as the beginning of a new era in painting. Major works in several Italian cities established Giotto's contribution to the new movement. He lived during a time when the Gothic spirit was at its peak, but his humanism and individuality were of such a quality that he can rightfully be called the link between the Gothic and the period to follow—the Renaissance.

Giotto's most famous work is the monumental fresco of the *Life of Christ* on the walls of the Arena Chapel at Padua. **Fresco** is a technique of painting on wet or fresh plaster. This is exceedingly difficult, for an error means that new plaster must be applied and then painted over. Another distinct disadvantage of fresco painting is that plaster has the tendency to crack and absorb moisture. The works in fresco of Leonardo da Vinci and Michelangelo (see chapter 7) have been damaged in this way.

Colorplate 19
follows p. 114.

One of the remarkable scenes from Giotto's *Life of Christ* is the *Lamentation of Christ,* the laying away of Christ's body in the tomb (colorplate 19). Giotto presented this theme in such a natural manner that the viewer becomes a witness to a real drama. He created a three-dimensional group that moves in space. Closed form centers attention on the body of Christ: every movement and every gaze is focused upon him, and even the angels are drawn toward him. There are expressions of grief on each face. In true Gothic tradition, facial expressions of grief are alike in each—lips parted slightly, eyes narrowed and drawn back. Giotto did not yet express the individuality of grief.

Although its clear lines sharply define the color, the *Lamentation of Christ* is still Gothic in its essential symbolic features. The halos and angels attest to this. The stylized humans are still unreal in comparison with the Greeks' portrayal of physical reality, yet there is more realism than was found in Romanesque sculpture or even in the Gothic sculpture of Amiens. Giotto was on the threshold of the Renaissance. He organized the elements of painting in much the same manner as later artists. However, in adherence to traditional scenes and symbols, he is tied to the spirit of the northern Gothic.

MUSIC

Gothic music, like Gothic art, broke with the past in its move toward humanism, yet it still held to the scholastic attitude of the Middle Ages. In this period are found the first formal expressions of one of the distinctive elements of western European music—the simultaneous sounding of tones of different pitch, or harmony. The way harmony is used is probably the most characteristic element that makes European music different from all other musical systems.

In the history of Western music, there have been two basic schemes whereby harmony is achieved. One, called polyphony or counterpoint, uses two or more independent, simultaneous melodic lines. The other, called homophony, can be described as a melody with chordal accompaniment. Both result in tones of different pitch sounding simultaneously and thus producing harmony (an element of music described in chapter 2).

Both of these schemes require systematic notation, so composers may communicate their ideas to musical performers. As long as music was made exclusively of single melodic lines, there was no need for a system of symbols that did more than remind performers of the traditional melodies. Notation, with Guido of Arezzo as one of its principal innovators, made possible the preservation of Gothic music. It became necessary with the advent of musician-composers who were concerned with the organization of musical sounds in complex tonal patterns.

The countless anonymous composers of the chants of the Middle Ages are an embodiment of a "God-inspired," mysterious, creative power disassociated from the humans through which it worked. Gothic composers, however, saw themselves as individuals struggling with artistic problems, and they needed to communicate their solutions to other people. Another manifestation of humanism was the composers' interest in assigning their names to their works. A final example of humanistic expression was the emphasis on the artistic treatment of secular music, both by recognized composers and by the great body of poet-musicians, the minstrel singers of the twelfth and thirteenth centuries.

In contrast to these humanizing tendencies, the rigid subscription to rules and devices of composition can be likened to the acceptance of the stylized symbols of Gothic painting. The organization of the musical materials by composers of the Gothic period was accomplished by strict adherence to arbitrary rules and practices, many of which had symbolic meanings. For example, Church music used triple meter for its rhythmic structure to symbolize the Trinity.

Gothic composers also developed **organum**, a strictly prescribed style of polyphony that was greatly influenced by the traditional music of the medieval church. One or more lines of melody were added to the ***cantus firmus*** (basic chant). At cadence points, all the melodies returned to the so-called perfect intervals of the unison, fifth, or octave. This is, in a sense, the musical parallel of the subdivisions of the Gothic tracery so characteristic of architecture. In the two-voice organum *Rex Caeli* (ex. 6.1), the *cantus firmus* is in the upper voice.

Example 6.1 *Rex Caeli, Domine,* organum, sequence

Original chant in upper voice, organum in lower voice

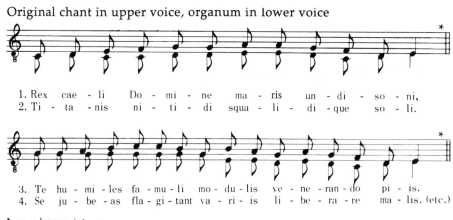

* = cadence point.

The weaving together of lines of melody, one of which is a traditional chant of the Church, is characteristic of the works of the composers of this style. In a polyphonic *Alleluia* by Perotin (ex. 6.2), the original modal chant, the *cantus firmus,* is sung as a slow-moving voice, while the added parts move in a decorative manner in faster note values, inevitably returning at the cadences to the perfect intervals of unison, fifth, or octave. The harmony, which results from combining the upper melodic lines with the traditional chant, is merely coincidental. To those accustomed to more recent music, this harmony might sound stark and simple at first, but in its intended setting in a Gothic cathedral, it enriched the worship service.

Example 6.2 *Alleluia,* Perotin From *The Montpellier Codex,* edited by Hans Tischler, *Recent Researches in the Music of the Middle Ages and Early Renaissance,* vols. 2, 3 (Madison: A–R Editions, 1978).

The rhythmic organization of this *Alleluia* illustrates the rigid application of an arbitrary poetic-rhythmic pattern, the dactyl (long-short-short), in the upper two voices. In the greater portion of this work, the lower voice is unmeasured. The form of the *Alleluia* is free.

While there are no instructions given by the composer for the performance of early polyphonic music, it is apparent from sculpture and paintings of the period that instruments were used. The voice parts could have been doubled or instruments substituted for voices in one or more parts. Certainly the slow-moving note values of a *cantus firmus* would be well adapted to rendition by such instruments as viols, sackbuts, or other wind instruments (see fig. 7.12).

A CLOSER LOOK

Machaut, *Messe de Notre Dame* (Kyrie)

In the Middle Ages, the music of polyphonic Mass movements was collected into large volumes organized according to movement type. Kyries were grouped together, and other movements were similarly grouped. Consequently, movements by the same composer did not appear together. The fact that Guillaume de Machaut's Mass is preserved in its entirety makes it a historical milestone. It is the first four-voice polyphonic setting of the complete Ordinary of the Mass known to be composed by a single individual.

Machaut was born around 1300, probably near Reims, whose cathedral played an important part in his life and for which he may have composed this Mass. After receiving a classical education, he served King John of Luxembourg and Bohemia for many years. He traveled widely throughout Europe, using his expertise in theology and diplomacy.

In 1337, Machaut became a Canon (clergyman) at Reims, where he spent much of the remainder of his life. Machaut was known primarily as a poet and, to a lesser degree, a composer. It is unlikely his Mass greatly influenced his contemporaries. It has gained its greatest renown in the modern era. Machaut is famous for assembling his musical works in an illustrated manuscript.

This manuscript contains 143 works, secular (virelais, ballades, and rondeaux) and sacred (motets and the Mass) and is an invaluable window on the late medieval period. Another important source of information about Machaut's personal life and his compositional process is the *Voir Dit,* a manuscript containing poetry and musical works, as well as writings expressing his love for a nineteen-year-old girl.

Machaut's Mass includes the usual movements of the Ordinary of the Mass: Kyrie, Gloria, Credo, Sanctus, Agnus Dei and Ite, missa est. The four voices are (from highest to lowest), triplum, motetus, tenor, and contratenor. In three of the movements, the upper voices are paired, as are the lower voices. The two other movements treat the voices in a more equal fashion. The interval of the third, so pleasing to the modern ear, is heard occasionally. These movements favor duple meters, a break with the dominating triple meter favored at the time because of its representation of the Holy Trinity. It also includes other numerical symbolism featured so frequently in the arts of the Middle Ages.

The first movement (Kyrie) consists of three sections: Kyrie eleison, Christe eleison, Kyrie eleison, each of which is performed three times, an

Example 6.3 Guillaume de Machaut, Kyrie from *Messe de Notre Dame*

Notated Polyphonic Version	A Performance Version
I. Kyrie eleison no. 1 (one polyphonic setting performed three times)	Kyrie eleison no. 1 (4-voice polyphony, triple meter, complex rhythms) Kyrie eleison no. 1 (monophonic chant, nonmetric, free rhythms) Kyrie eleison no. 1 (as in the beginning)
II. Christe eleison (one polyphonic setting performed three times)	Christe eleison (monophonic chant, nonmetric, free rhythms) Christe eleison (4-voice polyphony, triple meter, complex rhythms) Christe eleison (monophonic chant, nonmetric, free rhythms)
III. Kyrie eleison no. 2 (one polyphonic setting performed two times) Kyrie eleison no. 3 (one polyphonic setting performed one time)	Kyrie eleison no. 2 (4-voice polyphony, triple meter, complex rhythms) Kyrie eleison no. 2 (monophonic chant, nonmetric, free rhythms) Kyrie eleison no. 3 (4-voice polyphony, triple meter, complex rhythms)

immutable tradition (see ex. 6.3). This three-part division symbolized to the medieval mind the Holy Trinity. Each of the sections is based on an earlier Gregorian plainchant. In the performance practice of this period, considerable freedom could be exercised, allowing the original Gregorian plainchant to replace any of the polyphonic sections (see ex. 6.3, A Performance Version).

To a large extent, Machaut's Mass embodies the typical formal structure of the plainsong Mass of this period, in which repeating melodic units (**color**) (ex. 6.4) and repeated rhythmic units (**talea**) are part of a rational compositional procedure called **isorhythm**.

This music is complex and was written for the musical elite of that time. However, a careful study of the work will introduce the listener of today to many of its mathematical intricacies and its numerical symbolism, representative of Medieval music.

Example 6.4 Guillaume de Machaut, pitches of the color from Kyrie, *Messe de Notre Dame*

In contrast to these sacred works, there is a great wealth of secular songs from the Gothic period. Minstrel singers who were variously known as ***troubadours, trouvères,*** and ***minnesingers*** set poems with secular themes to melodies that they composed or to well-known tunes of the day. While not all medieval secular songs were the product of these aristocratic and courtly singers, it is from them that most of the settings have come down to us. Bernart de Ventadorn (fl. 1150–1180) was not an aristocrat, but he rose from mean circumstances to become the lover of Eleanor of Aquitaine and a poet of renown (ex. 6.5).

Example 6.5 Troubadour text by Bernart de Ventadorn. (From *The Lyrics of the Troubadour, Trouvères,* by Frederick Goldin. Copyright © 1973 by Frederick Goldin. Used by permission of Doubleday, a division of Bantam Doubleday Dell Publishing Group, Inc.)

> The winter that comes to me
> is white red yellow flowers;
> my good luck grows
> with the wind and the rain,
> and so my song mounts up, rises,
> and my worth increases.
> I have such love in my heart,
> such joy, such sweetness,
> the ice I see is a flower,
> that snow, green things that grow.

The *troubadours* originated in southern France, but their influence spread over all Europe. In northern France their counterparts were known as *trouvères* and, in Germany, as *minnesingers*. These minstrels were first and foremost concerned with poetic expression; the melodies were often secondary. From the *troubadours* and *trouvères* alone a treasury of more than 1500 melodies and 7500 poems are known today. The subjects of these lyrics vary from political satire to love, the latter being a favorite theme. Many secular Gothic songs portray religious topics. This is especially true of the **laudas** of neighboring Italy. Since they are nonliturgical, however, they are included in the category "secular."

A common characteristic of all these songs, whether from France, Italy, Germany, or Spain, is their restriction to a single melodic line; they are thus examples of **monody.** The *trouvère* song *Or la truix* is representative of this type of musical expression. It consists of a single line of melody, the form of which is dictated by the construction of the poetic text. The opening phrase contrasts with the second, which is followed by two repetitions of the first phrase. Various patterns of such repetition and contrast are found in all these secular songs, depending on the structure of the lyrics. The melody might have been sung to a simple accompaniment of harp or lute, for there are contemporaneous pictures showing singers and other performers with instruments capable of producing chordal harmony. The melodies, while predominantly modal, tend to fall into our present-day concept of minor and even major tonality.

Among the earliest composers of Gothic music known by name was the mystic, Abbess Hildegard von Bingen (1098–1197). Her work has been made available through recent research. She is one of the earliest identified women composers known. Her extant works are devoted primarily to religious music, which are settings of her own poetry, as documented in the recording, *A Feather on the Breath of God.*

Summary

During the Gothic period, the Church retained its position as the principal patron of the arts. It was still the most powerful political, economic, educational, artistic, and religious institution. While the canons and symbolism of religious art remained basically the same as in the Romanesque, there was more emphasis on magnificence and beauty. This trend brought greater focus on human creations. The rise of towns and the Crusades were developments that promoted increasingly secular ideas and foreign influences. Gothic churches were more the result of the communal effort of the towns than the product of the monasteries. The Gothic church was the educational, social, and religious center of the community. Its splendor was a testimony to the wealth and power of the Church.

The development of the Gothic arch provided a skeletal frame that made it possible to construct buildings of great height. It also made possible walls of magnificent stained-glass windows, usually with memorials to the donors placed in prominent positions. Gothic sculpture was usually freestanding, with movement of free-flowing drapery and some evidence of bodily movement. Sculpture was still somewhat distorted but more physically realistic than in the Romanesque. Real beauty was still of the spirit and not of the flesh. Painting also showed more three-dimensional character, albeit still very slight. Clearly defined lines and contrasting colors gave the effect of a controlled space with little sense of movement. Expressive feeling in painting, sculpture, and stained glass was conveyed more by symbolism than by the realism of emotional expression.

Developments in polyphony, rhythmic organization, and form were the major achievements of Gothic music, made possible through the invention of a system of notation. Still, music was more a science than an art. Rigid rules controlled intervallic relationships, rhythms, and formal organization in polyphonic sacred music, which was organized around liturgical texts. A great wealth of secular songs was set to the poems of *troubadours, trouvères,* and *minnesingers*. These songs were usually of a courtly nature, but many were related to religious subjects, especially to the love of the Virgin Mary.

Architecture, sculpture, painting, and music in the Gothic period expressed the religion, mysticism, and scholasticism that permeated the age. All art was part of a veritable encyclopedia of religious beliefs. Humanism was beginning to blossom, but it remained for the Renaissance artist to capture and fully express this new spirit.

Suggested Readings

In addition to the specific sources that follow, the general readings on pages 388 and 389 contain valuable information about the topic of this chapter.

Branner, Robert, ed. *Chartres Cathedral*. New York: W. W. Norton, 1969.

Branner, Robert, ed. *Burgundian Gothic Architecture*. London: Sothebys Publications, 1986.

Brown, Sarah. *Stained Glass: An Illustrated History*. Avenal, NJ: Outlet Book Co., 1992.

Brown, Sarah, and David O'Conner. *Medieval Craftsmen: Glass Painters*. Toronto: University of Toronto Press, 1991.

Ferguson, G. *Signs and Symbols in Christian Art*. New York: Oxford University Press, 1966.

Hoppin, Richard H. *Medieval Music*. New York: W. W. Norton, 1978.

Male, Emile. *Religious Art in France: The Thirteenth Century*. Princeton, NJ: Princeton University Press, 1984.

Martindale, Andrew. *Gothic Art*. New York: Thames Hudson, 1985.

Shaver-Crandell, Anne. *The Middle Ages*. Cambridge: Cambridge University Press, 1982.

Stubblebine, James. *Giotto: The Arena Chapel Frescos*. New York: W. W. Norton, 1969.

Thomson, James. *Music Through The Renaissance*. Dubuque, IA: Wm. C. Brown Publishers, 1984.

Chapter 7

·••◦•◦•◦••·

The Renaissance
(1400–1600)

Chronology

Visual Arts	Music	Historical Figures and Events
•Lorenzo Ghiberti (1378–1455) •Donato di Niccolò Donatello (1386–1466) •Fra Angelico (c. 1387–1455)		
	•Guillaume Dufay (c. 1400–1474)	•Rule of the Medici (1430–1495)
•Andrea Mantegna (c. 1431–1506) •Andrea del Verrocchio (1435–1488) •Sandro Botticelli (1440–1510)	•Josquin Desprez (c. 1440–1521)	
•Donato Bramante (1444–1514)		•Lorenzo de Medici (1449–1492)
•Perugino (1450–1523) •Leonardo da Vinci (1452–1519)	•Heinrich Isaac (1450–1517)	
•Tilman Riemenschneider (1460–1531)		•Gutenberg Bible (1454)
•Albrecht Dürer (1471–1528)		•Niccolo Machiavelli (1469–1527)
		•Nicolaus Copernicus (1473–1543)
•Michelangelo Buonarroti (1475–1564) •Tiziano Vecelli (Titian) (1477–1576) •Giorgione del Castelfranco (1478–1511) •Mathias Grünewald (1480–1528) •Sanzio Raphael (1483–1520)		•Martin Luther (1483–1546) •Henry VIII (1491–1547) •First voyage of Columbus (1492)
	•Johann Walter (1496–1570)	•Vasco da Gama voyage to India (1497) •Execution of Savonarola (1498) •Julius II as Pope (1503)

Chronology (*Continued*)

Visual Arts	Music	Historical Figures and Events
	• Thomas Tallis (c. 1505–1585)	• *The Prince* by Machiavelli (1513) • Luther posts his *Ninety-Five Theses* (1517)
• Jacopo Robusti (Tintoretto) (1518–1594) • Andrea Palladio (1518–1580) • Pieter Brueghel (c. 1524–1569)	• Andrea Gabrieli (c. 1520–1586) • Giovanni Pierluigi da Palestrina (c. 1525–1594) • Orlando di Lasso (1532–1594)	
		• Church of England separates from the Papacy (1534) • Founding of the Jesuit Society (1540)
• Domenico Theotocopouli (El Greco) (1548–1614)	• William Byrd (1543–1623)	• Council of Trent (1545)
	• Luca Marenzio (1553–1599) • Giovanni Gabrieli (c. 1555–1612) • Don Carlo Gesualdo (c. 1560–1613) • John Bennet (c. 1575–1625)	• William Shakespeare (1564–1616) • Drake starts world voyage (1577)

Pronunciation Guide

Botticelli (Baw-tee-chel´-lee)
Créquillon (Kray-kee-ö)
Dürer (Dü´-rer)
El Greco (El Gré-koh)
Erasmus (E-ras´-moos)
Farnese (Fahr-nay´-zay)
Fra Angelico (Frah Ahn-jay´-lee-coh)
Gabrieli, Andrea (Gah-bree-ay´-lee, Ahn-dray´-ah)
Gesualdo (Jez-wahl´-doh)
Ghirlandaio (Geer-lahn-dah´-yoh)
Gott Schöpfer, Heiliger Geist (Got Shöp´-fer, Hai´-li-ger Gaist)
Gozzoli (Gawt´-zoh-lee)
Grünewald (Grü´-ne-valt)

Isaac (Ee´-zahk´)
Josquin Desprez (Zhos-kä Deh-pray)
Machiavelli (Mah´-kee-ah-vel´-lee)
Magi (Mah´-jee)
Mantegna, Andrea (Mahn-teyn´-yeh, Ahn-dray´-ah)
Medici, Lorenzo de´ (May´-dee-chee, Loh-ren´-zoh day)
Michelangelo (Mih-kel-ahń-jel-oh)
Palestrina (Pahl-es-tree´-nah)
Palladio (Pahl-lah´-dee-oh)
Perugino (Pay-roo-jee´-noh)
Prinzen-Tanz, Proportz (Print´-zen Tahnz, Proh´-portz)

Riemenschneider (Ree-men-schnai-der)
Santa Maria delle Grazia (Sahn´-tah Mah-ree´-ah del-le Graht´-zee-ah)
Savonarola (Sah´-vohn-ah-roh´-lah)
Sforza, Ludovico (Sfor´-zah, Loo-doh-vee´-koh)
Simonetta (See-moh-net´-tah)
Tintoretto (Teen-toh-ret´-toh)
Titian (Tish´-an)
Veni Sponsa Christi (Vay´-nee Spon´-sah Krees´-tee)
Verrocchio (Ver-roh´-kee-oh)
Vicenza (Vee-chen´-zah)
Walter (Vahl´-ter)

Study Objectives

1. Understand how the Renaissance marks a return to the ideals of Greek humanism and individualism and how the search for personal identity dominated the arts during this period.
2. Study how scientific research influenced art through perspective and anatomy, and how it influenced music in harmonic structure.
3. Understand how Renaissance humanism is reflected in the creative efforts of its artists.
4. Learn how artists reveal themselves in the function, subject matter, and expressive content of those works of art recognized as among the greatest of all time.
5. Understand how the patronage of artists and musicians was divided between the Church and the aristocracy for similarly humanistic objectives.

The flowering of humanism, which had its beginnings in the Gothic period, reached full bloom in the succeeding epoch, called the *Renaissance* (a French word meaning, literally, "rebirth"). In its attempt to return to the spirit of Greek culture, the Renaissance spirit was one of worldliness, but it was quite different from the Greek in that individuality and the worth of human personality were its motivating forces. The Greeks were interested in the ideal human, but the Renaissance attitude was one of concern for the real human. Interest was shown in the individual's personality, mind, body, social relationships, personal religion, economic condition, and place in the political scheme of things. It was an idea, a philosophy, a way of life that changed and molded the individual's attitude toward self, community, and God. Although dominated by the artistic movements of Italy, the Renaissance found expression somewhat later in the rest of Europe.

Because of the complexity of the Renaissance, there have been numerous interpretations of its cultural fabric. The most popular has been that it was the period in history dedicated to the rebirth of classical learning. In fact, the term itself has this connotation. Such an interpretation is quite true: the scholars of the Renaissance did rediscover the classical learning of the Greeks, probably because they were interested in the things of this world, as were the Greeks. It was not merely a veneration for antiquity but a kindred spirit that inspired their interest. The Parthenon stood in Athens throughout the Middle Ages, but medieval people denied its beauty and value because of their asceticism. Renaissance artists did not "discover" Greek culture as if it had been long lost; they cultivated it because they found themselves in sympathy with Greek attitudes toward life.

To some writers and scholars, the Renaissance marks a resurgence of interest in people and the world in which they lived. It was a period when people began again to show interest in the knowledge of natural phenomena and in the techniques of civilization. The Renaissance spirit laid the foundation for the heliocentric theory of the universe, which established that the earth was round and moved around the sun. The voyages of Columbus and Vasco da Gama into unknown seas were outward, physical manifestations of the Renaissance spirit. The introduction into western Europe of gunpowder, the invention of the printing press, and the systematic progress of physical science were also proof that Renaissance people were concentrating on their own minds and their earthly problems. Scholars pursued political as well as natural science. Machiavelli's *The Prince* was much praised as a book of advice for the ambitious ruler.

Some see the Renaissance as a crucible of religious, economic, and social conflict. The Protestant Reformation, for example, was a manifestation of the humanistic spirit in northern Europe and was associated with trends in the economic, social, and political scene. The powerful ruling families of the Italian city-states were in a continuing struggle with each other for political and economic supremacy—a struggle that often had control of the Vatican itself as the ultimate prize.

The Renaissance was all of this and more. It was a time for change and integration, for new discoveries and for inventions that had a profound effect on every phase of human experience. Each of these ideas and events contributed to the Renaissance spirit of humanism and, at the same time, its result.

The result of these activities was a Renaissance individual confronted by change. The gradual spread of humanistic thought and the advances made in astronomy and other sciences removed some of the wonder and mystery from the then-current understanding of the universe. This, coupled with a weakening loyalty to spiritual authority (in part caused by the constant struggle between Church and State for supremacy), created a new materialism. The development of trade and commerce, with resultant increases in the standard of living, also strengthened materialistic philosophy. Set free from the authority of the Church, people began to question all authority. If they could no longer look to either the Church or the State for leadership, they felt free to have confidence in their own rationalizations. Consequently, they turned to more individualistic beliefs and pursuits.

Materialism and individualism brought new incentives for living. The acquiring of personal wealth became a goal worth striving for. Worldly wisdom and temporal power were cultivated for the personal satisfaction they could bring. New dreamers were born, but their dreams were of business, science, and politics rather than religion.

Because of its fortunate position along the trade route from the East, Italy was the center from which this tremendous activity spread. It was also the home of the financiers who made such activity possible, but the Renaissance movement was not confined to Italy. Northern Europe responded to the same forces in much the same way but with its own stamp of cultural personality. Throughout Europe there was great vitality, forcefulness, profit-driven business, and often extreme cruelty. Beauty, whether pagan or Christian, began to be cultivated for its own sake and not for the sake of what it could teach. The arts were enthusiastically cultivated by the rich patrons of the time—patrons who were often paganized princes, and popes who were seldom Christian in spirit. Piero de´ Medici, for example, commissioned Fra Angelico to create decorations for a silver chest that included the *Annunciation* (colorplate 22), a sacred subject on this secular object. As in the Middle Ages, the Church remained the greatest single patron of all the arts.

Colorplate 22
follows p. 146.

One of the most important results of the Renaissance spirit was the influence of wealthy patronage upon both the function and subject matter of art. The portrait, which had not been in favor since early Roman times, again assumed a prominent place as an art subject. No doubt this was due, in part, to the egotistic desire of the wealthy to leave likenesses of themselves as reminders of their worldly successes (as did the Romans). Patrons were eager to have artists present them in a most favorable light: as devout Christians or as benefactors of humankind, often without any real basis in fact. It was looked upon as a signal honor to be represented as a personage from pagan mythology or as a figure from a biblical scene. Botticelli included the whole Medici family in his *Adoration of the Magi* (colorplate 20) and included himself at the extreme right of the painting. As was characteristic in paintings of this period, all human figures wore clothing of their own time rather than of the time depicted in the painting. Their sumptuous dress and jewelry clearly depict the status of the powerful Medici family.

Colorplate 20
follows p. 146.

Artists were retained to furnish designs for elaborate costumes and even to plan parades and festivals to enhance the glory and prestige of the patron. They were called upon to make pictorial records of ordinary events, as well as events that were a part of the social activity of the upper classes. Consequently, much of this art was popular, descriptive, and at times superficial. The *Journey of the Magi* (colorplate 21) by Gozzoli is such a painting. Its purpose was to commemorate an elaborate parade in honor of Lorenzo the Magnificent of Florence and his honored guests. The title and subject matter, however, are religious, symbolizing the journey of the wise men to Jerusalem. Obviously, the title was a pretext for celebrating the wealth and power of the ruling Medici family, the artist's benefactors. The largest and most brilliantly colored figure in the group is Lorenzo himself, with the lesser personages painted in a splendor proportionate to their importance. Individual faces are shown realistically, but the landscape depicted is quite primitive from our point of view. This mood of worldly culture had little in common with the soul-searching mysticism of the earlier Gothic artists.

Colorplate 21
follows p. 146.

Although the Church was still the richest institution to patronize art, religious painting ceased to be the main concern of artists. There were still a great number of artworks being created with religious titles, but their religious purposes were frequently secondary. Pope Julius II (1503–1513) initiated the planning for a new St. Peter's Cathedral in Rome. It was to be a magnificent structure, not to the glory of God but to the glory of Julius himself. Ironically, Julius died before his plans could be executed.

Music in the Renaissance was also strongly influenced by secular patronage. It moved out of the Church and into the home as a necessary adjunct to social life. Great social importance was attached to making music after meals. Dance music gained popularity both in the home and at festivals and pageants. More composers were attached to wealthy households to provide music for entertainment and to teach youth. Even municipalities retained bands of musicians to announce honored guests and perform for special celebrations.

Art and music also reflected the new humanistic spirit through the personalities of their creators. The Renaissance has often been referred to as an age of geniuses, and, as we have seen, its humanism fostered individualism. For the first time in centuries, creative personalities created works of art admired not only by their contemporaries but by our age as well. Leonardo da Vinci, Michelangelo, Raphael, Botticelli—to mention a few— were artists of such strong character that they influenced much of subsequent art history. The awakening of artists to their creative powers and imaginations was an important phenomenon. From this time on, art was rarely a collective effort; it was instead the personal, creative product of an individual. Stylistic differences stemmed in large part from the individual differences of the artists. This is not to say, however, that immediate regional influences ceased to exist.

In addition to typifying the spirit of humanism, Renaissance artists also were profoundly inspired by scientific research and exploration. An added degree of realism in art was the direct result. Artists made extensive studies and measurements of classical architecture and sculpture to arrive at workable rules of proportion and balance. Rules of perspective and **foreshortening** were formulated with mathematical exactness. These enabled artists to create the illusion of space more realistically. Mantegna's (c. 1431–1506) *The Dead Christ* (fig. 7.1) is illustrative of the attention artists gave to this principle. The unique position of the viewer in relation to the body of Christ evokes a particularly strong emotional response.

Studies in anatomy were of fundamental importance to Renaissance art. Medieval prejudice and Church opposition to depiction of the body were overridden by the thirst for knowledge. Artists believed that realistic portrayal of the human form could not be fully attained without a sound knowledge of physical details. Laboratory dissections and laborious drawings

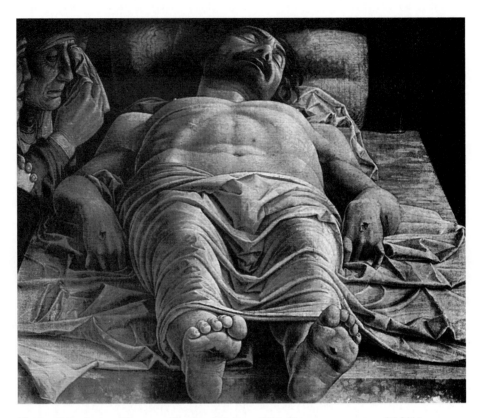

Figure 7.1   Andrea Mantegna, *The Dead Christ,* c. 1501. Tempera on canvas, 26 3/4 in. ×
31 7/8 in. Pinacoteca di Brera, Milan, Italy. (Alinari/Art Resource, NY)

of muscles, tissue, and bony structures were among the required studies of
young artists. The studies in anatomy made by Leonardo da Vinci were so
meticulously drawn that they were used in medical textbooks until modern
times. Because of the interest in the human form, the nude regained its place
in art and lost its medieval connotation of shame. The essence of humanism—
the entire human being with a perfectly proportioned body—could be completely represented only in the nude. For Renaissance humanists, as for the
Greeks, nudity was without self-consciousness.

Renaissance culture was so intimately mirrored in the works of its artists
that its history can be told in terms of their creative efforts. Time has proven
that of all Renaissance historical figures, its artists have left us the most valuable legacy and the finest interpretation of their age. There were more first-
rate artists during this epoch than during any preceding period. However, this
study will of necessity be confined to only a few great artists and their works.
This selection in no way questions the importance or the quality of others.

PAINTING

Renaissance artists used the same elements of line, space, color, and formal organization that were used by Gothic artists and by those in the ancient world. Humanism, however, brought a new, fresh approach to the organization of these elements. In order to emphasize form, the element of line was usually clearly defined and curvilinear, creating an effect of smooth-flowing motion. Although space was at first organized on several shallow planes, with little sense of recession into the distance, Renaissance artists increasingly explored linear perspective in their paintings (colorplates 22, 25, 30). In Gozzoli's *Journey of the Magi* (colorplate 21), perspective is naive. In this example of closed form the eye is directed inward, with attention focused on a central figure or point of interest. The formal organization juxtaposes disparate parts in a compositional whole. The colors are brilliantly polychromatic, a general characteristic of Renaissance painting. Gozzoli (1420–1497), like others, used color as a line to separate figures from one another. This led to a rich palette of contrasting colors that also detached principal forms from their backgrounds.

Colorplates 25 and 30 follow p. 146.

Several other stylistic conventions that became integral parts of painting in the Renaissance persisted until late in the nineteenth century. The first of these was the idea that all painting must be true to nature, a requirement stemming from the humanism of the period. Another was the use of objects symbolic of something not actually present in the scene but necessary to its complete understanding. For example, the headdress in the *Sistine Madonna* (colorplate 7) is common to the Eastern church and symbolizes its unity with the Western church. The last of these conventions held that the organization of an artwork reflects its function. This is illustrated in Gozzoli's work, where the wealthy Medici family is prominently portrayed in a religious procession. The Medici's importance in the painting expresses their social position.

Colorplate 7 follows p. 18.

An analysis of several paintings will show how they differ from the art of earlier periods and will reveal the differences among the cultures of each epoch.

Fra Angelico

Unlike many other Italian Renaissance painters, Fra Angelico (c. 1400–1455) chose sacred subjects almost exclusively. This was natural, in part, because of his commitment to the Dominican Order, and also because many of his works were designed to decorate churches and other religious buildings. A common subject for such buildings was the Annunciation. Fra Angelico's use of this subject (colorplate 22) to decorate a silver chest is not to be confused with his larger altarpiece devoted to the same subject. In this example, the angel of the Annunciation, Gabriel, gains the attention of Mary, who is wearing the traditional blue robe. The two figures are at the front of the picture plane and face one another across deep space, which convincingly, though naively, presents linear perspective. Except for these two figures and the footstool, the picture is entirely symmetrical. The presence of the Holy Ghost is depicted by a small dove at the top of the picture. Blue is the unifying color in this composition, expressing an intimate, quiet moment in the life of the Virgin. This cool serenity is broken by the angel's garish multi-colored wings.

Botticelli

Colorplate 23 follows p. 146.

Lyric style and a sensitive feeling for poetic beauty are major elements of Sandro Botticelli's *The Birth of Venus* (colorplate 23). He was enamored of the idealized beauty of pagan mythology and used it to express his own love for the beauty of the human form. Botticelli (1440–1510) was influenced by the Florentine monk and reformer Savonarola and turned to religious painting; he actually burned some of his paintings of mythological subjects. On the whole, though, his mythological works best represent his style. *The Birth of Venus* depicts the Greek myth that told of Venus born from the foam of the sea and gently carried to shore on a seashell, with personified Winds rippling the waves and mythical Hours waiting to cover her with a star-studded garment.

Pictorial representation is the dominant force in this painting. Objects, such as the seashell and the figures representing the Winds and Hours, are used symbolically. The function was to put the Greek myth on canvas and to reveal the beauty of Venus. It is probable that the model for Venus was Simonetta, a great Florentine beauty of the artist's acquaintance. The elements are organized by sharply drawn lines. They are curvilinear and sparkle with life and movement. The figures representing the Winds are almost as one, not blended, but each defined by structural line and color. There is great detail in this work, and each is made important by clear, flowing lines. The spatial depth in the painting is not convincingly real. The shoreline in the background is more artificial than nature's creation. The unreal landscape contrasts with the realism of the human form, even to the color of the flesh. The form is closed, for there is nothing to take the eye outside the picture. While removing any one of the objects would destroy the balance, such removal would not destroy the plasticity of the remaining objects. It is a painting of contrasting colors rather than a blend of different shades of the same color.

The Birth of Venus also demonstrates the principles of contrast and repetition. The vertically curved lines of Venus contrast sharply with the horizon and the diagonal lines of the figures. The straight lines of the trees repeat and also oppose the curved and vertical lines of Venus.

Botticelli has presented his story in a graphic manner, with all the essential symbols of the myth present. The viewer, however, is more enchanted by the physical forms than by the story. True to the Renaissance spirit, the artist reflects the Greek influence and humanism in both the subject and his treatment of it. The human body becomes the real subject. The painting is classic in style, arranging individual forms into harmonious unity. It is a painting devoted to the ideal of beauty for its own sake.

A Closer Look

Botticelli, *Adoration of the Magi*

The Adoration of the Magi was one of the most frequent subjects for altarpiece painting during the Renaissance. Sandro Botticelli painted four *Adorations* that have achieved lasting fame. Many common features of subject matter and design are shared among these paintings, but for several reasons, mainly historical, the *Adoration* in the Uffizi palace (colorplate 20) is particularly interesting. Its connection with the Medici family endeared it especially to the Florentines.

This modest-sized wooden altarpiece shows groups of men on either side of the central grouping of the Virgin and Child, registering little concern for the event they are witnessing. They stand on ground that slopes upward into the picture. The Virgin and Child are in a rude structure of tree trunks, rocks, and hewn stone, elevated above the adoring kings. In the distance to the left are some architectural ruins of decayed grandeur. An ambiguous landscape occupies a small corner in the distance to the right.

The human figures are carefully deployed to create a geometric design on the panel. There is a strong axial line running from the rays of the star (top center) down through the Holy Family and the kneeling figure (center front). The groups of adoring visitors on the left and right provide balance around the axial line and focus attention on the central figures. The proud young man to the left, with slightly bent leg, and with the classical ruins at the rear help to cast the viewer's eyes inwardly. This is balanced and countered by the right-most figure and the wall fragment above him. The men leaning toward the

Holy Family form two sides of a triangle whose apex is the Virgin's face. Botticelli seems not too concerned with linear perspective, although there is evidence of it, especially in the architectural elements.

Botticelli lived at a time when commissions dictated the amount of gold that was to appear in a painting or its frame. In this *Adoration,* however, color and texture are of more importance than gold in depicting the richness of the kings and others featured in the work. He depicts rich brown and white fur trim and embroidery with colored or golden threads and even shows pearls and rubies sewn into some of the costumes. Crimsons and some of the colors from natural dyes of the time mark the festivity of this occasion. The blue of the Virgin's cloak is traditional in Renaissance iconography.

This painting was commissioned for a funerary chapel in the church of Santa Maria Novella in Florence. The chapel, donated by Guasparre del Lama, was dedicated to the Epiphany. The donor's Christian name, Guasparre, was the same as that of one of the three kings, who is traditionally called "Caspar." These facts must have played a part in the choice of subject matter for the commission. In the middle of the sixteenth century Vasari, in writing of Botticelli's life, identifies the three kings of this painting as members of the Medici family. His conclusions have now been questioned by more recent scholarship, taking into account other portraits, medals struck in honor of the Medicis, and historical records. The identifiable figures in this early collective portrait are Cosimo de Medici, as the old king; Giuliano de Medici, the young man with the sword, left front; Lorenzo de Medici, clad in a black garment with a crimson strip across the shoulder, to the right of the young kneeling king; the patron Guasparre, represented as a gray-haired man facing outward and pointing with his right hand; and, finally, Botticelli himself, said to be represented by the man at the extreme right of the painting. The reasons for including each of these in the painting vary. Inclusion of the patron and the artist could be a matter of documentation. Representing the Medicis may have had more complex motivations: the artist, for example, might well have hoped for further commissions from the Medici family. (Adulatory prefaces to literary works of the Renaissance were another manifestation of the same impulse.) He later did forge a strong economic connection with the Medici family.

There are several levels of symbolism present in the *Adoration of the Magi*. The Medici family, perhaps in acts of self-flattery, were identified with the Magi. Simple objects within the painting had specific symbolic meaning to Botticelli's contemporaries; examples include the peacock (immortality) and the laurel branches (eternity). Collectively, the persons and their relationships, the setting, and the fragmented architecture reminded the faithful of the Epiphany, that moment when pagan kings came to recognize the Christ as Savior. The presentation of gifts by the kings reminded viewers of the bringing of gifts that was part of the Eucharist (the sacrifice portion of the Mass celebration) in the Renaissance church and still today in certain parts of the world.

Finally, there is a marvelous path of glances among the figures in this painting. If lines were drawn following these glances, a veritable labyrinth would be created. These gestures afford the artist opportunities to show the faces of the characters in varied positions. Not at all of least importance is the way the characters bring the observer into the life of this sacred scene. If the figure on the right is Botticelli, then he—perhaps most strongly of all—with his proud look continues to invite each generation of viewers to participate in this moment.

···◄━◉━►···

Leonardo da Vinci

If one person could be singled out as the quintessence of the Renaissance spirit, it would be Leonardo da Vinci (1452–1519). He was a painter, sculptor, scientist, engineer, and poet, to mention only a few of the fields of human endeavor that claimed his attention. Leonardo received his early training in the studio of Verrocchio, the most celebrated teacher of art in Florence. The studio Verrocchio maintained was a meeting place for the great intellectuals and artists of that time. Leonardo was able to make contact with the finest minds of the age—minds from which he acquired the skills of scientific investigation, as well as the finest training in the canons of painting and sculpture.

Leonardo left Verrocchio's studio to work as an independent artist in Florence. After painting his first masterpiece, *Adoration of the Magi,* he went to Milan under the patronage of the Duke of Milan, Ludovico Sforza. He remained there for seventeen years, and during this time he performed many duties, some artistic and some military. His later years were divided between Milan and Florence, and he maintained studios in both cities. Ironically, Leonardo did not live out his life in Italy. Disappointed by his relations with his patrons and willing to serve anyone who loved beauty, he accompanied Francis I to France, where he ended a long and useful career in 1519.

A recital of Leonardo's activities and accomplishments would fill many pages. He executed designs for public buildings; built dams and constructed a canal; rebuilt the fortifications of Milan and devised new instruments of war; invented an aircraft and a submarine; and wrote treatises on anatomy, optics, geology, physics, and painting. His notebooks, which have been preserved, are an encyclopedia of Renaissance thought and culture. Leonardo, of course, also found time to create some of the greatest art masterpieces of all time, including the portrait *Mona Lisa* and one of his greatest works, *The Last Supper* (colorplate 25).

In the same vein as the *Mona Lisa* is Leonardo's *Ginevra dé Benci* (colorplate 24). He succeeded in capturing her mysterious beauty by subtle gradations of light and dark, together with filigree lines that bring out the character of the subject. He has painted more than a portrait; his is a psychological study of the character of his subject.

Colorplate 24 follows p. 146.

Leonardo da Vinci believed that all art should have its roots in the scientific study of nature, human nature included. However, he had no intention of confining himself to surface qualities. His studies convinced him that nature's secrets were well hidden and could be revealed only by painstaking investigation. He spent weeks and often months exploring such minor details as anatomical and psychological peculiarities that less careful and patient artists would have ignored. In the process, he added a vast amount of knowledge to the art of painting and to the storehouse of human intellectual achievement.

Of the few completed works to come from the hand of Leonardo da Vinci, *The Last Supper* (colorplate 25) is one of the monumental artworks of all time. It is a large work painted on a wall in the refectory of the church of Santa Maria della Grazie in Milan. Because Leonardo used a flawed experimental method of painting on fresh plaster, the painting has not withstood the ravages of time very well, although it has recently been restored. *The Last Supper* is a major contribution of Leonardo to the science and art of painting. It is not a photographic study of the twelve disciples and Jesus but a psychological study of the effect of Christ's words, "One of you shall betray me." The sudden shock of those words and the varied response of each disciple, reacting according to his own nature, are the subjects of the painting. The disciples are not merely ordinary men used as models; they are individuals. Leonardo studied each person involved in the scene. He spent long hours

Colorplate 25 follows p. 146.

probing their personalities according to the biblical record. The whole work took years to complete because there were certain men, especially Judas, whose character and psychological makeup Leonardo had difficulty in grasping. In some ways this is not a religious picture but a psychological observation by one of the most perceptive artists of all time. It is a pictorial study of emotional responses to a shocking statement. It is a revelation of each man's physical and emotional reaction under the impact of this accusation.

From a formal point of view, the painting is classical in design. The figure of Christ is in the center, his head silhouetted against the sky through the open window. He is isolated physically as well as psychologically. By itself, the room is a masterpiece of linear perspective. The lines of the walls and table converge to a point behind the head of Christ. This is not infinite space but a carefully controlled chamber of space created by clearly defined lines. The form is closed, with all attention centered on the figure of Christ. The bodies of the men seem to merge, but their heads are separate and individual. Leonardo chose to present an individual portrait of each and yet mold the separate units into a whole. He did this by means of the table and the narrow room, which force the lines of perspective toward the center. The work is a monument not only to Leonardo's skill as a painter and his painstaking research as a scientist but to his profound understanding of human nature.

Michelangelo

One of the last of the great sixteenth-century painters was Michelangelo Buonarroti (1475–1564), who stood with Leonardo da Vinci at the pinnacle of the Renaissance ideal. Born in 1475 near Florence, Michelangelo entered the studio of Ghirlandaio at the age of thirteen. He later became a favorite of Lorenzo the Magnificent, who had in his private gallery a large collection of Greek sculpture. Michelangelo's preference for sculpture probably resulted from this experience. He also studied the usual canons of art and was given an opportunity to study scientific anatomy. Because of the kindness of a friendly monk, he was permitted to perform dissections of human and animal cadavers to discover for himself the mysteries of the human form.

Michelangelo, like Leonardo, had a variety of talents. He was a painter, architect, and sculptor, but it was as the latter that he primarily identified himself. He saw the human form through the eyes of one who worked with marble and a chisel. His omission of nature as a background, his manner of painting the nude in a strong three-dimensional form, and his preoccupation with the human form have all led to his painting being called "painted sculpture." He is said to have stated on more than one occasion, "The only fit subject for an artist is man." He could not have made a remark more in keeping with the Renaissance spirit, for the statement is humanism at its most eloquent.

Michelangelo's personal life was filled with hardship. Poverty was his faithful companion, made even more menacing by selfish relatives and friends. He suffered almost constantly from personality conflicts during his eighty-nine years, and many of his works reveal the conflicting forces of his own consciousness, though others communicate strength and solidity.

As an artist, however, he was generally above personal problems, for he was a universalist in outlook. His art transcends the superficial, and his painting and sculpture embody an awareness of the forces of universal tragedy. This is perhaps best expressed in the *Last Judgment* (colorplate 26), painted on the east wall of the Sistine Chapel. Here, human forms are the artistic motive, as Michelangelo depicts humankind on the day of judgment. There is wave after wave of rhythmic movement as the blessed are separated from the damned. There is also an unlimited variety of poses and gestures in the figures. The nature of fresco painting is apparent in the knots of figures that were rapidly painted before the plaster had time to dry, giving the work an additive character that contributes to its power.

Colorplate 26 follows p. 146.

The frescoes in the Sistine Chapel, with scenes depicting the epic of humankind from the creation to the day of judgment, were Michelangelo's greatest paintings. As a sculptor, he protested bitterly when Pope Julius II ordered him to this task, for he claimed he was not a painter. The completed work is testimony that he was a great painter as well.

The *Creation* (colorplate 27) is one of the panels on the ceiling of the Sistine Chapel. This composition clearly shows the artist's qualities in painting, as well as his absorbing concern for humanity. Adam rests upon the earth, symbolic of humanity, while his outstretched hand receives the life-giving touch from Jehovah. The figures, including Jehovah, have a quality of buoyancy that suggests the infinity of God's world. The face of Adam does not show the joy of life but appears pensive in recognition of the trials and sorrows of the earthly life he is gaining. The artist has made the physical figures of Adam and Jehovah the focal points of the panel. The bodies are plastic and seem molded in three-dimensional space. The anatomy is superb, perfect in every detail down to the rippling of flexed muscles. In general, the lines are sharply defined.

Colorplate 27 follows p. 146.

The form of the *Creation* is closed, and the effect of distance is canceled by the predominance of the two molded figures. The reaching gestures of Jehovah and Adam effectively bridge the distance between them. Despite all its symbolism, this is not a greatly religious painting although it portrays God's gift of life. It is, instead, one of the most perfect representations of the human form in all of art history; one feels that the subject is the form itself, not the act of creation suggested by the title. True to the Renaissance ideal, Michelangelo created a great work of art with a religious subject but a secular spirit.

For several centuries the paintings of the Sistine chapel have suffered from the prudery of people who objected to the nude figures, as well as from the smoke of incense and candles and the polluted air of Rome. Recently completed efforts to restore the frescoes to their original color and vibrancy have met with mixed responses. Colorplate 27, in fact, is a photograph of the newly restored—and brightened—*Creation*.

Titian

Florence and Rome were not the only centers of artistic activity in Renaissance Italy. One of the preeminent city-states, Venice, prospered artistically as a consequence of its commercial successes. The works of one of Venice's native sons, Titian (1477–1576), illustrate a departure from the sharply defined line and static quality of earlier Renaissance painting. There is more movement and energy in his work than is found in the paintings of Botticelli and Michelangelo. During his ninety-nine years, he created thousands of paintings, including portraits as well as religious and mythological subjects. His *Venus and Adonis* (colorplate 28) treats figures of mythology as human beings of flesh and blood, with a quality of sensuality usually lacking in earlier Renaissance painting. While the principle of design is still closed, with a pyramidal form, lines are less sharply defined and blend into a shadowy background. Titian was a colorist, and his forms, instead of being created with line, seem to be created with color. His art marked the end of the Renaissance and served as a transition to the Baroque painting of Tintoretto and El Greco. He anticipated the coloring and sensuousness of such later painters as Rubens and even Delacroix.

Colorplate 28 follows p. 146.

Raphael

Raphael (1483–1520) was born into an artistic family and received artistic training first from his father and subsequently from Perugino, with whom he served an apprenticeship. He, perhaps more than any other painter, epitomizes the later Renaissance in Italian painting. In 1508, following a competition, Raphael was commissioned to provide murals for the papal apartments of the Vatican. Though many of the walls were ultimately painted by his apprentices, the *School of Athens* (colorplate 6) was by his own hand. The concept and rendering are clearly those of a learned Renaissance master. The inclusion of Plato (left) and Aristotle (right) in the central arch among scholars, scientists, artists, and musicians places the two great Greek philosophers in a grand, theatrical environment. The architecture represented is reminiscent of that of Rome and, in its grandeur, at the same time seems to express something of the magnificence of St. Peter's. Furthermore, in its embodiment of the Renaissance use of perspective and anatomy, the *School of Athens* is also about space and its architectural definition. It is even perhaps about the major concern of Renaissance Christian thought—the reconciliation of the Christian with the pagan—depicting as it does Greek thought in what may be a Christian structure.

Colorplate 6 follows p. 18.

Raphael's *Sistine Madonna* (colorplate 7) is a typical example of Renaissance style; it is primarily linear, in closed form and with little depth. While the subject is religious, many viewers are aware more of the beauty of forms and color than of any religious meaning. The impression given is one of a humanistic expression, of the poetic beauty of human form, of beauty for itself.

Albrecht Dürer

Renaissance painters of northern Europe responded less quickly to the revival of Greek ideals than did the Italians. While the trend toward humanism and realism in the North was undoubtedly the result of Italian influence, the expressiveness was still Gothic. Religious subjects with an almost morbid focus on suffering and death were common. The Reformation was a great influence in northern Europe, and the problems of sin, suffering, and salvation were still very real. This was especially the case in northern Germany, where Luther's teaching precipitated strong religious feelings.

Albrecht Dürer (1471–1528) was a German Renaissance artist, a friend of Luther and Erasmus, who embraced the Protestant religion. His early studies in Italy brought him into contact with humanism and introduced him to the disciplined objectivity of line and perspective of the Italian Renaissance. Among the arts Dürer practiced, in addition to painting, were the **intaglio** arts of engraving and etching and the relief process of woodcutting. His engraving, *Knight, Death, and the Devil* (fig. 7.2), shows his careful molding of physical forms, the controlled spatial effect, and the clear character of line. The subject is the eternal struggle between good and evil, with the Christian knight journeying toward the Heavenly City in the remote distance of the picture plane. The knight is undaunted by the specter of the horseman of Death, who holds an hourglass to show the transitory qualities of life, and by the temptation of the grotesque Devil behind him. Even his faithful dog seems unafraid and confident in faith.

Mathias Grünewald

The Small Crucifixion by Mathias Grünewald (colorplate 29) communicates the essential spirit and style of northern Renaissance painting. Whereas Dürer represented the Protestant element, Grünewald (1480–1528) was associated with Catholic patronage in Germany. The artist's portrayal of the agony on the cross is medieval. The enlarged figure of Christ emphasizes its importance and is shockingly realistic as a festering corpse. On the other hand, the surrounding figures are softer, grieving humans. The sweeping curves and polychromaticism highlight the line. There is a limited sense of perspective and three-dimensional form, which were usually absent in medieval painting. The unity of separate parts is achieved by balancing the figures on either side with the central figure of the dead Christ.

Colorplate 29 follows p. 146.

Figure 7.2 Albrecht Dürer, *Knight, Death, and the Devil,* 1513. Engraving, 9 7/8 in. × 7 5/8 in.
Gift of Mrs. Horatio Greenough Curtis in memory of her husband, Horatio Greenough Curtis.
(Courtesy Museum of Fine Arts, Boston)

Pieter Brueghel

Pieter Brueghel the Elder (c. 1524–1569) represents the Protestant North in Renaissance art during the middle of the sixteenth century. Many of his works depict the struggle between the Catholics and Protestants in the Low Countries, now Holland and Belgium. The paintings were sometimes filled with symbolic figures related to those conflicts, which arose during the Spanish Inquisition.

The Flemish Brueghel was a master of landscapes, and some of his finest paintings recorded the scenery of the Low Countries. He was intimately familiar with the folk customs and the lives of humble people. *Winter, Return of the Hunters* (colorplate 30) shows a landscape with ordinary peasants in simple, everyday activities in the cold and damp of winter. The Renaissance idea of space, controlled by the repetition of similar shapes and recession into the distance, is very apparent.

Contrasting with the static and chilly atmosphere of *Winter* is Brueghel's *The Wedding Dance* (colorplate 31). Here peasants move in vigorous and colorful dance, their united purpose and gesture providing some of the unity of the painting. The natural, plain colors in the fabrics are characteristic of the peasant costumes of the period. The viewpoint is from several feet above the dancers, making visible to the viewer the variegated pattern of colors so typical of Brueghel's work. Both of these paintings exemplify the genre tradition popular in the Flemish art of this period. **Genre paintings** depict common people in common pursuits, and are especially associated with Renaissance painting in the Low Countries.

Colorplate 31 follows p. 146.

SCULPTURE

Renaissance sculpture reflects the same concern for humanism found in its painting. Because of the predilection for the molded form in all Renaissance art, it was not uncommon for an artist to be equally facile with a chisel as with a brush. Leonardo da Vinci and Michelangelo were examples of such artists. While the medium of sculpture is quite different from that of painting, Renaissance sculpture employs stylistic conventions similar to those in painting, such as the representation of the natural world, the use of symbolism to represent things not physically present, and the use of curvilinear lines instead of the stiff formality of the Middle Ages.

Donatello

Recognized as one of the premiere sculptors of fifteenth-century Florence, Donato di Niccolò Donatello (1386–1466) mastered several diverse artistic styles. In choosing the subject of David (fig. 7.3) for a sculpture commissioned by the Medici, Donatello created a life-sized, youthful figure in bronze.

Figure 7.3 Donato di Niccolò Donatello, *David*, c. 1430–40. Bronze, 5 ft. 2 1/4 in. high. Bargello Museum, Florence, Italy. (Alinari/Art Resource, NY)

Three important objects from the story of the slaying of Goliath are included in the composition: the stone, the sword, and Goliath's severed head, which rests beneath the triumphant David's left foot. Upon his shepherd's hat, David wears a laurel wreath, which in Greek mythology symbolized victory.

The artist has emphasized the immature qualities of David's body and the boyish candor of his facial expression. The posture emphasizes lightness and movement, with the application of **contrapposto,** a slight displacement of hips and straightening of one leg to show the weight of the figure resting on that leg. The artist was familiar with later Greek sculpture, which employed a similar style. The bent elbows and wrists and the slight tilt of the head also contribute to the relaxed pose of the figure.

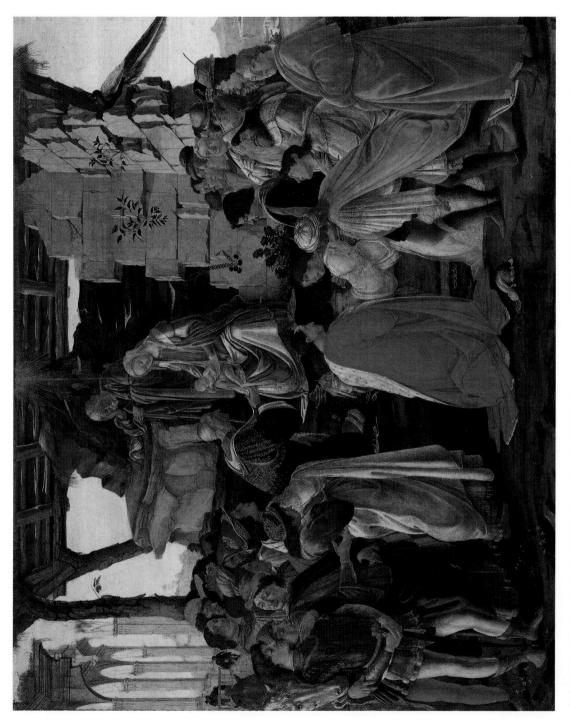

Colorplate 20 Sandro Botticelli, *Adoration of the Magi*, 1478. Tempera on wood, 43 3/4 × 52 3/4 in. Uffizi Gallery, Florence, Italy. (Scala/Art Resource, NY) (See p. 132, 137)

Colorplate 21 Benozzo Gozzoli, *Journey of the Magi*, 1469. Fresco, c. 12 ft. 4 1/2 in. long. Medici-Riccardi Palace, Florence, Italy. (Scala/Art Resource, NY) (See p. 132, 135)

Colorplate 22 Fra Angelico, *Annunciation*. Tempera panel on silver chest, 15 × 14 1/2 in. Museum of San Marco, Florence, Italy. (© Pierre Boulat/Cosmos) *(See p. 132, 135)*

Colorplate 23 Sandro Botticelli, *The Birth of Venus.* Tempera on canvas, 5 ft. 8 in. × 9 ft. 1 in. Uffizi Gallery, Florence, Italy. (Scala/Art Resource, NY) *(See p. 136, 356)*

Colorplate 24   Leonardo da Vinci, *Ginevra dé Benci,* c. 1480. Wood panel, 15 1/4 × 15 1/2 in. Ailsa Mellon Bruce Fund © 1994 Board of Trustees, National Gallery of Art, Washington, D.C. *(See p. 139)*

Colorplate 25 Leonardo da Vinci, *The Last Supper*, 1495–1498. Fresco (oil and tempera on plaster), 14 ft. 5 in. × 28 ft. 1/8 in. Refectory of S. Maria della Grazie, Milan, Italy. (Scala/Art Resource, NY) (See p. 135, 139, 175)

Colorplate 26 Michelangelo Buonarroti, *Last Judgment,* 1534–1541. Fresco on altar wall. Sistine Chapel, Vatican, Rome. (Scala/Art Resource, NY) *(See p. 141)*

Colorplate 27 Michelangelo Buonarroti, *Creation*, 1508–1512. Fresco, detail of the cleaned Sistine Chapel ceiling. Vatican, Rome. (© Nippon TV Network Corporation, Tokyo 1991.) (See p. 141.)

Colorplate 28 Titian (Tiziano Vecelli), *Venus and Adonis,* c. 1560. Oil on canvas, 42 × 53 1/2 in. Widener
Collection © 1994 Board of Trustees, National Gallery of Art, Washington, D.C. *(See p. 142)*

Colorplate 29 Matthias Grünewald, *The Small Crucifixion,* 1505–1510. Oil on panel, 24 1/4 × 18 1/8 in. Samuel H. Kress Collection © 1994 Board of Trustees, National Gallery of Art, Washington, D.C. *(See p. 143)*

Colorplate 30   Pieter Brueghel the Elder, *Winter, Return of the Hunters,* 1565. Oil on oak panel, 46 × 63 3/4 in. Kunsthistorisches Museum, Vienna, Austria. (Saskia Ltd./Art Resource, NY) *(See p. 135, 145)*

Colorplate 31 Pieter Brueghel the Elder, *The Wedding Dance*, 1566. Tempera on panel, 47 × 62 in. © The Detroit Institute of Arts, City of Detroit Purchase.

(See p. 145)

Figure 7.4 Michelangelo Buonarroti, *David*, 1501–03. Marble, 18 ft. high. Galleria dell' Accademia, Florence, Italy. (Alinari/Art Resource, NY)

Michelangelo

Michelangelo's *David* (fig. 7.4) is, on the other hand, a different person. The artist saw David as a mature man with great physical strength, emphasized by the monumental size of the statue. It is made from a huge block of marble and stands eighteen feet high. Michelangelo depicted his subject before the action took place, with a stone in his left hand, looking out over the scene in contemplation of the coming action. The highly developed bodily features show a greater degree of physical maturity. David also projects a strong personality; he looks determined to achieve his goal and shows confidence in his own physical prowess.

Both of these examples, Donatello's adolescent *David* and Michelangelo's adult *David,* express a similar spirit. The line and detail of both are clear and express movement within tranquility. Yet they represent the individual differences of their creators. (In the next chapter, we shall see how Bernini treats the same subject in Baroque style.)

Properzia de´ Rossi

Writers often mention the "Renaissance man" as an ideal. Properzia de´ Rossi (c. 1490–1530) was truly a "Renaissance woman." The contemporaneous painter-historian, Vasari, declared that Rossi could sing and play better than any woman in the city of her day. She was also so talented in the sciences that she was the envy of men. In the visual arts, her work began with the carving of peach stones into intricate biblical scenes. She was so successful that she was commissioned to create several portrait busts in marble. Later, she created marble bas-reliefs for San Petronio in Bologna. Finally, she took up copper engraving, and found success in it as well.

Joseph and Potiphar's Wife (fig. 7.5) is a bas-relief assumed to be the work of Rossi. The bas-relief is carved with substantial depth. Some of the limbs of the figures are nearly freestanding. Rossi captured the sense of movement using posture, gesture, and flowing costumes. The attempted seduction of Joseph is clearly illustrated by the eager pursuit of the partially-clad wife of Potiphar.

Tilman Riemenschneider

Much of the sculpture of the sixteenth century was executed in stone, but Tilman Riemenschneider's great works are in wood. Although the dates of his life (1460–1531) make him contemporaneous with the Renaissance in Italy, Riemenschneider's style and spirit, like those of his German compatriots, are much more akin to the Gothic. His *Assumption of the Blessed Virgin* (fig. 7.6), typical of his works, is an altarpiece representing a sacred event. Its pyramidal structure emphasizes symmetry and balance. The figures grouped at the bottom have some individuality, but the carving of the hair and the clothing are stylized. The multifaceted lines on the figures' robes create a rich texture that adds vitality and interest to the work. The subsidiary figures are carved in high relief, but the figure of Mary is more in the round and, thus, more realistic.

Figure 7.5 Properzia de′ Rossi, *Joseph and Potiphar's Wife,* c. 1520. Marble bas-relief, 19 ft. 1/4 in. × 18 ft. 1/8 in. Museo di San Petronio, Bologna, Italy. (Alinari/Art Resource, NY)

ARCHITECTURE

Although buildings for religious purposes were still created by Renaissance architects, they also devoted themselves to designing palaces and villas for elaborate and comfortable living. This function of architecture was an important element of sixteenth-century life. Along with individualism and the desire for worldly possessions, there was a natural trend among the wealthy toward elaborate domestic housing. In meeting this demand, architects increasingly employed elements of classical Greek architecture, including the orders, frieze, and pediment. As in classical architecture, the favorite proportion was the "golden mean," in which height and width are in the approximate ratio of 3 to 2.

Figure 7.6 Tilman Riemenschneider, *Assumption of the Blessed Virgin,* c. 1505. Linden wood, 73 1/4 in. wide. Herrgottskirche, Creglingen, Germany. (Foto Marburg/Art Resource, NY)

Figure 7.7 Andrea Palladio, Villa Rotonda, c. 1567. Vicenza, Italy. (Alinari/Art Resource, NY)

One of the architects to devote his talents to this type of building was the Italian, Andrea Palladio (1518–1580). The work of Palladio is frequently studied as the epitome of Renaissance architecture because he had the greatest influence on later generations. In both England and America, the "classic style" of the great estates from the seventeenth century can be traced directly to his work. They represent some of the finest examples of the Palladian style of architecture. Monticello, Thomas Jefferson's home, is in this style, and Jefferson even suggested a Palladian building for the White House. Like many other architects of his time, Palladio wrote treatises about his art, substantially based on the writings of Vitruvius. In his *Four Books on Architecture,* he laid down the classic canons of the builder's art in much the same fashion as Leonardo did for painting.

The Villa Rotonda (fig. 7.7) in Vicenza is the best known of Palladio's works and a fine example of his own theories of architecture. One of the most striking aspects of the Villa Rotonda is its debt to antiquity. Its dome is modeled after the Pantheon in Rome (fig. 4.2), and Greek influence is apparent in the use of freestanding columns that support the pediment of the porticos. The building is classic in proportion. Its various rooms are laid out symmetrically around the central rotunda. Palladio used the cube and cylinder as

Figure 7.8 Antonio da Sangallo and Michelangelo Buonarroti, Farnese Palace, c. 1535. Rome, Italy. (Alinari/Art Resource, NY)

his basic forms. It is a square plan with four identical porticos placed on the two axes of the rotunda. He did not obscure the simplicity of the plan with elaborate decoration but used ornament sparingly. The structure sits lightly upon the earth with none of the towering spires of the Gothic. This is a functional building, both spacious and formal. It is Renaissance in its classic proportion and dignity and in the absence of mystic symbolism.

Another example of classic proportion in architecture is the Farnese Palace in Rome (fig. 7.8). Michelangelo was responsible for a portion of this building, having designed the third story. The facade is symmetrical, with each story clearly separated from the others by a broad band. The window treatment of the first floor exactly repeats the lintel design, and the third floor uses the Grecian pediment design. The second floor, however, alternates the pediment with an arch motif. Repetition and contrast is the apparent principle of design for the facade. The eye is relieved as it moves from the top by the contrast of the second floor. In its visual appeal, as well as in its function and arrangement, the Farnese Palace mirrors the classic idealism of its age.

Just as Michelangelo came to the Farnese Palace only when it was near completion, he assumed responsibility for the completion of St. Peter's,

Figure 7.9 Bramante and Michelangelo Buonarroti, St. Peter's, 1546–64. Plaza by Giovanni Lorenzo Bernini, 1656–63. Rome, Italy. (Alinari/Art Resource, NY)

Rome (fig. 7.9) after the death of the original architect, Bramante. The final plan for St. Peter's was in the shape of a Greek cross, crowned with a magnificent dome that dominated the structure. Michelangelo himself did not live to see the completion of the structure, or the dome, which was modified and completed by yet another architect (Bernini) in the seventeenth century.

Many palatial residences in Italy continued to have the appearance of Greek temples or fortresses. In England, however, stately homes projected a very different image. As can be seen in Hardwick Hall (fig. 7.10), exterior walls were dominated by glass rather than by stone. Feelings of massive power were replaced by elegance and, at times, opulence. These homes were frequently of such scale that they dwarfed their predecessors. They often included enormous halls or galleries; that of Hardwick Hall was 166 feet long.

MUSIC

During the Renaissance, the performance of music began to move out of churches and into the households of the aristocracy and the upper classes.

Figure 7.10 Robert Smythson, Hardwick Hall, 1590–97. Derbyshire, England. (James Pipkin)

Music was still important in the Church but was no longer under its exclusive patronage. As a consequence, a large body of instrumental and vocal music devoted to secular purposes was created.

Sacred Music

The music of the Catholic church continued to serve much the same purpose in the Renaissance as in previous periods. In **motets** and masses, at this time, both polyphonic vocal compositions, composers continued to set those parts of the Latin liturgy that were permitted musical settings. Most Protestant churches regarded the use of music with Latin texts as popish and too reminiscent of the Roman liturgy. As a result, composers for the Lutheran and Calvinist churches gave music of greater simplicity—and with German texts—to congregations as their rightful heritage. Sixteenth-century Lutheran church music subsequently became a great fountainhead for the Baroque art of Bach and his contemporaries. Although the counterpoint of early Renaissance Catholic and Protestant music still had something of Gothic scholasticism, in the sixteenth century a complete mastery of technical devices made possible a truly expressive handling of musical materials.

Religious music spoke not only of the serenity of God but of human serenity, not only of the mysterious detachment of a supreme being but of the anguish, aspirations, and hopes of the human soul. On the other hand, secular music evoked the human joys and sorrows of this earthly existence in song and dance.

Despite the emphasis on humanism, which created the great wealth of painting, sculpture, and architecture, much of the religious music of the Renaissance was rarely heard outside the church until recent times. This is undoubtedly because of the stylistic disparity between the music of the fifteenth and sixteenth centuries and that of the eighteenth and nineteenth; the latter still constitutes the bulk of today's musical repertoire. The disparity lies primarily in the modal polyphony of the Renaissance, which sounds quite foreign compared to the more familiar tonal polyphony and homophony of later periods.

Although some dance and instrumental forms of secular music were homophonically constructed, most Renaissance composers—secular as well as sacred—dealt primarily with polyphonic treatment of musical ideas. They organized their melodic material not on an underlying or gravitational harmonic concept but on certain intervallic relationships among voices. As in the Gothic period, certain intervals (the unison, fourth, fifth, and octave) were considered consonant and were specifically named the "perfect" intervals; all others were in varying degree, dissonant. A great body of practical rules and regulations determined how the dissonant intervals were used and called for their careful introduction and inevitable resolution to perfect consonances. Renaissance composers achieved a greater variety of harmonies than were possible in the Gothic, yet the lack of depth in Renaissance painting is paralleled in music by the limited tonal variety. Toward the end of the Renaissance, certain practices already indicated the tendency toward a distinct feeling for tonality. In the seventeenth century, tonality became the harmonic system composers relied on. This system continued until the beginning of the twentieth century. It has substantially conditioned our listening attitudes. Therefore, Renaissance music must be listened to within its own stylistic context and not fettered by the stylistic conventions of subsequent centuries.

Josquin Desprez

One of the most important composers of polyphony, and indeed one of the great composers of all time, was Josquin Desprez (c. 1440–1521). Josquin traveled from his native Burgundy to Italy, where he sang at court as well as in the papal choir during the tenure of two different popes. He was an acclaimed composer in his day and was among the first to have his works published during his lifetime. The expressiveness of his music, despite the complex compositional rules required in the early Renaissance, partly explains his popularity among his contemporaries. His motet *Ave Maria* comprises a number of contrasting sections, each knit together by strict imitation among the several voices. The contrasting sections overlap one another as if to cover up the seams of the work. Actually, the entire work, both music and words, is derived from a Gregorian chant setting of the "Ave Maria." The composer treats the chant exhaustively, line by line, until its conclusion. While it would seem that several methods of organization are present, actually the principles of repetition (within each section) and contrast (among the sections) are the main techniques used. Joining rather unrelated and contrasting sections is characteristic of all the vocal forms of this period, whether secular or sacred. It is particularly well-suited to musical works that accompany a literary text; there seems no need for an overall principle of theme and variation or of repetition after contrast. Instrumental music, on the other hand, requires a larger overall design.

Palestrina

Giovanni Pierluigi da Palestrina (c. 1525–1594), with the exception of a few books of madrigals, devoted his compositions exclusively to sacred music. He has been regarded by the Catholic church as the ideal composer of liturgical compositions. His music has a certain detached and calm sublimity that makes it the sacred music *par excellence*. The lines of melody are smooth-flowing, quite limited in range, and characteristically devoid of wide intervals. The voice parts rarely cross each other, which tends to give a transparency to the texture of the whole work, and dissonance is handled in such a fashion as to make it very unobtrusive.

The Mass *Veni sponsa Christi,* of which the Agnus Dei is the final section, is based on a motet by Palestrina, which is in turn based on a Gregorian chant. There are three sections in the Agnus Dei, each developed in imitative style. The first section is set to the words *Agnus Dei* ("Lamb of God"); the second, to the words *qui tollis peccata mundi* ("who taketh away the sins of the world"); the third, to *miserere nobis* ("have mercy on us"). There is enough repetition of text to allow the composer to spin out his musical ideas. The three sections generally contrast with one another, but careful listening will be rewarded by the discovery of a rhythmic-melodic pattern of four notes in each of the three sections. Its appearance is varied; it occurs (1) both as an ascending and descending scale passage, (2) with varied note values, (3) at different pitch levels, and (4) on different accented rhythmic points in each of the four voice parts.

Music of the Protestant Church

Of the several Protestant groups arising from the Reformation, the Lutheran church most profoundly influenced the musical development of western Europe. The musical influence of Calvinism was largely restricted to French-speaking countries and to the hymn tradition of Scottish Presbyterianism. During the Renaissance, the Lutheran influence consisted almost exclusively of settings of hymn texts in what became known as the German Protestant (or Lutheran) **chorale.** Martin Luther gathered a large collection of these chorales because of his intense interest in music as a vehicle for religious expression and his immediate need for hundreds of German chorale texts. Chorale tunes came from several sources: the Gregorian hymn tunes of the Catholic church, the melodies of secular and folk songs, and tunes composed by Protestant musicians.

While the tunes with their vernacular texts served as unison hymns for the congregation, they also were the bases for compositions in motet style. An example is the chorale *Komm, Gott Schöpfer, heiliger Geist (Come, O Creator Spirit)*, composed by Johann Walter (1496–1570) to the old Latin hymn text, *Veni Creator Spiritus,* translated into German by Martin Luther. Although this is an elaborate use of the hymn tune, it was not long before regular four-part settings with the melody in the soprano became the conventional congregational hymn. Bach would make extensive use of such settings in the Baroque period.

The Reformation in England had different musical consequences, the most obvious of which was the development of the English anthem. Much of the music of Thomas Tallis (c. 1505–1585), who served four English monarchs, employed Latin texts and was composed for the Catholic Church. He was, however, the first composer to use the English language in musical settings for the new Anglican liturgy. His compositions range from works in very simple hymn style to grand motets, such as *Spem in alium,* a motet for forty separately written vocal lines.

William Byrd (1543–1623) may well be the greatest composer in all of English history. His prodigious output includes anthems, motets, and masses, as well as madrigals, consort music, and keyboard music. *Carmen's Whistle,* a composition for virginal, was especially popular. Beginning in 1575, he shared with Tallis the exclusive license to print and publish music.

Secular Music

Secular folk songs were often adapted by composers as the melodic basis (*cantus firmus*) for polyphonic settings both secular and religious. A folk song that has been used in this fashion many times is the tune for *Innsbruck, ich muss dich lassen (Innsbruck, I Must Leave Thee)*. In its original form, it was a love song. Its first notated setting was a polyphonic **Lied,** or song, by Heinrich Isaac to words by the Emperor Maximilian. It is in this form that it is known as the *Innsbruck Lied*. Isaac employed it in a polyphonic setting in the Kyrie of the *Missa Carminum,* a polyphonic Mass that employed a number of secular songs as melodies. Subsequently, the *Innsbruck Lied* was adapted to other words and choral settings, including Bach's *Passion According to St. Matthew.*

Figure 7.11   Clouet, *The Duc de Joyeuse's Ball,* 1581. (Stock Montage, Inc.)

Secular music served a society that actively participated in its production. It was not a mere pastime or entertainment for passive patrons. Instrumental and vocal secular music, chansons, madrigals, canzone alla francese, ricercare, and dance music, were played and sung by every refined gentleman and lady, whose educations always included some study of music making. During the Renaissance, no organized social event existed comparable to the public concert or opera of today. There were royal balls and other social functions that incorporated music and dance (fig. 7.11). However, Renaissance secular music was an intimate music meant for a small, interested, and (for the most part) participating group.

The texts of the chansons and madrigals reflect this intimacy. Even when they are humorous they are inclined to be wistful, and words such as *sighing, alas, sorrow, cruel, slay,* and *pain* tend to be stressed. All of this indicates a tendency to express particular human emotions.

There were no large forms comparable to the Mass in secular composition. The madrigal, chanson, and polyphonic *Lied,* however, were secular counterparts to the religious motet. The devices of polyphonic composition were the same as those used in sacred motets. In secular works, the vernacular texts often dealt with themes of love (usually unrequited) and exhibited more rhythmic freedom in an attempt to write music reflecting the spirit and emotions of the text.

A Closer Look

Bennet, *Thyrsis? Sleepest Thou?*

Italian religious influence on England diminished during the second half of the sixteenth century. Its secular influence continued, notably in music. In 1588, the year of the Spanish Armada, a major collection of Italian madrigals was published under the title *Musica Transalpina,* or *Music from Across the Alps.* This publication stimulated the composition of madrigals by English composers that continued into the second decade of the seventeenth century. The **madrigal,** like the chanson, was secular music meant to be sung and played by the upper and middle classes of society. Thousands of madrigals were composed and published in Italy, where the form originated, and later in England. In many madrigals, the style common to the motet and chanson is easily recognized. The same imitative devices unify each section of the textual setting. Pictorial musical writing, illustrating the emotional content of the words, marked the dissolution of the Renaissance style in favor of the more expressive and dramatic manner that was the hallmark of the coming Baroque era. John Bennet's *Thyrsis? Sleepest Thou?*, a narrative madrigal, is representative of this great flowering of English composition.

A common feature of many, but by no means all, madrigals was the inclusion of passages set to nonsense syllables, such as "Fa-la-la." Bennet's madrigal (ex. 7.1) introduces the nonsense words "Holla, Holla" in a short refrain. These passages were frequently written in a simple harmonic style. Another common feature of Renaissance composition is pictorial writing. This "word painting" may have descriptive pitch or rhythmic characteristics. Words such as *heaven, hell, love, running, skipping,* and *sighing* were accompanied by rhythmic and pitch activities appropriate to their meanings. The phrase "hold up thy head man" (ex. 7.2) is given a melodic fragment that ascends by a wide upward skip and is imitated in each voice.

Example 7.1 *Thyrsis? Sleepest Thou?* by John Bennet

Example 7.2 *Thyrsis? Sleepest Thou?* by John Bennet

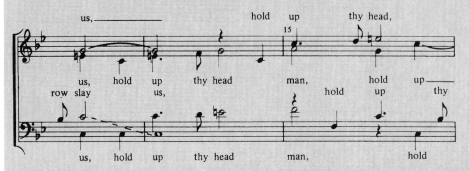

A more precise example of word painting appears in the setting of the phrase "hark how the cuckoo singeth cuckoo" (ex. 7.3). The last "cuckoo" is actually sung to the musical imitation of the cuckoo's call in the soprano and alto voices, even to the extent of keeping the call (a falling minor third) always at the same pitch as though it were an actual bird (see the bracketed tones in the example).

Example 7.3 *Thyrsis? Sleepest Thou?* by John Bennet

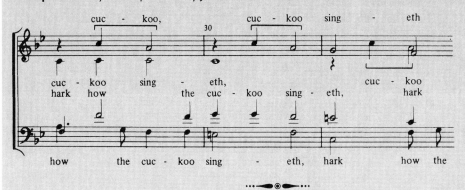

(fol. 142b) Die geschicklheit in der musiken und was in seinen ingenien und durch
in erfunden und gepessert worden ist.
(Cod. 3033.)

Figure 7.12 Renaissance instruments in an illustration from *Der Weisskunig*. Print of Hans Brugkmair. (The Metropolitan Museum of Art, NY. Gift of William Loring Andrews, 1888)

The French equivalents of the sixteenth century madrigal were called by that language's generic term for song, **chanson.** Their textual and musical materials are much more lightly treated than in their relative, the motet. In addition to the chanson's importance as a secular vocal form, it was the prototype for an instrumental form, the **canzona alla francese,** which was a precursor of several later forms, such as the capriccio, ricercare, and fugue.

Although the madrigal, chanson, and polyphonic *Lied* were all meant to be sung and, therefore, had no written instrumental parts, it was common practice to double the voice parts or even to substitute instruments for some or all of them. Among the favorite instruments (fig. 7.12) used for this purpose

Figure 7.13 German lute, c. 1596. Ivory, wood, 29 × 12 in. (The Metropolitan Museum of Art, NY. The Crosby Brown Collection of Musical Instruments, 1889)

were the large families of viols and recorders, the lute (fig. 7.13), and such keyboard instruments as the harpsichord or the virginal (fig. 7.14). Their size and construction were not standardized, and individual instruments of the same type varied greatly.

Together with wind instruments, such as shawms, crumhorns, cornets, and sackbuts (which were more often played out-of-doors), these instruments were also used for an ever-growing supply of purely instrumental music. The instrumental forms were largely based on dances and performed on various solo instruments and by small ensembles. One of the most common solo instruments of the Renaissance was the lute. Its importance during the fifteenth and sixteenth centuries corresponds to the position of the piano in the nineteenth century. Dances written for solo lute were extremely popular.

Figure 7.14 Double spinet or virginal made by Ludovicus Grovvelus (Lodewijck Grauwels). (The Metropolitan Museum of Art, NY. The Crosby Brown Collection of Musical Instruments, 1889)

Like the madrigals, the dances reflected a tendency toward major and minor tonalities. Unlike the more truly polyphonic vocal works, dance forms organized the melodic material in well-defined phrases that tended to balance one another in a symmetrical fashion. In the seventeenth century, such forms would have a profound effect on all music.

MANNERISM—A TRANSITION IN ART AND MUSIC

One art epoch is not usually clearly delineated from the epoch that follows. As the Renaissance ran its course, there were artists who chose only to imitate the accepted great masters of the time. There were also, however, the occasional few who sought to escape from the domination of such masters as Raphael, Michelangelo, and Leonardo da Vinci in the visual arts and

Josquin and Palestrina in music. Among such individualists there was a search for freedom from the rational objectivity of the Renaissance, a move toward greater subjectivity and mysticism, and the establishment of personal stylistic idiosyncrasies. Many art historians call this transitional style **mannerism.** The term actually has two meanings. First, it applies to those who rigidly imitated the masters of the High Renaissance. Second, it applies to those who were moving away from the past and were responding to new movements in religion, politics, economics, and science. Mannerism, consequently, can be interpreted both as the end of the Renaissance and the beginning of the Baroque. Tintoretto and El Greco are sometimes called "mannerists" because they hinted at the stylistic changes that were to come to fruition in the Baroque period. In music, Gesualdo and Monteverdi introduced chromatic harmonies that presaged the expressiveness of the composers of the Baroque. Another transitional composer, Giovanni Gabrieli, lived the greater portion of his life in the late sixteenth century, yet his music suggests the sonorities and major/minor tonalities of the Baroque period.

Summary

The Renaissance was an age of humanism and individualism characterized by a search for personal identity and a desire for wealth and power. It was also a period of insatiable searching for knowledge in science, natural phenomena, and human behavior. Because their interests were of this world, there was a reappropriation of the ideals of the Greeks, especially in philosophy, literature, and art.

The Church was still the most powerful patron of the arts, but artistic patronage came increasingly from wealthy families, such as the Medici, who ruled the various city-states. Secular and mythological subjects in art were often intertwined with religious subjects. Moreover, portrait painting was popular, even to the point of including prominent people in religious and mythological scenes.

Artists, such as Michelangelo and Leonardo da Vinci, became prototypes of the "Renaissance man." Their wide range of artistic activities and their intense quest for knowledge about science, nature, and humanity made them almost legendary, and they have remained so to this day.

During the Renaissance there was an emphasis on representational painting and sculpture. In painting, line was clearly defined, smooth-flowing, and curvilinear. Earlier, space was organized on a shallow plane, and the development of perspective during the course of the period gave the illusion of an orderly and controlled space. Brilliant, polychromatic coloring often separated figures from each other and from their backgrounds. Closed form was common, and separately articulated parts balanced one another.

Renaissance sculpture showed the same humanistic characteristics as did painting; in fact, some of the finest sculptors were also painters. Sculpture was closely modeled on that of the Greeks, with finely molded forms showing all the physical details of the human figure. Some were so delicately wrought that the observer can almost sense the living body beneath the stone and metal, yet in painting and sculpture, there was an absence of strong emotion. Feeling was expressed, but it was usually well controlled.

Churches continued to be the focus of Renaissance architects, but many palaces and villas were built for comfortable living and pleasurable pursuits. The influence of the classic Greek style, with Grecian porticos, symmetry, classic simplicity, and balanced design, was very strong. Religious architecture sometimes combined this classic style with the Romanesque dome and vault.

Sacred music retained its importance, but music also moved into the households of the aristocracy and the upper classes. As in the other arts, the Church was no longer the sole patron of music. As a consequence, a large body of secular music, vocal and instrumental, was created. Composers of sacred music continued to set those portions of the liturgy that had become standard. Polyphonic style was still used, but with more freedom and individualism. The sometimes barren and harsh intervals of the Gothic were softened to please the ear. Repetition and contrast constituted the most common principle of organization—repetition of melodic lines by various voices, with a contrast of melodies within the various sections of the text. Expression was often achieved by word painting. This was especially true in the madrigal and chanson. Vocal music was still dominant, but instrumental music was abundant, most often in the form of dances for keyboard instruments or instrumental consorts.

Suggested Readings

In addition to the specific sources that follow, the general readings on pages 388 and 389 contain valuable information about the topic of this chapter.

Blume, Friedrich. *Renaissance and Baroque Music*. New York: W. W. Norton, 1967.

Brown, Howard M. *Music in the Renaissance*. Englewood Cliffs, NJ: Prentice-Hall, 1976.

Cuttler, Charles D. *Northern Painting*. New York: Holt, Rinehart & Winston, 1968.

Gilbert, Creighton, ed. *History of Renaissance Art*. New York: Harper & Row, 1973.

Lowry, Bates. *Renaissance Architecture*. New York: Braziller, 1962.

Maynard, Winifred. *Elizabethan Lyric Poetry and Its Music*. Oxford: Oxford University Press, 1986.

Snyder, James. *Northern Renaissance Art: Painting, Sculpture, the Graphic Arts from 1350–1575*. New York: Abrams, 1985.

Thomson, James. *Music through the Renaissance*. Dubuque, IA: Wm. C. Brown Publishers, 1984.

Chapter 8

·····➧◉➧····

The Baroque and Rococo Periods
(1600–1775)

Chronology

Visual Arts	Music	Historical Figures and Events
•Tintoretto (1518–1594) •Domenicos Theotocopoulos (El Greco) (1541–1614)		
	•Giovanni Gabrieli (c. 1557–1612)	
		•Francis Bacon (1561–1626) •William Shakespeare (1564–1616) •Galileo Galilei (1564–1642)
	•Claudio Monteverdi (1567–1643)	•Johann Kepler (1571–1630)
•Michelangelo da Caravaggio (1573–1610) •Peter Paul Rubens (1577–1640)		
	•Heinrich Schütz (1585–1673)	•William Harvey (1578–1657)
•Clara Peeters (1594–1676)		
•Gianlorenzo Bernini (1598–1680) •Diego Velásquez (1599–1660) •Francesco Borromini (1599–1667)		•René Descartes (1596–1650)
•Rembrandt van Rijn (1606–1669)		•Galilei discovers law of falling bodies (1602) •*Macbeth* written by Shakespeare (1606) •John Milton (1608–1674) •Henry Hudson explores the Hudson River (1609)
	•J. J. Froberger (1616–1667)	•Thirty Years War (1618–1648) •Pilgrims landed at Plymouth (1620) •Jean Baptiste Molière (1622–1673)

Chronology (*Continued*)

Visual Arts	Music	Historical Figures and Events
	•Guarneri family makes violins in Cremona (1625–1744)	
		•Peter Minuit buys Manhattan Island (1626) •William Harvey discovers circulation of the blood (1628) •Boston founded (1630) •Baruch Spinoza (1632–1677)
•Taj Mahal begun (1634)		•Harvard University founded (1636)
	•First public opera house opens in Venice (1637) •Dietrich Buxtehude (1637–1707)	
	•Antonius Stradivarius (1644–1737)	•Isaac Newton (1642–1727) •End of the Thirty Years War (1648)
	•Arcangelo Corelli (1653–1713) •Henry Purcell (1659–1695)	
	•François Couperin (1668–1733)	•Reign of Louis XIV (1661–1715) •Milton writes *Paradise Lost* (1667) •Newton propounds Law of Gravity (1672)
•Christopher Wren begins St. Paul's Cathedral (1675)	•Antonio Vivaldi (c. 1678–1741) •First German public opera house opens in Hamburg (1678) •Jean-Philippe Rameau (1683–1764)	•Philadelphia founded (1682) •Peter (The Great), Tsar of Russia (1682–1725)
•Antoine Watteau (1684–1721)		
•Giovanni Tiepolo (1696–1770)	•Johann Sebastian Bach (1685–1750) •George Frideric Handel (1685–1759) •Domenico Scarlatti (1685–1757)	
•François Boucher (1703–1770)	•Sauveur measures musical vibrations (1700)	•Yale University founded (1701) •First public theater opens in Vienna (1708) •Jean Jacques Rousseau (1712–1778)
•Étienne Maurice Falconet (1716–1791)		

Chronology (*Continued*)

Visual Arts	Music	Historical Figures and Events
	• Cristofori builds the first pianoforte (1709) • Willibald von Gluck (1714–1787)	
		• Reign of Louis XV (1715–1774) • Pompeii rediscovered (1719) • First spinning machine patented (1738) • Methodist church founded by John Wesley (1738) • University of Pennsylvania founded (1740) • Frederick the Great rules Prussia (1740–1786)
	• First New York performance of *Messiah* (1742)	• Princeton University founded (1745)

Pronunciation Guide

Anhalt-Cöthen (Ahn´-hahlt-Koe´-ten)

Antoinette (Ăn-twah-net)

Bernini (Bayr-nee´-nee)

Borromini, Francesco (Boh-roh-mee´-nee, Franches´-koh)

Boucher, François (Boo-shay´, Frăn-swah´)

Calvin (Kal-vin)

Colbert (Kohl-bayr)

Corelli, Arcangelo (Koh-rel´-lee, Ark-ahn´-jel-loh)

Couperin, François (Koo-per-ă, Frăn-swah´)

Courante (Koo-rahnt)

Cythera (Si´-the-rah)

Descartes (Day-kahrt)

Diderot (Dee-de-roh)

Falconet (Fall-koh-nay)

Frescobaldi (Fres-koh-bahl´-dee)

Froberger (Froh´-ber-ger)

Giacomo della Porta (Jah´-koh-moh del-lah Por´-tah)

Gigue (Zheeg)

Giorgio Maggiore (Jor´-joh Mah-joh´-ray)

Giorgione (Jor-joh´-nay)

Gluck (Glook)

Ignazio (Eeg-naht´-zee-oh)

Il Gesù (Eel Jay-zoo´)

Laocoön (Lay-ah´-koh-wahn)

Leipzig (Lihp´-tzeeg)

Leucippus (Loo-tsip´-pus)

Loyola, Ignatius (Loy-oh´-lah, Eeg-nah´-tsee-us)

Monteverdi (Mon-tay-ver´-dee)

Orfeo (Or-fay´-oh)

Pascal (Pahs-kahl)

Passacaglia (Pah-sah-kah´-lee-yah)

Peri (Pay´-ree)

Pompadour (Pohm-pah-door)

Pozzo, Andrea (Poht´-zoh, Ahn-dray´-ah)

Ritornello (Ri-tohr-nel´-loh)

Rubens (Roo´-benz)

Scarlatti, Domenico (Skahr-laht´-tee, Doh-may´-nee-koh)

Schütz, Heinrich (Shütz, Hine-rikh)

Spinoza (Spi-noh´-zah)

Velásquez (Vay-las´-keth)

Versailles (Vayr-sigh)

Vignola (Vee-nyoh´-lah)

Vivaldi (Vee-vahl´-dee)

Watteau (Wah-toh)

1. Study the development of the forms and methods of creativity as revealed in specific works of art and music from 1600 through 1775.
2. Explore the continuing development of perspective in art and tonality in music, which were fully achieved during these periods.
3. Examine the ways drama and motion permeate all the arts in the Baroque and Rococo periods.
4. Recognize the Rococo as the final expression of the Baroque.

THE SPIRIT OF THE BAROQUE

The term **Baroque** (from the Portuguese *barroco*, "a pearl of irregular form") was first used to describe a style of art overladen with ornament. It was applied especially to the seventeenth-century style of architecture and meant to suggest vulgar or debased Renaissance style. In our own century, art historians have rescued the term from connotations of inferiority. It now simply designates an art epoch, along with such terms as *Gothic* and *Renaissance*.

The last decades of the sixteenth century were filled with doubt and contradiction, signaling the dissolution of the stability of the Renaissance. The State and the Catholic church were facing almost certain separation; indeed, their existence as authoritarian institutions was in jeopardy. New prophets in religion, politics, economics, science, arts, and letters were challenging the established authority of the Renaissance. The Protestant Reformation, the rise of the mercantile system, the establishment of absolutism in government, and advances in science were all movements out of which a new spirit began to emerge.

The Renaissance incompletely fulfilled many of the hopes, dreams, and ideals of its initial adherents. There had never been greater patronage of the arts by the Church and wealthy individuals, yet these patrons, many of whom had won the right to the cardinal's hat and the pope's chair, were among the age's greatest scoundrels and most corrupt politicians.

The struggle between the Church and the State had begun mainly as a battle of words. The next step was to cultivate action in every sphere of human endeavor. The seventeenth century was thus ushered in on a wave of tremendous intellectual, spiritual, and physical activity. The result in art was a style full of vigor, strong emotions, symbolism, and subtleties—qualities that typify the Baroque.

Some of those who made contributions to this flood of activity were scientists. Bacon's scientific method of inquiry, that of experimentation, laid the foundation for our modern scientific age. Descartes and Pascal made notable advances in mathematics, as did Kepler in astronomy. Harvey heralded a new era in biology, Newton founded the modern science of physics, and Spinoza systematized modern philosophy. Colbert established the mercantile system upon which the world empires of the seventeenth and eighteenth centuries were built. In short, all intellectual activity was concerned with order and the techniques for achieving that order. The Baroque was truly the beginning of the modern age.

There was also great religious activity, marking the seventeenth century as one of the most spiritually minded ages. The Thirty Years War (1618–1648) resulted in the establishment of Protestantism in northern Europe. Calvinism had risen in Geneva, spreading to England, Holland, and, eventually, America. All of Protestantism was engaged in a vast program of expansion. The Catholic Counter-Reformation responded to Protestant criticism and expansion; out of this movement there rose the powerfully militant order of Jesuits, which reached into every country of the world. Each of these great spiritual revivals was based on the same principle—a marshaling of religious forces toward a more profound and personal religious experience.

The English and Dutch colonization of the Americas and the East Indies is further evidence of the great political and commercial activity of the seventeenth century. The application of mercantilism to empire building resulted in a shift of wealth from southern European countries to the Low Countries and to England. Adventurers from all parts of Europe brought Western influences to the entire globe. Not the least of the effects of these activities was the establishment of absolutism in government, accompanied by a rising tide of economic and physical expansion. This expansion also depended on a systematic program of action that held great promise of personal rewards in fame and fortune.

The spirit of the seventeenth century exerted strong influences on the arts. One of the more tangible results was the impact of religion on music and art. The patrons of the Baroque were somewhat different from those of the Renaissance. Religion provided an impetus for many of the greatest works of art; such impetus came not from the Church as an institution, but from the Church as the source of personal religious experience. Rembrandt, for example, made his paintings of religious subjects personal and meaningful experiences to the beholder, not merely symbolic and beautiful scenes. His *Supper at Emmaus* (fig. 8.2) breathes the very spirit of personal faith and humility. The Protestant Reformation emphasized personal religious expression. To fulfill life's mission one must first conquer the self: suffering was part of life, and there was ecstasy and joy in pain. The artistic consequence of this Lutheran attitude was an intense, personalized expression of religious subjects in all the arts—an expression filled with the pathos and joy of human struggle and victory over the inner self.

The Jesuit Counter-Reformation, with its spiritual discipline and exercises, also closely linked artistic expression with personal religious experiences. The effect of such discipline, especially in Catholic countries, was profound. These exercises were a series of mental states the devout would assume as a part of daily religious experience. There were rules of conduct for every phase of life designed to intensify concentration on spiritual matters.

The artistic result of the Jesuit movement was a personalized expression of all human experience. Jesuit artists used all the techniques at their disposal to convey to the observer a profound intensity of emotional expression. Domenicos Theotocopoulos (1541–1614), known as El Greco because of his Greek origins, lived most of his creative life in Spain, a Jesuit stronghold. He became the ideal artistic voice of the movement, intensifying the mystic asceticism in all of his paintings, whether or not the subject was religious. His *Laocoön* (colorplate 32) expresses the struggle of the high priest of Troy and his sons through the elongation of the human form, the diagonal movement of line, and the upward movement of light with the view of Toledo in the background. The sallow body color adds to the feeling of mysticism and asceticism. Art became a living thing by taking on a new vitality. Art and music were luxurious in form, color, melody, and harmony so people might have an intense experience and emotional satisfaction. A useful comparison can be made between the depiction of the El Greco Laocoön and the Greek statue of the same mythical event (Fig. 3.18).

Colorplate 32 follows p. 194.

The Protestant Calvinist movement held a different attitude—one that had a negative effect on the arts. Calvin preached the doctrine of predestination and freedom of conscience. He placed a high value on the individual soul as the recipient of salvation. Education in spiritual and civil affairs was the Calvinistic technique of bringing God's will into reality on earth. This doctrine brought forth a group that was religious, narrow and rigid in personal conduct, and successful in business and government. Goodness was following certain rules of conduct, and all avenues of aesthetic perception were carefully guarded and often completely closed. The beauty that Catholicism had used as a religious force was considered evil. Images disappeared from the church and the home: they were considered idols, too easily worshiped for their own sake. Music, because it made its appeal directly to the emotions, was also looked upon with great suspicion. Except for psalm singing, "in one voice and with plain tune," music was banished from the Calvinist church. Organs were either destroyed or removed from places of worship. This religious doctrine explains the lack of Church patronage of music and art in Scotland and the Low Countries, in which Calvinism had a strong hold. It remained for the Lutheran and Catholic churches to encourage artists to embody their religious ideals in art.

In the seventeenth century, the center of wealth had shifted from Italy to Germany, the Netherlands, and Flanders, where Rembrandt and Rubens represented the Dutch and Flemish, respectively. The arts in these centers reached far greater heights of achievement than did the Italian arts of the same age. During the great religious struggles of the late sixteenth century, the Low Countries had been divided by religious persuasion. The Dutch were Protestant, whereas the Flemish remained Catholic and aristocratic. Consequently, in Holland we find a distinctly antiroyalist, anti-Catholic, middle-class society that prospered with the rise of the Dutch colonial empire and the merchant class. The art of Holland and North Germany represents this middle-class, Protestant point of view. On the other hand, Flemish artists such as Rubens painted their biblical and holy pictures with aristocratic models rather than the poor or middle-class people used by the Dutch painters.

Compared with Renaissance painters, Baroque painters turned increasingly toward common people for patronage because of the concentration of wealth in the emerging middle class, whether Protestant or Catholic. Everyday scenes, events, and experiences, such as a picnic or a drunken beggar, were sufficient reason for creative effort. As artists became more sensitive to experience, their art became more sensitive in its expression. As the horizon of experience became wider, the attention of painters turned from individuals to their surroundings. Landscapes became a prominent part of painting. Even portraits were often made with the subject standing next to a tree or on a riverbank, with the rolling expanse of an estate in the distance. This was especially true in the north, where much of the wealth was concentrated in the land.

For the same reasons that painting appealed to middle-class merchants and aristocrats, music reached out for the same audience. In the north, especially in Germany, music provided devout Protestants with personal religious experiences. Melodies were broad and singable; harmonies were rich and full of pathos. Bach and Handel, both representatives of Protestant Germany, gave us some of the world's most meaningful sacred music because of this appeal to the emotions. Handel's *Messiah* and Bach's *Mass in B Minor* are symbols of the spiritual expressiveness and power of music. In the southern countries, music was still more concerned with spectacle and dancing, reflecting the more aristocratic society for which it was written.

The Baroque urge toward systematizing every aspect of human experience had an effect on the arts. In science, philosophy, economics, government, and even religion, there was a strong urge to codify. Artists likewise explored a great variety of organizational techniques. The theme-and-variations principle of design became an artistic creed, whether in painting, sculpture, architecture, or music. The tendency to combine the arts to achieve a singleness of purpose can be seen in the fusion of Baroque architecture, sculpture, and painting. The purpose was personal expression, not only for the creator but for the observer. Artists invited observers to enter into the action and partake of the aesthetic experience, just as Jesuits were

Figure 8.1 *Coronation Service of King Louis XV,* 1715. (Spencer Collection; The New York Public Library; Astor, Lenox and Tilden Foundations. Photo by Robert D. Rubic, NY)

invited to enter into a religious experience and Lutherans to partake of an inner struggle. The Baroque was not a cult of beauty but an art of energetic realism. The realism of all aspects of Baroque life, from business to religion, is thus expressed in its art. The *Coronation Service of King Louis XV* (fig. 8.1) documents an important event in French life. It represents the pageantry of the event, including music making and a procession in the cathedral at Reims, decorated with magnificent tapestries for the occasion.

The rise of a wealthy middle class brought about a desire for opulence, an important characteristic of the Baroque. Ornamentation, often carried to vulgarity, was responsible for the low esteem of Baroque art until recent times. Architecture was often excessively ornamental; melodic lines in music were embellished with trills, turns, and other devices. Ornamentation did sometimes hide weaknesses in Baroque art, yet beneath these decorative effects are melodies and visual lines that are truly expressive and beautiful.

Because of the many facets of the Baroque, it is difficult to single out one artist, or even one art, as the quintessence of the seventeenth-century spirit. There are, however, a few artists whose works reveal the spiritual content of the age. Tintoretto, Rembrandt, Rubens, and Velásquez in painting; Bernini in sculpture and architecture; Monteverdi, Froberger, Corelli, Giovanni Gabrieli, Schütz, Vivaldi, Bach, Handel, and Domenico Scarlatti in music—all have won a place among the truly great artists.

PAINTING

Because of different influences on their lives and art, Baroque painters used the elements of art differently than had their predecessors. Line was generally diffused, one form melting into another without clear demarcation. Color was often monochromatic, with variations in the saturation and value of that one color. The tremendous vitality of Baroque painting was shown in open form, with action implied beyond the visible limits of the canvas. A strong sense of space opened the canvas into the deep distance.

Tintoretto

Tintoretto's *Last Supper* (colorplate 33), at the Church of San Giorgio Maggiore in Venice, exemplifies early Baroque style. Tintoretto (1518–1594) was a Venetian and, as such, was deeply indebted to the spectacular and colorful style that characterized all Venetian art. He was also one of the last great Italian painters, as artistic activity gradually moved toward the northern countries.

Colorplate 33 follows p. 194.

There is a marked difference in concept between Tintoretto's *Last Supper* and that by Leonardo da Vinci (colorplate 25). Tintoretto impresses us with the dramatic vitality of the moment. Not only is the spiritual impact apparent; so, too, is the human reaction of the disciples. The figures stand out in sudden lights, and the whole scene suggests a spiritual and emotional interpretation that is quite opposite to the more balanced and formal expression of Leonardo's work. Tintoretto moved away from the classic balance of earlier painters and made his figures move about the canvas, vibrant and alive. Space recedes diagonally into the distance, drawing the viewer into the action. Symbolically, this space is even more extended by the physical presence of angels in motion over the scene, as the figures melt one into another without any precise demarcation. There is variety of color, but without the sharp contrast usually present in Renaissance art. An analogy might even be suggested between this painting and Baroque music, where sheer sonority arouses and intensifies emotion; thus, Tintoretto, with his force of color, light, space, and dramatic action, leads spectators into the scene as participants in this deeply moving drama.

Colorplate 25 follows p. 146.

Rembrandt

From an early age, Rembrandt van Rijn (1606–1669) showed great sensitivity to beauty. Rembrandt's parents hoped that he would become a lawyer, a doctor, or perhaps a preacher. They were disappointed when he showed little interest in anything except art, but he was apprenticed to a painter and later sent to Amsterdam to study. After six months, Rembrandt left Amsterdam but returned in 1632 to begin his career in art.

Colorplate 34 follows p. 194.

He received many commissions from wealthy families for portraits and scenes representing the business and professional life of Amsterdam. His most famous work of this early period is *Dr. Tulp's Anatomy Lesson* (colorplate 34), in which he painted a well-known doctor demonstrating the technique of surgery. Although this painting is a record of a dramatic event, it is essentially a group portrait with careful attention to the individual characteristics of several famous citizens of Amsterdam. Their characteristics are made more apparent through the use of a focused, bright light on their faces, leaving the surrounding details obscure, an example of ***chiaroscuro***.

Rembrandt at this stage painted in a well-defined manner, but without his later expressiveness. He was popular and successful, buying a large home in the Jewish section of the city and marrying into a very wealthy family. Always a student of people, Rembrandt began to be influenced by the people around him. While his earlier style was largely designed to satisfy the demands of his patrons, his later style probed the personalities of the subjects. As a result, Rembrandt lost favor with many wealthy clients.

With a sense of direction born of the analytical and scientific spirit of the Baroque, Rembrandt strove systematically to make himself a master of reality. He sketched and painted hundreds of works in an effort to perfect a technique that would bring reality, action, and vigor to his art. With the aid of mirrors, he made innumerable sketches of himself in order to reduce the texture of flesh and hair to a systematic arrangement under various light conditions. He was one of the first artists to exploit the function of light and shade as a medium of extending space, both in recession and projection. He was also one of the first artists to recognize light and shade as a unifying agent in painting.

The works of Rembrandt's later period show the results of his intense studies. They are deep and require extended contemplation for a full realization of their meaning. From the standpoint of human sympathy and understanding, nothing can approach the quiet, compassionate beauty of his religious art (see p. 178).

A Closer Look

Rembrandt, *The Night Watch*

During the sixteenth and seventeenth centuries, the city of Amsterdam had an active citizens' militia. This militia was established during the Middle Ages and continued to play a role in protecting citizens. As time passed, that role became more ceremonial, and it became more important to its members as a source of political power and social status. During Rembrandt's life there were twenty of these militia units in the city.

The long-standing tradition for influential or wealthy people to have their portraits painted often included group portraiture, and one of Rembrandt's most noteworthy paintings, *The Night Watch* (colorplate 35, following p.194), belongs to this genre.

The Night Watch was commissioned as a group portrait of the Kloveniers, a militia company under the command of Frans Banning Cocq. The men whose likenesses appear in the portrait paid a fee according to their prominence in the picture. Of the figures in the painting, eighteen are such commissioned portraits. The others are "extras" in the same spirit as the anonymous spear carriers in a Wagner opera.

The most important figure, Captain Frans Cocq, is placed in the immediate center foreground. Cocq is dressed in the traditional formal black of the upper class. His white lace collar, red sash with brocade, and tethers at the knees are typical accoutrements of elegant upper-class attire. Cocq's lieutenant, Wilhem van Ruytenburgh, is immediately to his left, listening attentively as Cocq gives directions to assemble the company in preparation to march. The lieutenant is clearly secondary to the captain, indicated by his standing in profile slightly behind the captain, and his being shorter in stature, yet his sumptuous dress and prominence in the painting attest to his importance.

The brightly illuminated gold costume of van Ruytenburgh is balanced by the costume of the girl on the opposite side of Cocq, an allegorical figure representing the glory of the militia unit. From her splendid clothing hangs a chicken with clearly visible claws, the recognized symbol of the Kloveniers.

In *The Night Watch,* Rembrandt combined portraiture and pageantry, strong light and mysterious darkness, action and pose, important citizens and fantasy characters. At the time, portraits tended to be stiff and actionless, with focus on individual faces. *The Night Watch* avoids this actionless pattern of figures posing in a straight line. The picture is organized around the action of a group, with characters on different levels, in different body attitudes, at different depths in the pictorial space, and facing in several directions.

In further contrast with the current style of the time, Rembrandt did not portray each of the commissioned figures with sharp lines and clear features. Many of them are in shadow or partially obscured by other individuals, which was novel enough to elicit criticism. In sharp contrast to the partially obscured figures are the faces of those who paid to be included in the painting, especially the central figures.

A significant number of weapons are represented in the scene. Several men are holding muskets; one, whose torso is partially visible behind Cocq, is in the act of firing. Others are loading or otherwise handling muskets. The long pikes on the right, whose various angles suggest action and movement, remind one of their historical importance to militias. Helmets, many decorated with symbols, are also prominently featured. The powder boy running out of the picture at the lower left is busy keeping the group supplied with gunpowder. Some humor is added to the picture by his too-large clothes and helmet. The drummer at the right is unusually prominent for his minor role in the event.

Continued

Surprisingly, the original painting was reduced in size around 1715 so it would fit between two doors in the Town Hall. It was cut most severely on the left side, where the figures of two men and a child were lost. On the right side, most of the body of the drummer was sacrificed. On the top, the crown of the archway was eliminated and a small strip of the floor on the bottom was removed. We only know how the original looked from a copy that was made prior to 1715.

Rembrandt's use of balance, light, color, and line is distinctive here. This complicated group portrait is balanced around the central figure of the captain. The young musket loader on the left is balanced by the drummer, as the groups of men are balanced at the two edges of the picture and above and behind Cocq and the lieutenant. The painting is also balanced vertically: the human figures occupy the bottom half of the picture plane, while the flag, arch, and pikes fill the upper portion of the painting.

The light for the picture clearly originates from multiple artificial sources. These bring prominent figures to the attention of the viewer through selective illumination. The spots of light enliven the bottom half of the picture, where human figures predominate.

The predominant colors in the picture are dark earthtones, which early critics disliked. Lighter colors were employed primarily in the faces and the dress of the girl and the lieutenant but are also used to feature certain faces and to bring attention to the captain. In *The Night Watch*, Rembrandt demonstrated his understanding of how humans see. As a master of *chiaroscuro*, he demonstrated that in areas of high illumination color distinctions are readily apparent, but as the illumination diminishes, those distinctions are lost.

There are precise lines in the painting, although they were thought unusually imprecise by Rembrandt's contemporaries. The straight lines of the pikes, muskets, sword, and flagpole at various diagonals to the rectangular frame contrast with the horizontal parade of faces and bodies.

··-·-◉-◂-··

Colorplate 36 follows p. 194.

One of Rembrandt's great religious paintings, *The Descent from the Cross* (colorplate 36), uses light and shade not only as unifying agents but as means of intensifying the powerful emotional content of the painting. The figure of Christ is highlighted, but it still has lost edges and diffused lines. With colors of differing intensity, Rembrandt makes the faces of all participants in the action reveal their grief over the tragedy.

Supper at Emmaus (fig. 8.2) portrays the story of the disciples' meal at Emmaus, one of the tenderest scenes in the New Testament. The two disciples have come together, speaking of the Master who is no longer dwelling among them. Thinking of his words, "Where two or three are gathered together in my name, there am I in the midst of them," the disciples sit at the table with the apparition of the Lord, who has made himself known to them. Rembrandt retains the quiet, tranquil mood of the story. The architecture has solemnity, with the huge arch outlining the figure of the Master. There is only

Figure 8.2 Rambrandt van Rijn, *Supper at Emmaus,* Oil on canvas, 26 3/4 × 25 5/8 in.
(Scala/Art Resource, NY)

gentle action, including the soft movement of light coming from the halo. The
disciples are quiet and deeply touched. Christ is presented in the simplest
view, full-faced and in the highest light. Space has been dematerialized in this
work. Rembrandt has caught not only the spirit of the story but the atmosphere of the setting. It is a spiritual experience, not only for the disciples but
for the thousands who have seen and been moved by this great work.

This painting is only one of the more than three hundred works that establish Rembrandt's greatness. In the end, he had only a few friends, but
Rembrandt believed that his art was his destiny, and he was faithful to it. In

The Baroque and Rococo Periods (1600–1775)   179

1669, he painted his last picture, a self-portrait showing an old, wrinkled man smiling. Society forced him into a pauper's grave, but in catching the spirit of his own age, he left lasting memorials to it.

Rubens

Unlike Rembrandt, who was the product of Dutch Protestantism, Peter Paul Rubens, a Roman Catholic, (1577–1640), was one of the greatest painters to come from the Flemish Counter-Reformation. Combining the best elements of the Italian schools of art, he created some of the most stimulating and significant art of any period. From the point of view of sheer vigor, there is no painter more exciting than Rubens. As an interpreter of the violently anti-Protestant movement of Spanish Flanders, he has left some of the most moving religious art of that period.

At the age of twenty-three, and already a master painter, Rubens went to Italy, where he was given every opportunity to travel and to study the work of Italian masters. On one occasion, he made a trip to Spain on a diplomatic mission for the Duke of Mantua. The success of this trip brought great favor from both the Duke and the Spanish court—favor that proved profitable artistically. While in Spain, Rubens did a number of portraits and palace decorations. From there, he traveled to England in the service of the Spanish king and incidentally decorated the ceiling of the banquet hall in Whitehall Palace in London. He later settled in Antwerp, where artists and students came to him from all over Europe.

Because of his enormous popularity as a painter, Rubens had many more orders than he could fill by his own creative efforts. He organized a commercial art studio operated on the assembly-line method. This studio, which accepted all commissions and orders, reflects the Baroque spirit of systematization. The general structure or plan for a work was done by Rubens in preliminary sketches and cartoons, but the canvas was made ready by assistants who executed the underpainting, including the background and figures. Rubens then completed the painting. Rubens continued his creative work in a personal way, but the studio supplied a vast number of excellent pictures. The patron's ability to pay often determined the extent of Rubens' personal interest and, therefore, the painting's quality.

Rubens was not a Jesuit, but he was in great sympathy with the Jesuit movement. Consequently, he was commissioned to do a number of paintings for a Jesuit church in Antwerp. These works, typical of Rubens, abound in color and are filled with movement and suggest enormous vigor. The forms are made cohesive with subtle light and shade. He identified himself with his subjects in the Jesuit manner of intense concentration. His effects are so real that observers are drawn into the feeling and action of his pictures.

The *Rape of the Daughters of Leucippus* (colorplate 37) embodies the robust dynamism of the Baroque spirit. It is the essence of physical exuberance and sensual flesh. Everything moves with sheer delight in motion. The variation technique is employed, with movement expressed in the short, curved lines of arms, legs, and torsos. This technique is applied even to the contour of the ground and the clouds in the sky. The larger movement speeds diagonally across the canvas through the twisted and unnatural positions of the nudes. The physical reality of form is highlighted by the agitated torsos contrasted with swarthy masses of men and animals. Form melts into form through diffused line and sheer energy. The observer is drawn into the action by its sensuous appeal to the eyes, not to the mind.

Colorplate 37 follows p. 194.

In *The Assumption of the Virgin* (colorplate 38), the human figure is used almost as a repeated musical motive, with each person blending into the other either by motion or by light and shade. Each figure seems to have its own identity, yet the whole canvas is a fusion of figures into one grand diagonal movement. The movement expresses vividly the ecstasy of the Virgin's ascent into heaven, accompanied by the cascade of angelic cherubs. Rubens ingeniously uses color, diffused line, and a bipartite form that distinguishes between the heavenly and earthly facets of one event.

Colorplate 38 follows p. 194.

This most typical Baroque painter died in 1640. It is recorded that the Jesuits of Antwerp said seven hundred Masses for the repose of his soul. Like Rembrandt, Rubens's greatest works were those created in the service of the Church, but they were created also out of the sincere conviction of his own spiritual experience.

Velásquez

Diego Velásquez (1599–1660) lived and worked in Spain. He was not a mystic or a Jesuit, nor did he express the bold ornamentation and action of the Baroque. Like Rembrandt, he was a master of light and shade, with a feel for space and realism. *Maids of Honor* (colorplate 39) is a portrait of the Infanta Margarita and her attendants, but it is more than that. Velásquez paints a moment in his life as a portrait painter. He is standing on the left, palette in hand, before a large canvas. The King and Queen, who are not shown directly, are reflected in the mirror across the room. The soft pastel dress of the Infanta contrasts with the darker colors of the attendants. However, there are soft edges that blend one figure into another. The refined delicacy of the Infanta also presents a dramatic contrast with the dwarfed features of the figures on the right. Velásquez manages a fine illusion of reality by his treatment of space and his arrangement of the figures.

Colorplate 39 follows p. 194.

The Baroque and Rococo Periods (1600–1775)   181

Peeters

Colorplate 40 follows p. 194.

Clara Peeters (1594–1676), like Rubens, made her home in Antwerp. She is best known for her still-life paintings and is one of the early contributors to that genre. The genre itself had just emerged in Flemish painting and occupied the attention of many creative artists of the time. *Set Table* (colorplate 40) is painted with a technique that heightens detail almost beyond realism. The lighting is dramatic rather than realistic. Such theatrical manipulation of light frequently has been employed by artists of later periods.

Pozzo

Finally, some of the most spectacular examples of the Baroque's soaring energy and religious ecstasy can be found in the ceiling paintings of many churches, especially those of the Jesuit order. These ceilings were often created by relatively unknown artists or even by groups of artists. One such is the ceiling by Fra Andrea Pozzo (1642–1709) (fig. 8.3) in the Church of Saint Ignatius in Rome. The scene represents the ascension of Ignatius Loyola into heaven and is painted in a style resembling that of Rubens. The upward motion of saints, angels, and cherubs gives the impression that the dome has been opened to heaven and all its glory. The human figure is used as a motif in a gigantic panorama of religious mysticism.

SCULPTURE

Compared with the more reserved sculpture of the Renaissance, there is more action, expressiveness, and individuality in the sculpture of the Baroque. The most famous sculptor of this age is Gianlorenzo Bernini (1598–1680), a Jesuit whose works are imbued with a devout and intense personal religious expressiveness that was enhanced by his spiritual exercises. A comparison of Michelangelo's *David* (see fig. 7.4) with Bernini's *David* (fig. 8.4) demonstrates the contrast between Renaissance and Baroque styles. Michelangelo's work is monumental but static, while Bernini's shows nervous energy. In Bernini's work there is action—David is tense with pent-up energy about to be released. His eyes are focused on the object of the action, the figure of Goliath, which remains beyond the artwork itself.

One of the most famous works of Bernini is the *Ecstasy of St. Theresa* (fig. 8.5), the sculpture above the altar of the Cornaro Chapel, Santa Maria della Vittoria, Rome. The Baroque spirit of intense emotional ecstasy and imagination is expressed in this work. The subject is St. Theresa's dream, in which an angel appeared before her holding a dart, symbolic of divine life, with which he pierced her heart. The saint is in an ecstasy of pain; the pathetic expression on her face and the shoulder upraised in anticipation of

Figure 8.3 Fra Andrea Pozzo, *Apotheosis of St. Ignatius,* 1691–94. Ceiling fresco, Church of Saint Ignatius, Rome, Italy. (Scala/Art Resources, NY)

Figure 8.4 Gianlorenzo Bernini, *David*, 1624. Marble, life size. Borghese Gallery, Rome, Italy. (Alinari/Art Resource, NY)

the next thrust are testimony to the emotional sensitivity of Bernini's art. The artist has used every device at his disposal to intensify this expression. The impression of infinite space is created by the heavenly cloud on which the action takes place. Space is made even more real by the hanging draperies and the suspended feet of the saint. The poised dart, the angelic face, the flowing drapery—all combine to make this a work of dynamic but spiritual motion.

Figure 8.5 Gianlorenzo Bernini, *Ecstasy of St. Theresa,* 1646. Marble, 11 ft. 6 in. high. Cornaro Chapel. S. Maria della Vittoria, Rome, Italy. (Alinari/Art Resource, NY)

Figure 8.6 Michelangelo Buonarroti, stairway of the Laurentian Library, 1558–59. Laurentian Library, Florence Library, Florence, Italy. (Alinari/Art Resource, NY)

ARCHITECTURE

Architectural design remained classic in its fundamental forms well into the twentieth century, but the Baroque spirit added vigor and, at times, profuse ornamentation. The same predilection for movement, light and shade, and plasticity of form that characterizes Baroque painting and sculpture is present in its buildings. They were designed not only to enclose space but to present a dramatic spectacle to the eye. Differences between Renaissance and Baroque style are superbly manifest in the grand stairwells of the Laurentian Library in Florence and the Schloss Augustusburg castle at Brühl (figs. 8.6, 8.7). In the former a feeling of serenity and order is projected through uncluttered lines, balance, and symmetry. In the latter, the exuberance and excitement of the Baroque are achieved by an encrustation of ornament and decoration over the structural members of the architecture. The stairs are scarcely noticed in the visually embellished surroundings.

Figure 8.7 B. Neumann, stairway at Schloss Augustusburg 1687–1753. Brühl, Germany. (Foto Marburg/Art Resource, NY)

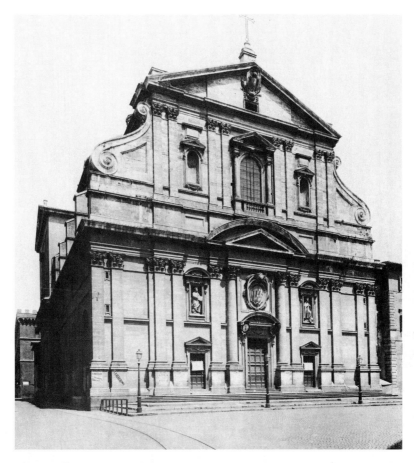

Figure 8.8 Giacomo della Porta, *Il Gesù* c. 1575–84. Rome, Italy. (Alinari/Art Resource, NY)

The dramatic spectacle of the Baroque particularly was apparent in its church buildings, with the glory and magnificence of heaven suggested to the eye by the facade and many interior features. The Greek temple and the Roman dome were almost always emulated by Baroque church builders. The way architects arranged and decorated these fundamentally simple forms, however, suggests the Baroque variation technique. An example of early Italian Baroque style, based on classical principles but energized by the Baroque spirit, is the church of *Il Gesù* in Rome (fig. 8.8). A Jesuit church, it was designed by Giacomo da Vignola (1507–1573), but the facade was redesigned by Giacomo della Porta (1541–1604). A mixing of Renaissance and Baroque styles can be seen in the triangular design over a low-arched pediment. The curved scrolls on either side act as buttresses. While *Il Gesù* is not excessively ornate, it did become a model for many other Baroque churches.

Figure 8.9 Francesco Borromini, facade of *Sant' Agnese*, 1657. Rome, Italy. (FPG International)

Sant' Agnese (fig. 8.9) in Rome, designed by Francesco Borromini (1599–1667), is a typical example of the middle Baroque period. One is immediately conscious of the classic columns and the huge dome. Some elements are included, however, purely for decoration. The columns have been doubled to make a richer appearance. The towers on either side of the dome are set forward and the facade is curved to connect with the central section. In a sense, this is comparable to the painter's use of light and shade for depth. While the bottom portion of each tower is square, the top is rounded, suggesting a twisting movement. The whole breadth of the facade is covered with repeated ornamental carvings to mold the components together, giving a sense of undulating motion.

Figure 8.10 Jacob Prandtauer, Monastery Church of Melk, c. 1702. Melk, Austria. (SEF/Art Resource, NY)

The Monastery Church of Melk in Austria (fig. 8.10) is an excellent example of the northern Baroque that followed the basic plan of *Il Gesù*. The richly decorative and ornamental interior (fig. 8.11) comprises a complex series of variations on the curves of the round arch. The effect is one of dynamic motion from the floor of the wide nave to the well-illuminated and elaborately decorated vaulting above, perhaps suggesting the splendors of heaven itself.

Bernini's Plaza of St. Peter's (fig. 7.9), situated in front of St. Peter's in Rome, illustrates the Baroque tendency to strive for monumental forms. It is an attempt to dominate great spaces, akin to the Jesuit idea of dominating the world. The facade of St. Peter's and the double rows of colonnades,

Figure 8.11 Jacob Prandtauer, interior of Monastery Church of Melk, 1702–c. 1738. Melk, Austria. (Foto Marburg/Art Resource, NY)

extending outward like great pincers, are all conceived as one gigantic work of art. The colonnades, topped by rows of figures of the saints, sweep up toward St. Peter's with a curvilinear motion that swiftly draws the observer into its portals.

Bernini was working in Paris on the Louvre in 1665 when he was visited by Christopher Wren, the English astronomer and geometrician. Wren was soon to become one of the greatest architects of all time. His response

Figure 8.12 Christopher Wren, St. Paul's Cathedral, 1675–1710. London, England. (© A. F. Kersting)

to the tragedy of the fire of London (1666) was to create a plan for a new city. While most of that design was never completed and is now lost, an enormous legacy of building remains. Perhaps the greatest single edifice designed by Wren is St. Paul's Cathedral (fig. 8.12). In a sense, its dome is the Anglican response to the dome of St. Peter's in Rome, and it was Wren's only church (among his many) to be without a steeple. Its flying buttresses, not a normal part of Baroque architecture, are uniquely concealed behind screening exterior walls. The massive rounded arches of the interior of the cathedral (fig. 8.13) reiterate the curve of the surmounting dome. The architectural vocabulary of the Greeks is evident in the repeated Corinthian capitals featured in the nave.

Figure 8.13 Christopher Wren, interior of St. Paul's Cathedral, 1675–1710. London, England. (© A. F. Kersting)

Many of the architectural features of Baroque secular buildings are identical to those of sacred structures. Memorable secular buildings include private residences, such as Versailles near Paris, Schönbrunn in Vienna, and Wilton House in England. Inigo Jones's penchant for geometric space is evident in the double-cube room (colorplate 41) at Wilton House. Its simple shape is disguised with decorative swags, murals, and ornate furnishings.

Colorplate 41 follows p. 194.

The Baroque and Rococo Periods (1600–1775)   193

MUSIC

There were two main lines of musical development during the Baroque. One was the evolution of dramatic vocal music: the opera, oratorio, and cantata. The other was the emancipation of instrumental music from its nearly exclusive use of vocal forms, leading it to a position of dominance by the end of the period. Moreover, for the first time in musical history, two styles were purposely used side by side, the older style of the Renaissance and the modern style of the Baroque. Composers became more conscious of musical conventions, and certain characteristics of style were developed that tied together such seemingly disparate composers as Peri, Monteverdi, and Frescobaldi from the early seventeenth century with Bach, Handel, and Domenico Scarlatti from the first half of the eighteenth century. These stylistic traits can be explained as the four unifying elements in Baroque music: (1) the establishment of tonality as the basis of harmonic organization, (2) *basso continuo,* or continuous bass above which the harmonies were played, (3) the declamatory recitative, and (4) the development of distinct vocal and instrumental idioms.

The first of these unifying elements, the establishment of tonality as the basis for harmonic organization, put Baroque music in complete contrast with Renaissance practice. Baroque music was conceived with carefully constructed harmonies and chordal progressions that fit this new practice. Renaissance music, on the other hand, had employed a style in which intervallic harmonies were merely the consequence of the melodic lines and not part of a harmonic plan. For example, the tonal sound centered around E minor in the opening chorus of the cantata, *Christ lag in Todesbanden* (*Christ Lay in the Bonds of Death*) (ex. 8.3) contrasts dramatically with the modal sounds of the *Agnus Dei* from Palestrina's Mass *Veni sponsa Christi.* They represent completely different concepts of tonal organization.

The establishment of tonality in Baroque music gave rise to a number of new methods of handling materials. Homophony, or musical compositions dominated by a single melody, became equal in importance to polyphony, that featured a richly imitative style. In opera and in instrumental music, such as the dance suite and those forms based on *basso continuo,* homophony reigned supreme. Tonality was applied to harmony with the construction of a series of chords under the melodic line. This chordal progression was designed to create a sense of tension and release, of motion and repose, through alternating dissonance and consonance. The tonal center, or tonic, acted as focal point for the harmony. This concern with tonality determined not only the organization of homophonic composition but also the treatment of counterpoint. The counterpoint of Bach and Handel was, for the most part, tonal rather than modal. The combinations of lines of melody in a Bach fugal passage, such as the "Hallelujah" at the end of the first chorus in the

Colorplate 32 El Greco, *Laocoön,* c. 1608. Oil on canvas, 54 1/8 × 67 7/8 in. Samuel H. Kress Collection © 1994 Board of Trustees, National Gallery of Art, Washington, D.C. *(See p. 172)*

Colorplate 33 Jacopo Tintoretto, *Last Supper*, 1594. Oil on canvas, 12 ft. × 18 ft. 8 in. San Giorgio Maggiore, Venice, Italy. (Scala/Art Resource, NY) *(See p. 175, 197)*

Colorplate 34 Rembrandt van Rijn, *Dr. Tulp's Anatomy Lesson,* 1632. Oil on canvas, 5 ft. 3 in. × 7 ft. 1 1/4 in. Mauritshuis–The Hague. (See *p. 176, 271*)

Colorplate 35 Rembrandt van Rijn, *The Night Watch*, 1642. Oil on canvas, 12 ft. 2 in. × 14 ft. 7 in. Rijksmuseum, Amsterdam. (See p. 177)

Colorplate 36 Rembrandt van Rijn, *The Descent from the Cross,* 1650–1655. Oil on canvas, 56 1/4 × 43 3/4 in. Widener Collection © 1994 Board of Trustees, National Gallery of Art, Washington, D.C. *(See p. 178)*

Colorplate 37 Peter Paul Rubens, *Rape of the Daughters of Leucippus,* 1618. Oil on canvas, 7 ft. 3 in. × 6 ft. 10 in. Die Alte Pinakothek, Munich, Germany. (Scala/Art Resource, NY)
(See p. 181)

Colorplate 38   Peter Paul Rubens, *The Assumption of the Virgin*, c. 1606. Oil on wood, 49 3/8 × 37 1/8 in. Samuel H. Kress Collection © 1994 Board of Trustees, National Gallery of Art, Washington, D.C. *(See p. 181)*

Colorplate 39 Diego Velásquez, *Las Meninas (Maids of Honor),* 1656. Oil on canvas, 10 ft. 5 1/4 in. × 9 ft. 5/8 in. Prado, Madrid. (Scala/Art Resource, NY) *(See p. 181)*

Colorplate 40 Clara Peeters, *Set Table,* c. 1589–1667. 21 1/2 × 28 1/2 in. Prado, Madrid. (Giraudon/Art Resource, NY) *(See p. 182)*

Colorplate 41 Double Cube Room, Wilton House, Wilton, Wiltshire, England, 1649–1653. 60 × 30 × 30 ft. (© A. F. Kersting) *(See p. 193)*

Colorplate 42 Antoine Watteau, *Embarkation for the Island of Cythera,* 1718. Oil on canvas, 51 × 76 in. Charlottenburg Castle, Staatliche Schlösser and Gärten, Berlin, Germany. (Erich Lessing/Art Resource, NY) *(See p. 214)*

Colorplate 43 François Boucher, *Madame de Pompadour,* 1758. Oil on canvas, 34 1/4 × 26 in.
(Victoria and Albert Museum, London/Art Resource, NY) *(See p. 214, 224)*

cantata *Christ Lay in the Bonds of Death,* were determined by chordal and tonal considerations. In contrast, the counterpoint of Palestrina's *Agnus Dei* was determined by the modal polyphony of the Renaissance.

To systematize tonality further, Baroque composers established a contrapuntal relationship between the bass line and the melody. A system of musical shorthand called **figured bass** was invented. This system of numbers and symbols indicated to the performer the chordal structure of the music. The figured bass was "realized" by the keyboard instrumentalist, who played the harmonies indicated by numbers under the bass line in support of the melody. The *basso continuo,* or bass line, was reinforced by instruments such as the viola da gamba, violoncello, bassoon, or string bass to supply color and volume. There thus was a sort of polarity between the bass and the melody, with the inner parts assuming lesser importance. This characteristic becomes a striking and readily recognizable feature of Baroque polyphonic music, whether vocal or instrumental from the early seventeenth or the early eighteenth century. The system of figured bass became so much a part of this new harmonic concept that it was, in one variant or another, the basis of the teaching of harmony for the next two hundred years.

One of the most striking and effective vocal devices originating in the early Baroque was the recitative. The **recitative** was a simple musical setting of a dramatic text so the words would be intelligible. The texts were set to a declamatory vocal solo in which the speech inflections were paramount. Recitatives were accompanied by either simple figured bass realized on a keyboard instrument or by a very plain orchestral texture. The recitative was developed by a literary and artistic group in Florence, known as the Camerata, who wanted to give effective representation to the words of their new dramatic venture, *dramma per musica,* later known as opera.

This new form, **opera,** fused drama and music through the use of recitatives, which carried the narrative text of the drama; arias and solo ensembles, which were the expression of highly emotional situations; and choral ensembles, which provided massed effects. The desire to fuse text and music into an indissoluble whole in the early music-drama was the counterpart of the same tendency to fuse elements of architecture, sculpture, and painting in the Baroque visual arts. For dramatic purposes, it is clear that a single vocal line conveys the meaning of words far better than a contrapuntal texture. This led, first, to the highly inflected declamation represented by the recitative. Gradually, more lyric and florid sections developed in contrast to the narrative character of the pure recitative until, by the middle of the seventeenth century, two distinct types of dramatic vocal settings were evident: the pure recitative and the **aria** (extended vocal solo).

The development of two musical idioms, one vocal and one instrumental, is another Baroque contribution. In earlier periods, most instrumental and vocal music could be played or sung interchangeably. In the Baroque, music was written specifically for instruments or for voices and could no longer be played or sung interchangeably. A *concerto grosso* or a sonata for violin and cembalo could not be conceived as vocal. The *Passacaglia and Fugue in C Minor* by Bach can be performed only as an instrumental work. On the other hand, such excerpts from Handel's *Messiah* as the recitative, "Comfort Ye My People" and the following aria, "Every Valley," (ex. 2.5) are suitable only for vocal performance.

With these general stylistic characteristics as their foundation, individual Baroque composers developed their technical mastery of chromatic harmonies and musically dramatic situations. They tried to lead the listeners out of and beyond themselves, to make them forget the limits of ordinary existence, and to open new aesthetic experiences through the emotions. The cultural and ultrarefined art of the elite was no longer satisfying. With the rise of the middle class came a desire among artists to identify with the new world of the spirit and intensified experience. The result can be seen in the music of the seventeenth-century Baroque, an art of ecstasy and exuberance, of dynamic tension and monumental forms, an art of longing and self-denial in contrast to the assuredness and self-reliance of the Renaissance. To achieve such effects, Baroque music was enriched by expressive melodies and recitatives, frequent **chromaticism** (melodic or harmonic use of tones not in the common scale), and energetic rhythm.

The growing humanism of the Renaissance had resulted in a greater interest in entertainment that would appeal to all classes of people, whether cultured or uncultured. However, the complexities of the polyphonic style in music did not appeal to ordinary people. They were more interested in dance forms and popular songs than in madrigals and Masses. Moreover, the Reformation had weakened the authority of the Roman church. Since ecclesiastical domination over the world of art was no longer possible, the work of the artist became increasingly secularized. Finally, the Renaissance veneration for classical antiquity, especially for Greek drama, set the stage for the invention of opera. Music was becoming an expression of human experience, an art of romantic idealism, a language of emotions. The beginning of the seventeenth century, thus, saw the fading of one epoch of music and the laying of the foundation for a musical revolution from which there eventually arose the whole edifice of modern music.

Vocal Music

Within the two main lines of musical development during the Baroque, the rise of the secular dramatic form of the opera was of earliest importance. In fact, the rapid increase of interest in this form created a renewed attention to instruments themselves as an accompaniment for the voice and for the staged drama and dance. The opera also led to the great wave of independent instrumental composition that was to dominate the latter part of the Baroque period.

Monteverdi

In his six books of madrigals, Claudio Monteverdi (1567–1643) explored the dramatic possibilities of diverse vocal groupings, presaging the Baroque opera. As the greatest of the early operatic composers, he set forth the principles for combining the most important innovations of the Baroque. In operas such as his masterpiece, *Orfeo,* Monteverdi used recitative as the vehicle for carrying the most intensely dramatic and emotional scenes of the drama. His use of the new recitative style was the realization of the desire of *Camerata* members to unify music, words and action into one form. In addition to the recitative, his operas include dances, madrigal-like choruses, and instrumental interludes called *ritornelli.*

This new musico-dramatic genre was so successful that by the end of the Baroque it had become the most popular form of musical entertainment. By this time, the original principles of Monteverdi and the Camerata had been laid aside; instead, vocal and visual thrills for a great popular audience became the norm. It was not until Gluck restated the principles of Monteverdi in the middle of the eighteenth century that opera gained a new vitality. By that time, despite their great earlier popularity, the operas of the Baroque (with a few rare exceptions) were completely forgotten. Recently, increasing numbers of productions of Baroque operas have begun to reverse this pattern of neglect.

One must listen to compositions such as Monteverdi's *Orfeo* within the framework of the early seventeenth century. Contrasted to the serenity and restraint of Renaissance choral music, *Orfeo* presents a dramatic power as dynamic as that of Tintoretto's *Last Supper* (colorplate 33). The unity of the opera depends upon several factors. Most important is the purposeful attempt to combine the music, text, and dramatic action into a unified expression. In much the same manner, Tintoretto repeated lines and masses of color to link his figures in the dynamic emotions of the *Last Supper.*

Opera's appeal, then, was in the vigorous, spectacular, and romantic dramas presented. The operas' plots, gleaned from Greek mythology and historic events, presented a variety of actions and emotions that could be intensified by music and staging. Everything about Baroque opera was impressive and dazzling. Ingenious stage machinery produced striking effects of supernaturalism and realism. Stage settings required Baroque painters to produce canvases that would reveal the excitement and pathos of the dramas. Music, staging, and the text were marshaled in a tremendous onslaught on the ear, eye, and mind. What began as an attempt to restore the ancient Greek drama by the *Camerata,* unwittingly created the new art form of accompanied monody (or song), and opera.

Gabrieli

While Monteverdi succeeded in arousing and intensifying emotion through a combination of words and music, another early Baroque composer achieved the same success by other means. Giovanni Gabrieli (c. 1557–1612), a Venetian like Tintoretto, overwhelmed the listener with sheer masses of sound. His musical style was in large measure determined by the performing spaces for which he composed. St. Mark's Cathedral was the site of countless ceremonies and pageants for the church, as well as for the ruling families of Venice. Gabrieli's music was designed for multiple ensembles that often occupied the four balconies of the interior of St. Mark's Cathedral. The resulting **antiphonal** sound is typical of Gabrieli's music. The effect of the rich and colorful sonorities he achieves in his *Symphoniae sacrae (Sacred Symphonies)* is intense and dramatic. Dissonant harmonies and rhythmic irregularities combine in a dramatic force different from that of Monteverdi but just as effective. The Baroque spirit of both masters is apparent in their power to move the emotions of their listeners.

The *Symphoniae sacrae* were published in two parts: part one contains forty-five vocal and sixteen instrumental compositions, while part two contains twenty-one purely instrumental compositions. The fact that some are instrumental and others vocal does not alter Gabrieli's preoccupation with tonal masses. The music is polyphonic; some of the sections have as many as sixteen independent parts. However, the obvious emphasis is upon a harmonic texture resulting from a purposeful and planned harmonic and tonal concept. This concept of tonal mass is truly Baroque in spirit. In these early Baroque instrumental works by Gabrieli, we sense the exploitation of sonority and masses of instrumental color, qualities that find even greater expression in the instrumental *concerti grossi* of the later Baroque composers—Corelli, Vivaldi, Bach, and Handel.

Schütz

The Baroque dramatic element was further revealed in religious music, especially in the oratorio, passion music, and cantata. The oratorio and passion music were, in effect, opera without staging and action. An early master of these forms for the Lutheran church was Heinrich Schütz (1585–1673), whose use of polyphonic choruses owed much to his Venetian teacher, Giovanni Gabrieli. His homophonic recitative and aria presaged the enormous output of Lutheran church music that came to full bloom with Bach. The **cantata** became particularly identified with the liturgy of the Lutheran church in Germany. In a sense it was a miniature liturgical oratorio, often based on a short hymn text. The massive strength of the Baroque church cantata often resulted from the Lutheran chorale tunes used as thematic material.

Instrumental Music

The Baroque musical activity most important to our musical heritage is the development of solo and orchestral music. The forms derived from the vocal styles of earlier times. Because of technical demands made by Baroque style, many instruments reached a degree of mechanical perfection that has never been surpassed. This is particularly true of the violin, viola, and cello. To meet the musical needs of the Church, the organ also reached a high state of refinement.

Baroque instrumental music has two equally popular textures. The first is homophonic texture, with an extended and predominant melodic line. The second is polyphonic texture, which develops thematic motives successively in various voices.

Homophonic Texture—Instrumental

In homophonic forms, the melodic line presents a simple statement of thematic material at contrasting dynamic levels in a few closely related keys. This gives unity and variety to the work, and it keeps the homophonic compositions, or movements, comparatively short and concise. As yet, themes and motives were not lengthened to extend a movement's length, as was common in the eighteenth-century classic sonata. As we have seen, the bass line and the chordal structure supported the melody.

The homophonic texture of Baroque instrumental music may be best observed in the forms of the solo sonata, the suite, and the concerto. The sonata derived its name from the Italian word *sonare,* meaning to sound, and was applied to instrumental music to distinguish it from vocal music. No specific form was implied in using the term, and compositions called sonatas varied from single-movement works for a solo instrument to works for small ensembles in several movements. Keyboard sonatas, played on the clavichord or harpsichord, were among the most popular. The hundreds of harpsichord sonatas composed by Domenico Scarlatti (1685–1757) are among the finest examples of this genre. These sonatas are typically binary, or two-part, forms. They begin in the tonic key, and the second part begins in the key of the dominant before returning at the close. The sonatas often are characterized by specific technical devices peculiar to the keyboard instrument, such as crossing of hands and both rapid scale and full-chordal passages.

The **suite** was made up of a number of short dances. It is found in its purest form in the many works written for the harpsichord during the

Baroque. In its final form in the late Baroque, it was based on four specific dances appearing in the following order: Allemande, Courante, Sarabande, and Gigue (Jig). The dance movements were often preceded by a Prelude, and sometimes additional dances were interspersed, usually when the suite was written for an instrumental ensemble or orchestra. Ensemble suites were often called by such names as "Sonata da Camera," "Sinfonia," and "Overture." The four dances included in the suite represented four different nationalities: German, French, Spanish, and English, respectively.

A typical suite for the keyboard, such as the *Suite in E Minor* by J. J. Froberger (1616–1667), includes the four basic dances, each in two parts, invariably repeated. Their common key is an important element of unity. Tempo, meter, and thematic material differ from one dance to the other. While each dance is essentially homophonic in texture, there are short, imitative figures that appear frequently and suggest a texture of several voices. This is especially true in the slower Allemande and Sarabande. **Ornamentation** is frequent, often notated but at other times merely suggested. Such ornamentation was an integral part of the Baroque performance technique and was one of the mannerisms affected by virtuoso performers, of whom Froberger was an early example. Later suites, such as those by Bach, retained the fundamental characteristics of Froberger's, but the dance movements were greatly extended, and almost without exception other dances were interpolated.

The **concertato** style of the early Baroque, in which competing or contrasting groups of instruments were played off against each other, developed gradually into the purely instrumental concerto in which a single instrument or a group of solo instruments was contrasted with a larger ensemble. The use of a single solo instrument with orchestra was called a **solo concerto.** When several solo instruments were used, the work was called a **concerto grosso.** The style and form in each case was similar. The music of the solo, or soloists, was contrasted with that of the orchestra. Passages in which all the instruments, orchestral and solo, were used were known as the **tutti** or **ripieno** passages, and passages in which the solo or soloists dominated were called the solo or **concertino** passages. These alternated in the course of each movement. **Concertos** were usually in three movements: fast, slow, and fast. Besides the contrast of dynamic and thematic material, there was also contrast of tonal color between the solo and the orchestra. Sometimes this was achieved by different use of the solo and orchestral bodies and sometimes by the use of totally different instruments in the solo parts. The latter was especially true in the *concerto grosso,* where several solo instruments were used, giving the composer an additional opportunity for tonal contrast.

Corelli

One of the earliest composers of the *concerto grosso* was Arcangelo Corelli (1653–1713). His twelve *concerti grossi* are written for a solo concertino group of violins and cello, with an accompanying group of violins and violas and a figured-bass part played by cellos, string bass, and harpsichord. *Concerto No. 8, Op. 6* is one of Corelli's most popular works. It is titled *Concerto fatto per la notte di Natale* (*Concerto Composed for Christmas Eve*). It has the usual three movements, fast, slow, and fast, and an additional movement labeled *Pastorale ad libitum* (*Pastorale to be played if desired*). Actually, this additional movement gives the work the character of a Christmas concerto, since the pastoral movement was commonly associated with works written for the Christmas season. Other examples are the Pastoral Symphony in Handel's *Messiah* and a similar movement in Bach's *Weihnachtsoratorium* (*Christmas Oratorio*).

The *Concerto No. 8* deviated from the pattern of only one tempo in each movement. Its composition begins with an introduction in two parts (marked allegro and grave), in which the concertino plays the same notes as the larger ripieno. The typical first movement then follows, with its alternation of soloists and accompanying orchestra. The slow movement, marked *adagio,* has a brief, fast passage in which the soloists and orchestra are again joined in unison. This separates the two presentations of the slow movement proper, in which the solo instruments are played off against the accompaniment. The final, fast section of the work is actually two very quick short movements. The second fast movement is characteristic of the driving rhythm usually associated with the final movement of the *concerto grosso.* Concluding the work is the pastoral movement in the rocking metric pattern often associated with lullabies and, hence, the nativity. Here the soloists are given even more conspicuous passages than those in the main body of the work.

The contrast of tonal color and dynamic levels among soloists and orchestra, the rhythmic drive of the fast movement in contrast to the expressive character of the slow movement, and the allusion to scene painting in the final movement all make this work a fitting musical counterpart of the highly ornamental and expressive Baroque murals of seventeenth- and eighteenth-century churches. Corelli was employed by a cardinal of the Church, and these compositions for church and festive occasions were in great demand.

Vivaldi

The concertos of Antonio Vivaldi (1678–1741) are perhaps the most varied and colorful of those composed in the last fifty years of the Baroque. In the Venetian tradition that relished tonal color, Vivaldi employed an exhaustive variety of solo and concertino instruments, as well as varied orchestral groups in the *concerto grosso*. He used brasses and woodwinds common during his time—trumpet, horn, flute, piccolo, oboe, and bassoon—as well as such little-used stringed instruments as the mandolin with equal success. While Vivaldi wrote over 450 concertos, the preponderance of the works are for solo instruments. Even in those works properly called *concerti grossi,* the solo instruments are given much that is in a virtuoso style and foreshadows the solo treatment in classical concertos of later times.

Among the concertos that Vivaldi wrote are a number grouped under specific titles that indicate the composer's acknowledgment of the Baroque tendency to combine the arts. This desire, expressed in the dramatic combination of word and music in vocal works for the stage and the church, finds a naive counterpart in some of the purely instrumental music of the period. Vivaldi wrote a series of twelve concertos, eleven for solo violin and one for oboe, under the title of *Il Cimento dell' Armonica e dell' Invenzione (The Contest between Harmony and Invention)* and grouped these works into sets of four. The first is entitled *The Four Seasons,* in which each season is represented by a single concerto. Apart from the evident desire to have the music portray the general events as well as specific details of the respective seasons, these are all cast in the traditional fast-slow-fast sequence of the concerto form.

Vivaldi wrote poems, or had them written, for each movement of these four concertos. In the first, called *Spring,* the poem sets the general tone of the movement and furnishes the detail for musical expression. It also relates in words what Vivaldi had already accomplished in music. Quotations from the poems are printed in accordance with Vivaldi's instructions at the beginning of the score, and where appropriate in the course of each movement. Translated, the poem for the first movement reads as follows:

> Spring has returned and the birds joyously salute it with their gay songs.
> The streams, set free by the breath of spring, flow again with their sweet murmur.
> Thunder and lightning cover the sky with veils of darkness and proclaim spring King.
> Their fury is soon spent and the birds once more sing sweetly.

Vivaldi had this poem printed line for line at the appropriate sections of the first movement for the instruction of the performers. In addition, specific program details are noted, such as the passage that designates the "Song of the Birds" (ex. 8.1). Other such details as the "Flowing of the Stream" and "The Thunderstorm" are also printed in the score.

Example 8.1 Canto de Gl'ucelli "Song of the Birds" from Concerto Grosso in E Major for Violin and String Orchestra op. 8, no. 1 by Antonio Vivaldi

The first movement contains as much material for the orchestra as for the solo instrument. Most of the solo passages are virtuoso sections that elaborate upon the musical material of the movement in very decorative fashion, accentuating the programmatic description of spring. The slow second movement is a two-part arioso that is played by the solo violin to an accompaniment of violins and violas. The solo part represents a sleeping goatherd, while the two violin parts are labeled "the murmuring of the forest trees" and the viola part "the barking of the goatherd's dog." The final allegro is a shepherds' dance in a gay jig tempo and rhythm, in which the solo violin is exploited and contrasted in virtuoso passages with the string orchestra.

Despite the naive program and the pictorial musical passages, Vivaldi has, with his usual mastery, written a work that is musically and aesthetically satisfying in its handling of form, brilliant tonal color, and expressive quality. He is certainly one of the great representatives of the Baroque love of dramatic tension and elaborate ornamentation. *The Four Seasons* is akin to the Renaissance word painting in the madrigal, now used in a purely instrumental manner.

Polyphonic Texture—Instrumental

The second type of Baroque instrumental texture, the polyphonic, develops motives and thematic subjects in various voices and is completely contrapuntal in nature. In fact, the **fugue,** which is one of the best known of these forms, can be regarded more as a device of contrapuntal writing than as an actual form. In addition, the fugue is not exclusively an instrumental form, since it is found in Baroque vocal music as well.

The devices of fugal writing were derived from earlier polyphonic vocal writing. The fugue itself is described as written in two or more "voices" even though designed exclusively for instrumental performance. The fugue is essentially a contrapuntal work built on a theme called the **subject.** Frequently, there are secondary themes, called **countersubjects.** Several compositional devices long associated with polyphonic vocal writing are used to achieve unity and variety in the presentation of the single theme. The fundamental unifying device is imitation of the subject in all voices. The subject is characteristically a melodic idea that is stated in the tonic key and ends in the dominant. Its **answer** is an imitation of itself that begins in the dominant key and ends in the tonic. The single subject is consistently treated in varied ways. The subject, or parts of it, may appear in different keys after varying time intervals. It may be played more slowly than the original statement **(augmentation)** or faster **(diminution).** The subject may be used upside down **(inversion)** or in reverse note order **(retrogression).** The subject and answer may appear separately in any of their forms, or they may overlap each other **(stretto).**

Bach

It would be difficult to propose a spot more fitting for the birthplace of Johann Sebastian Bach (1685–1750) than Eisenach. Romance, religion, and music had all put their special stamp upon this town in the heart of Germany. Just outside the town was the stately Wartburg Castle. Here lived the saintly Elizabeth of the Tannhäuser legend, here the famous tourney of song was held, and here the German *meistersingers* sang their songs. It was in this castle that Luther came to hide from the wrath of the pope and made the first translation of the Bible into German. Here also Luther composed many of the hymn tunes that were to shape the world's religious life, as well as provide material for the works of Bach. The most important influence on Bach was the work of Martin Luther; for without the foundations laid down by the Lutheran church, it is hardly possible that Bach would have done what he did. He was full of the vitality of Protestantism, yet steeped in the traditions of Catholicism, a combination that produced inspired works.

Bach devoted his life to composing music for the Church. Most of his great music was written from necessity. As an organist, he had to supply music for the Sunday services, and in order to have music he had to compose his own. Most of it remained unpublished until long after his death. He had little intercourse with other musicians of his time, being unable to travel and mingle in places where they were to be found. He did not comprehend his own greatness, and it never entered his mind that his music had qualities that would place it among the most inspired of the world.

At a very early age, Bach dedicated himself to the task of creating "a regulated Church music to the honor of God." By "regulated" he meant systematized musical form and expression. In the spirit of the Baroque, Bach achieved a technical mastery of all the available compositional devices and forms of his time and molded them into an expression of great religious faith. He invented nothing new, but he organized and codified the art of music in such a way that to this day he is looked upon as the final authority in the craft of Baroque musical composition. The subjective relationship between music and text makes his technical mastery more of a means to an end than an end in itself. His craftsmanship always served the meaning of the text. This is more apparent in his sacred music, where spiritual meaning was the objective. He used every compositional means to achieve this objective.

Bach was prolific. His music includes cantatas for every Sunday and Church festival of the year, three Passions (music for Holy Week, including the magnificent *Passion According to St. Matthew,*) the great *Mass in B Minor,* and many lesser choral works. Among the instrumental works are *The Well-Tempered Clavier,* violin sonatas, chorale preludes, orchestral suites, and numerous pieces for clavier and organ.

In addition to the fugue, other contrapuntal forms used by Bach are the canon, **chaconne,** and passacaglia. An example of one of these is Bach's *Passacaglia and Fugue in C Minor* (ex. 8.2), which provides an excellent study in the theme-and-variation method in Baroque polyphonic music. The composition was originally written for organ, but it has been transcribed for orchestra and is often performed as an orchestral work. A **passacaglia** is a dance form in which the melody appears in the bass and is constantly repeated in the other voices as well. The first announcement of the theme comes in the bass with no accompaniment (ex. 8.2).

Example 8.2   Passacaglia and Fugue in C Minor by J. S. Bach

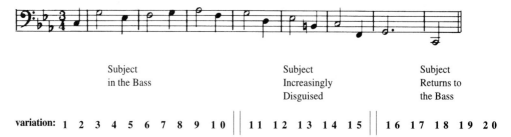

Subject	Subject	Subject
in the Bass	Increasingly	Returns to
	Disguised	the Bass

variation: 1   2   3   4   5   6   7   8   9   1 0   ‖   1 1   1 2   1 3   1 4   1 5   ‖   1 6   1 7   1 8   1 9   2 0

Subject:	Theme is stated alone in the bass in connected style
Var. 1:	Syncopated three-part treble accompaniment
Var. 2:	Syncopated three-part treble accompaniment, somewhat lower
Var. 3:	Continuous eighth-note motion in upper voices
Var. 4:	Rhythmic interest enhanced by sixteenth notes on second halves of beats
Var. 5:	Subject is disguised
Var. 6:	Subject returns to original rhythm; rapid ascending scale passages
Var. 7:	Rapid descending scale passages
Var. 8:	Continued active rhythms with contrary motion
Var. 9:	Subject altered rhythmically; gestures imitated in upper voices
Var. 10:	Subject becomes the basis for chords beneath a countermelody
Var. 11:	Two-voice texture with rapid motion in the lower voice
Var. 12:	Four-voice texture returns
Var. 13:	Three-voice texture; subject hidden in the inner voice
Var. 14:	Two-voice arpeggiated texture with contrary motion
Var. 15:	Ascending arpeggios
Var. 16:	Many dissonances in the accumulating chords
Var. 17:	Triplet figures dominate the three-voice texture
Var. 18:	Subject altered rhythmically; new irregular rhythms
Var. 19–20:	Rhythmic complexity and harmonic density increase; five-voice texture for much of the final statement (A double fugue follows)

The melody is characterized by rather large skips. In spite of these, it has a sustained quality and somber expressiveness. Bach is not trying to tell a story; he is creating a melody and using his skill to develop that melody. As the music progresses, the theme is constantly repeated, usually in the bass but on occasion in other voices. After a robustly climactic announcement of the melody, there follows a double fugue. For his fugue subject, Bach takes the first half of the main melody and combines it with a newly created theme, a countersubject. He then develops these two simultaneously. The music is repetitious but not monotonous, because he creates variety through vigorous contrasts in loudness, texture, and tempo. This is an example of the way Baroque music is organized. Its expressive qualities come from the sincerity of expression of the themes themselves and from the rich, full harmonic substance.

Harmonic contrast in Baroque music was achieved by dissonance and consonance in proper relation to each other. Dissonance sets up tension, while consonance affords release or repose. In the *Passacaglia and Fugue in C Minor,* Bach develops the melody in polyphonic style. He also varies the harmonic structure and, consequently, the relationship between consonance and dissonance as the work rises and falls and reaches a powerful climax. The listener is compelled by the flowing lines of melody and by the richly combined sounds.

A Closer Look

Bach, Cantata No. 4

The pathos and dramatic power of Bach's music are evident in the Easter cantata *Christ lag in Todesbanden (Christ Lay in the Bonds of Death)*, for chorus and small orchestra. While its structure is unique among the more than two hundred extant cantatas Bach wrote, it clearly illustrates one of his most consistent compositional devices: he linked the cantata both to the scriptural lesson of the particular Sunday's service for which it was written and to the entire musical tradition of the Lutheran church. In most cantatas, Bach was content to paraphrase a chorale tune—the text of which was a commentary on the scriptural lesson of the day—in the large-scale opening chorus. In this cantata, each of the first six choral movements is a variation on the chorale tune, and employs one of the first six verses of the original hymn text written by Martin Luther. The theme of these variations is found in the setting of the seventh and final verse, where it appears in the simple, four-part setting of the chorale or hymn (ex. 8.3).

Example 8.3 Cantata no. 4, *Christ lag in Todesbanden,* chorale variation by J. S. Bach

Sinfonia: 2 violins, 2 violas and *basso continuo* (organ and cello/bass). This short introduction is built from the opening two notes of the chorale melody.

Verse 1: Choir, strings, and *basso continuo*. Chorale form (AAB) is preserved with, as in all movements, added "Hallelujahs." Chorale melody in slow values in soprano voice. Other parts embellish with shorter note values.

Verse 2: Soprano and alto duet. The soprano carries the chorale melody in quarter- and half-note motion, while the *basso continuo* moves by eighth notes.

Verse 3: Solo for tenor voice moves in quarter-note motion with unison violins in sixteenth notes and basso continuo primarily in eighth notes.

Verse 4: Choir with *basso continuo*. The alto section carries the chorale melody in quarter notes, while other voices employ shorter note values.

Verse 5: Solo for bass voice accompanied by strings and *basso continuo*. This is the only verse in triple meter.

Verse 6: Soprano and tenor sing the chorale tune in duet, with some ornamentation. The *basso continuo* jigs throughout with dotted rhythms.

Verse 7: In the final chorale, the voices are doubled by the instrumental forces. Here the chorale tune is presented in its simplest form.

The formal structure of the cantata is symmetrical, following the instrumental sinfonia.

Sinfonia, then Verses:

The cantata's orchestral prelude paraphrases the chorale tune and presents a chromatically descending figure suggesting the pathos of death. In the opening verse, a decorative but vigorous statement of the chorale tune in the soprano voice contrasts with the complex counterpoint of the other three voices. The succeeding five verses in their variations on the chorale tune vividly support the text of each verse.

The second verse weaves the melody over a consistently moving **basso ostinato** figure. In the third verse, the driving and jubilantly decorative line of the unison violins goes far beyond the words set to the original tune in announcing Christ as the heroic conqueror of Death. A short interruption of rhythm at the word *Tod* (death) in the German text accentuates Christ's complete victory over death and contrasts with the subsequent jubilation of the final line and the "Hallelujah." Verse four depicts the struggle between life and death. The soprano, tenor, and bass voices in powerful fugal writing accompany the alto's presentation of the simple chorale tune. *Canon* and *stretto* tend to intensify the struggle between the opponents. This is especially true in the setting of the last line of the text, "The one death consumed the other," where the *canonic stretto* disintegrates to nothing, just as death was consumed and destroyed. The major chord at the final cadence of this verse confirms this victory. The elimination of death by the power of Christ calls for a "Hallelujah" on a cheerful major chord after the consistent minor tonality.

In verse five, the opening, haunting figure is again heard as the music depicts Christ on the cross in atonement for humanity's sins. The chromatic elements of melody and bass create a sense of harmonic tension that emphasizes the pathos of sin and death. Movement suggested by the impelling bass figure, along with the melody, creates a special sonority into which the listener enters. The total effect reflects the emotional state of the text.

There are similarities in the emotional expression of this cantata and that of Bernini's sculpture *St. Theresa*. The supernatural atmosphere that Bernini achieved by light and shade is achieved by Bach harmonically. With the chromatic motion of melodic line and energized rhythm, he established the same tension as does the implied motion of the angel and St. Theresa.

The completed cantata is a moving expression of the sense of sin and atonement and of the joyous hope of salvation by the cross. This was music that expressed not only Bach's own religious faith but the essence of Protestantism. The music exemplifies the peak of the Baroque spirit in religious music.

The influence of Bach's employers is plainly imprinted on his creative works. In spite of his avowed goal of writing music to the glory of God, Bach accepted a number of positions where church music was minimized. When he was organist at Arnstadt, most of his music was written for the organ. When he moved to the Court of Weimar as organist and violinist, he conformed to the wishes of the Duke. Because of that court's strong Lutheran emphasis, he wrote some church music, particularly for organ and for voices; it was, however, a court position with demands for entertainment music— music with a virtuoso display and music for dancing. His violin sonatas, concertos for chamber orchestra, and keyboard music filled these needs.

When Bach went to the court at Anhalt-Cöthen, he found a Calvinist establishment that did not have a chapel or an organ. Because the Calvinists permitted very little music in their churches, there was no opportunity for sacred music. Bach then turned his attention to the keyboard and orchestra and to secular music for voices. Because his duties included pedagogy, he wrote a number of pieces for teaching purposes, notably the *Inventions* and *Klavierübung*. When in 1723 he was finally granted the position at the Church of St. Thomas in Leipzig, his entire effort returned to sacred music. This was, without doubt, his greatest creative period.

Handel

George Frideric Handel (1685–1759) was born in Halle, Saxony, in the same year as Bach. Handel had to overcome the opposition of his parents to a musical career. He learned to play the violin, piano, and organ at an early age and studied law to satisfy his father's wishes. He studied music and law at the same time, but after the death of his father, he gave up law and went to Italy to study music. There he learned to write in the Italian style. After three years, he went to England, where he achieved financial success with the popularity of his Italian operas. He became an English subject and lived in England until his death in 1759.

We know Handel as a composer of instrumental and choral music as well as opera. Such compositions as the *Water Music Suite* and his organ concertos are part of the standard repertory. His operas are in the **opera seria** style, and include *Giulio Cesare* (*Julius Caesar*) and *Xerxes*. He became an opera director, but as conditions and public taste changed, he turned to writing oratorios. He admitted that he had always wanted to write in this form, but financial needs had kept him composing operas. In the dozen years before his death, he composed about nineteen oratorios, *Messiah* being the greatest of all. *Messiah,* written in 1741, is one of the most popular of all oratorios. There are generous borrowings from other Handel works in *Messiah;* nonetheless, it was a prodigious feat for Handel to have composed this oratorio in just twenty-four days. Its appeal to both singer and audience has made it a favorite with choral organizations, and it has probably been sung more often than any other choral work.

The style of music in *Messiah* is a combination of German polyphony and the Italian operatic tradition. The choruses are usually in polyphonic style. It is in the recitatives and arias that the Italian opera shows its influence. Handel's melodies are singable, although some have a somewhat instrumental character. His harmonic structure is blocklike and simple, suggesting a feeling of great majesty but not the intense pathos of Bach.

The recitative "Comfort ye my people" and the following air, "Every valley," exemplify the Baroque dramatic element as it was applied to the oratorio. The recitative is accompanied by a series of chords, giving the singer freedom to declaim in a personal manner. The air "Every valley" is built upon a short, lilting melody that is repeated and extended by a variety of quick-running passages and ornamental writing. It is an aria with a contrasting middle section and repetition of the initial melody. Handel does not repeat the first section exactly but makes a few changes for interest and to accommodate the text. The total effect is of great lyricism combined with vivid textural realism. The bass aria "Why do the nations" has been often quoted as a typical example of the florid, agitated "rage" aria of Baroque opera. Handel often achieves an objective realism by suggesting the meaning of the text in the music. "The people that walked in darkness" shows this realism by its writing, in which the bass voice, singing in unison with the lower strings on a wandering chromatic figure imitates the visual impression of groping in darkness.

Handel's knowledge of voices enables him to create maximum effect. The polyphonic chorus "For unto us a child is born"—with its climactic sonority on the words *Wonderful, Counselor, the Mighty God, the Everlasting Father, the Prince of Peace*—must certainly be included with the greatest choruses of all time. In the "Hallelujah chorus," one of the most exuberant choruses in all music, Handel captures the simple majesty of the text by clear-cut melodic motives stated in vigorous rhythmic patterns. In the development of this material, he never loses sight of this majesty. It is no wonder that, when *Messiah* was first performed in London, King George II rose from his seat when he heard this imposing chorus, thus establishing a custom that has become traditional whenever it is sung. (Incidentally, the "Hallelujah chorus" was included note-for-note in the *Foundling Hospital Anthem,* an example of Handel borrowing from himself.)

Although Bach and Handel were contemporaries, they never met. Both were considered among the greatest organists of their day; they composed in the conventional styles of their time and produced lasting choral music. Bach admired Handel. He knew Handel's music and was eager to know him personally. Handel, on the other hand, never had any desire to know Bach and probably knew very little of his music. Bach had no wish for fame and fortune, both of which were sought by Handel. They were, indeed, two very different personalities.

Handel's music is most often on a monumental scale. Having spent his apprenticeship in the school of Italian opera, he thought in elaborate and spectacular terms. His melodies are always broad, full of energy, and seldom obscured by technical devices. He often used the same melody in different compositions, gaining variety and interest in the manner of treatment rather than in the originality of the material. He did not have the personal touch that marks the music of Bach. As a Baroque composer, Handel was committed to the expressive content of music, and his expressiveness is in terms of broad, general emotions. Bach's music is more subtle and personal. The appeal of Handel to the present listening generation is the appeal of realism, of programmatic presentations, and of active rhythmic development. In the music of Handel there are fewer demands on the intellect than in the music of Bach.

Both of these men represent the Baroque spirit in art. If they seem to contradict, such contradiction is a part of that spirit. The horizons of art were being widened, and both the idealist Bach and the realist Handel were universal in their appeal.

THE ROCOCO PERIOD

Through the opening years of the eighteenth century, there came a gradual revolution in all phases of life. The seventeenth-century propensity for systematizing was carried to its ultimate. Utopia was thought to be the result of reason applied to every field from politics to art. This philosophy was so commonly held that the eighteenth century has often been called the "Age of

Reason." Indeed, it was a century of order and symmetry. Everything was codified and formalized through the intellect: economics, science, religion, politics, art. Even manners were affected. Diderot's *Encyclopaedia* was a compendium of eighteenth-century logic that reduced all areas of human endeavor to mathematical exactness. It was the supreme symbol of the era.

Common people were beginning to take their rightful place in society, and by the later decades of the century, freedom became the object of reason. There was an urge for intellectual, political, economic, spiritual, and artistic freedom. The struggle for liberty reached its catastrophic climax in the French Revolution near the end of the century. The artistic fruits of this struggle, however, are to be found later, in the Romantic movement.

A style of painting, sculpture, and decoration called **Rococo** flourished in the wealthy, despotic society whose greed and avarice were the cause of the forthcoming revolution. The term *rococo* derives from the French word *rocaille,* which refers to the delicate scroll of the seashell, a conspicuous motif in ornamentation. The style was characteristic of the courts of Louis XIV and Louis XV, but traces of it are also found in the Italian and German aristocratic circles that imitated the French manner. Rococo style dominated the period from about 1725 to 1775. With emphasis on pleasantness and prettiness, it forms a bridge between the grandeur of the Baroque and the poise and clarity of the Classic. It mirrored the beauty of life among the upper classes before the French Revolution and the rise of democracy. The Baroque, Rococo, and Classic periods overlap. While the Baroque spirit was still strong in Germany until near the middle of the century, the Rococo had already come of age in France.

The styles of the Baroque and Rococo flowed into each other without any great revolution in style. The intellectual life of the eighteenth century produced many scholars who were often more concerned with forms and niceties of expression than with the content of their works. The economy had produced a very wealthy middle class, which took on the attitudes of culture without discovering its real meaning. The absolutism of rulers was possible with the fruits of the mercantile system. Wealth was concentrated in a small group of people, with no provision or thought given to the welfare of average people. The systematic advances in science, political absolutism, and economics had nearly turned the hearts of the upper classes away from religion. There was a marked change in emphasis between the healthy, vigorous seventeenth century and the decadent court society of the later eighteenth century.

The change in emphasis was nowhere more evident than in the French court of Louis XV. At the royal residence in Versailles, the most elegant and, perhaps, the most mediocre people of France gathered. The aristocracy lived in great leisure and luxury on wealth squeezed out of the common people by unscrupulous tax collectors. Rococo art and music were naturally colored by the patronage of this society, taking on the light and frivolous character of the court. Artists acceded to the amorous and playful whims of their clients. Painters, sculptors, and decorators created charming and sentimental works designed to flatter and please. The delicacy and fragility of their art was a mirror of the facade of aristocratic life, as artificial as its art.

In this highly artificial setting, life seemed to imitate art. Society and manners were reduced to a formula, with elegance, grace, refinement, and love as motivating forces. The worship of wealth, pleasure, and power superseded the worship of God. The Baroque art of expression and spiritual values was cast out, for this society was interested in gossiping, conversing, dancing, and flirting. It preferred the *tête-à-tête* to large receptions; it preferred music for dancing to music for worship; it preferred paintings of sentimental love to paintings depicting the reality of human experience. The heart of Rococo aristocratic culture lay in this superficial manner of living, open only to the wealthy and devoid of great passion and noble pleasures.

Painting

There were a few painters whose works show more vitality and genuine expression than we would expect from such a decadent society. Watteau and Fragonard, both painters of the French Rococo, reveal a great debt to Rembrandt and Rubens in their styles. Boucher, who was a favorite at Versailles, painted in a delicately superficial manner that breathes the very air of aristocratic eroticism. The art of these painters was the frivolous surface of the Baroque without its depth. Emotion gave way to sentimentalism and love to flirtation. Art had to meet the demands of a society that was artificial, with insistence upon luxurious display and elegance, no matter what the cost in money or morals. It is a wonder that a period of such frivolity could produce art with any strength and vitality.

Given the functions of Rococo art, artists generally attempted to achieve effects of grace and refinement. After the lessons of the Baroque in the use of light, shade, and expanding space, there were few radical changes. The methods and organizations of the Rococo remained about the same but with less vigor and on a smaller scale. Spatial awareness was usually less strong. Lines were less diffused, and there was a tendency to break up masses into smaller fragments with shorter, more animated curves and more ornate detail. Formal organization was less open than in the Baroque, denoting less action as well as less space. In an examination of the works of Rococo artists, it is difficult to distinguish them from those of the Baroque on purely technical grounds. It is the degree of emphasis, coupled with subject matter and general attitude, that makes the style Rococo.

Watteau

Antoine Watteau (1684–1721) is perhaps the most important painter to mirror the elegant life of the Rococo. In his works, the courtly customs and morals take on a grandeur of sentiment that transcends the actual conditions of the time. He was active during the period of change from the Baroque to the Rococo; his work was imbued with the vitality of the Baroque, but at the same time, he was meeting the artificial demands of the French court. His *Embarkation for the Island of Cythera* (colorplate 42) is not only one of his best-known works but is representative of the era. The mythological subject tells the story of the successive courtly steps involved in convincing a lady to join the festivities and set sail for the mythical island of love. It was the kind of sentimental and amorous myth that court society loved to enact.

Colorplate 42 follows p. 194.

The outlook of the Baroque still prevailed in this work. The lines are diffused and edges are lost in the mass of color, but there is a partial return of the clearly molded lines, as in the treatment of trees and the outlines of the figures. The effects of light and shade, so strong in the works of Rembrandt, have been weakened greatly. Light seems more evenly distributed, giving an almost pastel quality to the color. Tension of movement seems to be lost; open form is less direct and more static. Action is lessened and is more delicate and restrained. There is little strong, expressive appeal in this work. It speaks gently and softly, murmuring amorous sentiments, in depicting the curious morals of the age.

Boucher

Although François Boucher (1703–1770) painted many miniature scenes of questionable taste for the King, his portrait *Madame de Pompadour* (colorplate 43) is a happy combination of his consummate skill as a painter and the Rococo spirit of elegance. Boucher was the favorite artist of this woman of intrigue and power in French aristocratic circles. It is said that he was her constant advisor in matters of interior decoration, in selection of costumes, and in all matters pertaining to the purchase and commissioning of works of art. In this particular portrait of Madame de Pompadour—he painted many—Boucher captured the spirit of aristocracy in every detail. Her posture and elegance of dress suggest her exalted position, even though she was not of noble birth. He gave her an aura of the intellectual by including an open book in her hand. Through a skillful use of light and shade, he has even painted the "feel" of the silken gown. The Baroque technique is still present, as it was in Watteau, but on a miniature scale and without as much feeling or sentiment.

Colorplate 43 follows p. 194.

Figure 8.14 Étienne Maurice Falconet, *Punishment of Cupid,* c. 1755.

Sculpture

Rococo sculpture merits but brief mention. The same general spirit that is found in painting prevailed. Gardens were generously supplied with marble cupids coyly chaperoning amorous couples in their games of love. Even painters included such statues in their paintings, as in Watteau's *Embarkation for the Island of Cythera.* Étienne Maurice Falconet (1716–1791) was an artist who applied his whimsical and light touch to the Rococo scene. The *Punishment of Cupid* (fig. 8.14) shows the spirit of frivolity and superficiality that prevailed. There is little expression and only a generalized modeling of form. The statue served only as a reminder of a playful attitude toward love.

Figure 8.15 Salon of Marie Antoinette (*Petit Trianon*), 1762–64. Palace of Versailles, France. (FPG International)

Architecture

The decorative aspect of Rococo style is most obvious in the interior decoration used in palaces and salons. The Salon of Marie Antoinette (fig. 8.15) is a striking example of the use of delicately curved motifs in interior design. A floral wreath pattern is used on the carved wall paneling and on the ceiling. This same pattern is repeated in the upholstery fabric of the chairs and divan. Another typical, decorative feature is the chandelier, with its crystal prisms that sparkle like diamonds in the light. The huge mirror, because of its height, could reflect the beauty and fashion of everyone in the room. The salon was a spacious and elegant setting for the charming conversation of an elite segment of court society.

Music

The musical counterpart of Watteau and Boucher is found in the delicately ornamented keyboard pieces of François Couperin (1668–1733). His work was personal, intimate music in miniature. It avoided passion and the grand manner; it was fragile in texture and luminous in color, like the canvases of Watteau and Boucher. Couperin's harpsichord piece *La Galante,* with its exquisite style, its playful ornaments, and restrained manner, is a musical symbol of the Rococo, as is *The Bells of Cythera.*

The pervasive spirit of the Rococo was present not only in the refined ornamentation of the music but also in the decorative details of the musical instruments. The shapes of the cases and their decorations incorporated architectural elements of the Rococo, as did many of the formal furnishings of aristocratic homes of the period. The sides and tops of keyboard instruments were also frequently painted with graceful, sentimental scenes by artists who are today largely anonymous.

Summary

The Baroque was an age of systematic pursuit in all areas of activity—intellectual, spiritual, technological, and artistic. It saw the beginning of the scientific method of inquiry that laid the foundations for the modern scientific age. All intellectual pursuits were concerned with the achievement of orderly systems, especially in mathematics, philosophy, and economics. There was also a wave of religious activity, and sects arose in both Catholicism and Protestantism that imposed strict rules on thought and conduct as an important part of the search for salvation.

The center of wealth had gradually shifted from southern Europe to northern Europe, where foreign trade and shipping flourished. The extensive program of colonization, especially in the Americas and the East Indies, helped build a middle class of wealthy merchants who became enthusiastic patrons of the arts. This rise of a wealthy middle class brought about a desire for magnificence, even to the point of vulgarity in ornamentation and decoration. This outward display of material wealth was partly responsible for the rejection of the Baroque until recent times.

While the Church, especially Catholicism, still patronized the arts, more and more of the middle class became patrons, and everyday activities became suitable subjects with which artists could appeal to the emotions of the common people. Music also reached out for a wider audience, speaking with expressive, singable melodies that could appeal to the average person.

Baroque painting was characterized by vitality, movement, emotion, and often mysticism. Lines were usually made up of short curves with lost edges, showing vigor and a merging of one figure with another. Color was often used monochromatically with varying values and intensities. Space was expanded through facile treatment of perspective. Evidence of action extended beyond the visual limits of the canvas, so form was usually open and without classic balance and symmetry. Moreover, expression and overt emotion were achieved by the combination of color, diffused line, and space combined with the emotional behavior of the figures. Baroque painters systematically explored the effects of light and shade on color, line, and space.

Baroque sculpture reveals the same action, expressiveness, and personalized feelings as does painting. In comparison with their Renaissance counterparts, Baroque sculptors depicted stronger emotion, more spatial quality, and more sense of movement in stone and metal. Deeply carved and flowing robes with elaborate decoration also enhanced the impression of movement. Sculptors did not hesitate to include sculptured backgrounds to make the illusion of space more real and to bring the observer into the scene.

It was in Baroque architecture that the desire for magnificence and dramatic spectacle showed itself in its most flamboyant form. Architects achieved vigor and motion by elaborate decoration of design. Undulating facades, scrolls, twisting columns, and other ornamental decorations created light and shadow and gave a feeling of motion to otherwise classic facades. Interiors were often complex variations on the curve of a rounded arch. The interiors, filled with ornate ceiling paintings, created the illusion of being open to the heavens.

Some of the more dramatic changes in Baroque art took place in music. While Baroque painting, sculpture, and architecture seem in a sense dated in our time, Baroque music seems almost timeless. Even today it remains as a foundation for much of our musical experience. There were two main lines of development in Baroque music. One was the development of vocal dramatic music, secular and sacred, that led to the cantata, oratorio, and opera. The other important development was that of pure instrumental music. Emancipating instrumental from vocal music made it necessary to develop forms based solely on melodic and harmonic considerations. Composers systematically organized tonal material into such forms as the sonata, concerto, suite, and fugue.

The Baroque also saw the technical improvement of most musical instruments. The violin, viola, cello, organ, and harpsichord reached high states of refinement.

Homophonic texture in music became equal in importance to polyphonic texture. In opera, oratorio, and cantata, the recitative and aria were homophonic, while choruses were more likely to be polyphonic. In instrumental music, such forms as the fugue were totally polyphonic. Other instrumental forms, like the sonata and *concerto grosso,* often alternated homophonic and polyphonic textures. The development of tonal harmony was also a Baroque accomplishment. This gave rise to a number of new devices for handling tonal materials. The system of chordal relationships around a well-defined tonal center emphasized the importance of dissonant harmony that created tension and its release through subsequent consonant harmony. Although Baroque composers systematically developed the tonal resources of music, the expressive content was aimed at the emotional experiences of the listener. With their technical mastery of chromatic harmony and musically dramatic situations, composers tried to lead the listener beyond the limits of ordinary existence to new aesthetic experiences through the emotions. The many new musical developments of the Baroque resulted in the creation of an immense body of musical literature by such masters as Bach, Handel, Vivaldi, and Scarlatti.

Rococo style was a contrast to that of the Baroque. It was mainly the product of the French court, but since the court at Versailles became the model for aristocratic life and manners, the Rococo was imitated in other places, especially in Germany and Italy. The Rococo developed naturally from the intense systematization of the Baroque. As a result of absolutism in government, wealth became concentrated in the hands of the nobility. Society and manners were reduced to a formula. There was an emphasis on elegance, refinement, amorous pursuits, and sentimental love. Gone were the great passions and noble pleasures of the Baroque. Gone also were the intense spiritual values of the past. Life at the court was artificial, and so was its art.

Amorous scenes, courtly life, and manners provided the most popular subjects for painters and sculptors. The method of organizing the elements remained much as in the Baroque; however, there was less vigor and everything was on a much smaller scale. Lines were broken up into smaller fragments. Spatial awareness was reduced, and color, while still monochromatic, was less intense and showed more of a pastel quality.

Decoration in architecture revealed the Rococo style at its best, where generous use was made of floral patterns with delicately carved motifs. These decorations were also found in the design of furniture and in almost every kind of household furnishing, including dishes, silverware, and other items in the homes of the aristocracy.

Suggested Readings

In addition to the specific sources that follow, the general readings on pages 388 and 389 contain valuable information about the topics of this chapter.

Bianconi, Lorenzo. *Music in the Seventeenth Century*. Cambridge: Cambridge University Press, 1987.

Clark, Kenneth. *Rembrandt and the Italian Renaissance*. New York: W. W. Norton, 1966.

Haskell, Francis. *Patrons and Painters: Art and Society in Baroque Italy*. New Haven, CT: Yale University Press, 1980.

Held, Julius, and Donald Posner. *Seventeenth- and Eighteenth-Century Art*. Englewood Cliffs, NJ: Prentice-Hall, 1972.

Palisca, Claude. *Baroque Music*. 3d ed. Englewood Cliffs, NJ: Prentice-Hall, 1991.

Rifkin, Joshua, et al. *The New Grove North European Masters*. New York: W. W. Norton, 1985.

Chapter 9

···➤◉◀···

The Classic Period
(1750–1800)

Chronology

Visual Arts	Music	Historical Figures and Events
•Sir Joshua Reynolds (1723–1792)		
		•Immanuel Kant (1724–1804)
	•Charles Burney (1726–1814)	
•Jean Honoré Fragonard (1732–1806)	•Franz Joseph Haydn (1732–1809)	
•Benjamin West (1738–1820)		
		•Maria Theresa, Empress of Austria (1740–1780)
•Jacques-Louis David (1748–1825)		
		•Johann Wolfgang von Goethe (1749–1832)
		•Benjamin Franklin experiments with electricity (1751)
	•Wolfgang Amadeus Mozart (1756–1791)	
•Antonio Canova (1757–1822)		
		•George III of England reigned (1760–1820)
•Constance Marie Charpentier (1767–1849)		
		•Watt's steam engine patented (1769)
	•Ludwig van Beethoven (1770–1827)	•Napoleon Bonaparte (1769–1821)
		•First Edition of the *Encyclopaedia Britannica* (1771)
		•Discovery of oxygen (1774)
		•Marie Antoinette's reign as Queen of France (1774–1793)
	•Burney's *History of Music* published (1776)	•American Declaration of Independence (1776)
		•Discovery of hydrogen (1776)

Visual Arts	Music	Historical Figures and Events
•Jean Auguste Dominique Ingres (1780–1867)		
		•Steamboat invented (1788)
		•Beginning of the French Revolution (1789)
	•Haydn's first trip to London (1790)	
		•White House built (1792)
		•Louis XVI and Marie Antoinette of France beheaded (1793)
	•Haydn's second trip to London (1794)	
	•Paris Conservatory founded (1795)	
	•Beethoven's First Symphony finished (1799)	

Pronunciation Guide

Beaumarchais (Boh-mahr-shay)

Borghese (Bohr-gay´-ze)

Canova (Kah-noh´-vah)

Charpentier (Shahr-păn-tee-yay)

Cherubino (Kay-roo-bee´-noh)

Cosí fan tutte (Ko-zee´ fan too´-te)

David, Jacques-Louis (Dah-veed, Zhahk-Louie)

Fragonard (Frah-goh-nahr)

Ingres (Ang-reh)

Mannheim (Mahn´-hime)

Val d´Ognes (Vahl dohn-yeh)

Study Objectives

1. Learn about the shift in attitude from the extravagance of the Baroque and Rococo to the simplicity, clarity, and balance of the Classic era.
2. Examine the relationship between the visual arts of the Greek and Roman classics and the images of the eighteenth-century Classic period.
3. Learn about the development of secular music, and especially the sonata as a classic form.

NEOCLASSICISM IN THE VISUAL ARTS

As the Rococo marked the end of an era of opulence and excess, in the late eighteenth century another movement arose that marked a return to rational principles. This was Neoclassicism (new classicism)—a return to the supposed classic ideals of the ancients. The French Academy was founded in the seventeenth century as a guardian and purifier of French intellectual life. For the most part, the Academy controlled art, education, and exhibitions and set "official" standards of taste and style. In the latter part of the eighteenth century, in protest against the superficial elegance of the Rococo, the Academy sponsored a return to classic ideals based on Greek and Roman models. The movement gained momentum at the time of the Revolution, when public opinion joined in the denunciation of almost anything that represented the court.

Neoclassicists sought to express classic ideals by using models from Greece, Rome, and the Italian Renaissance. These models encouraged artists to create forms that were more realistic and stripped of sentimentality. The art of Greece and Rome became a symbol of detachment from superficial feeling. Neoclassicism would be prized during the deluge of blood that was to follow.

Panini's *Interior of the Pantheon* (colorplate 11) is a Neoclassic painting of a classic subject. By presenting humans as inconsequential figures in a monumental building, the painter emphasizes the classic features of the Pantheon. The linear perspective is dramatic, receding through open doors into deep space. The distortion of perspective in the top half of the picture is largely responsible for the drama. Through the opening at the center of the dome a focused beam of light falls on the wall to the right of the entrance, contributing to the balance of the picture. However, the source of the light that bathes the interior is of uncertain origin.

Colorplate 11 follows p. 50.

Painting

David

Jacques-Louis David (1748–1825) was the leader of the Neoclassic movement in revolutionary France. After a visit to Greece and Rome, he returned full of enthusiasm for the glories of the ancient world. His first great success was the *Oath of the Horatii* (colorplate 44), painted four years before the French Revolution. Its subject is a Roman father pledging his three sons to fight against the enemies of Rome. Thus, Roman virtue and readiness to die for liberty became the subject of Neoclassic French painting almost on the eve of the Revolution. The style and forms within the painting show a return to Renaissance classicism. The lines are sharply defined, severe, and angular—conveying great strength. Separate groups make up the whole: the three sons to the left, the father and the weeping women on the right. The focal point (the swords) is exactly in the center. Each group is framed against the background of a Roman arch set on Greek columns. For all its heroism, there is little expressive feeling in this canvas. Its subject is from a bygone age; its style is formal, intellectual, and unreal. In many of his paintings, David emphasized the ideal of dedication to freedom and the glory of the sacrifice necessary to attain it.

Colorplate 44 follows p. 226.

Charpentier

Colorplate 45
follows p. 226.

Portrait of a Young Woman, called Mlle. Charlotte du Val d'Ognes (color-plate 45) was for many years attributed to David. Recent research assigns the painting instead to Constance Marie Charpentier (1767–1849), an artist given wide recognition among Parisian connoisseurs during her lifetime. In this portrait, Mlle. Val d'Ognes is presented as a willowy young woman seated before a window that provides the light. The work is realistic in its details, even to the broken pane in the window. The form is modeled firmly and clearly against the darkened background. The interior of the room is painted with virtually no detail. The static, dark wall against which the fig-ure is placed focuses the attention of the viewer on the face and hair of Mlle. Val d'Ognes and on the details of her clothing. Compared with Boucher's *Madame de Pompadour* (colorplate 43), the change from Rococo to Neoclassic is obvious. The lines are sharply drawn to emphasize the severity of the figure, in contrast to the fragile quality of Boucher's portrait.

Colorplate 43
follows p. 194.

Ingres

Colorplate 46
follows p. 226.

Jean Auguste Dominique Ingres (1780–1867) was among the last French painters to uphold Neoclassicism, continuing to work in that style well into the nineteenth century. He trained and worked in Italy and then returned to France, becoming an advocate of the Davidian style. In contrast to David, his own drawings and paintings are characterized by sensuousness of line and exotic color, as in *The Odalisque with the Slave* (colorplate 46). This theatrical painting is only one of many in which Ingres reflected his preoc-cupation with the exotic. The central figure of the nude concubine is placed in an opulent Turkish harem. The frontal plane is occupied by this "odal-isque" and her musician; a Moorish servant is barely visible behind the balustrade. The light from an unidentified source focuses on the two main figures, calling attention to the sensuous rendering of the flesh tones and the rich and lustrous fabrics in the room. A spirit of calm pervades the pic-ture, caused in part by the repeated horizontals of the reclining figure, the musical instrument, and the balustrade. The spirit is reinforced by the casual poses of the odalisque and musician, their sentimental gazes, and the lazy falling of the drape on the right. In opposition to the horizontals are the re-peated vertical lines of the column, the Moorish servant, and the individual balusters of the railing. Together the horizontal and vertical lines create a grid system that expresses formality.

Benjamin West

One of the first noteworthy painters from America was Benjamin West (1738–1820). He began his training in Philadelphia but subsequently studied in Italy and finally settled in England, where he became a close friend of King George III. He was not only a painter; he was also a pedagogue and was responsible for teaching a whole generation of American painters. Of his numerous paintings (he left over three thousand), *The Death of General Wolfe* (colorplate 47) is characteristic in style and content. Such historical subjects were the source of many of his commissions.

Colorplate 47 follows p. 226.

At the siege of Quebec, during the so-called French and Indian Wars that were noted with great interest in England, General Wolfe died. West represents this event with the characters in traditional classic poses and arrangement but with contemporary dress. The inclusion of the Indian connects the event unmistakably to the New World. The figures are arranged in three groups: two larger ones at the left and center and a third, smaller group on the right. These create a rhythm across the painting, vertically and horizontally. The bright sky above the burning city of Quebec is contrasted with the threatening darkness on the right. Between the foreground and the distant background, West simplifies and omits almost all detail. The concerned gazes of the figures, the line of the unfurled banner, and the theatrical lighting all focus attention on the dying general.

Sculpture

Neoclassic sculpture followed the lead of painting in its debt to the ancients. Antonio Canova (1757–1822) employed his technical facility to portray his patroness as the Greek goddess of love in *Pauline Borghese as Venus* (fig. 9.1). While the lines and plastic forms are classic, there is only the outward appearance of classic form. This sculpture does not portray the Greek ideal of beauty but that of a woman of the world. Canova's debt to the classic style is made all the more apparent by comparing *Pauline Borghese as Venus* with the *Odalisque* of Ingres.

CLASSICISM IN MUSIC

Unlike the visual arts, music never succumbed completely to the Rococo spirit. Rather, the Rococo ideal colored both the dying Baroque and the new Classicism in music in the same way that court practices of the kings of France colored the social and artistic customs of every court in Europe—both petty and great—during the eighteenth century. The great music of the Classic period was a product of Germany, not of France. It stressed perfection of form rather than the superficial lightness of the Rococo, although the latter was often present. The French monarchy was absolute and extreme in its disregard of its citizens; in Germany, there was an enlightened absolutism. This new absolutism influenced all fields of cultural activity, and the

Figure 9.1 Antonio Canova, *Pauline Borghese as Venus,* 1808. Marble, life-size, Galeria Borghese, Rome, Italy. (Giraudon/Art Resource, NY)

patronage of the French monarchy and the German courts promoted artistic progress. Music became more widely cultivated than ever before. This enlightened absolutism could claim as part of its enormous musical productivity the works of Mozart and Haydn. Haydn depended, either directly or indirectly, on the patronage of a court or aristocratic society of discriminating cultural and musical taste. In the works of these masters, traces of Rococo fantasy, the clarity and perfection of classic form, and the seriousness of the impending new Romanticism can be found.

During these periods, makers of musical instruments continued to refine the mechanical and acoustic properties of their instruments. Among the strings, the viol had earlier given way to the violin, but of equal importance for classic and romantic music was the movement away from the harpsichord, with its plucked strings, to the fortepiano and later, the piano, which

Colorplate 44 Jacques-Louis David, *Oath of the Horatii,* 1785. Oil on canvas, 10 × 14 ft. Louvre, Paris. (Scala/Art Resource, NY) *(See p. 50, 223)*

Colorplate 45 Constance Marie Charpentier (formerly attributed to Jacques-Louis David), *Portrait of a Young Woman, called Mlle. Charlotte du Val d' Ognes,* 1785. Oil on canvas, 63 1/2 × 50 5/8 in. The Metropolitan Museum of Art, NY. The Mr. and Mrs. Isaac D. Fletcher Collection, Bequest of Isaac D. Fletcher, 1917, 17.120.204. *(See p. 224)*

Colorplate 46 Jean Auguste Dominique Ingres, *The Odalisque with the Slave,* 1830. Canvas mounted on wood, 30 1/2 × 41 in. Courtesy of the Fogg Art Museum, Harvard University, Cambridge, Massachusetts. Bequest-Grenville L. Winthrop. *(See p. 224)*

Colorplate 47 Benjamin West, *The Death of General Wolfe*, 1771. Oil on canvas, 60 × 96 in. National Gallery of Canada, Ottawa. Transfer from the Canadian War Memorials, 1921. Gift of the 2nd Duke of Westminster, Eaton Hall, Cheshire, 1918. (See p. 225)

employed hammered strings. The inventor of the instrument we recognize today as the piano was Bartolommeo Cristofori (1655–1731). Ultimately, the piano, with its increased resonance, and possibilities for dynamic variety and lyric expression, was an important influence on chamber music, song, and the concerto.

The Classic era, in its revolt against the extravagant and diffuse expression of the Baroque, depended on two key features to achieve a near perfect unity: lyricism and regularity of form. Lyricism—melodic clarity and beauty—is that quality of music that appeals to the widest audience. It was frequently absent from the music of the Baroque. The folklike simplicity of the melodies of Haydn and Mozart supplied the lyricism that, when coupled with the formal perfection of their works, yielded some of the world's most beautiful music.

Composers after Bach found the complicated, contrapuntal textures of Baroque music too involved to express the refinement of the social scene in which they moved and worked. They resorted to the use of clearly defined and expressive melodic material easily grasped by their patrons, the cultured aristocrats. This lyricism lent fresh appeal to their art.

Eighteenth-century composers, it may be argued, were more fortunate than Neoclassic painters and decorators because they did not have models for the classic ideal they wanted to express, having no examples of how Greek and Roman music might have sounded. In music, Classicism was an abstract ideal, not a reworking of an earlier classic model as it so often was in the visual arts. However, the operatic and instrumental forms of the Italian Baroque were influential in the development of classic forms. Classicists used lyric and expressive melodies, often inventing musical forms designed to contrast one melody with a second. Harmonic and rhythmic accompaniment was always subordinate to these melodic lines.

The most striking result was the sonata. Originally, the term *sonata* meant the music was to be played, not sung. Little by little it was modified, and in the eighteenth century, composers were able for the first time to embody their ideals of formal structure in an abstract instrumental form of large proportions. While the sonata is built upon ideas from music's long association with ritual and dance, the music of the sonata stands free from these associations. The sonata as a form of musical expression must stand or fall on the handling of musical materials in the abstract medium of instrumental music.

The sonata of the Classic period is an extended composition in three or four separate movements written for a single instrument, such as the piano, or for a combination of instruments. In some cases, the sonata has taken the specific name of the group for which it was written. For example, a sonata written for four stringed instruments (two violins, viola, and cello) is called a string quartet; a sonata written for an orchestra is called a symphony; a sonata written for a solo instrument and orchestra is called a concerto.

The composer of the sonata lends unity and variety to the movements of the work by several means. Variety is achieved by contrasting tempos. The tempo of the first movement is usually fast; the second, slow; the third, stately to lively; the fourth, very fast. Harmonically, there is emphasis on unity, with the first, third, and fourth movements usually in the same key and the second in a closely related key. Another means of achieving variety is the formal organization for each of the movements. With few exceptions, the first movement is in what is known as **sonata-allegro** form. The second movement is often in **song form** (ABA) or **variation form** ($A^1A^2A^3A^4$). The third movement, the last to have been included in the sonata and the one often omitted, is a **minuet,** a stately dance in triple meter. The fourth movement is most often a **rondo,** with alternating and contrasting themes.

Of all these forms, the sonata-allegro is by far the most representative of Classicism in music and represents the inventive genius of the Classic period. The fundamental structural principal of sonata-allegro form is the presentation of two or more musical themes in a three-part plan: (1) a section called the **exposition,** in which themes are stated, (2) the **development** or elaboration of the themes, and (3) their final restatement in a **recapitulation**. The exposition, or A section, has sections in two contrasting keys, each of which contains at least one melodic theme. In Classic sonata-allegro movements, these themes were contrasting in melodic outline and affective style; a more vigorous theme was first presented in the tonic key and then a more lyrical theme appeared in a contrasting key. The B section of sonata-allegro form is called the "development" because the themes are broken into smaller bits and are subjected to various inventive musical techniques according to the ability of the composer. The third section is labeled A because the themes are repeated in the manner of the exposition, except that here the key difference is reconciled. This section (and thus the whole movement) is then brought to a close in the original key (ex. 9.1).

Example 9.1   Plan of the classic sonata-allegro form

(Th. I is first theme; trans. is transition; Th. II is second theme; Cl. Th. is closing theme (which is optional). The pattern below the line is followed when the movement is cast in a minor key.)

Exposition	‖:Th. I.	(maj.)	trans.	Th. II.	(dom.)	trans.	Cl. Th.:‖
	‖:Th. I.	(min.)	trans.	Th. II.	(rel.)	trans.	Cl. Th.:‖

Development	Varied treatment of material of the exposition in distant keys followed by a cadence leading to . . .

Recapitulation	Th. I. tonic maj.	trans.	Th. II.	tonic trans.	Cl. Th. tonic ‖
	Th. II. tonic min.	trans.	Th. I.	tonic maj.	trans. Cl. Th. tonic ‖

Sonata-allegro form gave composers the opportunity to present lyric melodies and tonal harmonies with clarity. They also could develop materials logically so listeners could more easily remember them.

In much of the music of the Classic period, the Rococo spirit shows up in the lyrical treatment of the material. The music is often light, gay, and full of rhythmic subtleties and bright melodies. The harmony is free flowing, without the prolonged dissonant tension of the Baroque. It appeals to listeners because of its purity of melodic invention and its simplicity of form. This music reflects the well-regulated society of which it was a part. With the coming Romantic movement and its dramatic struggle for freedom, music became strong, violent, and full of personal passion. The Baroque had experienced some of this in intense religious movements. The Classic period was an ebb between these two great tides; it provided time for reflective thinking, as demonstrated in the music of Haydn and Mozart.

Although vocal and instrumental music flourished together in the Classic period, instrumental genres commanded the greater attention of composers and represented the Classic spirit more vividly. The sacred-music tradition of the Baroque continued in the liturgical music of the Catholic church but virtually ceased to be of any importance in the services of the Protestant church. Choral works such as Haydn's *Creation* were influenced by Handel's oratorios but lacked the vigor of their Baroque models.

The operas of Gluck and Mozart, however, did set new standards for musical theater. Gluck honored the old themes of classical mythology in *Orfeo* (as did Monteverdi) and *Alceste,* while bringing about badly needed reforms of earlier Baroque excesses. Mozart's consummate skill and inherent dramatic sense enabled him to write masterpieces in a form similar to the Baroque models. In the Mozartian operas, the treatment of the form sets the works apart from all others and makes them the oldest and perhaps the most perfect in the standard repertoire of the modern opera house. The formal treatment is that of classic balance and restraint.

Because music is a temporal art, great amounts of time are needed for listeners to become thoroughly acquainted with major works. Therefore, the number of examples we use must be few in order to strike some reasonable balance with those of the other arts. Countless excellent works and whole areas of composition must be omitted.

Haydn

Franz Joseph Haydn (1732–1809) was in tune with the social conditions of his time. Born in a provincial village of the Austrian Empire, he turned early toward music. With the exception of a few months in which he was tutored by Nicola Porpora, a renowned Italian composer, he was chiefly self-taught, both in performance and in composition. His ability as a violinist and his early compositions for chamber ensembles caught the attention of an Austrian nobleman. In 1761, he entered the service of Prince Esterházy where he remained for twenty-eight years.

While this long period of employment in one household was not typical of most performers and composers, Haydn's long service to the aristocracy represents the normal career of the eighteenth-century musician. As one of the household servants, Haydn was responsible for composing and directing all music for the court. In line with his duties, Haydn wrote a prodigious amount of music—solo works, chamber music, orchestral music, operas, and church music of all sorts. Much of this great wealth of composition has been lost, but an enormous quantity has come down to us today. For example, there are over one hundred known symphonies of Haydn and some eighty-three string quartets.

In 1790, at the death of Prince Nicholas Esterházy, Haydn was pensioned and relieved of the duties he had so long performed at the Prince's court. A commission for the composition of a set of symphonies and their performance in London brought him to England for the first of two visits. While these last symphonies were more extended than most of the works written during his years with Esterházy, they still are excellent examples of the mature Classic sonata as written for the orchestra.

A Closer Look

Haydn, *Symphony no. 101 in D Major*

One of the best-known of Haydn's London symphonies is *Symphony no. 101 in D Major*, popularly known to concert audiences today as the *Clock Symphony*. It is scored for the mature Classic orchestra. Its instrumentation calls for the usual complement of stringed instruments; first and second violins, violas, violoncellos, and double basses. Depending on the wealth of the orchestral sponsor or patron and upon the physical conditions under which the orchestra performed, the number of string players varied from four to eight performers in each of the four groups, making a total of approximately twenty-five string players. This group formed the core of the symphony orchestra and has remained so to the present time. To this string foundation the composer added wind and percussion instruments as desired for each symphony.

In addition to the strings, the *Clock Symphony* is scored for a full complement of woodwinds—two flutes, two oboes, two clarinets, and two bassoons. With the exception of the clarinets, woodwinds were found regularly in various combinations in all the Classic symphonic works. The clarinets were the latest addition and were used only in some of Haydn's and Mozart's late works for orchestra. In this symphony, the brass choir comprises only two horns and two trumpets, used principally for sustaining harmonies, reinforcing volume, and marking rhythm. The percussion is represented by a pair of tympani, used to stress rhythm and reinforce loud and full orchestral passages.

In general, even in such a late work as the *Clock Symphony,* Haydn does little exploiting of the varied tonal qualities of the orchestral instruments. There is little dependence on instrumental color, or color for affective expression. Passages where the particular qualities of an instrument or group of instruments are exploited stand out, as in the trio of the minuet where flute and bassoon are used against a subdued string tone.

The first movement of this symphony is in sonata-allegro form. At the beginning of the movement, however, Haydn added a slow introduction to catch the attention of his London audience. It is in strong contrast to the sparkling, lively quality of the rest of the movement. The introduction is cast in a minor key, adding to its solemnity, and contrasting with the first theme of the exposition, which enters in the major key.

The first theme of the exposition, introduced in D major by the first violins, is driving and dancelike. (ex. 9.2). The first and second themes have strong similarities. They are rhythmically aggressive and employ similar instrumentation. As in the standard sonata-allegro movement, however, the second theme is in a contrasting key to the first theme.

In the development section, short motives from the second theme are traded back and forth among the strings. Then, the full orchestra subjects short bits of the first theme to musical development. In the recapitulation, a final repetition of the themes in the tonic reinforces the key. As in most sonata-allegro movements

a feeling of roundedness and completion is accomplished by the recapitulation.

The second movement, traditionally slow, is based on a three-part song form with a simple statement, contrast, and restatement. The first section of this movement, with its insistent, clocklike rhythm, suggests the name given to the symphony by Haydn's publisher. The middle section is characterized by contrapuntal devices and short melodic fragments, followed by the return of the first theme. This movement features a variety of woodwind instruments in combination.

The third movement, again in D major, is a traditional minuet and a good example of how a simple dance became a Classic form. Balance is achieved by two independent three-part forms united into a larger three-part form. The minuet and trio are essentially two independent minuets. At the conclusion of the trio, or second minuet, the first minuet is repeated, so the following scheme is realized:

Minuet (A repeated, B plus A repeated) ‖:A:‖:B A:‖
Trio   (C repeated, D plus C repeated) ‖:C:‖:D C:‖
Minuet (A-B-A, all without repetition)   A B A

The fourth movement, also in D major, is in rondo form, the essential idea of which is contrast and restatement. In this case, the thematic pattern is A-B-A-B-A. In contrast to sonata-allegro form, the rondo lacks an actual development section, and the form is based on the dominance and return of the principal theme (theme A). There are features within this movement that indicate Haydn's grounding in Baroque fugal practice. So skillful is Haydn in contrapuntal technique that one short section contains elements of both themes adroitly woven into a contrapuntal texture. Haydn's compositional style played the central role in establishing the Viennese Classic style.

Example 9.2 Symphony no. 101 in D Major, *Clock Symphony*, first movement by Franz Josef Haydn

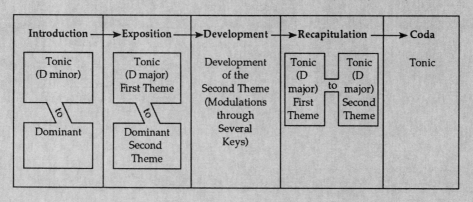

Introduction	Exposition	Development	Recapitulation	Coda
Tonic (D minor) *to* Dominant	Tonic (D major) First Theme *to* Dominant Second Theme	Development of the Second Theme (Modulations through Several Keys)	Tonic (D major) First Theme *to* Tonic (D major) Second Theme	Tonic

First Theme

Second Theme

In the Classic symphony, as represented by the *Clock Symphony*, the composer depended primarily on the logic of abstract design and formal treatment to communicate an aesthetic message. The classic ideals of restraint, balance, and formal design, as expressed in the idealized art of Greek sculpture and architecture, were expressed in the purely abstract form of this music. The composer had to invent the vehicle for the musical expression of classic ideals. The sonata and sonata-allegro form, as developed in the symphony, concerto, and chamber music, afforded the greatest opportunity for this expression.

Mozart

Mozart (1756–1791) was perhaps the most nearly perfect musical creator in the history of Western music. At four years of age he was already showing remarkable signs of musical precocity, and at ten he was composing works that ranked him with the masters of his time. Gifted as a performer on the violin and the keyboard instruments of his day, he worked in every known field of composition with equal genius. By the time of his death in 1791, at the age of thirty-five, he had left a remarkable wealth of masterpieces. Their beauty and timelessness have kept them as vital and fresh today as they were at the time of their creation.

His works so faithfully embody the Classic period's ideal of objectivity and balance that it is difficult to realize the personal tragedy that haunted most of Mozart's short life. There is frequently a note of deep personal feeling in the works of this master, but the consummate artistry of the creative genius so beguiles us that somehow we are never conscious of the person Mozart, only of his musical spirit. His works make him the personification of immortal youthfulness. Perhaps the most outstanding characteristic of his incomparable genius is his melodic inventiveness. Whatever musical material Mozart touched found expression in lyric beauty. His genius made everything sing, whether through instruments or voices.

Mozart, unlike Haydn, never successfully gained the position that would have pleased him most—that of court composer. He had only one regular appointment during his lifetime, with the Archbishop of Salzburg, and he resigned that at an early age. This left him at the mercy of a society that was passing through a revolutionary period and had made no provision for artists without aristocratic patrons. Mozart was compelled, therefore, to spread his compositional activities in many directions—from the operatic stage to the chamber music salon, from the church to the ballroom. Because his great desire for an operatic post was never realized, he was forced into many activities he might otherwise have passed by.

The *Clarinet Quintet in A Major* (ex. 9.3) reflects the personal detachment Mozart usually brought to his compositions. It was written two years

Example 9.3 Clarinet Quintet in A Major, K. 521, first movement by Wolfgang Amadeus Mozart

before his death and followed a bitterly disappointing tour of north Germany. He wrote despairingly to a friend of the dismal outlook for himself and his family, yet the work shows little but tranquil beauty in its musical expression. It is typical of the intimate mood of chamber music. The usual string quartet (two violins, viola, and cello) is joined by the clarinet, of which Mozart was especially fond.

The formal structure of the individual movements shows little departure from contemporary models. The first movement is a clearly defined sonata-allegro form. With a wealth of melodic invention, Mozart rarely repeated a melodic idea, even a short one, without some change sufficient to add a striking new beauty to the old idea. The opening measures of the first movement present the initial theme in the first violin part. These same measures are repeated after a very brief clarinet interlude. Only a single tone of the melody (note marked with * in ex 9.3) is changed in the repetition, and the harmonies are slightly altered, but a significant change in musical feeling is aroused by this inspired revision.

The forty-one symphonies of Mozart, composed from his early childhood to the last years of his life, demonstrate a continuous concern with this form. The first thirty symphonies, while typical of Mozart's individual style, follow the techniques of the Viennese and Mannheim schools and, particularly, those of Haydn. In these works, orchestration, form, and harmonic design follow the early Classic models. Of the final ten symphonies, the last three stand out as landmarks in the history of this form. *The Symphony No. 40 in G Minor,* composed in 1788, reveals Mozart as a mature orchestral composer. The Classic orchestra, though somewhat smaller than the full orchestra of the nineteenth and twentieth centuries, had now been established. While Mozart did not use all the instruments in any one of his last works, a variety of woodwinds, brass, percussion, and strings is present in the orchestras of his symphonies, concertos, and operas. This instrumental force became the orchestra of the next 150 years. Expansion of the various instrumental choirs occurred in the Romantic and Modern eras, but the Classic model was maintained.

The *Symphony in G Minor* is scored for the full complement of woodwinds (flutes, oboes, clarinets, and bassoons); but only two horns represent the brass choir, and percussion is absent. The strings are divided into the usual four parts: first and second violins, violas, and cellos, with the string basses simply doubling the cello line. This symphony is one of the most compact of Mozart's last great works. The first, second, and final movements are all in sonata-allegro form. The third movement is the traditional minuet and trio. There are no slow introductory passages to any of the movements, for each begins directly with the thematic material upon which it is built. The development sections of the three sonata-allegro movements are concise and compact, based solely on the material of the main themes, and employ contrapuntal treatment boldly.

Even opera in the Classic period shows the strong influence of restraint and formalism. This hybrid form was a child of the Baroque and assumed, during the seventeenth century, all the excesses (most prominently in extravagantly ornamented vocal solos) of an era known for its emphasis on the emotional and spectacular. Late Baroque operatic composers found it difficult to achieve or to maintain artistic value in the face of these excesses. In the last half of the eighteenth century, Gluck determinedly set about correcting the Baroque abuses of opera. Mozart had no preconceived ideas of reform, but his refined classic taste and his innate feeling for—and love of—the theater led him to write what are perhaps the happiest solutions to the problem of combining pure music and extramusical ideas. Baroque opera composers largely chose **libretti** (text of the opera) based on mythological subjects whose characters were, if not gods, at least larger than life. In contrast, Mozart's finest characters are human through and through. His most successful operas featured people whose life situations would have been familiar to his contemporaries and quite believable. Of his operas *Don Giovanni, Così fan tutte, The Abduction from the Seraglio, The Magic Flute,* and *The Marriage of Figaro* are the finest examples. The genius of Mozart enabled him to keep his operatic works in the tradition of theatrical entertainment, while composing music in the finest classical mold.

The overture and the first act from *The Marriage of Figaro* illustrate how Mozart applied Classic forms to nearly every component of traditional opera. The work is based on a comedy by the French dramatist Beaumarchais, whose convoluted story of romantic intrigue almost defies description. As the work opens, Figaro is about to marry Susanna, the Countess Almaviva's waiting maid. He realizes that Susanna is the object of the affection of his master, the Count (duets #1 and #2 of Figaro and Susanna). Figaro plans a counterplot against his master, as well as Don Basilio, one of the Count's aides, in his designs on Susanna (cavatina of Figaro). A secondary plot is introduced in the persons of Marcellina and Dr. Bartolo, who desire revenge on Figaro and Susanna (aria of Bartolo and duet of Marcellina and Susanna). Cherubino, the Count's page (a part sung by a mezzo-soprano), has a secret passion for the Countess, and becomes an eager assistant to Figaro. The page is in disfavor with the Count for flirting with Barbarina, a cousin of Susanna. He begs Susanna to intercede with the Countess (aria of Cherubino). During this scene, the Count arrives. Cherubino hides behind a large chair. The Count, not realizing that he is being overheard by Cherubino, tries to advance his designs on Susanna and is interrupted by the arrival of Basilio. Not wanting to be found alone with Susanna, he hides behind the chair. At the same time,

Cherubino slips around and curls up in this same chair, where Susanna covers him with a dress of the Countess. Basilio enters and tries to advance the Count's cause with Susanna, mentioning also Cherubino's love for the Countess. The Count, unable to contain himself any longer, jumps from his hiding place and, in a rage against Cherubino, tells how he discovered the page concealed in Barbarina's room. He illustrates his action by snatching the dress off the chair, only to find Cherubino again (trio of Susanna, Basilio, and the Count). But Cherubino has heard too much, and the Count is forced to forgive them. However, the Count succeeds in ridding himself of the page by commissioning him as a captain in the army. Figaro bids Cherubino farewell (aria of Figaro). Thus, the convoluted first act ends, building a framework of intrigue that finally resolves in the happy marriage of Figaro and Susanna at the end of the opera.

The music of the overture and the eight vocal numbers of Act One follow the same Classic design as the purely instrumental works of Mozart. The overture is a reduced sonata-allegro form lacking a development section. The vivacious spirit of the music makes a fitting prelude to the sparkling comedy that follows, although no attempt is made either through musical connection or extramusical device to connect the overture with the opera itself.

Recitatives carry the narrative of the story in the traditional operatic manner, but are of little significance in the formal structure. Mozart employed the style of *secco* (or dry) recitative, which uses only a keyboard instrument as accompaniment to the sung declamation. The arias and vocal ensembles are complete in themselves, unlike later nineteenth-century opera, which presented continuous music.

In addition to the formal beauty of each number, Mozart voiced the musical counterpart of each theatrical situation in a happy wedding of extramusical idea (text) and pure musical utterance. This is accomplished in the cavatina, in which Figaro says, "If you want to dance, Sir Count, I'll play the tune." The first part is actually a minuet. It gives way to a contrasting middle section that voices the determination of Figaro to outwit his master, only to return again to the suave minuet form in which Figaro restates his confidence in being able to make the Count bend to his desires. The whole is in three-part song form with a strikingly contrasting middle section.

Cherubino's aria, in which he voices his disturbance over the fevers of love that beset him, is another example of Mozart's ability to capture a specific mood in melody and form. In this case, he composes the musical counterpart to the breathless utterances of lovesick youth. The aria is a three-part song form with an extended **coda.** In the coda, the simple means of breaking the musical ideas into shorter and shorter repetitive patterns suggests a feeling of frustration that reveals more of the tender self-pity and hopelessness of first love than do Cherubino's actual words. The trio that follows this aria is a masterful musico-dramatic portrayal of the three characters within the formal musical structure of a free rondo form.

Figaro's final aria is another example of Mozart's use of a Classic form (in this case another rondo) to characterize the change that is to take place in the person of Cherubino. The first episode is a rhythmic march that parades before Cherubino the soft and carefree life of his past. This is done in the first section of the aria. A second episode presents the more grim and bombastic military character of the life he is soon to lead in the army. The whole is rounded out formally with the repetition of the opening section. The resulting rondo form is thus given by the scheme ABACABA.

Such is the skill of Mozart that perfection of musical form heightens the dramatic incident. He was a Classicist who, by pure musical handling of his materials, integrated music with the dramatic situation so adroitly that listeners are unaware of the genius of the artist concealing his craft. This is the goal of every operatic composer, but few have been as successful as Mozart.

Summary

In protest against the superficial elegance of the Rococo, the French Academy urged a return to classic ideals with models from the Greeks, the Romans, and the Renaissance. This calm, cool art became a symbol of the revolt against the frivolity and elegance of the French court. In place of amorous and artificial manners, the subjects of Neoclassic painters and sculptors were often patriotic or at least revealed intellectual pursuits. Lines were clear and formally balanced, in keeping with the Classic ideals of restraint and unity.

Music in the Classic style embraced the ideals of order and clarity. The finest music of the period was from Germany and Austria and stressed perfection of form, lyric melody, restrained emotional expression, and homophonic texture. Although Classic composers also composed for the opera stage, it was in instrumental music that the Classic style reached its culmination. The most important forms were sonata-allegro and the composite sonata. In these, composers embodied their ideal of unified structure in abstract instrumental forms of large proportions.

Suggested Readings

In addition to the specific sources that follow, the general readings on pages 388 and 389 contain valuable information about the topics of this chapter.

Held, Julius, and Donald Posner. *Seventeenth- and Eighteenth-Century Art.* Englewood Cliffs, NJ: Prentice-Hall, 1972.

Pauly, Reinhard G. *Music in the Classic Period.* 3d ed. Englewood Cliffs, NJ: Prentice-Hall, 1988.

Rosen, Charles. *The Classical Style: Haydn, Mozart, Beethoven.* New York: W. W. Norton, 1972.

Chapter 10

···──◉──···

The Romantic Period
(1800–1900)

Chronology

Visual Arts	Music	Historical Figures and Events
• Francisco José de Goya (1746–1828) • Marie-Guillemine Benoist (1768–1826)		
	• Ludwig van Beethoven (1770–1827)	
• J. M. W. Turner (1775–1851) • John Constable (1776–1837)		
	• Niccolò Paganini (1782–1840) • Carl Maria von Weber (1786–1826)	
• Théodore Géricault (1791–1824)	• Gioacchino Rossini (1792–1868)	
• Jean Baptiste Camille Corot (1796–1875)		
• Eugène Delacroix (1798–1863)	• Franz Schubert (1797–1828)	
	• Hector Berlioz (1803–1869) • Mikhail Ivanovitch Glinka (1804–1857) • Fanny Mendelssohn-Hensel (1805–1847)	• Napoleon becomes Emperor (1804)
		• Lewis and Clark reach the Pacific (1806)
• Honoré Daumier (1808–1879)	• Felix Mendelssohn (1809–1847)	• Abraham Lincoln (1809–1865) • Charles Darwin (1809–1882)
	• Frédéric Chopin (1810–1849) • Robert Schumann (1810–1856) • Franz Liszt (1811–1886)	
		• Charles Dickens (1812–1870) • *Fairy Tales* by the Grimm Brothers (1812) • War of 1812 between England and the United States (1812)
	• Richard Wagner (1813–1883) • Giuseppe Verdi (1813–1901)	
		• Battle of Waterloo (1815)

Visual Arts	Music	Historical Figures and Events
		• Karl Marx (1818–1883)
• Gustave Courbet (1819–1877)	• Clara Wieck Schumann (1819–1896)	• Walt Whitman (1819–1892)
		• Louis Pasteur (1822–1895)
	• Bedřich Smetana (1824–1884)	• Monroe Doctrine promulgated (1823)
		• First performance of Goethe's *Faust* (1828)
		• Beginning of antislavery movement (1831)
	• Johannes Brahms (1833–1897)	
		• Froebel founded the first kindergarten (1836)
		• Morse invents the telegraph (1837)
		• Queen Victoria's reign in England (1837–1901)
• First photograph taken by Daguerre (1838)		
	• Modest Mussorgsky (1839–1881)	
	• Piotr Ilyitch Tchaikovsky (1840–1893)	
	• Antonin Dvořák (1841–1904)	
	• Saxophone invented by Adolphe Sax (c. 1841–1842)	
• Thomas Eakins (1844–1916)	• Nikolai Rimsky-Korsakov (1844–1908)	• Friederich Nietsche (1844–1900)
		• Marx and Engels publish the *Communist Manifesto* (1848)
• Elizabeth Thompson Butler (1850–1933)		
		• Japan opened to the West (1853)
		• Thoreau's *Walden* published (1854)
	• Giacomo Puccini (1858–1924)	
		• Darwin's *Origin of Species* published (1859)
	• Hugo Wolf (1860–1903)	
	• Gustav Mahler (1860–1911)	
		• Russia emancipates the serfs (1861)
		• American Civil War (1861–1865)
	• Richard Strauss (1864–1949)	
	• Jean Sibelius (1865–1957)	• Slavery outlawed in the United States by the Thirteenth Amendment (1865)
		• Site of Troy excavated (1870)
		• Edison invents the phonograph (1877)
		• Automobile engine patented by Daimler (1883)
		• Universal adoption of solar day as unit of time (1884)
		• Koch discovers the tuberculosis germ (1885)
		• Roentgen discovers the X-ray (1895)

Pronunciation Guide

Balzac (Bahl-zahk)
Baudelaire (Boh-de-layr)
Benoist (Ben-wah)
Chopin (Shoh-pǎ)
Corot, Camille (Koh-roh, Kah-meel)
Delacroix (Duh-la-krwah)
Dvořák (Dvor´-zhahk)

Eroica (Eh-roh´-i-kah)
Géricault (Zhay-ree-koh)
Goethe (Goe-te)
Goya (Goy´-ah)
Heine (High´-ne)
Hugo (Ü-goh)
Mendelssohn (Men´-del-zohn)
Paganini (Pah-gah-nee´-nee)

Puccini (Poo-chee´-nee)
Rousseau, Jean Jacques (Roo-soh, Zhan Zhahk)
Sand (Sŏn)
Schubert (Shoo´-bert)
Schumann (Shoo´-mahn)
Verdi (Ver´-dee)

Study Objectives

1. Learn how the revolutions in Europe and America influenced the Romantic period.
2. Learn about the conflicts and contradictions expressed in the individualism and emotionalism of Romantic artists.
3. Study the added tensions in harmony, melody, and rhythm characteristic of most Romantic music.

ROMANTICISM

Romantic is the term used to designate the style of art and literature of a large part of the nineteenth century. The word itself has a vague and mysterious connotation of sentimentality. In fact, the first use of the term was to designate the chivalrous and what at that time was thought to be sentimental writings of medieval Italy, France, and Spain. These "romances" displayed a preference for moonlit forests, enchanted castles, dragons, and objects, lending mythical atmosphere to the stories.

By the turn of the nineteenth century, Romanticism had come to mean something very different. As a movement, it did not exclude inspiration from legends and myths, but its emphasis was on the search for free expression of personal feelings. Romanticism became a revolt against convention and authority in personal, religious, civil, and artistic matters. The search for individual freedom was its motivating force, even when that freedom was at the expense of formal perfection. This search distinguished the Romanticist from the Classicist, who sought perfection of form and design and preferred intellectuality to personal feelings. Romantic artists used classic design when it served their artistic purposes, but personal feelings were primary and design was secondary in importance.

Artists explored ways to express their individualism and to intensify the emotional expressiveness of their art. One means was to be realistic, both visually and musically, creating a movement now known as Realism. Another trend that became especially strong in music was Nationalism: the expression of the individuality of ethnic groups in folk music, legend, and historical events. Nationalism in music was the application of the Romantic spirit to the musical heritage of sovereign states.

The eighteenth century had been an age of reason, and all phases of intellectual activity were to a great extent dominated by the scientific attitude. People extended this attitude to government, economics, art, society, and even to religion. However, they did not take into account human personality and emotions, one of the major consequences of which was the French Revolution.

Reason had not solved all of society's problems, nor had it been enough to satisfy the human longing for spiritual consciousness. Reason may have been overcultivated at the expense of sentiment and liberty and may have directed the thinking that led to the Romantic attitude. The urge for freedom that started in the eighteenth century had finally matured to a point where it had an effect on human life. Central to the Romantic spirit was the notion that everyone was an individual with feelings and had the right to agree or disagree.

Jean Jacques Rousseau was the popularizer of the Romantic movement. His *Social Contract,* written in 1762, set forth his philosophy of individualism. He asserted that science and civilization had taken people away from nature and that natural instincts should be their guide. In order to "return to nature," the taboos and artificialities of civilization must be cast aside. Previous philosophies held that people are inherently evil and must be subordinated to the beneficial laws of society. Rousseau asserted that humans are inherently good, and they are evil only to the extent that they are influenced by evil. To be one's natural self should be the guiding principle of life. The following lines from Rousseau's *Confessions* represent the Romantic spirit as it applies to individualism: "I am different from all men I have seen. If I am not better, at least I am different." Paganini, the great Romantic virtuoso of the violin, said it another way when he said, "Paganini avoids mediocrity in everything."

The emphasis on individual feeling led to feverish activity in all phases of life. European society was experiencing a demand for a fresh interpretation of humanity and nature. There was a revival of the "cult of feeling" that became the basis for much nineteenth-century poetry, drama, art, and music. To no creative activity did intense emotion mean so much as to music and the visual arts. As might be suspected, the French Academy—the guardian of Classic aesthetic values—opposed the new Romantic movement for this very reason.

The philosophy of Romanticism gave people the freedom to give voice to their passions, fears, love, and longing. Artists could now celebrate "natural man" and break the bonds of formalism imposed by Classicism. This meant that new subjects for art were now available; all kinds of subjects and experiences previously considered inappropriate now found artistic expression. With the renewed interest in nature, landscape again became a favorite theme for painters, as it had been in the seventeenth century. Folklore and folk song were borrowed as the unaffected expression of the peasantry. The mysteries of love and death brought passion and drama back into the arts. The new ideals of freedom were dramatized both visually and tonally. Atypical experience fascinated Romantic artists because of its mystery or supernaturalism. Violence and shocking events were often used because such subjects gave more opportunity for the projection of strong emotions. Romantic subjects were almost unlimited, for any subject seen through an individual temperament could be highly charged with passion and intense emotions.

There was also a tendency to combine the arts. Painting and sculpture often depended on literary and poetic ideas and sometimes were actual illustrations of literary works, such as Delacroix's paintings of scenes from *Hamlet* and the *Divine Comedy*. In this style period, much music was written that was descriptive, some of which is known today as program music—music that recreates a story or scene in terms of melody, rhythm, and harmony. Whatever the subject or art, the listener or spectator was able to feel the whole scale of emotional sensations.

Because Romantic art expressed the individual temperaments of its creators, the personal lives of artists took on new importance. Biographical details can thus serve as keys to the motivating experiences in their art. Artists' lives came to be as romantic as their works as freedom extended to personal behavior. Their love affairs, relations with publishers and museum directors, economic problems, and eccentricities became an integral part of the record of their creative lives. The life of Beethoven is such a case. Every recorded scrap of information regarding his personal ideals, his love of nature, his illness, and his unfortunate love affairs has contributed to his Romantic persona.

Delacroix's literary associations with George Sand and Baudelaire, his friendship with Chopin, his travels, and his political friends reveal facts that influence our concepts of the Romantic qualities of his paintings. One must, however, beware of creating fantasies about the lives of artists at the expense of appreciating their works. After all, creative artists stand or fall on the quality of their works, not on the nature of their personal affairs.

There was also a change in the patronage of art. Artists were no longer attached to courts to provide entertainment in keeping with courtly customs, nor was the Church a particularly active patron of the arts. Romantic artists depended on their abilities to arouse the interest of a greater public—the common people. Composers and writers relied on performances and the sale of published works. Painters and sculptors depended on the sale of their works to the public and upon fees for exhibitions. Although they were not bound by the demands of the court or Church, they were influenced by public taste. Because there were very close economic ties with the general public, artists were very sensitive to public reaction. Fortunately, the public generally favored the new Romantic works of art and music and supported their creators.

This new patronage also brought changes in the social status of artists. They were no longer servants; instead, they held a place in society commensurate with their artistic and economic success. Haydn was a servant at the court of Prince Esterházy; but Beethoven, only a few decades later, was a free, independent, and financially successful composer. In general, successful artists were honored members of society and often reaped abundant rewards for their efforts. Not all achieved financial success early enough to be of much benefit to them, however. This was the case with Schubert, who died at the age of thirty-one, apparently on the threshold of worldly success, although artistic success came much earlier.

There are many contrasts and paradoxes within Romanticism. It is almost impossible to formulate a set of rules for evaluating the arts of the Romantic era because it reflects a spirit of revolt and individualism. However, a comparison with the arts of the Classic era provides a useful model for study. For example, the Classic tendency in music and visual arts was toward centralization and closed form; the Romantic tendency was toward action, soaring emotions and open form. The Classic was logical and intellectual, while the Romantic was irrational and often experimental. The Classic dealt in sharply defined lines and melodies, the Romantic in vague, shadowy, conjectural forms and suggestive harmonies. One can also contrast the strong, positive objectivity of Classicism to the often loosely formed subjectivity of Romanticism.

The art and music of previous epochs reflect certain elements of romanticism. The Gothic cathedral, Leonardo da Vinci, Rembrandt, Bach, and even Mozart demonstrated evidence of the Romantic spirit. Perhaps this is what gives these works and artists the expressive values that have made them timeless. It was not until the nineteenth century, however, that a true Romantic spirit dominated the arts.

PAINTING

The painters of Romanticism turned their attention to a wide range of subject matter, treating it with greater individuality than did artists of the Rococo and Neoclassic periods. Art was finally free, unfettered by previous standards of taste; it could express the personal feelings of the artist. The emotions of violence and excitement replaced the social niceties of the previous era.

Painters turned to the Dutch art of Rembrandt and Rubens for inspiration in the use of color, light, and shade in depicting strong emotions.

Géricault

Colorplate 48 follows p. 258.

Théodore Géricault (1791–1824) was one of the first painters of the French Romantic movement. *The Raft of the Medusa* (colorplate 48) was inspired by a newspaper account of the sinking of the ship *Medusa* off the coast of West Africa. After many days on a raft in the storm-tossed ocean, only a handful of survivors reached safety. In an effort to recreate the emotions of the tragedy, Géricault dramatized in his imagination the scenes aboard the raft. It was reported that he even hired the survivors as models and made studies of corpses in order to render the victims accurately. He endeavored to express the despair, the hunger and thirst, and the struggle for life aboard the raft. He tried to engulf the observer in the whole range of emotions in the disaster. Through color, twisting diagonal lines, and the emotional postures and gestures of the participants, he made this painting a profound experience for viewers. He chose a supremely appropriate Romantic subject—humans against the sea—in which the odds against the human spirit seem overwhelmingly unfavorable.

Delacroix

Colorplate 49 follows p. 258.

Eugène Delacroix (1798–1863) became the leader of the Romantic movement in painting. In his famous work *Liberty Leading the People* (colorplate 49), Delacroix recaptured the spirit of the Romantic revolution. He symbolized the struggle for freedom against the forces of tyranny by portraying an allegorical goddess, Liberty, leading the people of France over the barricades. The event that suggested this work was the July Revolution of 1830 and not the Revolution of 1789, as is popularly supposed. Some Romantic aspects of the work are immediately apparent. This is more than a group of people engaged in a scene of violent action. The goddess, tall and placed in a central position, dominates the scene. She is not a static figure but is going forward, raising the tricolor of France high above everything else. She symbolizes the energy and action necessary to gain freedom and retain it. The figures around her represent the various classes of people that make up a nation. They, too, under the leadership of the ideal, are forging ahead, trampling over the fallen bodies of their enemies and their own comrades.

The elements are arranged in much the same manner as was typical in the Baroque. While the goddess is the central figure, spatial awareness is enhanced by the diffused lines and forms melting into one another. Patches of color and light contrast with the predominant somber hues of the painting. The repeated and varied human forms are important features of its design.

Delacroix himself was regarded as a revolutionary. As an artist, he was described as a barbarian and a savage with a paintbrush. He never thought of himself, however, as a leader of the new movement or as a particularly savage Romanticist. He merely desired to express his unfettered feelings about subjects and scenes that attracted him. He came from a wealthy family and was a well-read, sensitive, and intelligent person. He numbered among his friends such literary figures as Balzac, Victor Hugo, and George Sand. He was also a friend of the composer Chopin. Undoubtedly, these connections with fellow Romanticists helped implant the elements of Romanticism more deeply into his personality. The hostility of the French Academy did not deter him; it only confirmed his own ideals.

The Romantic artists' attraction to literary works for inspiration is shown in Delacroix's illustrations for Dante's *Divine Comedy*. *Dante and Virgil in Hell* (colorplate 50) depicts the two poets being ferried through a murky and bloody hell, with anguished and tortured souls clinging to the boat. Delacroix shocked viewers with a painting of horror; even the two poets are appalled by the scene before them. The shadowy background with its faint spot of light gives a sense of the magnitude of hell. There is action, both physical and emotional: the raised hand, the twisting torsos, the waves, and the flowing robes all suggest a feeling of motion. The agony expressed in the faces provides a powerful emotional climax. The artist used masses without line drawing to mold the subject. Theatrical lighting calls attention to the people clinging to the boat. Delacroix expressed human feelings; the forms are only a means to that end. The whole canvas intensifies the horror of the story that Dante related.

Colorplate 50 follows p. 258.

Benoist

The French portrait painter Marie-Guillemine Benoist (1768–1826) received tutelage first under Lebrun and later under the Neoclassic painter Jacques-Louis David. Among the notable persons she painted was Napoleon Bonaparte. Her *Portrait of a Negress* (colorplate 51) was painted in the middle of her career. The subject is an exotic figure with a regal bearing, confidently looking out from the canvas. Several large fields of color create the form: the brown body, the white cloth of her costume with the shadows created by draping, the blue cloth over the chair, and the simple ecru background. The partially concealed crimson belt provides contrast in this serene portrait.

Colorplate 51 follows p. 258.

Goya

The Romantic movement was not confined to any particular country, but each nation developed its special expression of Romantic feeling and its own artists who portrayed that feeling. Francisco Goya (1746–1828) was one of the great Spanish individualistic painters. He was an artist of extraordinary imaginative and technical powers with the courage to paint whatever his feelings dictated. He painted a wide range of subjects, from meticulous portraits to scenes of violence and horror. As a Romanticist, Goya felt art should do more than entertain or decorate. He was convinced that painting must focus attention on moral issues. He made a set of prints called *Disasters of War* in which he suggested, with unbelievable literalness, the rape, mutilation, and desecration that took place during the French invasion of Spain in 1808. This series of prints remains one of the greatest artistic comments on the tragedy of war. In his works, Goya appealed to the emotions through the power of suggestion. He was not a physical realist, but through his subjective treatment Goya not only supplied the details of action but also intensified the impact of the subject upon the viewer's feelings.

Colorplate 52 follows p. 258.

In *The Third of May* (colorplate 52) Goya portrayed the drama of terror, blood, and violence, and moralized on the event at the same time. The subject is the execution of Spanish loyalists by the French. It is said that the artist, who witnessed the terrible event, went by night to sketch the pile of bloody corpses in preparation for his painting. Goya used great economy of line and color to suggest the impact of his message of horror. The lighting adds a feeling of terror to the scene as the lantern illuminates the shirt of the central victim. The dim outline of the building and the sloping contour of the hill in the background impart a sense of space. There is little detailed line in either the soldiers or their victims. They are huddled masses rather than realistic bodies. The upraised arms of the central victim, highlighted in white, symbolize the sacrifice of life for liberty. There is action in the line of soldiers with pointed rifles and in the crowd that turns toward the executioners in resignation. Goya used color and mass to intensify the drama of death for liberty.

Turner

This influential English painter of landscapes and seascapes worked in both oils and watercolors. Whereas the Dutch painters of seascapes rendered works that were almost photographic in their realism, J. M. W. Turner (1775–1851) employed loose brushstrokes, an almost violent application of paint, and a high degree of abstraction to create works that anticipated the French Impressionists by several decades. Although most of these predated by some fifty years the painting by Monet of *Rouen Cathedral, West Facade* (colorplate 63), both artists used rapid brush techniques to create the spirit of the object rather than a mere photographic likeness.

Colorplate 63 follows p. 290.

A Closer Look

Turner, *Rain, Steam, and Speed: The Great Western Railway*

The Train

A green eye—and a red—in the dark.
Thunder—smoke—and a spark.
It is there—it is here—flashed by.
Whither will the wild thing fly?
It is rushing, tearing thro' the night,
Rending her gloom in its flight.
It shatters her silence with shrieks.
What is it the wild thing seeks?
Alas! for it hurries away
Them that are fain to stay.
Hurrah! for it carries home
Lovers and friends that roam.
Where are you, Time and Space?
The world is a little place,
Your reign is over and done,
You are one.

This poem, written in 1895 by Mary Coleridge, a distant relative of the more famous English poet Samuel Taylor Coleridge, reflects something of the pervasive preoccupation with the vehicular speed made possible in the nineteenth century by the Industrial Revolution. The poem, which concludes with a poetic intuition of some of the space-time theories of Albert Einstein, was set to music for voices by Charles Villiers Stanford as his Opus 119, No. 4. Charles Dickens also wrote picturesquely, one might even say extravagantly, about trains and their effect on society in *Dombey and Son*. Similarly, many composers of the nineteenth century assigned picturesque titles about trains to their small orchestral works: Johann Strauss Sr., *Railway Delight Waltz*, Op. 89; Eduard Strauss, *With Steam—Fast Polka*, Op. 70; and Hans Christian Lumbye, *Copenhagen Steam Railway Galop.*

The forward-looking English painter, Joseph Mallord William Turner, must have been considering the train in thoughts similar to those of Mary Coleridge when he painted *Rain, Steam, and Speed: The Great Western Railway* in 1844 (colorplate 53, following p. 258). In that year, the average speed

on the Great Western was thirty-three miles per hour, and the famous English engineer Brunel was predicting speeds of up to one hundred miles per hour. The recently completed railway brought England's west country much closer to London, but at great societal cost.

The subject matter of this painting is not simply the train but both the physical world (rain and steam) and the passage of time—both major concerns of the nineteenth century. While the rain in the title is not very apparent on the canvas, the steam and speed are convincingly represented. The steam engine bursts toward the foreground of the painting on a diagonal from left to right. The steam it produces obscures the distant landscape in the center of the canvas. The sense of speed is achieved by the bold application of linear as well as aerial perspective to the bridge on which the train travels, as well as to the train itself. The angle at which a second bridge in the left of the picture intersects the railway bridge also communicates a sense of speed. True, it is out of our vision, obscured by the rain or steam, but our visual imagination completes the angle.

A more difficult aspect of speed is less easily discovered. In the lower right corner, there is a hare racing over the bridge, ahead of the train. (While the painting is not large, reproductions are sufficiently reduced to make this less apparent.) This naturally swift animal is pitting its speed against that of the mechanical monster. In a way, this is an almost archetypical representation of nature being overtaken or subdued by human engineering. To further heighten the sense of speed, Turner included on the extreme right of the picture a farmer with two horses plowing a field, and a lazy, drifting boat on the river to the left. Our familiarity with the slow pace of these activities makes obvious the contrasting speed of the train. A contemporary critic said of this painting, "There comes a train down upon you, really moving at the rate of fifty miles an hour, and that the reader had best make haste to see, lest it should dash out of the picture . . . The rain . . . is composed of dabs of dirty putty slapped on to the canvas with a trowel: the sunshine scintillates out of very thick, smeary clumps of chrome yellow." There were other critics less enthralled by Turner's loose technique and creative use of color; they did not hesitate to fault his work.

The atmosphere of the painting suggests a visual experience that is no longer precisely replicable. When people were caught in the steam created by a passing locomotive, the visual results were similar to being caught in a temporary fog. This effect was achieved by the artist in his choice of colors and the heavy, generous application of pigment to the canvas. Line has become secondary, as both texture and color have been used to create the atmosphere of the painting. Therefore, the objects in the painting are loosely defined. Turner's technique allowed him to capture successfully the speed and power of the Great Western Railway.

···—◆◎◆—···

Corot

One of the characteristics of Romantic painting was the return of the landscape as a favored theme. Jean Baptiste Camille Corot (1796–1875) was one of the prominent and prolific painters of Romantic pastoral scenes. There is a sentimental quality about his landscapes, for the mood is always gentle. His painted fields and trees seem immersed in mist, and their forms are dissolved in soft light, color, and lines. His *A View Near Volterra* (colorplate 54) shows Corot's personal interpretation of nature. It displays a Romantic feeling for light, space, and color. A strong sense of structure is shown in the solid mass of rocks and in the figures of horse and rider. Sentiment, however, overtakes structure to create an escape from the stuffiness and turmoil of the city in favor of the quiet peace of a shepherd's world.

Colorplate 54 follows p. 258.

ARCHITECTURE

There was no one style to distinguish architecture as Romantic. It could, perhaps, be called revivalist architecture because most architecture created during the nineteenth century consisted of revivals of past styles, such as the Gothic, Renaissance, and Baroque. The Gothic revival is very apparent in the Neo-Gothic style of the Houses of Parliament in London (fig. 10.1), designed by Charles Barry and A. Welby Pugin and built during the period 1840–1860. There is a symmetry about the main structure that encloses the governmental spaces. The Gothic influence is evident in the various towers that give the building an irregular appearance.

Figure 10.1 Charles Barry and A. W. N. Pugin, Houses of Parliament, 1840–60. London. (Department of the Environment, London)

Another example of revivalist architecture is the Paris Opera (fig. 10.2), designed by Jean-Louis-Charles Garnier and built in the years 1861–1874. It is often referred to as a Neo-Baroque structure, partly because of the multiplicity of sculpture and ornaments both outside and within. The opulence of the building reflects the tastes of the newly rich and powerful captains of the Industrial Revolution.

There were a few structures that reflected the technological developments of the Industrial Revolution in their use of cast iron and glass. One of the most famous of these was the Crystal Palace in London, built in 1851 for the Great Exhibition of the Works of Industry of all Nations. Unfortunately, it was destroyed by fire in 1937. Another technological tour de force is the Eiffel Tower in Paris, constructed in 1889.

MUSIC

In the Romantic period, music was an effective medium for personal artistic expression. Although music deals with only tones in the abstract, listeners translate these sounds into specific personal feelings and experiences. In the nineteenth century, with its emphasis on individual freedom, music gave artists the greatest opportunity of all the arts to exercise such freedom.

Figure 10.2   Jean-Louis-Charles Garnier, Paris Opera, 1861–74. Paris. (Bulloz, Paris)

There is a great quantity of sculpture, painting, and architecture of the Romantic period that is exaggerated, irrational, or sentimental. This is partly because of a desire to appeal to the individual's emotional response. It is possible for music, however, to sustain a feeling of intensity that no visual art can without becoming exaggerated or irrational. In fact, we often approve of things in music that would be intolerable in literature or the visual arts. It is thus possible for music to be the most Romantic of all the arts.

In earlier periods, the social and professional positions of such composers as Palestrina, Bach, and Haydn colored their creative efforts. With the Romantic struggle for freedom came the emancipation of composers, as well as other artists, from the system of Church or aristocratic patronage. From this period on, composers responded either to their public or to their own impulses. A number of works in the nineteenth century were commissioned by a small, elite, and discriminating musical aristocracy. By and large, however, most works were written either for public performance or to satisfy the individual composer's intense feeling for expression.

Because Romantic composers wrote works that appealed to the general musical public, they achieved a degree of material success. Because they wrote to satisfy their personal desires and express their personal musical thoughts, they could experiment with new materials and forms. They should not have been surprised, however, if such a path led to popular neglect, if not to outright antagonism or obscurity, during their lifetimes.

Democratic society became the patron whose acceptance, or at least tolerance, the artist of the nineteenth century had to win. Failing this, composers had to write for a continually shrinking circle of admirers who were incapable of sustaining them economically. This condition became more aggravated throughout the nineteenth and twentieth centuries.

As in the field of the visual arts, it is impossible to formulate a set of rules that describes Romantic music. However, all Romantic music is based on the premise that musical tension is necessary to achieve a corresponding intensification of emotional response. Romantic music, therefore, concentrated on achieving this tension. This meant that the exploitation of sonorities and dynamics and the exploration of sheer masses of sound were of deep concern to the composer. Tone color—the use of instruments in combination, and the use of individual instrumental qualities, until then unexplored—was also a focus. Romantic composers were interested in all the means for creating harmonic tension. The further exploitation of the duality of key, so neatly couched in the sonata-allegro form of the Classic period, was developed into a plethora of keys. This is reflected in the rich harmonic texture of Romantic music with its chromaticism and dissonance. With this increased richness of harmony came an increased richness of melodic line. Melodies were intensified by choice of tone color and often seemed inseparable from their initial association with a particular instrument or voice. Schubert's song *Erlkönig* is unthinkable for a soprano voice, and a performance of the English horn solo from the Largo movement of Dvořák's *New World Symphony* would miss the musical pathos of the original if played on any other instrument.

Nineteenth-century composers devised no new formal musical structures. However, the breaking-up of thematic ideas into motives and the detailed development of themes and motives indicates a concern with musical tension. Beethoven and Wagner are particularly noteworthy in this respect.

Apart from these common concerns, it is difficult to generalize about musical Romanticism. There were Romantic idealists and Romantic realists. The idealists insisted that music could exist for its own sake; the realists insisted that music must tell a story that could be verbalized or visualized. There were Romanticists who excelled in spectacular virtuosity, dazzling listeners with their brilliant technique. There were also those who emphasized intimacy in chamber music and solo songs as the best expression of personalized feelings. Others combined literature and landscape with music in the invention of the symphonic poem.

There were three favorite media of expression for Romantic composers—the orchestra, the piano, and the human voice. Most composers wrote for all three. The orchestra became the favorite large ensemble of the century. It had those qualities of size, color, and brilliance that accomodated Romantic expression. It could present musical sounds from a whisper to an overpowering thunder and, therefore, lent itself well to the descriptive desires of certain composers. The piano, with its newly developed dynamic range, offered many of the same characteristics, and could be played by one person. Consequently, the piano became almost a musical symbol of the Romantic spirit of freedom and individualism. The voice is also a personalized instrument, and it combined with the literary element of Romanticism to give an added intensity to the poetic text. Of course, other instruments were also used during this period, particularly those (such as the violin) that lent themselves to virtuoso exploitation.

Beethoven

While arguments can be justifiably made for placing Beethoven in the Classic period or between the Classic and the Romantic, it is clear from an analysis of his music that his compositions reveal characteristics generally recognized as Romantic. Ludwig van Beethoven (1770–1827), born in Bonn, Germany, exhibited strong musical gifts as a young boy. He suffered severely from a father who hoped to exploit his son's talents by launching him on a musical career. His father, an incompetent manager, failed in this attempt. Despite his father's role of taskmaster, Beethoven developed a deep love for music and acquired great skill as a pianist, organist, and violinist. Because of his musical skill, he was employed as a court musician in his early teens and was the sole family support until his final departure from Bonn in 1792. From then on, his residence in Vienna was interrupted only in the early years by concert tours of Germany and Austria. The last twenty years of his life were spent within the city and suburbs of the Austrian capital.

Although he began to devote himself to composition before his twentieth birthday, he was known in Vienna primarily as a magnificent concert pianist. Beethoven's creative life falls conveniently into three periods. Roughly speaking, the "Early" period ends about 1802. This was the period of the pianist-composer, and the works written during this time are substantially in the Classic style of Mozart and Haydn. The composition of the Third Symphony in the years 1802–1804 ushered in the "Middle" period, which was truly Romantic in character. Beethoven cast Classic restraint aside whenever intensity of expression demanded. Increasing deafness forced Beethoven to abandon his concert career in favor of composition. What performance could have accomplished in personal expression had to find voice through writing, and his works of the "Late" period (1815–1827) became the vehicle for individualized personal expression.

A Closer Look

Beethoven, *Symphony no. 3 in E-flat Major*

The *Symphony no. 3 in E-flat Major,* op. 55 (*Eroica*) is based on the Classic precepts of Haydn and Mozart, but it goes far beyond the Classic style in its expressive quality. Countless pages have been written concerning the meaning of this work. Much has been made of the destruction by Beethoven of the dedication to Napoleon Bonaparte when he heard of the latter's assumption of the crown. The title given to this work, *Eroica,* was undoubtedly prompted by the desire to dedicate a work to Napoleon, whom the composer had admired purely as a liberator. Disgust with Napoleon's act of crowning himself Emperor prompted Beethoven to reword his dedication, but the title remained as a concession to the promise that remained unfulfilled. It is extremely doubtful if Beethoven ever had anything more in mind than this when he wrote the symphony. The *Eroica Symphony* is a purely musical expression of the spirit of Romanticism as surely as is Delacroix's *Liberty Leading the People.*

The work itself is in the tradition of Classic models. It has the traditional four movements, the first of which is in a greatly expanded sonata-allegro form. Particularly noteworthy are the musical materials of both the first and second theme of the first movement. These are not melodies as those found in the themes of the Haydn symphony or the Mozart quintet discussed earlier but are themes made up of melodic fragments that lend themselves, in a most spectacular way, to development. The first theme group of Beethoven's Symphony no. 3 is more a collection of melodic and rhythmic motives than a complete melody. Its first appearance combines the cellos and violas (ex. 10.1). From these motives, Beethoven constructed the entire first section of the exposition in the tonic key.

There are not just two contrasting themes but two groups of thematic motives, none of which can be lifted from context (as can a melody from Haydn or Mozart) and still remain a complete entity. Moreover,

Example 10.1 Ludwig van Beethoven (First theme group, partial score) Symphony no. 3 in E-flat Major, *Eroica*

these are themes in a purely instrumental idiom. The second theme group is in the key of B-flat, the dominant of E-flat, in keeping with tradition. Beethoven felt no great need of harmonic deviation from tradition—as yet. He relied on striking dynamic contrasts and violent accentuations of regularly weak rhythmic beats to secure tension. This is particularly noticeable in the extraordinarily long development section. This section was not simply an excursion away from and then back to the tonic key to restate the first theme in its original form. Rather, it was used to exploit the composer's ingenuity and imagination. After the lengthy and violent development, the thematic material is restated, and Beethoven added to it a very lengthy musical summary in the coda. No longer content to close the restatement with a climactic cadence, Beethoven reiterated his ideas in the coda in ever new guises, as if his inventive genius knew no limits.

The second movement, in the relative key of C minor, is a funeral march with the distinctive rhythmic pattern associated with funeral music. It does not rely on dynamic contrasts alone but exploits tone color and melody. The opening melody, for example, is first played in the lower register of the violins and then is given to the oboe, with its mournful timbre. The form is loosely that of a march and trio. The trio in this instance is in the contrasting key of C major, which accentuates the somberness of the C minor on its return. The conclusion of this movement produces a complete disintegration of the thematic material. Repose is finally achieved only by the gradual dissolution of the main theme.

The third movement is one of the most striking examples of Romantic transformation: from an originally simple dance form into a vehicle for violent and intense action. The basic form of the movement is the minuet, but its speed, length, and entire melodic character belie its origin. Beethoven employed the term *scherzo* (Italian for "joke") to characterize the spirit of the movement. This significant alteration of the character of the third movement and its consequent renaming was continued by later Romantic symphonists. The trio, with its main theme given to three horns, shows Beethoven's interest in tone color as a means of Romantic expression.

The fourth movement is a brilliant set of variations freely composed on a theme the composer had used in three previous works. After an opening flourish of strings and full orchestra, the theme is presented in the bass. The subsequent variations exhibit the remarkable skill with which Beethoven adds contrasting material. Again, dynamic contrast, rhythmic complexity, and brilliance of thematic invention all unite in a blaze of spectacular musical expressiveness.

···━◉◖━···

While Beethoven's expressiveness is revealed best in his orchestral works, it is equally present in other genres as well. The poignant relationships in his opera *Fidelio* are a case in point, as is the *Piano Sonata no. 23,* op. 57. Because of this sonata's character, it is commonly known as the *Appassionata*. The terseness of the thematic material of the first movement and its driving, motoric energy are as evident in this sonata as in the *Symphony no. 3*. This sonata exhibits certain compositional devices that Beethoven applied to the piano to make this instrument an expressive vehicle for his music. The extended pitch range of the first twenty-five measures of the first movement, the great use of the low register of the instrument, the heavy thick chords placed low in the bass, the wide skips between consecutive motive groups, the abrupt dynamic changes, the sweeping chordal passages—these pianistic compositional devices displayed Beethoven's complete command of the instrument. In this sonata, and in many others as well, Beethoven made the piano a more expressive instrument than it had been before, setting the stage for its Romantic exploitation and making the piano second in importance only to the orchestra as a musical means of personal expression.

The *String Quartet no. 16,* op. 135 was written only a year before his death. Shorter, and in some respects less radical in deviation from Classical form than the other quartets of this period, it is nevertheless an example of the intensely personal, late style of the composer. Beethoven brought to the limited timbral palette of the string quartet a magnificent range of expressive qualities, from the wild, incessant rhythm and leaping melody of the trio of the second movement to the tender, exquisite melodic line of the third movement. The continuous changes of rhythm and key are typical of Beethoven's late compositions. He seemed to be searching for all means at his disposal to give full scope to his inventive genius. No Romantic composer to follow Beethoven wrote for the string quartet in such an expressive manner. Most attempts by later Romanticists resulted either in weak imitations of Beethoven or in works that failed to realize the potential of the medium.

Schubert

Another Romanticist and a contemporary of Beethoven was Franz Schubert (1797–1828). He was the only great Viennese composer who could claim that city as his birthplace. Schubert's life illustrates a certain kind of bohemianism often associated with the age of Romanticism. He was never in the employ of any institution or aristocratic patron. Moreover, he did not even have the security of benevolent patronage that Beethoven enjoyed. He eked out a slim existence as a private teacher, sold a few compositions to publishers, and had a few commissions for works. Throughout his life he was dogged by poverty, so most of his compositions could be ascribed to "art for art's sake." This is particularly true for his more than six hundred *Lieder* or art songs. These were not written on commission; few of them were published during his life, and most were largely unknown until years after his death. While his chamber, piano, and orchestral works are significant contributions to Romantic music, Schubert's art songs illustrate his most important contribution to the field of Romantic musical expression.

Individual solo songs were not an invention of the Romantic era. However, the great wealth of nineteenth-century German lyric poetry, with its tendency toward the sentimental, stimulated the Romantic trend toward combining music with extramusical ideas. This contributed to a great interest in art-song settings through the entire nineteenth and even into the twentieth century. Similarly, the Romantic love for the intimate and small form encouraged this medium of composition. Two distinct forms of the art song were used by Schubert. The first, known as the strophic song, is illustrated by Schubert's *Heidenröslein*. In this form, the strophes or stanzas of the poem are each set to the same melody. Actually, Schubert's song—though entirely original with him—is so much in the folk tradition that it is often thought to be a German folk song. The poem, by Goethe, is simple and whimsically philosophical. Schubert matches its simplicity with a charming, straightforward melody and an accompaniment that, while written for the piano, might be realized on any chordal instrument, such as the guitar or lute.

A Closer Look

Schubert, *Erlkönig*

In contrast to *Heidenröslein*, Schubert's *Erlkönig* is a powerful, dramatic ballad on a poem by one of Germany's greatest authors, Johann Wolfgang von Goethe. The poem consists of eight four-line stanzas, in each of which the first and second pairs of lines rhyme. In this *Lied*, a narrator introduces the story of an anxious father riding through the night carrying his sick son in his arms. As the father journeys through the dark forest, the erlking, the spector of death, entreats the child to come to him.

N: Narrator F: Father; C: Child, E: Erlking

1. N: Wer reitet so spät durch Nacht un Wind?
   Es ist der Vater mit seinem Kind;
   Er hat den Knaben wohl in dem Arm,
   Er fasst ihn sicher, er hält ihn warm.

   Who rides so late through the night and the wind?
   It is the father with his child.
   He holds the boy in his arm,
   He holds him safe, he keeps him warm.

2. F: 'Mein Sohn, was birgst du so bang dein Gesicht?'
   C: 'Siehst, Vater, du den Erlkönig nicht?
   Den Erlenkönig mit Kron und Schweif?'
   F: 'Mein Sohn, es ist ein Nebelstreif.'

   "My son, why do you hide your face so anxiously?"
   "Don't you see there, Father, the erlking?
   The erlking with crown and tail?"
   "My son, it is only a wisp of mist."

3. E: 'Du liebes Kind, komm, geh mit mir!
   Gar schöne Spiele ich mit dir;
   Manch bunte Blumen sind an dem Strand,
   Meine Mutter hat manch gülden Gewand.'

   "You dear child, come away with me!
   I will play wonderful games with you.
   Many colorful flowers grow by the shore:
   my mother has many golden robes."

4. C: 'Mein Vater, mein Vater, und hörest du nicht?
   Was Erlenkönig mir leise verspricht?'
   F: 'Sei ruhig, bleibe ruhig, mein Kind:
   In dürren Blättern säuselt der Wind.'

   "My father, my father, don't you hear?
   what the erlking is saying softly to me?"
   "Be calm, be calm, my child,
   the wind is rustling in the trees."

5. E: 'Willst, feiner Knabe, du mit mir gehn?
   Meine Töchter sollen dich warten schön;
   Meine Töchter führen den nächtlichen Reihn
   Und wiegen und tanzen und singen dich ein.'

   "Will you, my fine lad, go with me?
   My daughters will take special care of you.
   They will lead the nightly dance
   and rock you, dance with you and sing you to sleep."

6. C: 'Mein Vater, mein Vater, und siehst du nicht dort
   Erlkönigs Töchter am düstern Ort?'
   F: 'Mein Sohn, mein Sohn, ich seh es genau:
   Es scheinen die alten Weiden so grau.'

   "My father, don't you see there

   the erlking's daughter in the dark place?"
   "My son, I see it clearly;
   It is the gray gleam of the willows."

Colorplate 48 Théodore Géricault, *The Raft of the Medusa*, 1818–1819. Oil on canvas, 16 ft. × 23 ft. 6 in. Louvre, Paris. (Giraudon/Art Resource, NY) (See p. 246, 272)

Colorplate 49 Eugène Delacroix, *Liberty Leading the People*, 1831. Oil on canvas, 8 ft. 6 3/8 in. × 10 ft. 8 in. Louvre, Paris. (Giraudon/Art Resource, NY) *(See p. 10, 246)*

Colorplate 50   Eugène Delacroix, *Dante and Virgil in Hell,* 1822. Oil on canvas, 6 ft. 1 in. × 7 ft. 10 in. Louvre, Paris. (Giraudon/Art Resource, NY) *(See p. 247)*

Colorplate 51 Marie-Guillemine Benoist, *Portrait of a Negress,* 1800. Oil on canvas, 31 5/8 × 25 5/8 in. Louvre, Paris. (Agence Photographique de la Réunion des Musées Nationaux, Paris) *(See p. 247)*

Colorplate 52 Francisco Goya, *The Third of May, 1814.* Oil on canvas, 8 ft. 8 3/4 in. × 11 ft. 4 in. Prado, Madrid. (Scala/Art Resource, NY) *(See p. 11, 248)*

Colorplate 53 J. M. W. Turner, *Rain, Steam, and Speed: The Great Western Railway*, 1844. Oil on canvas, 36 × 48 in. National Gallery of Art, London. (See p. 249)

7. E: 'Ich liebe dich, mich reizt deine schöne
Gestalt;
Und bist du nicht willig, so brauch ich Gewalt.'

C: 'Mein Vater, mein Vater, jetzt fasst er mich an!
Erlkönig hat mir ein Leids getan!'

8. N: Dem Vater drauset's, er reitet geschwind
Er hält in Armen das ächzende Kind,
Erreicht den Hof mit Müh und Not;
In seinen Armen das Kind war tot.

"I love you, your beauty excites me,

and if you don't come willingly, I shall force you."
"My father, now he is seizing hold of me!
The erlking has hurt me."

The father is consumed with fear, he rides swiftly,
he holds the moaning child in his arms;
He reaches the manor in much distress—
In his arms, the child was dead.

This poem was set to music by over fifty composers, including a number of Goethe's contemporaries, and Schubert's setting was, surprisingly, by no means Goethe's favorite. While some would see a connection with German mythology in this frightening poem, there is no *Erlkönig* in any mythology. There may be a connection between the Danish ElfKing and the *Erlkönig*, although that would require a mistranslation of the Danish word, *Ellekonge*, and a complete mutation of the character. Schubert found that the dramatic poem demanded more particularized treatment than the strophic repetition of other songs. A single rhythmic and melodic statement could not adequately convey the many emotions contained in its eight stanzas. Schubert wanted distinct musical characterizations for the narrator and the three persons involved in the story, and simple repetition would have made that quite impossible. There are repetitions of melodic and rhythmic gestures, to be sure, but they accompany the reappearance of the participating characters or the recurring expressions of profound emotion.

Underlying the vocal setting is a piano part that, in true Romantic art-song fashion, is an essential part of the song's musical expression. The piano part in *Erlkönig* suggests, with both rhythmic and melodic motives, a ceaseless and driving quality that sets up musical tension, creating a powerful metaphor for the dramatic poem. (In example 10.2, the letters *a* through *e* mark the various piano textures.) Each of the four characters—narrator, father, son, and erlking—is distinguished musically, although represented by a single singer. Together these elements lend remarkable unity to the song.

Formally, the piece is quite clear, yet it would be incorrect to call it obvious. Its 149 measures appear to fall into three large sections (ex. 10.2). The first embraces stanzas 1 and 2; the second, stanzas 3 through 6; and the third, stanzas 7 and 8. The order in which each character speaks was dictated by the poet, but Schubert's use of that order makes a strong musical structure.

In the long piano introduction, the agitation of the drama and the galloping horse is suggested by rapid triplet note movement in the key of G minor. The right hand, here and at frequent intervals throughout much of the song, plays reiterated octaves against a memorable rhythmic-melodic gesture in the left hand:

The narrator sets the scene in stanza 1, and is not heard again until the conclusion of the *Lied* in stanza 8. In stanzas two through seven, the essential action of the drama takes place. Schubert has chosen key, range, tessitura (the range of most of the notes), dynamics, and rhythmic texture to convey the feelings of each character. The erlking alone has music that centers in the major mode. There are moments of major tonality in the music of the father during moments of encouragement for his dying son, but much of the father-son dialogue is in the minor mode. Bearing in mind that this was to be sung by one person, Schubert created distinct vocal ranges for each of the characters. The father has the lowest

Example 10.2 Graphic analysis of *Erlkönig* Franz Schubert.

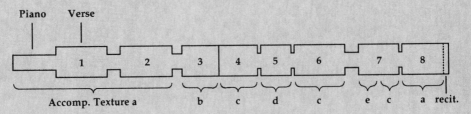

—Piano Introduction

Verse 1: Narrator sets the stage for the story.

    (Four measure piano interlude)

Verse 2: Father questions the son's fears. Son sees the Erlking.

    (Three measure piano interlude)

Verse 3: Erlking invites the child to join him in play.

    (No interlude)

Verse 4: The son hallucinates and the father comforts him.

    (One measure piano interlude)

Verse 5: Erlking promises his daughters as nannies.

    (One measure piano interlude)

Verse 6: Son becomes more hysterical and sees the Erlking's
daughters. The father quietly reassures him.

Verse 7: Erlking declares his determination to have the child.
The son screams, "My father, he now is seizing hold of me!"

    (One measure piano interlude)

Verse 8: Narrator describes the father's arrival at home only to
find his son is dead.

260

range, and the narrator and erlking share an almost identical range. The child is assigned a range of one octave, and is the highest of the group. Indications of dynamics are placed exclusively in the piano score, and range from *ppp* to *fff*. Such a wide range of dynamics was exceptional for the time. The import of the text and the dynamic indications in the keyboard provide the singer with clues for appropriate performance.

The first entry of the erlking (stanza 3) is set to a jaunty triplet accompaniment that creates an entirely different feeling than what precedes it. His second entry (stanza 5) presents another variant, emphasizing arpeggiation in the right hand. Upon the third and final entrance of the erlking (first half of stanza 7), the rhythmic material is closely akin to that of the child. In music clearly deriving from the opening, the narrator moves toward the tragic conclusion, but with a musical twist. As if only a complete break with the old texture would suffice to communicate the fateful truth, the narrator in a dramatic three-measure recitative declares, "In his arms, the child was dead."

There is a certain theatricality about *Erlkönig*. Some of this must be projected through the use of vocal coloring. This is the contribution of the singer in performance and is not indicated in any way in the score. For this the singer must rely on intuition. In keeping with some theatrical traditions, the distribution of the roles appeared to be of some concern to the composer. The father, who is unable to rescue his son from the clutches of death, can only carry the sick child and attempt to comfort him. His role is considerably shorter than those of the narrator, child, and the erlking.

In addition to his wealth of songs and orchestral works, Schubert was also a composer of piano and chamber music. His eighth and ninth symphonies give him a permanent place in the history of symphonic literature. The eighth symphony, known as the *Unfinished,* is a work in only two movements that would normally be considered the first and second movements of a typical symphony. Whether it was Schubert's intention to add two more movements or whether he considered the work complete remains forever an unanswered question. The continued inclusion of the *Unfinished* symphony in the orchestral repertoire attests to the satisfaction it gives as a complete work. Both movements are rich in lyrical melodies. The *Symphony in C Major* (*The Great*), Schubert's last work in this form, is a typical Romantic symphony in its great length and its deep, expressive power. In it, Schubert rivals Beethoven. The C Major Symphony is both a realization and a promise of Schubert's growing command of symphonic form, which his untimely death unfortunately left unfulfilled.

Fanny Mendelssohn-Hensel, Felix Mendelssohn, Frédéric Chopin, Robert Schumann, Clara Schumann

Fanny Mendelssohn-Hensel (1805–1847), Felix Mendelssohn (1809–1847), Frédéric Chopin (1810–1849), Robert Schumann (1810–1856), and Clara Schumann (1819–1896) are each representative of the Romantic trends of the nineteenth century. Like Beethoven and Schubert, they all represent a certain Classic restraint in an age of Romantic emphasis. Their respective lives are indicative of the new place musicians were forced to find in nineteenth-century society. Robert Schumann became a conservatory director and musical journalist. Both occupations became possible in the nineteenth century, which saw the founding of the first state music schools, or conservatories, in the face of the withdrawal of patronage by the Church and the aristocracy. Mendelssohn, privately wealthy, founded one of the first public orchestral societies and served as its director. Chopin and Clara Schumann made substantial portions of their incomes through widespread concertizing in which their own works were often featured.

In his piano works, Robert Schumann employed small forms as vehicles for the poetic moods usually suggested in their titles. *Carnaval* is a series of such short works connected by extramusical ideas. It is a musical representation of a pre-Lenten carnival ball. Most of the twenty-two short pieces are in dance rhythms, particularly the waltz. The individual names of the pieces suggest Schumann's desire to give musical characterization to certain individuals, real and fictitious. Besides this descriptive element, Schumann set himself the task of using the notes A, E-flat, C, and B, which in German represent the letters ASCH, the name of a town where an early sweetheart lived. They also represented four letters of his own name, that could be musically stated. Practically every one of these short pieces is based on these four notes in one order or another. Most of them are in a three-part song form or a simple rondo form. Harmonies are enriched with chromatically altered tones to lend color through dissonance. There is no actual program to give specific meaning to the individual pieces other than the often ambiguous titles. The parts most stimulating to the imagination are those most dancelike, in which the listener may project the movement of appropriate dance figures into the musical work. *Pierrot* and *Arlequin* are examples. While in general *Carnaval* represents nineteenth-century tonal painting for the piano, there is an obvious concession to formal considerations characteristic of all Schumann's compositions.

Schumann also made an impressive contribution to the literature of the German *Lied*. In 1840, an unusually productive year, he composed many songs, including the song cycle *Dichterliebe (Poet's Love)*, sixteen songs on texts by the Romantic poet, Heine. In it he treated the various emotions of love, from humor, intimacy, and irony to unrequited love and pathos. Each poem deals with some aspect of love. Most of them are through-composed; that is, new music is presented continuously throughout the composition. A notable characteristic of Schumann's *Lieder* is the independence of the piano part. Schumann captured the mood of the text through imaginative writing for the piano as an equal partner with the voice.

The bulk of Mendelssohn's great works—the symphonies, the piano and violin concertos, the oratorios—show a deep regard for Classic form. However, Romanticism is particularly apparent in one specific musical mood: the fanciful nature of his scherzo movements. In fact, this particular stylistic invention of Mendelssohn is the distinguishing feature of many of his compositions, including his songs, even where the term *scherzo* is not used.

Mendelssohn was only seventeen when he composed the atmospheric *Scherzo* from *A Midsummer Night's Dream.* Written to be used with the performance of the Shakespeare play, it has become one of the great orchestral virtuoso pieces of symphonic literature. With Mendelssohn, the scherzo was no longer a piece of boisterous humor, such as those Beethoven wrote, but a dancelike bit of imagery, in which the actual tones dance as if they were imaginative sprites. The short movement is based on the alternation of two closely related themes, both of which are developed briefly and restated. This work represents another facet of nineteenth-century musical Romanticism, the invoking of literary fantasy through musical technique and invention.

Two remarkable women composers also emerged in the first half of the nineteenth century. One was the sister and the other the wife of the now-famous composers just discussed. Both were virtuoso pianists. Fanny Mendelssohn-Hensel was as gifted as her brother Felix, and she composed in a style nearly indistinguishable from his. When his songs of Opus 8 and Opus 9 were published, six of her songs were included but not identified as hers. Recent scholarship attributes approximately five hundred compositions to Mendelssohn-Hensel, but many of her works remain unpublished.

Clara Wieck Schumann was one of the most highly regarded virtuoso pianists of her time. Liszt and Chopin were admirers of her pianistic talents, and she carried on a long friendship and correspondence with Brahms. Among her many works are songs, preludes and fugues, a piano concerto, and some chamber music, as well as cadenzas for some of the concertos of Beethoven and Mozart.

Chopin was the poet of musical fantasy. With the exception of some songs rarely heard today and the orchestral parts of his concertos, Chopin composed exclusively for the piano. The fact that a composer of such enormous talent could find realization for that talent through a single instrument is evidence of how greatly the piano's expressive possibilities had been expanded. This was not accomplished merely by mechanical perfection but by newer concepts of pianistic composition and performance. By the middle of the nineteenth century, the varied possibilities of the instrument had been so thoroughly developed that Chopin could find complete expression through it. For Chopin, the piano was capable of expressing all varieties of musical moods and feelings. His more typical writing style, however, exploited the tender, singing quality of the instrument through compositions that shrouded the melodic line in patterns of harmonic fantasy. Typically, his works were short and often carried titles that suggested a mood. They were of an intimate character, meant for performance in the salons of the nineteenth-century aristocracy and literati rather than for the large public concert hall. Such compositions were the nocturnes, scherzos, preludes, études, and many dance forms, such as the polonaise, mazurka, and waltz, which were elevated from their folk background to a refined level of sophistication. Besides Chopin's great importance in the exploitation of the piano, his use of harmony is noteworthy. His small works illustrate the use of harmonic tension and release so readily translated into poetic feeling.

The *Ètude in C Minor,* Op. 10, no. 12 is known as the *Revolutionary Ètude.* It is so named because of the circumstances prompting its composition and its fiery, martial rhythmic gestures. It was written in 1831 on the occasion of the Russians taking the city of Warsaw, Poland. Its bravura nature has made it a favorite of virtuoso pianists since its creation.

Brahms, Mahler, Verdi, Puccini

A large number of composers continued the Romantic practices of the first half of the century. Such creative spirits as Brahms (1833–1897), Mahler (1860–1911), Verdi (1813–1901), and Puccini (1858–1924) are still among the most widely performed in concert halls and opera houses of the twentieth century. They are part of a large group of composers who neither broke with tradition nor repudiated Romantic practices. On the contrary, they presented a more highly-charged emotional content by expanding the traditional forms and calling for added volume, especially in the enlarged orchestra. They expanded the harmonic and expressive language of their time and made use of Romantic themes expressed in literature and art when using texts for their works.

Brahms, one of the great masters of contrapuntal writing, preferred Classic forms in his instrumental works. Many of his orchestral works are of importance in orchestral programs today. Among them are the *Academic Festival Overture,* Opus 80, the *Hungarian Dances,* and *Variations on a Theme by Haydn,* Opus 56a. His four symphonies are among the greatest works in the orchestral repertoire. They follow the Classic forms developed by Haydn and Mozart and expanded by Beethoven. Brahms, fearful of comparison with Beethoven, allowed twenty-one years to elapse between the initial work and the completion of his *Symphony no. 1 in C Minor,* Opus 68. In the ensuing decade, he completed three more symphonies. The *Symphony no. 4 in E Minor* is characterized by rich harmonic structure, the use of motivic repetition in all the movements (as introduced by Beethoven in his Fifth Symphony), the introduction of folklike melodic themes, and the frequent use of old forms and devices, such as fugal passages and the passacaglia. While he did not contribute to the genre of opera, he wrote large-scale works for orchestra and chorus, such as the *Alto Rhapsodie,* Opus 53 and *Ein Deutsches Requiem,* Opus 45, based on nonliturgical Biblical texts in the German language. Other important contributions include a significant body of chamber and piano music and songs.

Gustav Mahler, known chiefly for his compositions of symphonic dimension, took his cue from Beethoven's *Symphony no. 9* in his great love for combining choral and solo voices with symphonic form. With Mahler, the symphony often became a symphonic cantata. The selection of Romantic literature and the frequent employment of folk tunes and poems indicate his devotion to Romantic ideals. The formal structure of his symphonies reflects his respect for tradition and for Beethoven. Mahler's symphonic writing features folk themes, and texts from Romantic authors. He also expanded the individual movements of the symphony to enormous lengths, and added significantly to the timbral palette of the orchestra. His obsession with death in the selection of literary as well as musical material is indicated by the funeral march in his *Symphony no. 4 in G Major,* and overwhelmingly, in the song cycle for voice and orchestra, *Kindertotenlieder (Songs for the Death of Children).*

In opera, Verdi shared center stage with Wagner (whose works are discussed in chapter 11 under "Romantic Realism"). Verdi remained faithful to the tradition of the Italian opera in which the solo voice was the dominating vehicle; he also brought the Italian opera to its zenith. His last operas, *Aida, Otello,* and *Falstaff,* represent his ultimate achievement.

Otello and *Falstaff* epitomize tragedy and comedy on the operatic stage. While both retain the vocal character of Italian opera, the orchestra had become a vital part of the work; it was no longer primarily an accompaniment. The individual characters of the opera still sang closed arias, but these were less differentiated than previously. Recitative passages as understood in the eighteenth century disappeared. There were fewer set arias that can be lifted from the works as independent songs. Each of these libretti was chosen by Verdi from a drama of great literary significance. However, not all of his choices for libretti were of this same high quality. While he did not use the Wagnerian device of *Leitmotif* (see chapter 11), he did use thematic material to relate dramatic events by means of music. The melodic theme in the love duet of Act One of *Otello,* for example, is recalled in the death scene at the end of the opera, thereby providing a psychological as well as musical link between the two scenes. His compositions apart from opera were few indeed. One of his last great works, however, was a mass for the dead. This *Requiem,* scored for four soloists, choir, and large orchestra, is thoroughly operatic in dimension and thrust.

Puccini was the foremost Italian opera composer at the close of the nineteenth century. His style was labeled *verismo* ("realism"), in reference to his choice of realistic stories and melodramatic musical settings. Whether tragic or comic, they were dramas not about heroic historical figures but rather about ordinary people. *La Boheme,* a story of the life struggles of young artists in the Latin quarter of Paris and the tragic love story of two of them, represents the *verismo* style in Puccini's works. Puccini retained the traditional predominant role for the singers with some set arias; the continuous musical line, however, generally does not differentiate recitative from aria. The colorful orchestration and the use of a chorus accentuate the roles of these two components of opera writing, which had been diminished in the Classical Italian operas of the eighteenth century.

Any discussion of nineteenth-century opera must make reference to Bizet's *Carmen* and Gounod's *Faust.* The former is perhaps the most popular opera ever written, and the latter is based on Goethe's famous *Faust* legend.

Summary

The revolutions of the late eighteenth to the mid-nineteenth centuries caused a great upheaval in the political and economic systems of Europe. The urge for freedom of all kinds, begun in the eighteenth century, had a profound effect on all activities of society. New movements in politics, religion, philosophy, social life, and the arts arose in revolt against the past.

Romanticism in the arts was also a revolt against the past. It was anti-Classic, repudiating symmetry, simplicity, and emotional restraint. Romantic artists strove to express emotion rather than rationality and individualism rather than conformity. There was greater individuality expressed in Romantic style than previously, for each creative artist had a personal way of expressing the ideas and feelings of the new movement.

Art patronage also changed. The courts of the nobility and the wealthy merchant class were no longer major patrons. For the first time, the general public became the primary consumers of the arts. Creative artists sought to interest common people in their works through publications, exhibitions, and concerts. Romanticism encouraged new sources of subjects for the arts. Subjects and experiences previously considered in bad taste became acceptable; violent and shocking scenes provided the opportunity for representing strong emotions. There was a renewed interest in nature in all its variety. Atypical experiences fascinated artists because of their mystery and supernaturalism. The arts were often mixed, with painting and sculptural illustrations of literary and poetic ideas. Even purely instrumental music attempted to recreate stories or scenes in melody, rhythm, tone color, and harmony. Whatever the subject, the aim was to make the spectator or listener feel the whole range of emotions by whatever means the artist could muster.

Romantic painters often turned to the Dutch and Flemish art of Rembrandt and Rubens for inspiration in the use of color, light, and shade. Subjects often had a moral message or were based on political or social issues. Violent scenes of carnage captured the imagination of both artists and the public, especially if they were related to actual events.

Like Romantic visual art, Romantic music was a revolt against the Classic. As in the visual arts, the evocation of emotion was its principal aim. Romantic music was based on the premise that a feeling of musical tension is necessary to achieve an intense emotional response. As a consequence, the music reveals a rich harmonic texture, with chromaticism and dissonance to create tension. Melodies are sometimes fragmentary or extremely long, often intensified by particular tone colors that support their character and mood.

While formal organization of some Romantic music was based on the Classic principle of sonata-allegro form, the sections were often enlarged by detailed developments of motives and harmonic sequences. Many short, ambiguous forms also emerged in solo instrumental and vocal music.

The most popular media for Romantic music were the orchestra, the piano, and the human voice. Most composers wrote for all three, which suggests a wide variety of musical expression. A great body of music currently in the concert and opera repertoire comes to us from Romantic composers such as Beethoven, Schubert, Schumann, Mendelssohn, Chopin, Verdi, and Brahms.

Suggested Readings

In addition to the specific sources that follow, the general readings listed on pages 388 and 389 contain valuable information about the topics of this chapter.

Clark, Kenneth. *The Romantic Rebellion: Romantic vs. Classic Art*. New York: Harper & Row, 1973.

Dalhaus, Carl. *Nineteenth-Century Music*. Berkeley: University of California Press, 1989.

Gossett, Philip, et al. *The New Grove Masters of the Italian Opera*. New York: W. W. Norton, 1986.

Hamilton, George H. *Nineteenth- and Twentieth-Century Art: Painting, Sculpture, Architecture*. Englewood Cliffs, NJ: Prentice-Hall, 1988.

Licht, Fred. *Goya, The Origins of the Modern Temper in Art*. New York: Harper & Row, 1983.

Longyear, Rey M. *Nineteenth-Century Romanticism in Music*. 3d ed. Englewood Cliffs, NJ: Prentice-Hall, 1988.

Reich, Nancy B. *Clara Schumann: The Artist and the Woman*. Ithaca, NY: Cornell University Press, 1985.

Rosenblum, Robert, and H. W. Jansen. *Nineteenth-Century Art*. New York: Abrams, 1984.

Vaughan, William. *German Romanticism and English Art*. New Haven, CT: Yale University Press, 1979.

Chapter 11

···──◉──···

Nineteenth-Century Realism
and Nationalism
(1840–1900)

(For a chronology of Nineteenth-Century Realism and Nationalism, refer to pages 240–241.)

Pronunciation Guide

Berlioz (Bear-lee-ohz)

Courbet, Gustave (Koor-bay, Gus-tahv)

Daumier, Honoré (Dohm-yay, Oh-nor-ay)

Dies Irae (Dee´-es Ee´-reh)

Eulenspiegel (Oy-len-shpee´-gel)

Glinka (Gleen´-kah)

Grieg (Greeg)

Godunov, Boris (Goh´-doo-nuf, Boh´-ris)

Idée fixe (Ee-day feex)

Lamartine (Lah-mahr-teen)

Liszt (List)

Moldau (Mohl´-dow)

Mussorgsky (Moo-sohrg´-skee)

Les Préludes (Leh Preh-lüd)

Pushkin (Poosh´-keen)

Rimsky-Korsakov (Rim´-skee Kor´-sah-koff)

Smetana, Bedřich (Sme´-tah-nah, Bed´-rikh)

Tchaikovsky (Chai-kof´-skee)

Vltava (Vul´-tah-vah)

Wagner (Vahg´-ner)

Study Objectives

1. Study the ways nineteenth-century composers suggest realism in their music.
2. Learn how artists confronted important social issues in a realistic way.
3. Study nationalistic music as a Romantic expression of ethnicity.
4. Learn about the conscious effort to incorporate folk melody and folklore into musical composition.

Romanticism focused attention on human feelings and sentiment. As the century progressed, artists appeared who, while still adhering to tenets of Romanticism, began to address physical and social realities. There was a growing consciousness of the physical world and its problems.

The Industrial Revolution created great social and economic changes, and it had positive and negative effects on society. The poverty of industrial workers and the concentration of population in urban centers drew attention to human relationships. The social problems of the mid-nineteenth century were the problems of the masses, and the artists of Realism made them their concern.

Realism was not anti-Romantic. On the contrary, it was an integral part of the Romantic ideal. Visual artists sought to be more "photographic" than was appropriate to Classicism. Human feeling was still a primary consideration, but it was feeling about specific problems or events that touched the lives of real people. However, because of the prevalence of sentiment, form was still of secondary importance, and feelings about the subject remained the motivating force of art. Similarly in music, the same concern with the "real" world was evident in extramusical connotations and in a desire to depict features of specific ethnic groups in the new nation-states of Europe.

VISUAL REALISM

Visual Realism dealt with the burning issues of social injustice, poverty, labor, and morals. In revealing these issues in simple, realistic forms, public sentiment was intensified. Visual art also dealt realistically with simple acts of everyday living, portraits, or scenes from nature. Realism was not an epoch of art in the manner of the Gothic or the Baroque. It was a style within a style, for it observed the basic tenets of Romanticism. Its aim incorporated Romanticism, and its patronage was essentially the same.

Courbet

Colorplate 55
follows p. 274.

Gustave Courbet (1819–1877) was one of the first painters to use the term "Realism" in connection with his art. He chose subjects from nature and from the simple acts of ordinary people. As a Romanticist, he was a supreme egoist, taking great care that he and his works had the greatest possible publicity. He did not hesitate to proclaim realism, purportedly saying to a friend, "Show me an angel, and I'll paint one." One of his famous paintings is the *Burial at Ornans* (colorplate 55). There is nothing literary or spectacular about this work. It is a simple, straightforward account of a common social act, the burial of the dead. It communicates nobility melded with humility. The lines of the faces are clearly drawn to emphasize the sentiment of the moment. The blue sky and the gray and violet coloring of the figures produce a monochromatic effect broken by patches of red and white. Space is controlled by the arrangement of the mourners positioned around the grave. The painting is a realistic portrait of those who mourn a departed member of their group. Its sentiment is Romantic, but its feeling is aroused through Realism.

Daumier

Honoré Daumier (1808–1879) was one of those Realists who emphasized the social and economic inequalities of the Industrial Revolution. His *The Third-Class Carriage* (colorplate 56) is not a pretty picture. It depicts the weariness, poverty, and futility of the working class. Crowded into the dark carriage are people with tired, empty faces. They are poor, but they are also imitators of the elite, with their tall hats as symbols of respectability. The drabness of the garments and the almost empty countenances seem to express a life of toil and hardship. The lines denoting form are vague, but short, curved lines emphasize the facial and physical features. Monochromatic browns fill the atmosphere with drabness not unlike that of its occupants. Most of Daumier's works depict lower-class, hard-working people who are at times miserable. His representation of them going through their weary days can be interpreted as a protest against the social and economic conditions of the time.

Colorplate 56 follows p. 274.

Eakins

Thomas Eakins (1844–1916) was an American painter whose realism bordered on the photographic. *Max Schmitt in a Single Scull* (colorplate 57) suggests the detailed clarity attainable with a telephoto lens. Eakins shows minute detail, from the foreground to the distant horizon. The subject, Max Schmitt, is turned toward the viewer as if posing for a camera portrait. An unearthly stillness pervades the canvas, evoked by careful balance, water without the slightest ripple, long horizontal lines, and diagonal lines that are themselves nearly horizontal.

Colorplate 57 follows p. 274.

An instructive comparison can be made between Eakins's *The Agnew Clinic* (colorplate 58), a Realist painting completed in 1889, and Rembrandt's *Dr. Tulp's Anatomy Lesson* (colorplate 34) of 1632. In the earlier work, Rembrandt used the event as an opportunity to create a group portrait. The dissected arm of the cadaver is of minor importance to the painting; the viewer's eyes are much more forcefully drawn to the faces of the individual participants and their personalities. In Eakins's painting, the focus is on the drama of the instruction. In the foreground, the isolated figure of Dr. Agnew provides psychological balance for the surgical team on the right. The attentive students, while rendered with considerable detail, constitute only a patterned background.

Colorplate 58, follows p. 274.

Colorplate 34 follows p. 194.

Thompson

Colorplate 59 follows p. 274.

Elizabeth Thompson (1850–1933), like many English women of the nineteenth century, traveled widely throughout the British Empire. She lived in India with her husband, Sir Francis Butler (hence her formal title, Lady Butler). Her paintings chronicle the military exploits of the British Empire with an uncanny realism and an eye for detail that documented many aspects of military life at that time. In *The Remnants of an Army* (colorplate 59), the subjects are a war-weary horse and rider. Their depiction in an expansive and arid landscape lends poignancy to the work. The realism is not only physical but also psychological, evoking a response in the viewer consonant with the desolate scene. The Romantic spirit is indicated by the idealized mountains in the distance and by the artist's capturing such a moment on canvas.

Homer

Colorplate 60 follows p. 274.

Like Eakins, Winslow Homer (1836–1910) was an American Romantic Realist. The subjects for his paintings range from scenes from ordinary life (genre painting) to dramatic scenes, such as *The Gulf Stream* (colorplate 60). In this painting, Homer unites two of his favorite subjects: humans against the sea and black people. Through the use of a high horizon, the magnitude of the ocean overwhelms the disabled boat and its solitary passenger. Two diagonals of dark blue water strengthen the sense of turbulence in the ocean and emphasize the shape of the boat.

Colorplate 48 follows p. 258.

Homer's approach to the subject of humans against the sea differs in some remarkable ways from that of Géricault (colorplate 48). Not the least of these is the way oil pigment is applied to the canvas, with Homer using techniques already being practiced by the Impressionists. Géricault's dramatic lighting evokes highly charged emotions, while Homer's more uniform light contributes little to the drama yet is more realistic.

REALISM IN MUSIC

Three kinds of musical realism can be identified: (1) **program music,** instrumental music with an accompanying literary description; (2) **descriptive music** devoid of any literary program but associated in the title with people, objects, and events; and (3) music with identifiable musical gestures (e.g., *Leitmotifs*) associated with specific ideas, events, objects, and feelings. Realism in music can be regarded as the musical counterpart to visual Realism. Much of the music of the nineteenth century was associated with extramusical subjects. Various musical devices were used; the most common were motives, melodies, or harmonic sequences identified with specific ideas or objects. The composer could then tell or suggest a story "realistically" by the use of these symbols and could convey the story to the audience through both the music and the literary suggestion. The most suitable medium for descriptive music was the orchestra, with its colorful tonal palette. Listeners were impressed by the ability of composers to portray specific ideas through orchestral sound.

Since the harmonic, melodic, and rhythmic materials used by composers to affect their descriptive aims were essentially those of the Romantic period, listeners came to expect all nineteenth-century music to have extramusical meanings. They even read into the works of Beethoven and Brahms the same kind of descriptive ideas that Berlioz and Wagner consciously tried to express in their compositions.

Berlioz

Hector Berlioz (1803–1869) was one of the significant composers whose works illustrate the techniques of program music. He and his great contemporary Richard Wagner were men of distinct literary ability. As a music critic, Berlioz wrote extensively for Parisian newspapers. His *Evenings in the Orchestra* is a collection of important essays expressing his philosophy of music as well as then-current ideas about the arts of the nineteenth century. Berlioz composed in all of the large forms popular in the nineteenth century: opera, oratorio, mass, symphony, and overture. In all cases, he is most remembered for his innovative use of orchestral instruments, singly and in ensemble.

A CLOSER LOOK

Berlioz, *Symphonie fantastique*

Berlioz's *Symphonie fantastique* (Fantastic Symphony) was avowedly written to create a musical representation of a literary idea. The following is a translation of Berlioz's "program," published in French with the musical score.

Program of the Symphony

A young musician of an unhealthy, sensitive nature endowed with vivid imagination has poisoned himself with opium in a paroxysm of lovesick despair. The narcotic he took was too weak to cause death, but it has thrown him into a long sleep accompanied by the most extraordinary visions. In this condition his sensations, his feelings, and his memories find utterance in his sick brain in the form of musical imagery. Even the Beloved One takes the form of a melody in his mind, like a fixed idea [*idée fixe*] which is ever returning and which he hears everywhere.

First Movement—[Dreams, Passions]

At first he thinks of the uneasy condition of his mind, of somber longings, of depression and joyous elation without any recognizable cause, which he experienced before the Beloved One appeared to him. Then he remembers the ardent love with which she suddenly inspired him; he thinks of his almost insane anxiety, of his raging jealousy, of his reawakening love, and of his religious consolation.

Second Movement—[A Ball]

In a ballroom, amidst the confusion of a brilliant festival, he finds the Beloved One again.

Third Movement—[Scene in the Meadows]

It is a summer evening. He is musing in the country when he hears two shepherd lads who play, in alternation, a *ranz des vaches* (the tune used by Swiss shepherds to call their flocks). This pastoral duet, the quiet scene, the soft whisperings of the trees stirred by the zephyr wind, some prospects of hope recently made known to him—all these sensations unite to impart a long unknown repose to his heart and to lend a smiling color to his imagination. And then She appears once more. His heart stops beating; painful forebodings fill his soul. "What if she should prove false to him?" One of the shepherds resumes the melody, but the other answers him no more . . . sunset . . . distant rolling of thunder . . . loneliness . . . silence.

Fourth Movement—[*March to the Scaffold*]
He dreams that he has murdered his Beloved, that he has been condemned to death and is being led to execution. A march that is alternately somber and wild, brilliant and solemn, accompanied without modulation by measured steps. At last the fixed idea returns—for a moment a last thought of love is revived, which is cut short by the death blow of the axe.

Fifth Movement—[*Dream of a Witches' Sabbath*]
He dreams that he is present at a witches' revel, surrounded by horrible spirits, amidst sorcerers and monsters in many fearful forms who have come together for his funeral. Strange sounds, groans, shrill laughter, distant yells, which other cries seem to answer. The Beloved melody is here again, but it has lost its shy and noble character; it has become vulgar, trivial, a grotesque dance tune. It is she who comes to attend the witches' meeting. Riotous howls and shouts greet her arrival . . . She joins the infernal orgy . . . Bells toll for the dead . . . A burlesque parody of the *Dies Irae* . . . The witches' round-dance . . . The dance and the *Dies Irae* are heard together.

The opening of the first movement, entitled *Dreams, Passions*, portrays the ephemeral quality of dreams through the vague manner in which the thematic material is presented. The principal theme, Berlioz's *idée fixe,* is not presented in its complete form until about four minutes of the first movement have passed, although the music hints at it with fragmentary motives derived from the theme itself. The music evokes the vague feelings one has in remembering a dream. This is coupled with an explicit literary program and the title *Dreams, Passions.*

Although the first movement has the general outline of the sonata-allegro form traditional for symphonic first movements, Berlioz felt no compulsion to restrict himself to formal devices. The *idée fixe* (ex. 11.1) is the source of musical material for the whole movement and is presented in various episodic passages; it is first played by violins and flutes. The success of this movement, however, is achieved by the realistic combination of musical and extramusical ideas and the masterly use of harmony, rhythm, dynamics, and instrumentation in the development of themes and motives.

Example 11.1 *Symphonie fantastique, Dreams and Passions* (First Movement) by Hector Berlioz

Colorplate 55 Gustave Courbet, *Burial at Ornans*, 1849. Oil on canvas, 10 ft. 3 in. × 20 ft. 10 in. Louvre, Paris. (Giraudon/Art Resource, NY) *(See p. 270)*

Colorplate 56   Honoré Daumier, *The Third-Class Carriage,* c. 1862. Oil on canvas, 25 3/4 × 35 1/2 in. The
Metropolitan Museum of Art, NY. Bequest of Mrs. H. O. Havemeyer [1929] The H. O. Havemeyer Collection,
29.100.129. *(See p. 271)*

Colorplate 57 Thomas Eakins, *Max Schmitt in a Single Scull,* 1871. Oil on canvas, 32 1/4 ×
46 1/4 in. The Metropolitan Museum of Art, NY. Purchase 1934, Alfred N. Punnett Fund and
Gift of George D. Pratt, 34.92. *(See p. 271)*

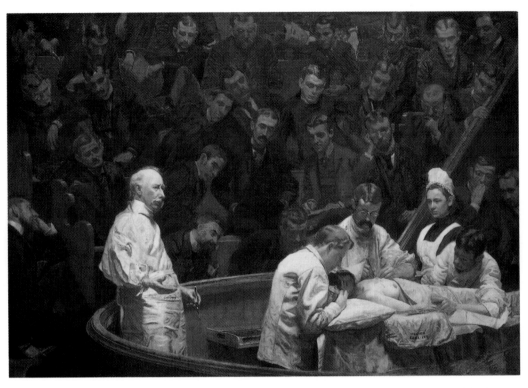

Colorplate 58 Thomas Eakins, *The Agnew Clinic,* 1889. Oil on canvas, 6 ft. 2 in. × 10 ft. 6 in. University of Pennsylvania School of Medicine. *(See p. 271)*

Colorplate 59   Elizabeth Thompson (Lady Butler), *The Remnants of an Army.* Oil on canvas, 52 × 92 in. The Tate Gallery, London. *(See p. 272)*

Colorplate 60 Winslow Homer, *The Gulf Stream*, 1906. Oil on canvas, 28 1/8 × 49 1/8 in. The Metropolitan Museum of Art, NY. Wolfe Fund, 1906. Catherine Lorillard Wolfe Collection, 06.1234. (See p. 272)

In the second movement, as in all subsequent movements, the *idée fixe* reappears, but each time in a different guise. The choice of a waltz rhythm is apt for a movement depicting a ball. The opening makes use of vague harmonic progressions that are finally resolved when the waltz begins. The first part of the dance, introduced by the violins, has its own theme closely allied to the *idée fixe*. The altered *idée fixe* itself is soon introduced (ex. 11.2) by the woodwinds to form a contrasting middle section. The first part returns, this time almost in a frenzied manner. A coda, in which the *idée fixe* is once more recalled in dramatic fashion, brings the movement to a fiery and impetuous close.

Example 11.2 *Symphonie fantastique, A Ball* (Second Movement) by Hector Berlioz

In the third movement, Berlioz is concerned almost exclusively with tone color. Three sections particularly illustrate this treatment: the pastoral duet played by the English horn and the oboe at the opening of the movement, the thunderstorm played by the tympani, and the lonely utterance of the oboe at the close of the movement, when this instrument repeats its portion of the opening duet. The *idée fixe* elicits only a faint reminiscence of the "Beloved One" in the tonal atmosphere of a pastoral scene (ex. 11.3). Through the use of woodwinds (traditionally associated with the outdoors) and high strings, Berlioz paints a touching musical scene of nature.

Example 11.3 *Symphonie fantastique, Scene in the Meadows* (Third Movement) by Hector Berlioz

The fourth movement is a grotesque and noisy march. Its grotesque quality is achieved mainly by the use of unusual instrumental combinations and even more unusual demands upon these instruments. In the opening measure, two sets of tympani employing two performers, along with cellos and string basses, set the march rhythm. The basses fix the tonality by repeating the tonic chord of G minor in their lowest range. The first theme of the march grows out of this ominous-sounding background. By using the extreme low ranges of the bassoon and string basses, Berlioz creates strange tonal colors that lend credence to his program. The second theme of the march is noisy and blatant, employing the brasses and woodwinds as if they were a wind band. These two themes alternate brilliantly in cleverly distributed rhythmic patterns. The fixed idea appears in this movement only at the climax, played by the clarinet, precisely following Berlioz's program (ex. 11.4).

Example 11.4 *Symphonie fantastique, March to the Scaffold* (Fourth Movement) by Hector Berlioz

In the final movement, Berlioz stakes everything on the virtuosity of his orchestration. This is particularly true in the opening measures, where he tries to set a mood through sound effects achieved by extraordinary demands upon the orchestral instruments. The demands are made not only upon individual performers but also upon the orchestra as a whole, which is treated as a huge palette with enormous resources. The opening measures, for example, divide the string section into ten parts, and the score calls for such unusual instruments for that time as the E-flat clarinet, valve cornets, tuba, four tympani, bells, and bass drum; what a change from the Classical orchestra of the eighteenth century, or even Beethoven's orchestra. Berlioz also employs new effects, such as muted horns, the playing of strings with the wood of the bow instead of the hair, and the playing of tympani with sponge mallets. The grotesque is heightened in this movement by the parodying and burlesquing of two thematic ideas: the fixed idea (ex. 11.5) played by the high E-flat

Example 11.5 *Symphonie fantastique, Dream of a Witches' Sabbath* (Fifth Movement) by Hector Berlioz

clarinet to portray the "Beloved One," and the ancient Gregorian chant of the *Dies Irae* from the *Mass for the Dead* (ex. 11.6) and its parody, played first by tubas and bassoons and eventually by shrill, mocking strings and woodwinds (ex. 11.7).

Example 11.6 *Dies Irae* from the *Mass for the Dead*, traditional Gregorian chant adapted by Berlioz

The parody is attained by rhythmic and melodic distortion of these two themes. The last movement climaxes with a witches' dance that, strangely enough, Berlioz commences in fugal fashion. One suspects the fugue is used to emphasize the parody, for Berlioz is known to have disliked the fugue as a musical form. This vigorous fugue subject is finally joined by the *Dies Irae*, and the symphony ends in a wild setting of musical frenzy.

Example 11.7 Parody of the *Dies Irae, Symphonie fantastique, Dream of a Witches' Sabbath* (Fifth Movement) by Hector Berlioz

Wagner

Even more than Berlioz, Richard Wagner (1813–1883) sacrificed formal musical considerations so that all the arts, including music, might be synthesized into a new and compelling medium of artistic expression. His last great music dramas (he disliked the term *opera*) are examples of his realization of such an "artwork of the future."

One of these later music dramas, *Die Meistersinger von Nürnberg* (*The Mastersingers of Nuremberg*), illustrates Wagner's theories concerning the "artwork of the future." It also illustrates Wagner's technique of realistic expression. In this, as in his later works, he employed the device of the **Leitmotif,** a short musical fragment with a specific nonmusical association (e.g., a sword). It is a means of musical organization that realistically expresses literary-dramatic implications. *Leitmotifs* are further reinforced (or may be suggested) by the libretto, dramatic action, or even manipulation of stage properties or lighting. In *Die Meistersinger,* one motif opens the Prelude and represents the mastersingers themselves. Another, immediately following, is associated with the lovemaking of Walter. The overture itself contains many more, such as the motifs of David, apprentices, the call of spring—all of which become extramusically significant in the course of the drama.

Wagner needed many *Leitmotifs* because they have very specific dramatic significance and are called for by the necessities of the action. Their musical treatment can be either vocal or instrumental. In fact, Wagner used the orchestra rather than the voice as his primary vehicle for musical expression. As a consequence, the motifs are rarely sung in their pure form but are treated symphonically by the orchestra.

The voice parts are conceived as continuous, decorative melodies that express the outward meaning of the drama by means of texts. The vocal part is neither aria nor recitative, as in traditional operas, but a sort of spoken melody in no specific traditional form.

Wagner's realism is convincing to the degree that the *Leitmotifs* are satisfactory musical expressions of the ideas to which they are attached. If the musically strong rhythmic and harmonic quality of the mastersinger *Leitmotif* can be persuasively linked in our minds to the actual characters of the mastersingers, we are likely to be willing to accept Wagner's realism. If the musical device of long-delayed resolutions, achieved by the use of continuously altered and dissonant harmonies, can be perceived as the realistic expression of longing, renunciation, and other psychological states, then Wagner's realism is successful. Despite great opposition to his works in the latter half of the nineteenth century, Wagner not only persuaded his listening public of the validity of his aesthetic principles but influenced many composers of his time and those immediately following him, particularly those who wrote music for the operatic stage.

In the last analysis, listeners must allow themselves to become willing partners in a fascinating and delightful illusion. The tones comprising the opening theme of the Prelude to *Die Meistersinger* do not actually depict the mastersingers, but this musical conjurer, this tremendous creative spirit, convinces listeners that they do.

No other nineteenth-century Romanticist achieved such convincing realism and, at the same time, such well-knit musical expression. The fact that Wagner's works are heard so frequently on the concert stage, apart from all dramatic action, indicates the superb compositional craft with which he constructed them. On the other hand, this very fact also indicates that Wagner failed to achieve his own goal. Despite his contention that the "art of the future" was to be a synthesis of all the arts and that his own works were of this nature, the music still is of greatest import in his drama.

In addition to his impact on opera and the harmonic language of the second half of the nineteenth century, Wagner's prose writings on political topics were important in the development of German nationalism. His choice of ancient German historical and mythological themes for his operas reinforced the nationalistic spirit.

Liszt, Richard Strauss

Franz Liszt (1811–1886) combined virtuosity with Realism in his compositions and in his performance as a pianist. He was the greatest technical virtuoso of his age, and his piano compositions, whether in a realistic vein such as *La Campanella* (*The Bell*) or in a more classical form such as the *Piano Concerto no. 1 in E-flat,* exploit the virtuosity of the pianist. His thirteen tone poems for orchestra are virtuoso pieces that were deliberately realistic. In these works, he used the *Leitmotif* to effect his realistic purpose, relating the motifs to the poem or other program that he attached to the work. In *Les Préludes* Liszt tried to express, through the musical idiom of nineteenth-century Romanticism, the poetic ideas of the French poet Lamartine's poem of the same name. Liszt attached the text of the poem to the published score of the work. With the *Leitmotifs* that correspond to the ideas of the poem and the technically elaborate and spectacular orchestration of these motifs, Liszt wove a musical counterpart to the poetic idea.

Richard Strauss (1864–1949), a composer in the tradition of Wagner and Liszt, used the same devices of realistic expression in his operas and symphonic poems. He made harmonies richer and more dissonant, and he expanded the orchestra even more than had his predecessors. The symphonic poem *Till Eulenspiegel* is a composition of wit and humor, quite apart from any program that has been attached to it. Till was a half-real character of the German Low Countries who was at least as well known then as Robin Hood is today. Everyone knew of his more famous pranks, which fill several volumes. It was easy for listeners to associate them with their obvious musical references.

The traditional pranks ascribed to Till—upsetting the market ladies' baskets, parading as a priest, having a love affair, and many others—and his eventual trial, judgment, and execution at the close of the work must all be supplied by the listener familiar with his escapades. Strauss refused to write an explicit program for the work, but he did give it a complete title that, when translated, reads: *Till Eulenspiegel's Merry Pranks, in an Old Roguish Manner—in Rondo Form.* When pressed for an explanation of the work, Strauss merely said he would leave it to the listeners to "crack the nuts that the rogue gives them." He indicated that the two motives (exs. 11.8, 11.9) represented Till in his many disguises, moods, and situations, and that the whole story ends in a catastrophe when he is condemned and strung up on the gallows.

Example 11.8 *Till Eulenspiegel's Merry Pranks* by Richard Strauss

Example 11.9 *Till Eulenspiegel's Merry Pranks* by Richard Strauss

Musically, the work is in a free rondo form. The two motives constantly recur in various guises—changed in their melodic and harmonic forms, put into new tempos, or rhythmically and tonally altered, always in a gay or wistful manner. The success of *Till Eulenspiegel* rests upon Strauss's artistic skill as a creative musician and his ability as a storyteller.

NINETEENTH-CENTURY NATIONALISM

Romantic and Realistic art often expressed individualism and the struggle for freedom from tyranny. Nationalism in the arts is the expression of the same impulse applied to sovereign states. In a way, it is the application of individualism on a national scale.

After the defeat of Napoleon, the national boundries of Europe were completely revised. His conquests had so changed the political map that for any particular faction to gain back some of its territory, innumerable treaties had to be written. In the ensuing process, there was a tendency to draw lines according to language. One after another of the European states and districts began the slow process of national unification. Germany, the last of the major national groups to achieve unity, finally became united in 1871 under Bismark. Smaller states, such as Poland, Bohemia, Norway, and Finland, did not realize this goal immediately, but growing patriotism kept a feeling of national identity alive.

Romanticism and Realism had much in common with Nationalism. The difference was in emphasis and subject matter. Anything that could inspire pride and patriotism was a legitimate subject for art. Folklore reappeared in concert music. For centuries it had been repressed because of its association with common people; it had not been considered a fit subject for courtly life. Nationalist art had propaganda value for the sovereign state because it glorified its traditions. National power and culture have been both a blessing and a curse; German Nationalism, born with Bismark, was one of the major causes of two world conflicts. Nationalism is not a period of time but an attitude that will remain as long as there are strongly nationalistic feelings within nations. Often, the smaller the state, the stronger the Nationalist movement in art. Small nations cannot boast of military, political, or economic power, but art does not depend on large armies.

As Romanticists, artists of the Nationalist movement made no marked changes in techniques or methods of organizing the elements of the arts. Nationalism appears in the artistic function of the work and in the use of materials indigenous to a particular country. For example, listeners can identify Spanish music by a particular rhythmic pattern, Russian music by a certain Eastern quality of melodic intervals, and Polish music by the use of folk dances, such as the polonaise and mazurka.

The visual arts of Nationalism appeal less to the world today than does its music. The pictorial depiction of contemporary events limits the appeal to those who are familiar with the history of the period. Beyond the borders of the specific country and beyond the span of memory, these events often lose their significance. When music of artistic worth was combined with Nationalistic Realism, however, it found wide audiences. Within the confines of its own immediate national group, it spoke to a people sympathetic with its musical and extramusical topics. Outside its own national confines, it appealed to the romantic sense of all people as a style with a distinct and unusual musical language. This is perhaps the key to the widespread acceptance of the works of nationalistic composers, even where people are unsympathetic to the nationalistic ideas the composer tried to express.

In music, Nationalism was not only an attempt to express the political independence of groups but also a conscious movement toward musical independence. German music had grown in its domination over European music, particularly that of central and eastern Europe, since the beginning of the eighteenth century. By the beginning of the nineteenth century, Germany provided practically all of Europe's performing musicians and teachers, as well as the music itself. The numerous smaller national groups, therefore, desired musical independence.

Composers began to identify themselves with their nation's histories. Music had always contained elements of Nationalism, and there were always traces of Italian, German, and Spanish influence, but never before had there been such a conscious effort to exploit national traits as during the last half of the nineteenth century. Wagner used in his music dramas elements of old German epics and legends, and composers of other nations began to do the same.

Nationalism, as would be expected, was strongest among those who were politically or culturally dominated by foreign forces. The largest national groups to feel such domination were the Slavic peoples. As a consequence, there was a very conscious Nationalism in the music of the Russians, Poles, Czechs, and Slovaks. The Czechs and Slovaks were the smallest numerically and the most completely dominated by a foreign people. Since the first part of the seventeenth century, Germanic culture and political organization had been imposed upon them. The liberating tendencies of nineteenth-century Romanticism, however, gave hope to an unquenchable desire for freedom that could find expression only in art—and particularly in music—until the twentieth century. As a result, music in eastern Europe was intensely Nationalistic in the middle of the nineteenth century.

Smetana

Bedřich Smetana (1824–1884) was a strong fighter for independence, particularly in artistic and musical matters. He was, in many respects, a disciple of the musical aesthetics of Wagner and Liszt. He tried to use their techniques, (coupled with the national folk songs, dances, folktales, and patriotism cherished by his people) to express the extramusical ideas of Czech nationalism. His great cycle of tone poems, *Ma Vlast (My Fatherland)*, represents his adaptation of Romantic musical procedures to this purpose. The work consists of six symphonic poems, each dealing with certain aspects of Czech landscape, life, mythology, and history.

Vltava (The Moldau), the second poem of the cycle, is an example of nationalistic expression that has won acceptance in concert halls everywhere. A reading of Smetana's own program reveals the same detailed realism found in Berlioz's *Symphonie fantastique*. In this case, however, the composer appeals specifically to the patriotic sentiments of his fellow Czechs. The Vltava River, which flows through the length of Bohemia, was a symbol of national unity and patriotism long before this work was written. The castles on its banks, the countryside along its broad valley, the rapids that interrupt its swift course were very close to the hearts of the people.

The Russian Five

Russia, while it was not under the political domination of a foreign power, had been dependent on western Europe for its art music until the performance of Mikhail Glinka's opera *A Life for the Czar* in 1836. After this first essay into the field of musical Nationalism, Russia soon produced a number of composers who were determined to free Russian music from the bondage of German Romanticism.

Russian composers adapted the techniques of German Romanticism, flavoring their work with the melodic, harmonic, and rhythmic idioms of Russian folk music. Two groups of composers arose, strongly antagonistic to one another. The one group, the Russian Five, felt themselves the true representatives of Russian Nationalism. They opposed other composers, such as Tchaikovsky, who in their minds represented an alliance with German Romanticism.

The Russian Five	*Others*
Mily Balakirev (1837–1910)	Anton Rubinstein (1829–1894)
Alexander Borodin (1833–1887)	Piotr I. Tchaikovsky
César Cui (1835–1918)	(1840–1893)
Modest Mussorgsky (1839–1881)	
Nikolai Rimsky-Korsakov (1844–1908)	

Tchaikovsky, Mussorgsky

Piotr Ilyitch Tchaikovsky wrote extensively in the traditional forms of nineteenth-century Romanticism. Among his many works are six symphonies, extensive chamber music, piano works, several very popular concertos, over one hundred songs, and nearly a dozen operas. While it is true that his style was greatly influenced by German Romanticism, his works reflect a strong commitment to his Russian heritage.

An examination of a work by Tchaikovsky and one by Modest Mussorgsky, the most original genius of the Russian Five, reveals their differences. In the *Symphony no. 4 in F Minor* Tchaikovsky used Classic forms, illustrating his close relationship to the German symphonic tradition. However, his Nationalism is also very evident in the use of Russian folk melodies in several movements. In the fourth movement, for example, Tchaikovsky used a popular Russian tune (ex. 11.10), and he acknowledged the composition's Russian Nationalism in his letters.

Example 11.10   *In the Field There Stood a Birch Tree* (Russian Folk Song) used in Tchaikovsky's *Symphony no. 4 in F Minor*

Such attempts at Nationalism were not acceptable, however, to the Russian Five, who felt that Russian composers must not only employ the idioms of Russian folk music but that they must link the musical ideas to Russian subject matter and, above all, create a musical tradition of their own. Perhaps the most original example of such purpose is the opera *Boris Godunov* by Mussorgsky. In this opera, Mussorgsky portrayed the Russian people as the central heroic characters, making it a work of nationalistic significance. The musical language is that of nineteenth-century Romanticism. He set out on a rather narrow nationalistic path yet, despite the dangers of such a restrictive procedure, succeeded in writing a work of musical artistry and magnificence. Its nationalistic ideas, both musical and extramusical, are evident throughout. It is in essence a set of choral-symphonic scenes. The irregularity of meter characteristic of eastern European and Slavic music is pervasive. The song of the pilgrims that ends the first scene introduces the liturgical music of the Russian church, which had a long history and was an important part of the lives of most Russians. The second scene, commonly called the "Coronation Scene," simulates the sounds of the great bells of Moscow. Mussorgsky based his libretto on a drama by Pushkin, which in turn was based on actual events in Russian history. The entire dramatic context of the opera was intensely Russian.

Summary

Realism is one facet of the Romantic spirit. Emotion was still a primary consideration, but the aim of Realism was to arouse emotions about a specific object or event, often mundane but sometimes urgent, that touched the lives of ordinary people. Visual Realism often dealt with issues of poverty, social injustice, labor, or morality. Most Realist painters tried to present their subjects in an almost photographic manner; there was little mystery, only the scene as they saw and experienced it objectively.

Descriptive (or programmatic) music was the counterpart of visual Realism, and composers used various devices to portray objective reality. The orchestra, with its vast resources of tone color and harmony, was the most popular medium for descriptive music. By suggesting that certain melodic configurations, harmonic progressions, tone colors, or rhythmic patterns were identifiable with poetic ideas, physical movement, or specific personalities, composers could tell a story or paint a picture in tone. However, their music had to be based on a secure formal structure in order to survive. In most of the more successful program music, the work was probably conceived before the program it was to illustrate was completed.

Nationalism was yet another facet of Romanticism. The ingredients of Nationalism in music were the folk songs and dances of particular countries or ethnic groups. When true folk material was not used, composers created their own melodies in the spirit and style of folk music. Additionally, legends or stories of historical events were often used as programs. The extramusical ideas, added to the music itself, make such pieces dear to those of particular national origins.

Numerous nationalistic works engaged composers in the nineteenth century. Sometimes, as with Smetana, Mussorgsky, Grieg, and others, the traits of Nationalism never seem absent from the composer's music. Others, such as Chopin and Liszt, paid some respect to this phase of Romanticism but were not entirely given over to it. For those groups struggling for cultural independence, however, this great nationalistic music literature was, and still is, of tremendous significance.

Suggested Readings

In addition to the specific sources that follow, the general readings listed on pages 388 and 389 contain valuable information about the topics of this chapter.

Dalhaus, Carl. *Realism in Nineteenth-Century Music*. Cambridge: Cambridge University Press, 1985.

Licht, Fred. *Goya, The Origins of the Modern Temper in Art*. New York: Harper & Row, 1983.

Longyear, Rey M. *Nineteenth-Century Romanticism in Music*. 3d ed. Englewood Cliffs, NJ: Prentice-Hall, 1988.

Rosenblum, Robert, and H. W. Janson. *Nineteenth-Century Art*. New York: Abrams, 1984.

Chapter 12

····───◉───····

Impressionism and Post-Impressionism
(1860–1900)

Chronology

Visual Arts	Music
•Edouard Manet (1832–1883) •Edgar Degas (1834–1917) •Paul Cézanne (1839–1906) •Auguste Rodin (1840–1917) •Claude Monet (1840–1926) •Berthe Morisot (1841–1895) •Pierre-Auguste Renoir (1841–1919) •Mary Cassatt (1845–1926) •Paul Gauguin (1848–1903) •Vincent van Gogh (1853–1890) •Georges Pierre Seurat (1859–1891)	•Claude Debussy (1862–1918) •Maurice Ravel (1875–1937) •Lili Boulanger (1893–1918)

Pronunciation Guide

Boulanger (Boo-lăn-zhay)
Cassatt (Kah-sáht)
Cézanne (Say-zahn)
Debussy (Deh-boo-see)
Degas (Day-gah)
Gauguin (Go-găn)
Grande Jatte (Grănd Zhaht)
Jas de Bouffan (Zha de Boo-fă)

Mallarmé (Mahl-lahr-may)
Manet (Man-ay)
Monet, Claude (Moh-nay, Klohd)
Morisot, Berthe (More-ee-so, Bear-tuh)
Moulin de la Galette (Moo-lăn duh lah Gah-let)
Nuages (Noo-ahzh)

Ravel (Rah-vel)
Renoir, Pierre-Auguste (Ren-wahr, Pee-air Oh-goost)
Rodin (Roh-dă)
Scriabin (Skree-yah´-been)
Seurat (Soe-rah)
van Gogh (van Gokh)
Verlaine (Ver-len)
Vétheuil (Vay-tuh-ee)

IMPRESSIONISM

As the Romantic spirit ran its course, there was an increased effort among artists to express "feeling." A commonly held view was that art was an expression of the soul, a communication of emotional states from one soul to another.

In the first half of the nineteenth century, people had found emotional release and spiritual value in Romantic art. Well before the end of the nineteenth century, however, the conventions of Romantic art were exhausted. The later nineteenth century has been called a period of "culture-weary art" because there had been such a concentration of emotional expression that feelings had become desensitized.

Impressionism was one result of this emotional desensitization. It was a reaction to the exuberance and the excess of Romanticism, and yet it was Romantic. It was realistic in its attempts to portray the subject, but now as seen through the eyes of the artist at a particular moment and under the particular conditions of that moment. Its final aim was to evoke an image, to suggest an emotion. There was less passion and deep feeling. It was a cult of suggestive colors, lines, and sounds, a fleeting glance, an incomplete melody; the viewer and the listener supplied the details and completed the art object. Impressionism was a sensuous art without the moral and emotional content of earlier Romanticism.

Literature provided both painters and composers with evocative poetry to inspire their works of art. Just as painters and composers rebelled against the structural patterns of Classic and Romantic art, the Symbolist poets rebelled against the restrictions of poetic forms. Words were used for their melodious and sensuous qualities rather than for their meanings. They became a means of suggesting musical sounds and visual colors. Both painters and composers were strongly influenced by the symbolic imagery of Verlaine and Mallarmé, the chief Symbolist poets. Their poetry was fragile and sensual, stimulating the imaginations of their fellow artists.

The relationship between artists and the public was also a factor in the rise of Impressionism. Artists were demonstrating greater independence from the public. Some of the previous functions of art were no longer pertinent. Photography, for example, was replacing the painter in portraiture.

Official academic painting and sculpture were stilted, but they enjoyed public approval. The first Impressionists, on the other hand, presented a new and fresh view of reality but were scorned by the public. While it did not ignore social conditions, Impressionism avoided preaching and moralizing. Instead, artists focused on the act of seeing the everyday world as it changed under the influence of light and movement. It was some time before public taste approved of these new ways of seeing. Experiments with new art theories and methods of painting were the immediate concerns of the early Impressionists. Gaining public attention and approval was also a strong motivation for their creative activity.

POST-IMPRESSIONISM

The fact that **Post-Impressionism** has a name derived from Impressionism indicates both its connection to, and its difference from, the earlier style. The term refers to the styles of several artists painting in the mid-1880s: Gauguin, van Gogh, Cézanne, and Seurat. The work of these artists constitutes a bridge from Impressionism to such early twentieth-century movements as Expressionism and Cubism. These painters had individual styles, and their works resist simple categorization.

PAINTING

The innovations that led to Impressionism in art were made by a group of painters in France. In their protest against the traditional methods and exuberance of Romanticism, they concerned themselves primarily with the perceptions of the eye, painting what they saw under specific conditions of light and shade. At first glance, an Impressionist painting seems unreal, but a close observation of nature suggests that this is realistic art. Our perception of color changes according to atmospheric conditions that control the intensity and amount of light. There is a difference, for example, in the color of grass in sunlight and in shade. The grass itself does not change, but the lighting causes it to take on different shades of green. Distance not only has the effect of making objects appear smaller, but cuts out details that we know are present but cannot actually see. The Impressionists explored almost every possibile effect of light on color and mass.

By calling attention to the delight of momentary vision, Impressionist painters opened a new area of human experience for artists to explore. This played an important part in the development of the various "-isms" of twentieth-century painting.

Landscapes, houses, people—anything that could be observed—were legitimate subjects for Impressionist paintings. The only stipulation was that it must be presented as it appeared at the moment of artistic creation. This caused artists to change their techniques. Design, space, line, and formal organization were subordinated to color. Artists no longer confined painting to the studio; they brought their work out into nature, and they had to devise methods of working that were quick and sure. They used only a few basic colors and applied them quickly to the canvas with bold strokes, for they realized that the blending of colors took place in the eyes of the viewer. A canvas had to be finished before the light effects changed. At times it was necessary for the artists to wait days, even weeks, for the same conditions of light and atmosphere to return so that a painting could be completed. Landscapes with water were particularly popular with painters because of the way water responds to the slightest changes of light and wind.

Manet

The immediate precursor of the Impressionist painters was Edouard Manet (1832–1883). One of his most important contributions to painting was his unrelenting attention to the effects of light on objects in space. Another was his commitment to paint the world without idealizing it. Although he was trained in an academic style, Manet regularly chose subjects considered scandalous by the establishment and public alike. As a consequence, it was necessary to band together with other experimental artists to exhibit rejected works in the *Salon des Refusés* ("Exhibit of the refused").

In 1863 the *Salon des Refusés* hung Manet's *Le Déjeuner sur l'Herbe* (*Luncheon on the Grass*) (colorplate 61), creating an uproar because of its nude female in the presence of formally dressed gentlemen. Copying masterpieces was a standard part of an artist's training, and Manet had spent a year studying and copying Giorgione's *Pastoral Concert,* which formed the basis for Manet's *Le Déjeuner.* Many of the objects in the painting, especially the vegetation, are defined by loose application of pigment, which only suggests line. The sharp contrasts in the painting are achieved by Manet's use of extremely light and dark colors, with few colors of middle value.

Colorplate 61 follows p. 290.

Monet

It was a painting of Claude Monet (1840–1926), *Impression: Sunrise,* exhibited in 1874, that gave Impressionism its name. The *Banks of the Seine, Vétheuil* (colorplate 62) is one of his color studies of the effect of light and atmosphere on water, trees, and foliage. The painting contains no people, action, or social problems—only the quiet beauty of shimmering reflections on the water. Monet applied colors in bold patches, with no attempt to

Colorplate 62 follows p. 290.

integrate them on the canvas. Details of the trees and foliage are vague and obscure. Space is made apparent in various ways. By placing the horizon high in the painting, the artist created a large area of foliage in the foreground. He also used a technique that left clear brush marks on the canvas. Each leaf is only a bit of color; there is no outline for individual leaves or flowers. The formal organization is not obvious, for the painting is an impression of a segment of real life and not a carefully arranged pattern.

Colorplate 63
follows p. 290.

In *Rouen Cathedral, West Facade* (colorplate 63), Monet caught the full intensity of bright sunlight on the facade of the cathedral. This is one of some thirty canvases he painted of the cathedral, each under different light conditions. Intense light has a tendency to detract from the massiveness of the building. In this painting the lines are imprecise, and the design is determined by an impressionistic image of the architectural mass itself. Color is in patches of grays and tans that mean little when viewed closely but integrate into a whole when viewed from a distance. Monet only suggests to the spectator the idea of the cathedral in the brilliance of the noonday sun.

Morisot

Colorplate 64
follows p. 290.

Berthe Morisot (1841–1895) was one of three women in the first group of Impressionist painters. (The others were Mary Cassatt and Eva Gonzalès.) Morisot participated in most of the Impressionists' shows. She championed the new movement vigorously and may have had an artistic influence on Manet and others in the group. *Young Girl by the Window* (colorplate 64) is readily identified as an Impressionist work because of its loose brush strokes and blurred lines. The heavy brush work creates an active surface even as it articulates pattern and form. The entire canvas is infused with light. The colors chosen by the artist are largely unsaturated and of many hues, giving the painting a feeling of serenity.

Renoir

Colorpate 65
follows p. 290.

Pierre-Auguste Renoir (1841–1919), another French Impressionist, carried on the tradition of structural form from the Romantics. Consequently, there is more emphasis on the plastic quality of figures in his work, even though he painted them with the colors and techniques of Impressionism. *By the Seashore* (colorplate 65) is such a canvas. Renoir placed his subject against the background of sky and water. There is a fragile and scintillating quality about the landscape. Pastel colors scarcely define anything except the rocky cliff. The woman, however, is boldly modeled in a traditional fashion, except for the effect of light and color apparent in the soft tones of flesh and the reflecting folds of her dress.

Colorplate 61 Edouard Manet, *Le Déjeuner sur l'Herbe*, 1863. Oil on canvas, 7 ft. × 8 ft. 10 in. Musée d'Orsay, Paris, France. (Erich Lessing/Art Resource, NY) (See p. 289)

Colorplate 62   Claude Monet, *Banks of the Seine, Vétheuil,* 1880. Oil on canvas, 28 7/8 ×
39 5/8 in. © 1994 Board of Trustees, National Gallery of Art, Washington, D.C. Chester Dale
Collection. *(See p. 289)*

Colorplate 63 Claude Monet, *Rouen Cathedral, West Facade,* 1894. Oil on canvas, 39 1/2 × 26 in. © 1994 Board of Trustees, National Gallery of Art, Washington, D.C. Chester Dale Collection. *(See p. 248, 290)*

Colorplate 64 Berthe Morisot, *Young Girl by the Window,* 1878. Oil on canvas, 30 × 24 in. Musée Fabre, Montpellier, France. (Art Resource, NY) *(See p. 290)*

Colorplate 65 Pierre-Auguste Renoir, *By the Seashore,* 1883. Oil on canvas, 36 1/4 × 28 1/2 in. The Metropolitan Museum of Art, NY. Bequest of Mrs. H. O. Havemeyer, 1929. The H. O. Havemeyer Collection, 29.100.125. *(See p. 290)*

Colorplate 66 Pierre-Auguste Renoir, *Le Moulin de la Galette*, 1876. Oil on canvas, 51 1/2 × 69 in. Musée d'Orsay, Paris. (Art Resource, NY) (See p. 291)

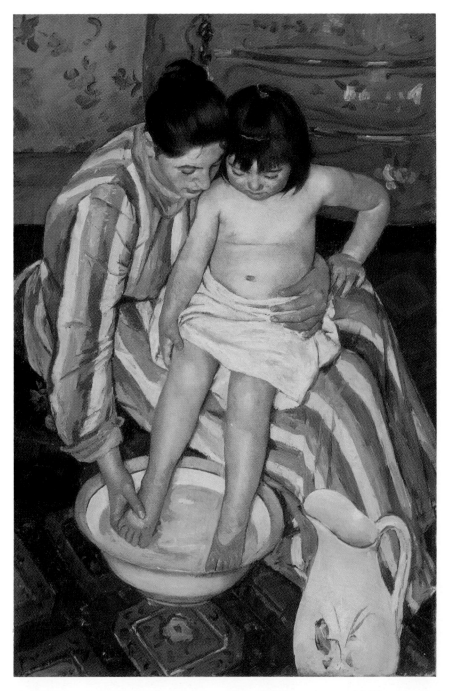

Colorplate 67 Mary Cassatt, *The Bath*, c. 1891–1892. Oil on canvas, 39 1/2 × 26 in. Robert A. Waller Fund, 1910.2. Photograph © 1994 The Art Institute of Chicago. All Rights Reserved. *(See p. 291)*

Colorplate 68 Paul Gauguin, *Mahana No Atua (Day of the Gods)*, 1894. Oil on canvas, 27 3/8 × 35 5/8 in. (Helen Birch Bartlett Memorial Collection, 1926.198. Photograph © 1994 The Art Institute of Chicago. All Rights Reserved.) (See p. 292)

Colorplate 69 Georges Pierre Seurat, *Sunday Afternoon on the Island of La Grande Jatte*, 1884–1886. Oil on canvas, 6 ft. 3 in. × 10 ft. 3/8 in. (Helen Birch Bartlett Collection, 1926.224. Photograph © 1994 The Art Institute of Chicago. All Rights Reserved) (See p. 292)

Colorplate 70 Paul Cézanne, *The Card Players*, 1891. Oil on canvas, 3 ft. 2 in. × 4 ft. 3 in. Courtauld Institute Galleries, London. Courtauld Collection. *(See p. 292)*

Colorplate 71   Paul Cézanne, *Chestnut Trees at Jas de Bouffan in Winter,* 1886. Oil on canvas, 29 × 36 in. The Minneapolis Institute of Art. *(See p. 293)*

Colorplate 72 Vincent van Gogh, *The Starry Night,* 1889. Oil on canvas, 29 × 36 1/4 in. The Museum of Modern Art, NY. Acquired through the Lillie P. Bliss Bequest. Photograph © 1996. The Museum of Modern Art, NY. *(See p. 11, 293)*

Le Moulin de la Galette (colorplate 66) shows Renoir's treatment of a group of figures. There is an intentional blurring of outlines, for here he paid little attention to the details of form. The effect of light on color and form is the most important impression one receives. Patches of light contrast with dark shadows. The striped dress of the figure at the table is flooded with light. Background figures are merely brushstrokes of pastel color. The feeling of formal balance is concealed by the busy activity of the figures and by the dappled light of the canvas. Renoir painted the gaiety of color, creating a realistic impression of a whirling throng in the sunlight. Unlike the Baroque, in which the viewer is usually a spectator, Impressionism forces the viewer to synthesize and complete the picture.

Colorplate 66 follows p. 290.

Cassatt

Though the Impressionist movement was begun in France by French painters, it attracted adherents from all over the Western world. Two noteworthy examples from North America were James Whistler and Mary Cassatt. Cassatt (1845–1926) was born in Pittsburgh, Pennsylvania. She traveled to France initially to study in the academic style of the day. Very soon, however, she was attracted to the works of Manet and Degas. In 1877, she met Degas, who invited her to exhibit her works with the Impressionists. She accepted, showing her works in at least four exhibitions between 1879 and 1886. Her style is bold, with broad brush strokes and vivid colors.

A CLOSER LOOK

Cassatt, *The Bath*

Mary Cassatt painted a wide range of subjects typical of Impressionists, including outdoor scenes and portraits. The subject matter she chose most often, however, tended toward the domestic. She is most widely esteemed for her many paintings of mothers and their children, as in *The Bath* (colorplate 67, following p. 290). The painting is dominated by two figures. The formal composition of the painting is established by the S-curve formed by the figure of the mother and made subtle by the figure of the child. With the pitcher, they create a bright diagonal from upper left to lower right. Cassatt has established a high perspective for the viewer. Interestingly, this affords a view quite similar to that of the two figures, both of whom are also looking down. The downward glances of the two figures make *The Bath* a tender, innocent scene that is reinforced by Cassatt's choice of colors, which are for the most part muted.

The picture includes four dominant textural areas: the gaudily patterned rug, the flowered taupe background of wallpaper and chest, the striped gown of the mother, and the delicate flesh of mother and child. The four areas are differentiated not only by texture but by color. Two of the four areas have geometric design (the carpet and the dress), while the other two are devoid of such patterns. A loose brush technique is employed in all areas except the flesh of the two subjects, where more refined brush strokes render the texture in a realistic manner. In *The Bath*, Cassatt's technique is effectively placed at the service of expression.

Gauguin

Paul Gauguin (1848–1903) is generally called a "Post-Impressionist." Disenchanted with the industrial civilization of his time, he escaped to Tahiti in search of the unspoiled life of the South Seas. There he used color in flat, two-dimensional surfaces with strong outlines. The juxtaposition of patterns of vibrant color suggest sensual, primitive forms. His *Mahana No Atua* (*Day of the Gods*) (colorplate 68) gives viewers a vicarious experience of a simple lifestyle in a faraway setting. Many saw in Gauguin's work the powerful symbols of the "exotic" world that fascinated nineteenth-century artists and public alike.

Colorplate 68 follows p. 290.

Seurat

Georges Pierre Seurat (1859–1891) seemed to exploit Impressionistic theories to their logical ends forming a bridge to the twentieth century. Consequently, he is sometimes included among the Post-Impressionists. He was still mainly concerned with color and light, but in a particularly disciplined manner he built up his colors with thousands of small dots of pigment. These dots were of uniform size and were designed to merge into shapes in the eye of the beholder, much like the bold patches of color used by Monet. Seurat's style is called "pointillism" and is sometimes compared to the fragmentary musical fabric of Anton Webern. *Sunday Afternoon on the Island of La Grande Jatte* (colorplate 69) is one of his best-known paintings. The forms are geometrically stylized and integrate dots of color in varying hues and values. A strong sense of spatial recession is achieved by the progressively smaller size of background figures. The painting has little sense of movement and is a static portrait of people in a park; the characters truly came to life in the 1984 Broadway musical by Stephen Sondheim that used this painting as its subject.

Colorplate 69 follows p. 290.

Cézanne

More than any other Post-Impressionist, Paul Cézanne (1839–1906) explored the spatial possibilities later employed by the Cubists. For Cézanne, nature was not what it seemed when photographed, but was something that could be reduced to simple geometric forms. He tried to reveal the character of objects, people, and landscapes through cylinders, cubes, cones, and spheres. Although landscapes were his favorite subject, Cézanne also painted still-life subjects and group pictures. One common subject frequently depicted by Cézanne was men playing cards. In one of the simpler versions, *The Card Players* (colorplate 70), he created an intimate arch by his arrangement of the two elongated figures. A triangle is created by the men's forearms and the

Colorplate 70 follows p. 290.

table top. Such geometric forms are, together with solid blocks of color, typical of Cézanne's style. The artist was not interested in the act of card playing but strove only to make an interesting arrangement of three-dimensional forms. He modestly distorted nature and simplified it by bringing out its natural forms. *Chestnut Trees at Jas de Bouffan in Winter* (colorplate 71) employs similar painting techniques. Cézanne distorted reality by eliminating details: many limbs were left out of the painting to emphasize the cylindrical shapes of the trees, and buildings were used sparingly, and then only as simplified shapes. The mountain, Ste. Victoire, shows clearly through the trees as a block of earth in nature. Cézanne's painting creates an artistic pattern of angular lines that define the volume and mass of geometric, rather than natural, forms.

Colorplate 71 follows p. 290.

van Gogh

This forerunner of Expressionism lived out his short life before the turn of the twentieth century. Vincent van Gogh (1853–1890) was a deeply religious man aware of the cosmic, or divine, forces of the universe. He attempted to paint his feelings about the natural world—not only what he could see of it but what he knew of it. Van Gogh thought of himself as a missionary of kindness. He lived a simple, humble life with miners, giving away his meager funds to the needy. He even shared his rooms with a prostitute and her child because he could not bear to let their suffering go unheeded. He was tormented by the suffering of the human race and finally, to escape the reality of life, committed suicide. Van Gogh had a profound conviction that his destiny was to try to bring humanity closer together.

The Starry Night (colorplate 72) expresses van Gogh's feelings about nature. The twisting cypress, the stark simplicity of the horizon and houses, and the swirling forces of the night atmosphere combine to make this canvas an expression of the rhythm of the universe. Indeed, one can almost feel the movement of the earth against the stars. The realism, however, is not photographic; it is the realism of the painter's feelings about the scene. Van Gogh sought to reveal the moving forces of nature. He used heavy oil paint in pure colors, which he applied in bold strokes and heavy lines. He did not bother with detailed drawings but preferred instead to portray the elemental character of nature with strong, contrasting curves of color. The inconsistent directions of the curves give the canvas a swirling rather than a directional motion. Van Gogh painted the motion of the atmosphere, which we know exists but cannot actually be seen. His use of color is daringly polychromatic, with brilliant blues, yellows, and oranges. Color, line, and texture are of almost equal importance in this painting. All other elements seem quite unimportant as van Gogh concentrated on depicting his feelings about the forces of the universe.

Colorplate 72 follows p. 290.

Figure 12.1 Edgar Degas, *Arabesque Ouverte Sur La Jambe Droite (Open arabesque on the right leg)*, c. 1880. Bronze, 11 3/8 in. high. Los Angeles County Museum of Art/Mr. and Mrs. George Gard De Sylva Collection

SCULPTURE

The feeling for luminous color and fragmentary form was expressed primarily in painting. However, sculpture was also touched by the spirit of Impressionism, as sculptors such as Degas and Rodin captured the fleeting and fragmentary nature of their subjects.

Degas

Ballet dancers and horses were favorite subjects of the painter-sculptor Edgar Degas (1834–1917). Movement in space was his true preoccupation, as demonstrated in the *Arabesque Ouverte Sur La Jambe Droite (Open Arabesque on the Right Leg* (fig. 12.1)). The figure's balance, poise, and gesture create a bouyant, graceful sense of movement. The lines of the torso and limbs contribute to its dynamic effect. Degas created his sculptures originally in wax and even exhibited them in that form. Cast later in bronze, they are eminent examples of Impressionist sculpture.

Rodin

Auguste Rodin (1840–1917) was, without a doubt, one of the greatest sculptors of the nineteenth century. While he cannot be truthfully called an Impressionist, his later works show this influence. He began to "suggest" in stone and bronze. He liked to leave something to the imagination of the spectator—something that could be completed only at the moment of viewing. To achieve this effect, Rodin sometimes left the plastic modeling of form incomplete and let his figures emerge out of the material. He also tended to dematerialize form by modeling surfaces into hollows and projections that catch light and produce shadows.

The Kiss (fig. 12.2) illustrates the influence of Impressionism on sculpture. The play of light and shadow over the surfaces of the entwined figures suggests warm flesh tones. The same effect of light lessens the sense of weight and hardness of the marble and breaks up the volume into suggestive fragments. Rodin made his figures less graphic by reducing the detail. While the subject is sensual, the passion of the scene is only suggested to the spectator.

MUSIC

Claude Debussy, the chief exemplar of musical Impressionism, associated regularly with French poets and painters and was significantly influenced by their views. Composers—like their painter colleagues—experimented with new means of achieving coloristic effects. Cyril Scott, an English composer, developed a scientific analogy between the color spectrum and vibrations of sound and then proceeded to compose in his new system. Scriabin, a late nineteenth- and early twentieth-century Russian composer, decided to include the sense of smell in his appeal to the senses. The performance of his last work, *Mysterium,* which he never completed, was to include a screen with changing colors and the release of certain perfumes as an accompaniment to the music. Such experiments were generally failures.

Debussy

Like the French painters, Debussy (1862–1918) protested against the emotionalism and exuberance of Romanticism. Debussy was greatly stimulated by the paintings of Monet and the literary Symbolists. He was also influenced by Asian music, notably the sounds of the Javanese *gamelan* orchestra he heard at the Paris Exposition of 1889. Naturally, the materials and

Figure 12.2 Auguste Rodin, *The Kiss* 1901–1904. Marble, over life-size. Rodin Museum, Paris, France. (Tate Gallery, London, Great Britain/Art Resource, NY)

techniques of music differ greatly from those of the visual arts, and Debussy did not attempt to imitate the effects of coloristic scenes. He did, however, try to suggest the same kinds of feelings in music that his colleagues did in painting and poetry. He sought to express the shimmering effects of light and shade through tone color, dynamics, and chordal structure and, as a result, sacrificed lyric melody, traditional form, and polyphonic complexity for suggestive harmonic progressions. In order to achieve a more luminous tonal coloring, he destroyed the traditional relationships of the successive scale steps. This he accomplished sometimes using the **whole-tone scale,** which included no half-steps, thus endowing each note with nearly equal importance. He weakened musical cadences by parallel chord progressions that helped avoid harmonic tensions. Debussy's music is almost kaleidoscopic in its meandering melodies and harmonies.

His *Prelude to the Afternoon of a Faun,* written in 1894, was perhaps the most popular of his orchestral music. It is a brief symphonic poem based on Mallarmé's poem of the same title dealing with a faun, a mythical creature half-man and half-beast. Debussy captured the fanciful spirit of the poem with a tonal fabric that suggests the feeling implied by Mallarmé's words.

The formal organization of this music is not obvious. Debussy wrote three contrasting melodic ideas and repeated the first more than once. This main melody (ex. 12.1), played by the flute, rises and falls gently and chromatically, at first alone, then weaving in and out of subtle harmonic progressions that seldom reach a complete cadence.

Example 12.1 *Prelude to the Afternoon of a Faun* by Claude Debussy

Climaxes are only anticipated, for they never reach the full force of the tonal power promised. The rhythm of *Prelude to the Afternoon of a Faun* is exceedingly complex, moving in and out of measures of nine, six, twelve, and four beats without establishing an easily recognizable pattern in any one meter. The fragile and lazy melodic line of the flute, the soft sweep of slightly dissonant chords on the harp, the restrained climaxes of the full orchestra—all suggest the feeling of blissful drowsiness the poet implies.

Like Monet's paintings, *Rouen Cathedral* and *Banks of the Seine,* Debussy's music is illusive. It suggests a "feeling," thereby drawing the listeners into the creative process. The music is bathed in the soft glow of subtle harmonies, outlined by delicately shaded melodic lines that fade into the shadow of musical imagery. Debussy reflected the oversensitive, restless mind of the late nineteenth century. He avoided the passion and sentiment of earlier composers, yet there was little hint of the harsh, brittle materialism to come. His work is the quintessence of musical Impressionism. Debussy himself, however, disliked being called an "Impressionist" because he felt confined by the term.

Ravel

No other composer, with the possible exception of Maurice Ravel (1875–1937), so consistently created works in the Impressionist style. Suites I and II from Ravel's ballet *Daphnis et Chloe* are excellent examples of his style and skill in orchestration. His orchestration of Mussorgsky's set of piano pieces, *Pictures at an Exhibition,* overshadowed the original for decades. The exotic coloration of this orchestration is shared in any number of Ravel's other works, including *Bolero* and, to even greater effect, in *Scheherazade,* for mezzo-soprano and orchestra.

Boulanger

Lili Boulanger (1893–1918) lived a short yet productive life. Her musical promise was enormous. In 1913, she became the first woman awarded the first prize in the Prix de Rome competition. Lili Boulanger's works are in a transitional style, moving somewhat beyond Impressionism. They possess formal clarity and abundant chromaticism; when they involve texts, as in *La Tempête* and *Les Sirènes,* they incline toward exotic subjects. Her sister, Nadia, was to achieve great fame in Paris as a teacher of many twentieth-century European and American composers.

Summary

Impressionism and Post-Impressionism formed a bridge between Romanticism and twentieth-century art. On one hand, they were reactions against the emotional exuberance of Romanticism; on the other hand, they were realistic attempts to capture the perceptions of the moment, both visually and in terms of tone color in music. Painters were interested in the phenomena of transient vision: the integration of color and line in the eye of the spectator. Artists painted what they saw at a particular moment, under the immediate conditions of atmosphere, light, and shade and from a specific angle or perspective. In landscapes and water scenes, the play of light and wind could change colors and forms; these were the Impressionists' favorite subjects. There was little movement, for the subject remained static. There was, likewise, no passion or deep feeling evoked. Line, spatial concepts, and formal organization, combined with the technique of juxtaposing bold strokes of color that would blend in the eyes of the beholders, replaced feeling as the painter's primary concern.

Like painting, music reflected the influence of Impressionist poets. In fact, some composers tried to suggest the same kinds of feelings in music as those evoked in poetic and other literary texts. In many instances, tone color and rhythmic freedom took precedence over formal organization, polyphonic complexity, and lyric melody. Composers weakened the strong tonal center of earlier music, thereby lessening the sense of tension and release associated with the emotion and passion of the Romantic period. Impressionist music was written to suggest "feeling" through vague melodic lines, static harmonies, and rhythmic complexities. It invited listeners to participate in the mood of a piece in much the same manner as color and line in Impressionist painting invited the beholder to catch a glimpse of a particular moment.

Suggested Readings

In addition to the specific sources that follow, the general readings listed on pages 388 and 389 contain valuable information about the topics of this chapter.

Arnason, H. H. *History of Modern Art: Painting, Sculpture, Architecture, Photography.* New York: Abrams, 1986.

Canaday, John. *Mainstreams of Modern Art.* 2d ed. New York: Holt, Rinehart & Winston, 1981.

Lockspeiser, Edward. *Music and Painting.* London: Cassell, 1973.

Rosenblum, Robert, and H. W. Janson. *Nineteenth-Century Art.* New York: Abrams, 1984.

Chapter 13

···➤●◀···

Modernism in the Arts to 1945

(1900–1945)

Chronology

Visual Arts	Music	Historical Figures and Events
		•Sigmund Freud (1856–1939)
•Gustav Klimt (1862–1918)	•Leoš Janácek (1864–1928)	
•Wassily Kandinsky (1866–1944)		
•Käthe Kollwitz (1867–1945)		
	•Scott Joplin (1868–1917)	
•Henri Matisse (1869–1954)		
•Frank Lloyd Wright (1869–1959)		
•Ernst Barlach (1870–1938)		
•Georges Rouault (1871–1958)		
•Julia Morgan (1872–1957)		
•Piet Mondrian (1872–1944)	•Ralph Vaughan Williams (1872–1958)	
	•W. C. Handy (1873–1958)	
	•Arnold Schoenberg (1874–1951)	
	•Charles Ives (1874–1954)	•Winston Churchill (1874–1965)
•Constantin Brancusi (1876–1957)		
•Raoul Dufy (1879–1953)		•Josef Stalin (1879–1953)
•Paul Klee (1879–1940)		•Albert Einstein (1879–1955)
•Pablo Picasso (1881–1973)		
•Wilhelm Lehmbruck (1881–1919)	•Béla Bartók (1881–1945)	
•Natalya Goncharova (1883–1962)		
	•Igor Stravinsky (1882–1971)	•James Joyce (1882–1941)
•Walter Gropius (1883–1969)	•Anton Webern (1883–1945)	
		•Franklin D. Roosevelt (1884–1945)
	•Alban Berg (1885–1935)	
	•Edgar Varèse (1885–1965)	
•Diego Rivera (1886–1957)		
•Charles Eduard Jeaneret (Corbusier) (1887–1965)		

Chronology (*Continued*)

Visual Arts	Music	Historical Figures and Events
•Marc Chagall (1887–1985) •Georgia O'Keeffe (1887–1986) •Malvina Hoffman (1887–1966) •Jean Arp (1888–1966)		
	•Sergey Prokofiev (1891–1953)	•T. S. Eliot (1888–1965)
•Palmer Hayden (1893–1973) •Joan Miró (1893–1983)		
	•Paul Hindemith (1895–1963) •Ragtime (c.1897–1915)	
•Alexander Calder (1898–1976) •Henry Moore (1898–1986)	•George Gershwin (1898–1937)	•Bertold Brecht (1898–1956) •Ernest Hemingway (1898–1961)
	•Duke Ellington (1899–1974) •Aaron Copland (1900–1990) •Louis Armstrong (1900–1971)	
•Alberto Giacometti (1901–1966) •Salvador Dali (1904–1989) •Peter Blume (1906–1992)	•Glen Miller (1904–1944)	
		•First World War begins (1914) •Panama Canal opens (1914)
	•First printed use of the term *Jazz* (1917)	
		•First World War ends (1918) •Nuclear fission discovered (1938) •Atomic bomb destroys Hiroshima and Nagasaki (1945)

Pronunciation Guide

Bartók (Bahr´-tok)
Bauhaus (Bow´-hows)
Berg (Bayrg)
Bloch (Blokh)
Brancusi (Bran-koo´-zee)
Chagall (Shah-gahl)
Corbusier (Kohr-boo-see-ay)
Dali (Dah-lee)
Gabo (Gah-boh)

Giacometti (Jah-koh-met´-tee)
Gropius (Groh´-pee-oos)
Guernica (Gwer´-nee-kah)
Kandinsky (Kahn-din´-skee)
Klee (Klay)
Kollwitz (Kohl´-vitz)
Lehmbruck (Laym´-brook)
Mahler (Mah´-ler)
Matisse (Mah-tees)

Miró (Mee-roh´)
Mondrian (Mon-dree-ăn)
Petrouchka (Pe-troo´-shka)
Picasso (Pee-kah´-soh)
Pogany (Poh-gah´-nee)
Rouault (Roo-oh´)
Schoenberg (Shoen´-berg)
Stravinsky (Strah-vin´-skee)
Webern (Vay´-bern)

Study Objectives

1. Learn about the revolt against the excesses of Romanticism.
2. Learn about the various named movements among the arts.
3. Study the technical development of new materials and new sounds.
4. Learn about the rise of jazz as a phenomenon of the early twentieth century.

The first decades of the twentieth century brought drastic changes to the Western world. Many of these changes were the result of technological and scientific advances, but others are attributable to political, social, economic, and even moral developments. Society was in many ways chaotic and almost brutally indifferent to individual human interests. The two world conflicts in the first half of the century showed the twentieth century to be an age of doubt, distrust, uncertainty, dissatisfaction, and disillusionment.

Despite the technological nature of modern civilization artists generally were expected to function as they had in previous times, producing art of feeling and sentiment. Although people were living in a mechanized world, they often condemned artists who embodied in their art the technological values of the time. Artists have always been social critics, documenting the present and using their intuitive power to sense relationships and trends.

The trends in music and art at the beginning of the century represented growth and change, which came about through breaking down old boundaries and the broadening of the horizons of artistic expression. The Renaissance was a response to the medieval period; Romanticism was a reaction to Classicism; and Impressionism was a rebellion against Romanticism. Modern art, some of whose proponents even issued manifestos, might similarly be called a "revolt"—a revolt against the sentimentality of Romanticism and an affirmation of the technological age.

After the turn of the century, artists began to question not only the emotionalism and sentimentality of the Romantics but also the material world that had seemed so real to their predecessors. There arose a demand for some sort of artistic response to the new scientific phenomena being explored. Research with X-rays and the microscope, the splitting of the atom, new concepts of time and space, the psychological research of Freud and Jung—all these challenged Western artists. The results were twofold. First, some artists rejected the idea that personal feeling or emotion had a dominant place in artistic expression. Perhaps this attitude was born of the scientific age, dominated by machines. Second, artists rejected the Renaissance notion that art should mirror nature. In their attempts to understand and express what lay beyond natural appearances, artists developed a conception of the world based on inner experience, not outward appearance. The essence of things was of greater importance than their outward forms. Some artists emulated scientists, and others tried to make of art some sort of universal vision, freed from physical appearances and a truthful mirror of their age.

It is difficult for people of any period to judge whether contemporary artists are reflecting the conditions of their time with integrity. People of all periods must endeavor to understand what contemporary artists are trying to do. It is impossible to state with finality which contemporary artists are destined to be called "great," but there are certain trends that can be observed and evaluated.

It might be useful, for example, to group artists into three categories. One type can be called the "sensationalists." Sensationalists break down artistic conventions and reject most accepted values. They might be brilliant, but because their art is most often aimed at gaining attention through shocking subjects and techniques, their works frequently lack expressiveness and sometimes even sincerity. The second type can be called the "experimentalists." As is the case with most innovators, they seek new methods and combinations of materials to express themselves. They break new ground and base their art on untried theories. They may be sincere, but their art often lacks unity and coherence. Experimentalists, like most innovators, seldom perfect what they begin. The third type consists of artists who are great enough to combine what is good from the first two types and what is valid from the past in new artistic expressions. Their art shines with a more steady light than that of the sensationalist or experimentalist.

One of the chief characteristics of early twentieth-century art was its diversity. Many experimental styles left their marks. Because of the accelerated tempo of life, there were rapidly changing movements in art. The styles overlapped and cannot be separated chronologically. A few principles, however, typify the work of twentieth-century artists. These principles were not adopted by all artists, nor were they applicable to all the works of those who did accept them.

The first principle held that artists must break with the past. For many artists working in the early half of the twentieth century, this required the rejection of nineteenth-century Romanticism. The so-called Modern movement was a revolt against Romantic techniques, subjects, and expressions. If these artists had any attachment to the past, it was to the Classic ideal that method was more important than subject.

The second principle was the rejection of realism. Modern art could thus represent interior psychological states or abstract patterns rather than suggest physical reality.

The last principle rejected unnecessary ornaments. "Form follows function" became the new motto. As a result, there was a demand for simplicity, terseness, and often brutality of expression. Because of this interest in reducing detail, abstraction became pervasive in the visual arts. There was little attempt to please or entertain, only a desire to reflect the age directly and unashamedly.

Based on the preceding paragraphs, it might appear that most twentieth-century art would be cold, intellectual, and perhaps cynical. This was sometimes true during the early decades, but there followed a softening, a realization that feelings do have a place in art. From about 1930, some artists were returning to Romantic ideals—not to a point of sentimentality but to the recognition that people have souls, and even machines must be guided by human hands.

Another factor to consider in the study of twentieth-century art is the relationship of artists to their public. Creative artists are sometimes alienated from a public that cannot keep pace with changes in style. It takes time to become acclimated to a style, and in this fast-moving century, the public often accepts a particular style just when it is no longer current. Consequently, the gulf between patrons and artists widens, and patrons often seek aesthetic pleasure in art that is more firmly established in the past.

Technical advances in mass production have made prints and recordings available to a wider audience. The gallery and concert hall are no longer the only centers of artistic experience. Mass education and mass communication offer an unprecedented range of artistic creations from all eras. Book publishing, recordings, radio, television, and movies make available to the public the work of artists and old masters previously unknown.

In the twentieth century, there have been many personal or social bonds among artists in different genres. Some painters have composed music, and some musicians have experimented in the visual arts. Schoenberg was a talented painter, for example. Another relationship among artists is expressed in the poetry of Eluard, whose *Le Travail du Peintre* (*The Work of the Painter*) pays tribute in individual poems to the painters Picasso, Chagall, Braque, Gris, Klee, Miro, and Villon. These were set to music for voice and piano by Francis Poulenc in 1950.

Many artists have had to depend on teaching or some other means of making a regular income. Seldom could they live by their creative efforts alone. Architects, however, are among the few remaining artists whose works receive broad recognition and who generally reap reasonable rewards from society. This is due in part to the functional nature of architecture: the new architecture evokes an enthusiastic response from a society that treasures efficiency and usefulness.

PAINTING

There was no dominant style in painting during the first half of the twentieth century. Because of the burgeoning number of styles and artists, not all of them can be represented in a one-volume survey. Three of the most important movements that seem endowed with the spirit of the Modern age are Expressionism, Cubism, and Surrealism. Other movements that flourished in the first half of the century were *Fauvism,* Constructivism, *Der Blaue Reiter* (Blue Rider), *Art Nouveau,* and *Dada.*

Expressionism

The movement in which artists went beyond natural appearances to present the inner meaning of natural phenomena is called **Expressionism.** Expressionist artists gave primary attention to the expression of intense, elemental feelings rather than to a description of the visible world. They were neither Romanticists nor realists. They had no desire to depict the world as they saw it but rather as they perceived it emotionally. As a consequence, their style included distortion of color, line, and form and, often, an almost violent application of paint to the canvas. They were aware of the conflicts inherent in the world and sought to express them in their art.

Matisse

Art historians place Henri Matisse (1869–1954) in the French Expressionist school called ***Fauvism*** (wild beasts), a style that used brilliant colors in a wild manner scorned by some art critics of the time. During the course of his life, Matisse was not committed to one style but experimented with several, including pointillism. His simple but strong forms, combined with his innovative use of color, were startling to his contemporaries. He used color without reference to three-dimensional forms or to the reality of forms. *The Blue Window* (colorplate 73) reflects his interest in strong color contrasts, decorative motifs, and the elimination of detail. It is an abstract still-life that blends into a stylized landscape. Perspective is suggested by the reduced intensity of color in the background. The colors do not fuse, but retain their own intense identities.

Colorplate 73 follows p. 322.

Klimt

An imaginative Austrian painter representing both Art Nouveau and Austrian Expressionism, Gustav Klimt (1862–1918), painted rich, decorative surfaces in his often erotic works. The surfaces frequently appear flat, denying the third dimension, and rely on pattern to create intense visual images. *Expectation* (colorplate 74) has the appearance of a rich, gold, Oriental quilt. The human figure is rendered almost invisible in the two repeated patterns. The flat surface decorations are strongly suggestive of Egyptian wall painting and even contain the repeated figure of an Egyptian eye. The result produces a two-dimensional surface that is sensuous and in many ways unique.

Colorplate 74 follows p. 322.

Rouault

Colorplate 75
follows p. 322.

An example of late Expressionism is found in the works of Georges Rouault (1871–1958), an original member of the *Fauvist* group. *Christ Mocked by Soldiers* (colorplate 75) is one of his religious paintings. The artist used broad heavy lines of black to give a forceful linear quality to the figure of Christ. He expressed the confrontation between Christ and the soldiers with deep reds and greens and by minimal but dramatic use of cobalt blue, colors characteristic of stained-glass windows. In fact, Rouault worked at the trade of stained glass for a time and carried over this technique into his paintings. Somewhat like van Gogh, he conveyed the feeling for his subject by heavy applications of colors and forceful lines. Organization and spatial depth seem secondary. In addition to the psychological realism of the incident, Rouault saw in the mocking of Christ a symbol of the mocking brutality of the modern world.

Kandinsky

Wassily Kandinsky (1866–1944) was an important figure in the cultural politics of the 1917 Russian Revolution. He was forced to leave Russia when the Soviets decided that nonrepresentational art did not fit their plan of Marxist propaganda. He went to Germany, where he was associated with **Der Blaue Reiter,** a school of painting centered in Munich around 1910, and taught at the Bauhaus School until the Nazi regime closed it. He eventually went to Paris, where he worked until his death.

Colorplate 76
follows p. 322.

In his abstractions, Kandinsky used color as the basis for artistic expression. In fact, he wrote extensive essays on the psychological and expressive meaning of color. *Painting Number 198* (colorplate 76) is one of a series of nonobjective paintings in which he used a complex rhythmic flow of line and color that seems to move from the bottom to the top of the work with energized movement and dramatically contrasting colors. The viewer's eye constantly moves along the line from color to color in much the same manner as the ear absorbs the line and tonal coloring of the contemporaneous music by Schoenberg and Webern.

Kollwitz

Käthe Kollwitz (1867–1945), a contemporary of Rouault, was one of the major artists of the first half of the twentieth century. She focused on the harshness of life, particularly as it was experienced by the poor. She found the world of graphics, with its dependence on black and white, a powerful medium of expression for such themes. The *Circle of Mothers,* a sculpture done in 1937, and such graphics as *Home Industry* and the *Peasants' War* series demonstrate her lifelong commitment to themes representing the downtrodden. In *Call of Death*

Figure 13.1
Käthe Kollwitz.
Call of Death, 1934.
Lithograph, 15 ×
15 in. (Art
Resource, NY)

(fig. 13.1), the black, deep-set eyes and the sparse use of detail in the face create a cadaverous appearance. Kollwitz uses black, gray, and white with great economy of line to express the imminence of death.

Cubism

Cubism was a style of twentieth-century art that reduced nature to basic geometric patterns such as circles, squares, triangles, and rectangles, and to three-dimensional forms, such as the cone, sphere, cube, and cylinder. The Cubists eliminated all superficial detail to reveal these patterns. Again, the artists painted what they knew, not what they saw. In pursuing this style, they were concerned more with *how* a work was painted and less with *what* was painted.

Picasso

The best-known painter of the twentieth century is Pablo Picasso (1881–1973). He did not limit himself to one idiom but experimented and changed his style many times. He was one of the first artists influenced by the sculpture of primitive Africa and artifacts from other non-Western cultures. Three of the five faces in *Les Demoiselles d'Avignon* (colorplate 77) are

*Colorplate 77
follows p. 322.*

in varying degrees Cubist renderings of African masks. The female figures are an early experiment with the faceting so characteristic of Cubism. They are distinguishable from the background to a large degree only through their color.

Building upon Cézanne's approach to forms and shapes, Picasso made notable advances in the techniques of Cubism. In addition to breaking natural objects into their basic geometric forms, he expressed new space relationships by reordering the components of the subject matter. He rejected all rules of perspective and showed several points of view at the same time. *Girl Before a Mirror* (colorplate 78) is one of Picasso's best-known paintings in Cubist style. He not only divided the female figure into its elemental forms but presented it from different points of view simultaneously, cleverly employing the mirrored image, an old formal device. He also reflected the recent scientific discoveries in the field of time-space relationships by destroying the traditional sense of time and space in painting. He superimposed a profile view of the body on a frontal view of the face and then reflected the image in the mirror. In reducing the figure to geometric forms, Picasso emphasized the breasts, abdomen, and hips, symbolic of womanhood. His lines are sharply emphasized with brilliant hues of black, red, yellow, green, and purple, suggesting, as did Rouault, the techniques of stained glass. Picasso created a nonrealistic painting of the idea of woman, using geometric forms.

Colorplate 78 follows p. 322.

A CLOSER LOOK

Picasso, *Guernica*

In 1937, the Spanish Republic commissioned Pablo Picasso to paint a mural for the Spanish pavilion at the International Exposition in Paris. This was a singular honor for the Spanish artist, who had been an expatriot for decades. Picasso's original intention for the mural was a large studio scene of a painter and a nude model. It would be joined in the exposition hall by the works of other famous artists, such as Joan Miró and Alexander Calder.

On April 26, 1937, the German Air Force, flying for Franco in the Spanish Civil War, bombed the Spanish village of Guernica as an experiment in modern warfare (the *Blitzkrieg*). Because of the speed and brutality of the air attack, the number of people killed, and the destruction caused, the experiment was a military success and the technique was to be used again and again.

This was an event of such shocking proportions that its repercussions were felt politically and artistically for decades. Paul Eluard, the outstanding French poet, wrote a poem, later set to music by Francis Poulenc, in response to this tragedy.

Picasso's previous art had been apolitical, but his response to the attack was to jettison the idea of the studio mural in favor of a strong protest against this savage event. The resulting work, *Guernica* (fig. 13.2), follows in a long succession of paintings protesting war, such as Delacroix's *Liberty Leading the People*, Goya's *The Third of May*, and Blume's *The Eternal City*.

Guernica was unlike anything Picasso had done before. In the past, his favorite subjects had included nudes, still lifes, and portraits. On May 1, a bare twenty-four days before the exposition opened, Picasso began a lengthy series of sketches. In them, he experimented with different sizes and proportions for the canvas and a variety of figures in various forms and shapes. Ultimately, he used drawings of fragments to symbolize the manifold horrors of destruction.

In the completed masterpiece there is no three dimensional depth; rather, there are only patterns on a two-dimensional plane. The colors are gray, black, and white—colors symbolic of death and mourning. Symbolic forms abound: a woman with her dead child, a broken sword, a dying horse, newsprint telling the horrible story. Other forms are clothed in the mystery of a dream world: the illuminated light bulb and the hand with a lamp (both perhaps revealing these horrors to the world), the violent but pathetic bull. The recognizable fragments of human and animal bodies attest to the dismemberment created by the bombing.

Two traditional symbols of Spanish culture, the bull and the horse, are metamorphosed in the painting. The bull is transformed into a brutish symbol for the thoughtless forces of war, while the horse, in the center of the mural, shrieks as a victim. Two human faces in the shape of teardrops are thrust into the picture, one from a burning building. They represent the people of the world gazing in shock on the horrors of the suffering. Finally, a small, inconspicuous flower seems to grow from the broken sword.

All this and much more make up Picasso's artistic protest against twentieth-century brutality. Every symbol does more than suggest a scene of terror; it also fits into the organization of abstract patterns of pure design. Despite his strong feelings about the subject, Picasso retained the abstract quality of twentieth-century painting, including stylistic elements from Cubism and Surrealism.

Figure 13.2   Pablo Picasso, *Guernica*, 1937. Oil on canvas, 11 ft. 6 in. × 25 ft. 8 in. Prado, Madrid, Spain.
© 1995 Artists Rights Society (ARS), New York, SPADEM, Paris.

Goncharova

*Colorplate 79
follows p. 322.*

Natalya Goncharova (1883–1962) was one of a large group of artists who fled from Russia to Paris during the tumultuous time of the Russian Revolution. Her early artistic efforts were directed to sculpture. Later, her interests in abstraction and the visual process led her in different directions. With her compatriot Larianov, she wrote the *Rayonist Manifesto* in 1913. This treatise expounded their theories of light and its effects on physical objects. *Linen* (colorplate 79) was painted in 1912 in the style of Analytical Cubism. The many textures that linen can take in slick, stiff collars and cuffs, decorative lace, and pleated napkins fill the pictorial space. The Russian word for laundry, using cyrillic letters, is prominent, as is an old-fashioned flat iron. Both contribute to the balance of this strongly two-dimensional painting and help to identify the subject for her contemporaries whose familiarity with Cubism was minimal.

Mondrian, Klee

*Colorplate 80
follows p. 322.*

Composition in White, Black, and Red (colorplate 80) by Piet Mondrian (1872–1944) carries Cubism to the point of abstraction. Mondrian dispensed with all suggestion of real objects and even eliminated an objective title. This painting is purely abstract art and not a realistic representation of nature. It suggests that just as music can appeal to one's aesthetic sense through its melody, harmony, and rhythm, painting can appeal through line, color, and organization. While the painting appears simple, it is actually very complex. Every line is of a different thickness (although this is difficult to detect in such a small reproduction), and each area of white is of a different size. The whole is organized and balanced with a mathematical exactness that makes it very difficult to imitate.

*Colorplate 81
follows p. 322.*

An important painter whose works verged on Surrealism, but were based on Cubism, is Paul Klee (1879–1940). His art uses delicate lines with subtle pastel coloring. *Twittering Machine* (colorplate 81) is almost a comic-strip drawing. By linear means, it amuses viewers with symbolic birds operated by a mechanical device, satirizing the mechanistic world. By the same devices, Klee even suggested the experience of sounds: the exclamation point coming from the beak of one of the birds suggests loudness. The sensation of piercing shrillness is suggested by an arrow through the beak of one of the "twitterers."

Surrealism

Perhaps the most spectacular movement of the twentieth century is **Surrealism,** a style of art that portrays the reality and intensity of the subconscious mind. This movement was inspired by scientific research and was linked closely to post–World War I developments in Freudian psychology and

dream interpretation. Surrealism freed those drives that are usually sup-
pressed in normal life and laid bare the motivating forces that influence our
thoughts, actions, and desires. It used stream-of-consciousness techniques to
record feelings or thoughts that are normally considered outside the realm
of expression, using symbols to convey the meanings of dreams. As a result,
all sorts of fantastic and unreal forms appear in Surrealistic art.

Dali

Salvador Dali (1904–1989) is the best-known and most sensational of the
Surrealists. *The Persistence of Memory* (colorplate 82), with its fantastically
limp watches, is an unforgettable painting. Dali painted everything with the
greatest detail; even the rocks in the distance are almost photographic in
their realism. Space seems limitless because of the elimination of atmosphere or aerial perspective. The most unnatural parts of this painting are
the limp watches hanging over a barren tree limb and over the edge of a
table; they are evidently Dali's idea of the symbolic nature of time. The distorted central figure and the juxtaposition of unrelated objects (ants and
pocket watch) evoke the feeling of a dream. The observer may not immediately understand all that Dali symbolized but will never forget the painting.

*Colorplate 82
follows p. 322.*

Blume

Contemporary events provided many subjects for early twentieth-century
artists. This was especially true of the rise of Fascism, Nazism, and Commu-
nism. Modern wars were frequently chosen as subjects for Expressionistic
and Surrealistic treatment. In the early thirties, the young American artist
Peter Blume (1906–1992) spent time observing the rise of Fascism in Italy
and came home to put on canvas what he had seen and felt. *The Eternal
City* (colorplate 83), an allegorical picture of wartime Rome complete with a
church, Mussolini, and the crushing weight of Fascism, was the result. Blume
gathered together a variety of symbols to remind viewers of the lost beauty
and tradition, the decadence and violence of Mussolini's Rome. The painting
is divided in half on the diagonal from the upper left to the lower right. The
ancient, stable past, represented in the upper right background, is painted in
a style and technique that would have been the envy of many fifteenth- and
sixteenth-century Italian painters. Its illumination and clarity contrast starkly
with the detailed Fascist world presented in the lower-left half of the painting. The symbols are painted in detail and sharply contrasted colors. The
bright green head of Mussolini contrasts with the blinding white of broken
marble. Christ, placed in a bright grotto in a dark wall with the symbols and
medals of war, overlooks the murky chasm into which humanity has been
plunged and from which the monster Jack-in-the-box head originates.
Blume's message is transmitted by the juxtaposition of incompatible objects.

*Colorplate 83
follows p. 322.*

This is an intentionally ugly picture. Blume wanted to make clear his prophecy of the end of Mussolini and Fascism years before it happened.

Miró

Colorplate 84 follows p. 322.

An artist who painted in both Surrealist and Abstractionist styles was Joan Miró (1893–1983). He suggested Surrealistic symbols by forms that appear as if they had developed as living organisms. Such forms are often called "biomorphic." In Miró's *Person Throwing a Stone at a Bird* (colorplate 84), the title stimulates certain expectations, and a whimsical fantasy is created by color and the almost childlike biomorphic forms. Its most striking aspects are the two-dimensional organization, the sharply defined curvilinear lines that define original shapes, and the brightly contrasting colors.

Chagall

Colorplate 85 follows p. 322.

Marc Chagall (1887–1985) was a Russian artist who never abandoned his affinity for Russian life and folklore. Although he was influenced in his early works by Cubism and its geometric forms, he revolted against its rationalism. His preference for irrational arrangements of natural objects led to a use of dream imagery in his paintings. *I and the Village* (colorplate 85) grew out of memories of his youth. The painting transports the viewer magically into the world of childhood dreams associated with Russian folklore. The composition consists of simple peasant figures, roosters, and floating cows, with a richly colored, cubistically treated irrational organization of figures that seem to hover in space.

Chagall was responsible for decorations for the opera house at Lincoln Center in New York and for the Paris Opera. Earlier, he was active in the Yiddish theater in Moscow where he designed scenery and costumes and painted decorative murals for theater interiors. The *Green Violinist* (fig. 13.3) was one of several studies of this "Fiddler on the Roof," the subject of a Yiddish folktale, and was used by Chagall in one of the murals of the Yiddish theater. The violin and the figure's location on the roof were symbolic of the precarious position of the Jews in a very repressive society. The painting is another example of his deep immersion in fantasy.

The works of the following three painters are of such stature that they deserve inclusion in this study. However, their individualistic styles do not place them in any of the artistic schools discussed earlier.

Rivera

One of Mexico's greatest twentieth-century painters was Diego Rivera (1886–1957). In many of his works, his populist political commitment is evident. Although he was an easel painter as well as a graphic artist, he is

Figure 13.3 Marc Chagall, *Green Violinist,* 1923–24. Oil on canvas, 78 × 42 3/4 in. (Solomon R. Guggenheim Museum, New York, Gift of Solomon R. Guggenheim 1937. Photo: David Heald)

best known in the United States as a muralist. He created frescoes in San Francisco, Detroit, and New York. Those decorating the Detroit Institute of Arts teem with twentieth-century machines, workers, and the activities of industry (colorplate 86). Even in the incomplete detail presented here, the visually busy nature of the work is apparent. While many murals by Rivera remain in Mexico, the Detroit mural is his most important work in the United States.

Colorplate 86 follows p. 322.

Figure 13.4   Palmer Hayden, *When Tricky Sam Shot Father Lamb,* n.d. Oil on canvas, 30 1/2 × 39 7/8 in. (Photo courtesy of the Los Angeles County Museum of Art)

Hayden

Palmer Hayden (1890–1973) was trained as an artist in the United States and France. In Paris, he enjoyed success as an exhibitor in several shows, including a one-man show of his own works. His earliest paintings were maritime scenes, but he turned more and more to scenes from African-American life. *When Tricky Sam Shot Father Lamb* (fig. 13.4) explores the folk idiom in painting. Hayden worked in a realistic style that might even be called "genre painting." Using flat, decorative color, much as did Matisse, there is little modeling of faces or figures. The psychological focus is achieved by the intense lighting on the tenement wall and the attention of the concerned neighbors.

O'Keeffe

There is a surrealistic quality in many of the works of Georgia O'Keeffe (1887–1986). This renowned American painter lived in New Mexico for much of her life, and the landscapes and artifacts of that region strongly influenced the content of her paintings. In *Cow's Skull with Calico Roses* (colorplate 87), a background of sand-colored rocks separated by a black void divides the background into two vertical sections. The chalky gray-white of the skull and roses lends a pallor to the whole. The gentle colors are interrupted by the tan section in the broken nose of the skull and the black vertical void. The bold symmetry of the painting is challenged by the slightly off-center void and the flower superimposed on the right horn of the skull. O'Keeffe's paintings seem to move between the fecundity of opulent flowers and the desolation of arid symbols of the desert.

Colorplate 87 follows p. 322.

SCULPTURE

Sculptors reacted to twentieth-century life in much the same manner as did painters. Cut loose from the patronage of the Church and the aristocracy, they also had to seek new functions and markets for their works. They too were alienated from the public because of the abstractness of their art and public conservatism. Like painters, sculptors experimented with new techniques and materials, seeking new expressiveness.

Artists began to create works in scale and design that fit into the modern home. In the past, they had conceived monumental pieces for the Church, for the palaces and gardens of the nobility, or for public buildings and memorials. With the virtual disappearance of these patrons, they turned to the home as a gallery, creating works especially designed as decorative pieces for modern living. New timesaving tools with which to work and new processes of reproduction also increased the availability of sculpture.

Unlike painters, who generally used the same materials as in the past, sculptors had a variety of new materials and processes at their disposal. Aluminum, chrome, and plastic are but a few that were successfully used. The physical characteristics of these new materials provided artists with the possibility of many new forms and surfaces with which to express modern life.

In general, sculptors followed the lead of painters in their attempts to go beyond natural appearances and to express inner meanings. They also subscribed to the same artistic creed—the revolt against Romanticism. Expressionism, Cubism, and Surrealism in painting had their counterparts in sculpture. Sculptors expressed their feelings about events and experiences in the same manner as their colleagues of the canvas and brush, but with different techniques and media.

Figure 13.5 Ernst Barlach, *The Avenger,* 1914. Bronze, 17 1/2 × 8 1/2 × 23 1/2 in. (Gift of Mrs. George Kamperman in memory of her husband Dr. George Kamperman, © Detroit Institute of Arts, 1989)

Barlach

The German sculptor Ernst Barlach (1870–1938) exemplifies early twentieth-century sculpture through the use of elemental planes, reduction of detail, and expressive distortion. *The Avenger* (fig. 13.5) is a dynamic image, infused with power through the appearance of imbalance and motion. As in many of Barlach's works, line plays a critical role. Although *The Avenger* has an aggressive stance with its raised sword, there is a benign spirit present, as in so much of Barlach's other work.

Lehmbruck

The Expressionist movement in sculpture is well represented by the works of Wilhelm Lehmbruck (1881–1919). He distorted and elongated forms in order to realize the expressive feeling he was seeking. In the *Kneeling Woman* (fig. 13.6) of cast stone, Lehmbruck endowed his figure with a feeling of simplicity and naturalness without being literal or objective. His mild distortion of the neck, torso, and limbs suggests an almost medieval asceticism. The open spaces add to the linear quality and to the feeling of elongation. Like van Gogh, Lehmbruck was not realistic about anything except the expression of humanity, pathos, and serenity of his subject.

Moore

Many sculptors employed Cubist style in their works. Some broke up their subjects into cubes and spheres while retaining the recognizable features. Others reduced their forms to almost complete abstraction. Henry Moore's

Figure 13.6 Wilhelm Lehmbruck, *Kneeling Woman*, 1911. Cast stone, 69 1/2 in. high, at base 56 × 27 in. (The Museum of Modern Art, NY. Abby Aldrich Rockefeller Fund Photograph © 1996 The Museum of Modern Art, NY)

(1898–1986) *Family Group* (fig. 13.7) typifies a style of organic free forms, with just enough physical realism to be representational. Moore was strongly influenced by primitivism, and this work shows a predilection for smooth, rounded forms that symbolize the shapes of the human figure without realistic detail. Moreover, there is unity among the figures that gives strength to the expressive idea of the family unit.

Brancusi

Constantin Brancusi (1876–1957) used highly polished surfaces of silver and bronze to show the play of light and dark in bringing out the natural shapes of geometric forms. *Mlle. Pogany* (fig. 13.8) is one of his best pieces in the Cubist tradition. The woman's head is a prolate spheroid, and the eyes are two great curves that meet at the nose. Contrast is provided by the texture of the hair and the elegantly attenuated wrists and hands. There is little decoration, emotion, or realism, but there is a play of light and shadow over the surface of the metal that gives rhythmic movement to the mass. There is also a formal organization of the sculptural masses that clearly suggests a human head.

Figure 13.7 Henry Moore, *Family Group,* 1950. Bronze, 59 1/4 × 46 1/2 in. high, at base 45 × 29 7/8 in. (The Museum of Modern Art, NY. A. Conger Goodyear Fund.) Photograph © 1996 The Museum of Modern Art, NY

Figure 13.8 Constantin Brancusi, *Mlle. Pogany, Version I,* 1913. After a marble of 1912, bronze, 17 1/4 in. high. (The Museum of Modern Art, NY. Acquired through the Lillie P. Bliss Bequest) Photograph © 1996 The Museum of Modern Art, NY

Figure 13.9 Malvina Hoffman, *Bengali Woman,* 1933. Bronze, 13 1/2 in. high. (The Field Museum, Chicago, –MH39T)

Hoffman

One of Rodin's American students of sculpture was Malvina Hoffman (1887–1966). After beginning her studies of painting and sculpture in New York, she went to Paris, where she became fascinated, much like Degas, with dancing figures. It was, however, as a portraitist that she became most famous. Her 105 busts of all racial types, commissioned by the Field Museum in Chicago, were a monumental effort and secured her place in twentieth-century sculpture. The *Bengali Woman* (fig. 13.9) from that series exudes dignity and serenity, hearkening back to a more traditional, realistic style of sculpture.

Arp

Human Concretion (fig. 13.10) by Jean (Hans) Arp (1888–1966) employs Surrealistic techniques of symbolic imagery. The softly molded, abstract forms are rhythmically balanced by the repetition of similar shapes of different sizes. These would be purely abstract but for the title *Human Concretion,* which implies the concreteness of something that is human and relates the forms to organic matter. Arp brought Surrealism into his work by his choice of title, creating both interest and confusion but nevertheless introducing an element of the subconscious.

Giacometti

Alberto Giacometti (1901–1966) was an important sculptor who joined the Surrealist movement. *Man Walking* (fig. 13.11) typifies his commitment to reducing objects to their elemental form. Elongation of line and rough, unpolished texture characterize his human and animal figures.

Figure 13.10 Jean (Hans) Arp, *Human Concretion,* 1935. Original plaster, 19 1/2 × 18 3/4 in. (The Museum of Modern Art, NY. Gift of the Advisory Committee. Photograph © The Museum of Modern Art, NY)

KINETIC ART

Kinetic Art, visual art that employs movement, has opened new avenues of creativity for artists, especially for sculptors. Some Kinetic artworks move by means of motors while others depend on the movement of air against delicately balanced forms. *Twittering Machine* (colorplate 81), by Paul Klee, may have suggested such mechanized kinetic artwork.

Calder

The American sculptor Alexander Calder (1898–1976) was a pioneer in Kinetic Art and is the best-known artist to use this medium. Using air currents to set his **mobiles** in motion, he introduced what amounted to a new art form in the 1930s. He suspended metal plates, painted with primary colors and black and white, from metal rods in such a way that they could move in any direction. When set in motion by currents of air, they revolve and exhibit a varied pattern of forms and colors in motion. His last monumental mobile was created for the Central Courtyard of the new East Building of the National Gallery of Art in Washington (colorplate 99). Calder's mobiles have become very popular with the public and are widely imitated as objects for home decoration.

Colorplate 99 follows p. 354.

Figure 13.11 Alberto Giacometti, *Man Walking,* 1960. Bronze, 71 3/4 × 10 1/2 × 38 in. (Albright-Knox Art Gallery/Buffalo, NY. Gift of Seymour H. Knox, 1961)

ARCHITECTURE

In architecture, the scientific and mechanical influences of the twentieth century have had their most obvious and most practical effects. In the first half of the century, the changes in industrial life, transportation, and communication—as well as those in economic and social life—all greatly influenced the function of architecture. Builders tried to adapt the planning, style, and construction of their architecture to meet the demands of a complex society. The new standards of living that made it possible for the average family to own its own home challenged architects to build efficient, comfortable, low-cost dwellings. In urban society, the large apartment house was developed into an economic and efficient edifice for modern living. Mass education required the building of educational plants in keeping with current philosophies of education. Supermarkets and large department stores were created to assist in the distribution of the enormous production of farms and factories. Factories became architectural achievements, providing open space for the machines of production and safe, pleasant surroundings for the workers. Skyscrapers became symbols of the rationally organized business life of the twentieth century.

In dealing with these changes, architects subscribed to the motto "Form follows function." For example, they viewed family dwellings from a sociological point of view. They made their plans according to the personalities of the owners, taking into consideration their professions, hobbies, social, and cultural preferences. Consequently, houses were designed to fit the needs of their occupants. This was also true for other kinds of structures, as architects let the efficient function of buildings determine their outward form. They eliminated superfluous decoration; they rejected traditional or derivative styles; they dared to let the inside speak for the outside. In general, the appearance of new buildings was a straightforward and simple expression of their functions. For their efforts, architects received more consistent patronage than any other artists. Conservatism was their great barrier for a time, but the efficient practicability of their designs soon won the approval of the doubtful.

Architectural innovations were possible because new materials and processes were developed, including steel, aluminum, reinforced concrete, glass, plywood, and plastics. In addition, central heating, the elevator, and electrical appliances helped make new designs more practical. The influence of the automobile on the construction and location of modern buildings was also great.

New materials encouraged new methods of construction, notably the **cantilever** method and **steel cage** construction (fig. 13.12). The cantilever is the projection of a slab, or beam, anchored at only one end. This was accomplished by the use of steel and reinforced concrete, materials of great tensile strength. The steel cage is just what the name implies—a cagelike skeleton consisting of steel beams. Both of these new methods made it possible to use glass for outside wall surfaces, for the weight is not borne by the walls but by the steel cage or by the cantilevered projection and its anchor.

Colorplate 73   Henri Matisse, *The Blue Window*. Issy-les-Moulineax, summer 1913. Oil on canvas, 51 1/2 × 35 5/8 in. The Museum of Modern Art, Abby Aldrich Rockefeller Fund. Photograph © 1996 The Museum of Modern Art, NY. © 1996 Artists' Rights Society (ARS), NY. *(See p. 305)*

Colorplate 74 Gustav Klimt, *Expectation,* c. 1905–1909. Mixed media and silver and gold leaf on paper, 76 × 45 3/8 in. Vienna, Austria. The Austrian Museum of Applied Arts. *(See p. 305)*

Colorplate 75 Georges Rouault, *Christ Mocked by Soldiers,* 1932. Oil on canvas, 36 1/4 ×
28 1/2 in. The Museum of Modern Art, NY. Given anonymously. Photograph © 1996 The
Museum of Modern Art, NY. *(See p. 306)*

Colorplate 76   Wassily Kandinsky, *Painting Number 198*, 1914. Oil on canvas, 64 × 36 1/4 in.
The Museum of Modern Art, NY. Mrs. Simon Guggenheim Fund. Photograph © 1996 The
Museum of Modern Art, NY. *(See p. 306)*

Colorplate 77 Pablo Picasso, *Les Demoiselles d'Avignon,* 1907. Oil on canvas, 8 ft. × 7 ft. 10 in. The Museum of Modern Art, NY. Acquired through the Lillie P. Bliss Bequest. Photograph © 1996 The Museum of Modern Art. ©1996 Artists Rights Society (ARS), NY/SPADEM, Paris. *(See p. 307)*

Colorplate 78 Pablo Picasso, *Girl Before a Mirror,* Boisgeloup, March 1932. Oil on canvas, 64 × 51 1/4 in. The Museum of Modern Art, NY. Gift of Mrs. Simon Guggenheim. Photograph © 1996 The Museum of Modern Art, NY. © 1996 Artists' Rights Society (ARS), NY/SPADEM, Paris. *(See p. 308)*

Colorplate 79 Natalya Goncharova, *Linen*, 1912. Oil on canvas, 37 5/8 × 33 in. Tate Gallery, London. *(See p. 310)*

Colorplate 80 Piet Mondrian, *Composition in White, Black, and Red,* 1936. Oil on canvas,
40 1/4 × 41 in. The Museum of Modern Art, NY. Gift of the Advisory Committee. Photograph
© 1996 The Museum of Modern Art, NY. *(See p. 310)*

Colorplate 81 Paul Klee, *Twittering Machine (Zwitscher-Maschine)*, 1922/151. Watercolor
and pen and ink on oil transfer drawing on paper, mounted on cardboard, 25 1/4 × 19 in. The
Museum of Modern Art, NY. Purchase. Photograph © 1966 The Museum of Modern Art, NY.
(See p. 310, 320, 372)

Colorplate 82 Salvador Dali, *The Persistence of Memory (Persistence de la mémoire)*, 1931. Oil
on canvas, 9 1/2 × 13 in. The Museum of Modern Art, NY. Given anonymously. Photograph
© 1996 The Museum of Modern Art, NY. *(See p. 311)*

Colorplate 83 Peter Blume, *The Eternal City,* 1934–1939 (dated on painting 1937). Oil on composition board, 34 × 47 7/8 in. The Museum of Modern Art, NY. Mrs. Simon Guggenheim Fund. Photograph © 1996 The Museum of Modern Art, NY. *(See p. 311)*

Colorplate 84   Joan Miró, *Person Throwing a Stone at a Bird,* 1926. Oil on canvas, 29 × 36 1/4 in. The
Museum of Modern Art, NY. Purchase. Photograph © 1996 The Museum of Modern Art, NY. © 1996
Artists' Rights Society (ARS). NY/ADAGP, Paris. *(See p. 312)*

Colorplate 85 Marc Chagall, *I and the Village,* 1911. Oil on canvas, 6 ft. 3 5/8 in. × 4 ft. 11 5/8 in.
The Museum of Modern Art, NY. Mrs. Simon Guggenheim Fund. Photograph © 1996
The Museum of Modern Art, NY. *(See p. 312)*

Colorplate 86 Diego Rivera, "Detroit Industry," north wall, 1932–1933. Fresco. (© The Detroit Institute of Arts Founders Society Purchase, Edsel B. Ford Fund and Gift of Edsel B. Ford) (See p. 313)

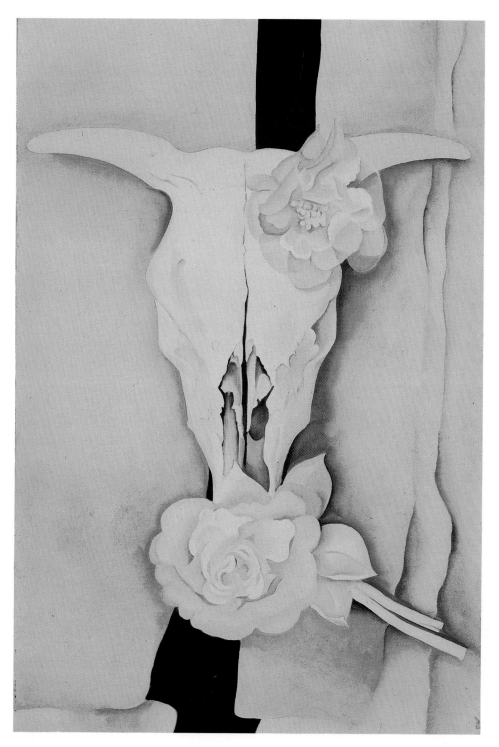

Colorplate 87 Georgia O'Keeffe, *Cow's Skull with Calico Roses*, 1932. Oil on canvas, 36 × 24 in. Gift of Georgia O'Keeffe, 1947.712. Photograph © 1994, The Art Institute of Chicago. All Rights Reserved. *(See p. 315)*

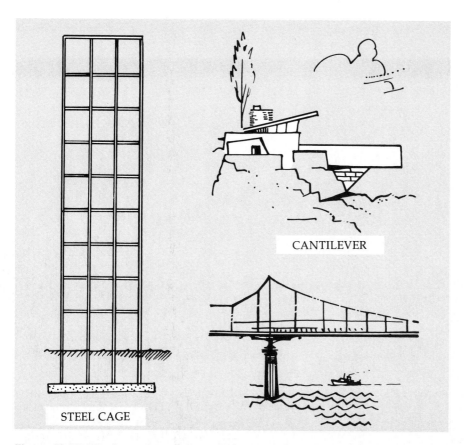

CANTILEVER

STEEL CAGE

Figure 13.12 Steel cage and cantilever construction—Sandgren

Wright

Another important trend, especially in domestic architecture, was the attempt to bring the outdoors into the building. Nature was no longer shut out of the house but was brought inside with large walls of glass. Nature also became part of the living space, with enclosed patios for outdoor living. The public became more conscious of view as well, and there was a tendency to integrate homes with their natural surroundings and to use materials indigenous to the locale. One of the finest examples is the famous Kaufmann House (fig. 13.13) in Bear Run, Pennsylvania, designed by Frank Lloyd Wright (1869–1959) for Edgar Kaufmann. Wright made the most of a stream and a waterfall that were on the site. He used cantilevers for overhanging balconies and brought nature into the house with large expanses of glass. Wright used elemental forms without decoration to express the function and simple beauty of the house in its natural surroundings.

Figure 13.13 Frank Lloyd Wright, Kaufmann House, 1937–39. Bear Run, Pennsylvania. (FPG International)

Frank Lloyd Wright also used glass and concrete to solve the problems of an industrial office building in the Johnson Wax Building (fig. 13.14) in Racine, Wisconsin. To support the great weight of the ceiling, he used hollow concrete piers that taper at the bottom and flare at the top. Indirect lighting through a diffused glass ceiling gives equal illumination without glare. The tapered piers provide maximum space for the desks, which were also designed by Wright.

Another striking example of integration with natural surroundings is the Watzek House (fig. 13.15) in Portland, Oregon, designed by the firm of Yeon and Doyle. The house was built on a hill overlooking the city and majestic Mount Hood. The lines of the structure imitate the contours of the distant mountain, making the building a form in a well-organized visual design. An exterior finish of natural wood helps the building blend into its

Figure 13.14 Frank Lloyd Wright, Interior of Johnson Wax Building, 1937–39. Racine, Wisconsin. (Courtesy Johnson Wax Company)

Figure 13.15 John B. Yeon and Albert E. Doyle, Watzek House, 1938. Portland, Oregon. (Courtesy Boychuk Studio)

Figure 13.16 Walter Gropius, Bauhaus at Dessau, 1925–26. Dessau, Germany. (Foto Marburg/Art Resource, NY)

setting among the shrubs and towering trees. This style has become one of the standards of domestic construction in the Pacific Northwest.

Gropius

The Bauhaus (fig. 13.16) at Dessau, Germany, is important not only from an architectural point of view but also because of its function. It was designed by Walter Gropius (1883–1969) as a technical school for creating designs and techniques for the twentieth century. Each workshop was a separate unit and its design was compatible with its activities. All the units were connected with covered passageways. Gropius used steel cage construction with glass for the outer walls. The exterior has the appearance of a curtain of glass hung over a masonry frame. The lack of ornament and the simple, angular pattern of the bands of glass and masonry are obvious.

Morgan

The impact of the first woman architect to graduate from the Ecóle des Beaux Arts in Paris was felt throughout the western United States. Julia Morgan

(1872–1957) founded a firm in California that had as many as sixteen architects, and she designed and supervised the construction of hundreds of homes, churches, and institutional buildings. Her legacy includes such impressive buildings in California as the Hearst Castle in San Simeon, Berkeley City Club, countless residences in the San Francisco area, and several buildings on the Mills College campus in Oakland.

MUSIC

At the start of the twentieth century, music—like the visual arts—was influenced by a number of forces, all of which were used to break with the nineteenth century and the Nationalist, Realist, and Impressionist movements. This was as true for popular music and music of the theater as it was for concert music.

The musical techniques employed in the nineteenth century were thought by many composers to be exhausted by the opening of the twentieth century. They had to find new ways to express their musical ideas.

Melodically and harmonically, there were at least two ways to change: divide the octave into smaller intervals to create more tones, or find new principles of construction so the old materials could be used in new ways. While the former was attempted by a few composers, it did not succeed in winning any significant number of adherents. The other solution, to find new principles of construction, has been applied in various ways throughout the century.

In a sense, all the attempts grew out of the practices of the nineteenth century. Harmonically as well as melodically, later Romantic composers created ever more dissonant harmonies to increase musical tension and expressiveness. However, these dissonances were part of a system of harmony that functioned around a central tonality. Twentieth-century composers came to appreciate the musical value of dissonant treatment for the sake of the dissonance itself. They found a certain expressive beauty in dissonance that seemed compatible with twentieth-century ideas and justified its use by various principles of construction. Among these were the use of free dissonant tones (greatly expanded but still within traditional harmonic principles), the use of two or more keys simultaneously **(polytonality),** the principle of the twelve-tone row **(serialism),** or the deliberate denial of tonality as a principle, without any formalized system to replace it **(atonality).**

The result of these practices was the dissonance that characterizes much of twentieth-century music. After listening to a representative work, most people would describe it as extremely dissonant and would be unable to reconcile its harmonies with the familiar—and therefore "correct"—harmonic practices of eighteenth- and nineteenth-century music.

In reshaping the element of rhythm, composers began to write more irregular and asymmetrical phrases and frequently employed mixed meters. These changes began in the music of some late nineteenth-century composers. Nationalist composers, in particular, exploited the unusual rhythmic and metric patterns of folk music, especially those of eastern Europe. Meters such as 5/4 were commonly found in the music of Slavic composers, such as Tchaikovsky and Mussorgsky. Twentieth-century composers have expanded these rhythmic irregularities to an enormous degree. In the works of some composers there is scarcely a set meter, and some have even written without meter signatures. Such metric patterns as 5/4, 7/16, and 11/8 are commonly used, not always consistently, but liberally interspersed with the other conventional patterns, so the total effect is one of great irregularity. Moreover, many works achieve rhythmic complexity by the juxtaposition of one or more independent rhythms. While such rhythmic complexities can be difficult for the performer, average listeners are not as disturbed by them as they are by dissonances. Difficulties in performance, however, have prevented widespread acceptance of contemporary music by many musicians and often result in poor performance by others.

Tone color was exploited by even the most traditional twentieth-century composers. Some composers added immeasurably to the tonal palette of the orchestra by making new demands on old instruments or by calling for new sound devices, such as wind machines, electronic instruments, sirens, and noisemakers of all sorts—even to the dropping of glass in a bucket and shaking it.

Music from outside the concert hall began to influence what happened inside. Most influential was the new popular style known as jazz, which distinctly influenced a number of twentieth-century composers. Some elements of jazz derived from African music. African drums of all types, the sitar from India, and bronze instruments from the Indonesian *gamelan* (orchestra) stimulated the new interest in exotic tone colors. The use of electronics in music began in the first half of the twentieth century, but its main influence was not felt until after World War II. In each of these ways, twentieth-century music has challenged the listener. Most early twentieth-century composers were interested in doing away with Romanticism. Their efforts led in many different directions, each of which challenged the listener in a different way.

Schoenberg

Arnold Schoenberg (1874–1951) was one of the most controversial composers of the early twentieth century. At first a vigorous follower of the Wagnerian tradition, he soon felt the necessity for a new system of composition. As a result, he devised a technique based on the independence and equality of each of the twelve tones of the chromatic scale, often referred to as the dodecaphonic or **twelve-tone system.** In it, harmonic and melodic relationships were governed not by procedures of traditional harmony but by an arbitrary pattern of twelve tones. This "tone row" was the unifying element of the composition. It served as a theme for countless variations. Its constant reappearance provided a new kind of unity; its constant variation provided interest. The resulting works were compositions alien to the harmonic style of the eighteenth and nineteenth centuries, in which harmony was the result of a closely knit, formal organization. Schoenberg's work, on the other hand, purposely avoided any suggestion of traditional tonality. It sounds thoroughly dissonant if one uses traditional harmonic sonorities as a frame of reference. For this reason, it is often referred to as "atonal" music. Nonetheless, he thought of his works as following in the tradition of Wagner and Strauss.

One of the early works of Schoenberg from the period of 1921 to 1923 is the *Serenade,* op. 24. In this Expressionist work, Schoenberg experimented with his new technique. Several of the seven movements were based on the same twelve-tone row (example 13.1). The formal organization of each movement was traditional: march, variation, minuet, song, and dance. However, the composer's treatment of the tonal material was in no way traditional. Melody, even when given to the voice as in the fourth movement, was not easily performed. Rhythm was one of the principal means of varying the tone row and was, therefore, very free and irregular. The unusual combination of instruments for which the *Serenade* is scored (clarinet, bass clarinet, mandolin, guitar, violin, cello, and bass voice) indicated Schoenberg's interest in timbres. Moreover, each of the instruments was exploited in most extraordinary ways.

Example 13.1　Tone row in *Serenade,* op. 24 by Arnold Schoenberg

A number of factors join together to keep music of this kind from frequent performance. Among them are the aggressive departure from tradition, the difficulty of its performance, a lack of sympathetic and willing performers among those technically capable, and the resulting bewilderment of the public. In the last quarter of the twentieth century, there are very few advocates of dodecaphonic music.

Berg

One of the most successful of Schoenberg's pupils was Alban Berg (1885–1935), an exponent of the twelve-tone system of composition. He eventually used this technique in operas, chamber music, and orchestral and vocal works. In all of these, he succeeded in tempering the strict dissonance of the twelve-tone system with a freedom that has made his music widely accepted.

The *Violin Concerto*, written in 1935, was his last completed composition. It was commissioned by the American violinist Louis Krasner and dedicated to the memory of Manon Gropius, the eighteen-year-old daughter of Alma Mahler, the widow of Gustav Mahler, and Walter Gropius, the architect. The young girl had died after a year of poliomyelitis, and the concerto's form and expression were influenced by the affection and admiration Berg held for this lovely girl.

The work is based on a most extraordinary tone row (ex. 13.2) that enabled the composer to combine the modern dissonance of twelve-tone music with traditional harmony. It also included a complete Bach chorale and fragments of a second. The concerto falls into two large parts, or movements, each of which is further divided into sections joined without pause. The first movement describes the beauty of the young Manon, and the second movement describes her suffering and death.

Example 13.2: Tone row in the Violin Concerto by Alan Berg

In the first movement, the introduction is a dialogue between the violin and the orchestra that exposes the tone row in various forms. The second section of the first movement depicts the youthful character of the girl with its ready reference to Viennese waltz rhythms and the eventual inclusion of an Austrian folk dance toward the end of the movement.

The second movement recalls the tragic death and ultimate deliverance of Manon. The incorporation of the two familiar German chorale tunes made this complicated work more accessible to the Viennese audience. Both of them, *O Ewigkeit, du Donnerwort (Oh eternity, thou thunderous word)* and *Es ist genug so nimm, Herr (It is enough, Lord, set me free)* lend comfort to the bereaved. By including these chorales, Berg tied the present to the past.

Webern

Anton Webern (1883–1945) not only adopted the twelve-tone technique of his teacher, Schoenberg, but extended its implications to what could be called completely organized serialism. Not only is each of the twelve tones used before any one is repeated, but the tonal qualities are organized so that no instrument plays two successive tones of a theme; dynamics are similarly constrained. The thematic material is extremely terse and concentrated, not unlike the paintings of Klee.

The *Five Orchestral Pieces,* op. 10 were written in 1913 before Webern had adopted the twelve-tone system of composition. They illustrate the succinct manner of Webern's writing, which he never abandoned and which influenced other composers of the twentieth century, such as Stravinsky and many later electronic composers.

Some facts concerning the fourth piece of the set will give an idea of Webern's economy of means. The entire piece is only six measures long, and in it nine instruments perform only fifty-seven printed notes. With a metronomic marking of sixty beats to the minute, and allowing for the two *ritardando* (slowing-down) passages, the total playing time does not exceed twenty-four seconds. Based on such economic structural and formal means, Webern fashioned an extremely concise expression of fleeting, kaleidoscopic tonal changes.

Vaughan Williams

While it would be wrong to underestimate the importance of the so-called Second Viennese School, of which Schoenberg, Berg, and Webern are the most famous adherents, there were other important musical styles being explored. In his vocal and instrumental music, Ralph Vaughan Williams (1872–1958) continued to write in a more Romantic-Nationalist style. He was drawn to the folk music of the British Isles and, like Bartók, was a major collector of traditional songs. His orchestral works are enriched by the inclusion of many British folk melodies and the spirit of British folk song. His *Fantasia on Greensleeves* and *Fantasia on a Theme by Thomas Tallis* continue to be popular and important in the concert repertoire.

Stravinsky

Of all twentieth-century composers, Igor Stravinsky (1882–1971) has unquestionably been the most successful in winning acceptance from the public. This was not accomplished easily, however, and many of his finest early works are, after almost one hundred years, still rarely heard. Stravinsky's music stems from a different tradition than did that of Schoenberg. His musical education was in the school of the realistic Nationalism of the Russian Five. One of them, Rimsky-Korsakov, was his teacher, whose influence is particularly evident in the works he wrote in the first twenty-five years of the century. His important compositions were ballets or at least stage works, many with Russian themes. *L'Oiseau de feu (The Firebird)*, *Petrouchka,* and *Le Sacre du printemps (The Rite of Spring)* are the most famous.

Two of these, *Petrouchka* and *The Rite of Spring,* have become standard works in the field of ballet, and all three are widely heard in Stravinsky's own versions for orchestral performance. *The Rite of Spring* created a near riot at its first performance in Paris in 1913 and is an important landmark of twentieth-century music.

In *The Rite of Spring,* as in almost all of his subsequent works, Stravinsky neither followed nor formulated any set theory of composition. Much of his work was characterized by a free use of dissonance that reached the extreme of atonality in only a few instances. Rhythmic drive, often resulting in brutal reiteration within very complex and irregular patterns, characterized his works. They were also known for an inventive and daring use of timbres, combining instruments with great effectiveness. Stravinsky not only combined instruments in unusual ways but also explored the extreme ranges of instruments for timbral effect, creating tone colors that run the gamut from great beauty to cruel ugliness. The primitive costumes provided by the designer Roerich, and the eccentric and unconventional postures and movements of the choreographer Nijinsky, contributed to the riotous rejection of its first performance (fig. 13.17).

Bartók

Béla Bartók (1881–1945) was drawn early to the folk music of his native Hungary and all Balkan peoples. So great was his interest in traditional music that he even studied the music of North Africa. The harmonies and rhythms of the musicians of the Balkan states, untouched by the concert-music tradition of western Europe, intrigued Bartók. Many of his piano pieces are derived from folk songs and dances. Moreover, his large works for orchestra also were influenced by his long and serious study of folk music, which led him to collect over ten thousand of these works.

The *Concerto for Orchestra* was one of the last great works of Bartók, composed during his terrible final years of illness in New York. It was written for the Boston Symphony on commission by its conductor, Serge Koussevitzky. Bartók explained his use of the term *concerto* in the title as a wish "to treat the single instruments in a concertante or soloistic style," returning to the Baroque concerto style of the early eighteenth century.

The *Concerto* consists of five movements. The first contains a slow introduction in the grand manner of the eighteenth-century, followed by an allegro-vivace section. The introduction is based on an intervallic motive of a fourth. Bartók was particularly fond of using this interval in many of his compositions, since it frequently occurred in the folk-song traditions with which he was familiar. The first movement is built on the traditional sonata-allegro form, and the use of the interval of the fourth is prominent in the thematic

Figure 13.17
Costumes and movements for Stravinsky's *Le Sacre du Printemps*, 1913. The Joffrey Ballet Dancers: Jill Davidson, Julie Janus, and Meg Gurin. Choreography by Millicent Hodson. (Photo by Herb Migdoll)

material. The second movement has the title *Game of Pairs,* and Bartók features five pairs of wind instruments in a series of short sections. Each pair is combined at a specific and individual interval: bassoons at the sixth, oboes at the third, clarinets at the seventh, flutes at the fifth, and trumpets at the second. In the restatement of the five sections, Bartók wrote a more elaborate instrumentation. The third movement, *Elegia,* is a song of death. The fourth movement, *Interrupted Intermezzo,* begins with a tune of folk character followed by a lyric melody; after an interruption by a tune in a more popular style, the first part returns. Characteristic of the rhythm of the entire movement is its alternation of 2/4, 3/4, 5/8, 6/8, and 7/8 meters, making an obviously asymmetrical scheme. The *Finale,* marked *pesante* (heavy) brings the work to a close with folk-tune material. The interval of the fourth is again prominent and the movement includes a fugue-like section that uses all the devices of counterpoint. Dissonances and rhythmic and timbral complexities give this a freshness and spontaneity typical of twentieth century music.

Ives

Charles Ives (1874–1954) used the traditional songs and gospel hymns of his native New England in much the same way that Bartók used Hungarian music in his compositions. Ives is one of those creative spirits who came from a traditional background and whose works foreshadowed musical techniques that became widely used and accepted years later. Almost his entire compositional output predates World War I, yet most of it was never heard until after World War II. The orchestral work *Central Park in the Dark in the Good Old Summertime* represents Ives's predilection for quoting folk tunes and popular songs. These are used contrapuntally, usually in different simultaneous tonalities and polyrhythms. Written early in the twentieth century (the composing of the work continued from 1898 to 1906), it is, in the words of Ives, "a picture in sound of the sounds of nature and of happenings that men would hear when sitting on a bench in Central Park on a hot summer night."

Gershwin

The music of George Gershwin (1898–1937) was profoundly influenced by jazz. He achieved stature with his scores for the concert stage and theater, as opposed to the predominantly improvised and spontaneous music of his jazz contemporaries. In *Rhapsody in Blue, An American in Paris,* and the *Piano Concerto in F,* he successfully integrated the jazz idiom with the more-or-less traditional forms of concert music. Because of its pictorial qualities, the symphonic poem *An American in Paris* has been successfully adapted for the dance, and the film of the same name. His works for the musical theater, such as *Of Thee I Sing* and *Girl Crazy,* supplied many hit tunes popularized throughout the world by jazz bands, but they also instilled a new life into the fading romantic operetta form that resulted in a new era of Broadway musicals. His opera *Porgy and Bess* is a successful amalgam of jazz, blues, spiritual, and folk song with a highly dramatic quality that can be called "folk opera." Its musical achievements place it favorably among the more traditional operatic masterworks.

Popular Music

In the first half of this century, there were at least five major movements in popular music, as well as numerous smaller movements, some of which are very well known. These five are ragtime, blues, jazz, swing, and the Broadway musical. Although the term *jazz* was once used to denote all the phases of twentieth-century American popular music, that usage is no

A Closer Look

Ives, *The Unanswered Question*

The Unanswered Question (1908) was an experimental work. It was written for string quartet (or chamber strings), woodwinds, and trumpet. Ives suggested that the strings should be placed either off stage or apart from the other instruments. The three sonorities (strings, woodwinds, trumpet) all maintain separate identities, though they sometimes overlap (ex. 13.3). The strings present a quiet background (designated by Ives as "The Silence of the Druids—Who Know, See, and Hear Nothing") against which a solo trumpet reiterates an angular but quiet melodic gesture ("The Perennial Question of Existence"). The woodwinds respond with increasing agitation ("The Fighting Answerers"). The string and trumpet parts are marked *Largo molto sempre* (very slow throughout). The woodwinds have no less than eight different tempo indications, each one faster than the previous one and independent of the strings and trumpet.

Similarly, the dynamics are almost imperceptibly but constantly changing. The strings have a very modest dynamic range, beginning with *ppp* and concluding with *pppp*, maintaining the muted background. The trumpet, too, has little dynamic variety. It begins and continues *piano* in its repetitious melody and concludes with a final *pianissimo* statement of "the question." The woodwinds have terraced dynamics. Their first response to "the question" is marked *piano*, and each successive response is louder and faster until the final response, which concludes *ffff*.

Example 13.3 Graphic analysis of *The Unanswered Question* by Charles Ives

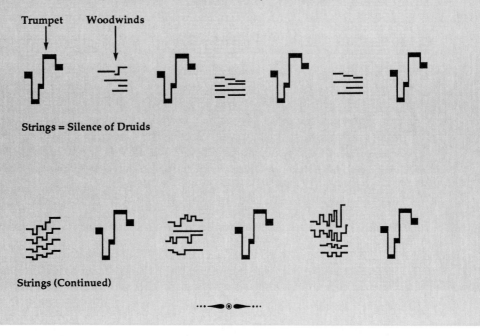

longer accurate. The phrase *popular music* will therefore be used here, although that term has difficulties as well. Since popular music is a musical practice and not a form of composition, it tends to be ever-changing in character and style. If success is judged by financial reward and acceptance by large numbers of people in many cultures, this music has become the most successful music of the twentieth century.

Among the most important sources of ragtime, blues, and jazz were the spirituals of African-American religious communities and the work songs, called "hollers," of the African-American fieldworkers of the South. Other sources included African religion and music, American popular music, Civil War musical instruments, and the creative talents of early African-American musicians themselves.

Ragtime was a name that appeared in the 1890s to describe a style that was to become popular through the first two decades of the twentieth century. It was largely a style of piano playing in which syncopation and at least two layers of rhythmic activity were applied to the slow, duple rhythms of march music. The works of Scott Joplin (1868–1917), which were revived after World War II, are good examples of this early ragtime. Many of his works, such as "Maple Leaf Rag" and "Pineapple Rag," are well known today.

Although many aspects of blues style have their roots in the nineteenth century and the rural life of southern African Americans, blues came to the attention of white American listeners around 1920. It became one of the dominant movements of jazz during the next few decades and continues today.

Blues tunes typically are based on twelve-measure patterns that allow much improvisation. In addition to the twelve-measure phrase, some blues lyrics are written in iambic pentameter, a common classic poetic scheme. Certain alterations in the major scale, namely, the lowering of the third and seventh degrees, gave rise to the term *blue notes,* which led to the term *blues* as a name of this type of song. The interplay between these flatted notes in the melody and those of the normal scale in the harmony is a characteristic of the blues. Another common characteristic is the double meaning of many lyrics (for example, expressing pain over the misery of life while simultaneously laughing at the same problem). "Memphis Blues" and "St. Louis Blues" by W. C. Handy (1873–1958), two examples of this style, have become classics in the repertoire of popular music.

Toward the end of the first decade of the twentieth century, another popular musical style began to emerge, and a word of obscure origins was used to describe it. The word was **jazz,** and it originally was applied to the popular tunes of eight and sixteen measures length into which ragtime and blues were incorporated. These were regularly performed by small groups of instrumentalists consisting of cornet, clarinet, trombone, drums, and piano. The music was highly syncopated and relied heavily on improvisation by the various soloists. It was, above all, dance music and had for many years a very unsavory reputation associated with drinking, promiscuous sex, and "loose" living. One style during this time was known as Dixieland jazz, which emphasized polyphonic improvisation by the performers. In the 1920s, jazz became the accepted name for all types of popular music and remained so until challenged by the rock and roll style of the post–World War II era.

The movement of African Americans to northern cities after World War I moved the centers of jazz from New Orleans to St. Louis, Chicago, and Kansas City, each of which developed a style of its own. Several of the original instruments were superseded—for example, the banjo, which had been occasionally used, was replaced by the guitar, the cornet by the trumpet, and the tuba by the string bass. The band was built up of melody and harmony sections. The clarinet, trumpet, trombone, and saxophone usually made up the melody section; the piano, string bass, and percussion comprised the harmony and rhythm sections.

One common form of jazz was based on the traditional three-part song typical of the music of western Europe since the sixteenth century. This form was used for the chorus (or refrain) of popular song. The verse was rarely used as part of the instrumental rendition. In the chorus, four eight-measure phrases (A-A-B-A) made up the dance tune; these were repeated a number of times to allow for improvised solos based on the tune by various members of the ensemble.

Personal appearances, as well as recordings, made such performers as Louis (Satchmo) Armstrong, Duke Ellington, and Bix Beiderbecke known to a worldwide audience. Paul Whiteman directed a jazz orchestra that premiered Gershwin's *Rhapsody in Blue,* thereby establishing itself as one of the leading groups in the 1920s.

Just prior to World War II, a new jazz style called **swing** emerged. While it was not an abrupt departure from earlier performance practices, swing emphasized danceable, easy-flowing rhythms. It suited the timbres of dance orchestras of around fifteen members rather than the smaller combos (combinations) of four, five, or six players so popular earlier. Swing also featured compositions by white band leaders rather than those of the African-American composers who had dominated previous styles.

In this new era of big bands and swing, improvisation gave way in some degree to written arrangements. The big bands of Guy Lombardo, Benny Goodman (the "King of Swing"), Duke Ellington, Tommy and Jimmy Dorsey, Harry James, and Glenn Miller, to name but a few, dominated popular music, particularly on the radio and in the recording business. Other styles, such as bebop and funky jazz, as well as the return of the small combo, led to the rock and roll era of post–World War II.

In the 1920s and thereafter, there developed an important field of musical entertainment known as "musical comedy" or the "Broadway musical." Closely related to the European tradition of the operetta in the late nineteenth century, these musical plays incorporated the popular musical styles of the day so successfully that many current hit songs were drawn directly from the plays. Such teams as George and Ira Gershwin, Rodgers and Hart, Rodgers and Hammerstein, and Lerner and Loewe created a treasure-trove of musical plays squarely in the popular musical tradition.

Summary

Summarizing any period of twentieth-century art and music is made exceedingly complicated by the rapid changes that occurred in every area of life. Technological and scientific developments, as well as dramatic economic, political, intellectual, and social changes have come about since the turn of the century. The arts responded to and were affected by all these developments. Technological innovations have had an especially important impact on the arts, both in patronage and in communicating the artist's message to the public. The advances made in transportation and the media, as well as printing, recordings, and color photography, have made it possible for the public to experience artworks that in the past were available only to a few people.

There have been a number of movements, especially in visual art, that have captured the spirit of the twentieth century in one way or another. Expressionism, Cubism, and Surrealism have in their own ways focused attention on some of the important facets of twentieth-century culture.

While music cannot be defined in terms of the same movements, there are certain analogous relationships that can be discerned. For example, some music by Webern can be considered analogous to the art of the Surrealists, and Stravinsky had a close working relationship with Cubist painters such as Picasso. Schoenberg was not only a composer but a painter as well, and was closely associated with the artistic ideas of Kandinsky. Furthermore, Schoenberg's compositional style, called the twelve-note system, was of seminal influence in music of the time.

Jazz, blues, ragtime, and Dixieland are also facets of the spirit of the early twentieth century. The improvisational style of this music is reminiscent of the Renaissance and Baroque periods. The music, however, is thoroughly modern in its use of new instrumental and compositional techniques.

There are a few abiding principles that prevail in almost all twentieth-century art. One is the denial of the emotional excesses of Romanticism. Instead, there is an emphasis on technical developments and new principles of construction. Decoration and ornamentation were discarded in favor of the inherent beauty of paint, stone, metal, plastic, color, simple lines, and even individual sounds in music. New concepts of time and space were suggested by various means in all the arts, including music.

The arts of the first half of the twentieth century were a reaction to the Romanticism and Impressionism of the nineteenth century and revealed the spirit of change taking place in the technological and sociocultural arena. World War II and its dramatic aftermath, however, precipitated even more radical departures from tradition in the following decades.

Suggested Readings

In addition to the specific sources that follow, the general readings listed on pages 388 and 389 contain valuable information about the topics of this chapter.

Austin, William W. *Music in the Twentieth Century*. New York: W. W. Norton, 1966.

Barr, Alfred, Jr. *What Is Modern Painting?* 6th ed. New York: Museum of Modern Art, 1975.

Brett, Guy. *Through Our Own Eyes: Popular Art and Modern History*. Philadelphia, PA: New Society Publishers, 1987.

Butler, Christopher. *Early Modernism: Literature, Music, and Painting in Europe, 1900–1916*. New York: Oxford University Press, 1994.

Jones, LeRoi. *Blues People: Negro Music in White America*. New York: Wm. Morrow and Co., 1963.

Machlis, Joseph. *Introduction to Contemporary Music*. 2d ed. New York: W. W. Norton, 1979.

Neighbor, Oliver, Paul Griffiths, and George Perle. *The New Grove Second Viennese School: Schoenberg, Webern, Berg*. New York: W. W. Norton, 1983.

Salzman, Eric. *Twentieth-Century Music: An Introduction*. 3d ed. Englewood Cliffs, NJ: Prentice-Hall, 1988.

Slonimsky, Nicholas. *Music Since 1900*. 5th ed. New York: Schirmer, 1993.

Somfai, Laszlo, et al. *The New Grove Modern Masters: Bartók, Stravinsky, Hindemith*. New York: W. W. Norton, 1984.

Wilder, Alec. *American Popular Song: The Great Innovators 1900–1950*. New York: Oxford University Press, 1972.

Chapter 14

····•◦●◦•····

The Arts Today
(1945 to the Present)

Chronology

Visual Arts	Music	Historical Figures and Events
•Fernand Léger (1881–1955)		
•Mark Rothko (1903–1970)		
•Barbara Hepworth (1903–1975)		
•Willem de Kooning (1904–)		
•Luigi Dallapiccola (1904–1975)		
•David Smith (1906–1965)		
	•Elliott Carter (1908–)	
	•Olivier Messiaen (1908–1992)	
	•Benny Goodman (1909–1986)	
•Jackson Pollock (1912–1956)	•John Cage (1912–1992)	
	•Benjamin Britten (1913–1976)	
	•Leonard Bernstein (1918–1990)	
•Roy Lichtenstein (1923–)	•Gyorgi Ligeti (1923–)	
•Robert Rauschenberg (1925–)	•Gunther Schuller (1925–)	
•Agam (1928–)	•Karlheinz Stockhausen (1928–)	
	•Thea Musgrave (1928–)	
•Claes Oldenburg (1929–)		
•Andy Warhol (1930–1987)		
•Bridget Riley (1931–)		
	•Krzysztof Penderecki (1933–)	
	•Morton Subotnick (1933–)	
	•Peter Maxwell Davies (1934–)	
	•Elvis Presley (1935–1977)	
	•Arvo Pärt (1935–)	
	•Steve Reich (1936–)	
	•Philip Glass (1937–)	
•Robert Smithson (1938–1973)		
	•John Lennon (1940–1980)	
		•First assembly of the United Nations (1946)
•Pop and Op Art (c. 1950)		
•United Nations Building completed (1950)		
	•Rock and Roll begins (c. 1955)	
	•The Beatles (Formed 1955)	

Chronology (*Continued*)

Visual Arts	Music	Historical Figures and Events
		• First satellite (*Sputnik*) launched by Russia (1957)
• Solomon R. Guggenheim Museum opens (1959)		
	• Wynton Marsalis (1961–) • Woodstock (1969)	• First man landed on the moon (1969)
	• John F. Kennedy Center for the Performing Arts opens (1971)	• First space shuttle launched (1971)
• Hiroshima Museum and Sculpture Garden opens (1974)		• Richard Nixon resigns U. S. presidency (1974) • Vietnam War ends (1975)
• Centre National d'Art et de Culture Georges Pompidou opens (1977)		
		• China's Tiananmen Square riots (1989)
• National Cathedral, Washington D.C. completed (1990)		• Germany reunited; USSR collapsed (1990) • South Africa ends apartheid (1994)

Pronunciation Guide

Agam (Ah´-gahm)
Berio, Luciano (Bay´-ree-oh, Loo-chah´-noh)
Bernstein (Bern´-stine)
Boulez (Boo-lez)
Dallapiccola (Dahl-lah-peek´-koh-lah)
Henze (Hen´-tse)
Krenek (Kre´-nek)
Léger (Lay-zhay)

Lichtenstein (Likh´-ten-stine)
Ligeti (Li-get´-ee)
Messiaen (Mes-ee-yă)
Milhaud (Mee-yoh)
Nono (Noh´-noh)
Pei (Pay´-ee)
Penderecki (Pen-der-et´-skee)
Rauschenberg (Row´-shen-berg)
Rochberg (Rokh´-berg)

Rothko (Roth´-koh)
Schuller (Shool´-ler)
Stockhausen (Shtock´-how-zen)
Tinguely (Tăn-glee)

Study Objectives

1. Study cultural trends since World War II as revealed in the visual arts and music.
2. Become familiar with the principles of design and composition and the various styles in the arts of the last five decades.
3. Learn about the influence of pop culture upon the visual and musical arts.

The end of World War II in 1945 marked a watershed in the development of artistic expression. The arts were altered by the consequences of World War II, especially by the resulting migrations of millions of people and the changes in political boundaries and alliances. It would be an error, however, to suggest that postwar art and music represented something entirely new. As suggested earlier, all artistic developments have roots in the past, and the roots of postwar art lay deep in the soil of the late nineteenth and early twentieth centuries.

A veritable explosion of technology drastically changed the lifestyles of people the world over. While the mass media had been powerful before 1939, they became even more pervasive as a result of developments related to television and satellite communication. Data processing and computers made instant information possible. Refinements in the techniques and psychology of advertising have made household words of a vast variety of products over the entire world. The mobility of people also increased dramatically. Air transportation made travel to every part of the globe easily accessible. As a result, there has been a cross-fertilization of cultures that threatens to destroy the long-standing integrity of racial and ethnic groups and their indigenous cultures. Countless terms, such as *Coca-Cola* and *jazz,* that in the first half of the twentieth century had been symbols of American culture have been adopted by the rest of the world. Some recent international icons include Andy Warhol, Michael Jackson, Madonna, and Rambo. What was formerly peculiar and exclusive to the people of a certain nation or culture has been spread worldwide.

As technology changed, so have the moral and ethical values by which people regulate themselves and relate to each other. The use of drugs as a protest and escape, and the corruption of expressive language are regrettable but undeniable. The denial of individual freedom has prompted social concern for civil and human rights worldwide. Terrorism, kidnapping, murder, and bombing have become commonplace responses to grievances in all parts of the world. The protests in the United States to the Vietnam War, and more recently, the response of students and citizens to years of oppression in such places as South Africa and China, have been timely responses to injustice.

Another recent development has been the emphasis on environmental issues, such as clean air, land use, preservation of wilderness areas and endangered species, and the effects of nuclear power. Moreover, concern for consumer protection has had an important influence on the health and economic welfare of people everywhere.

Artists respond to technological, social, and economic changes in creative ways. However, they interpret and relate to them individually. In Rauschenberg's *Quote* (fig. 14.2), the artist combined street signs, photographs of parachuting figures, and the image of John Kennedy in a silkscreen print of somewhat ambiguous intent but provocative power. The technological and engineering skill employed to create the Glass Cathedral (see figs. 14.16 and 14.17) forcefully brought the symbolism of light into an imaginative structure. Penderecki's reaction to the atomic bombing resulted in *Threnody in Memory of the Victims of Hiroshima* (see ex. 14.1). Benjamin Britten's *War Requiem* (1961) was a musical comment on war with its tragedies and victories, and *The Death of Klinghoffer* (1991) was John Adams's response to a recent terrorist act. The rapid development of computer technology and electronic synthesizers has made possible the exploration of electronic music by numerous composers.

The civil and human rights movements of the 1950s and 1960s and the opposition to the Vietnam War resulted in a wave of protest songs that became an important part of popular music. Pop culture was exploited by the mass media, which recognized the enormous purchasing power of the youth of the United States, Europe, and parts of Asia. They have championed rock music, with all its styles and fads, as a constantly changing and, therefore, highly profitable industry. In the visual arts, the mass media and mass production caught the attention of pop artists who turned to banal, everyday subjects such as that portrayed in Warhol's *Green Coca-Cola Bottles* (colorplate 88). More recently, pop culture has exploited MTV, a continuous presentation of rock music and surrealistic television imagery; it is an important innovation in this volatile industry. Pop culture, both musical and visual, generates fads at a tremendous rate. The speed with which these popular arts change results from incompletely developed ideas and styles, making it easier to replace the popular with the new.

Colorplate 88 follows p. 354.

One recent positive trend has been increased federal, state, and foundation support for cultural activities of all kinds. Laws requiring that a certain percentage of the cost for public buildings be assigned to the visual arts have provided opportunities for many artists while visually enriching the environments of cities. Foundations and corporations have become aware of the public relations impact of their support of the arts. This has resulted in the purchase of individual artist's works and in the underwriting of cultural activities, such as symphony concerts. There has been an unanticipated consequence of this corporate involvement in the arts as investors have acquired works not for their artistic merit but for their value as investments. Cultural exchange programs between nations have dramatically widened the horizons for artistic creativity. Serious art and music, as well as popular art forms, have benefited from these programs.

There is now an overwhelming abundance of music, popular and classical. It pours out at us day and night through the mass media. Ranging from opera and staged classical concerts to a surprising variety of popular, folk, and rock presentations, music has become almost omnipresent.

PAINTING

Some of the styles of earlier twentieth-century art have continued since 1945; others have evolved into new styles. Expressionism gave way to Abstract Expressionism, only to be succeeded by Pop Art, Op Art, Kinetic Art, Minimalism, and Photo-Realism. All these movements, however, are rooted in the Modernism of the early twentieth century. As Abstract Expressionism came out of Expressionism and Surrealism, Pop Art developed out of Surrealism. Op and Kinetic Art are related to the works derived from the Bauhaus School of Design in the 1920s and 1930s. **Conceptual Art** and **Photo-Realism** are at opposite poles in their attitude toward visual objects; the former rejects material reality for the "more important" artistic concept, and the latter reproduces material reality with eerie accuracy. *Post-Modernism* is a term widely used to describe anything from sociology to philosophy, including architecture and the fine arts. Its nature is eclectic, combining in myriad forms elements from classic Greek art to Modernism.

In more recent decades, there has been an emphasis on artists' uniqueness, on originality at any cost, and on what appears to be an effort toward sensationalism. Art "performances" (happenings), assemblages, minimal art, and even non-art catch public attention. In this industrial-technological age, some painters represent humanity in an environment of their own creation rather than in natural surroundings.

Léger

Fernand Léger (1881–1955) combined the machine and other industrial images in a style derived from Cubism but with colors associated with Expressionism. *The Great Constructors* (fig. 14.1) glorifies one of the marvels of twentieth-century architecture, the skyscraper. Through the use of strong lines and simplified images, Léger illustrates an important aspect of life in the second half of the twentieth century. Despite the visual impact of the building, human figures capture the viewers' eyes immediately.

Lawrence

Colorplate 89 follows p. 354.

The African-American artist Jacob Lawrence (1916–) makes people of central importance in his paintings. *Vaudeville* (colorplate 89) presents two entertainers before a "staccato" decorative screen. Three-dimensionality is kept to a minimum. There is no apparent source of illumination, although the character on the left casts a shadow while the one on the right does not. Its colors are playful and arbitrary.

Figure 14.1 Fernand Léger, *The Great Constructors,* 1950. Oil on canvas, 9 ft. 11 in. × 7 ft. 1 in. Fernand Léger Museum, Boit, France. (Giraudon/Art Resource, NY)

Bearden

Colorplate 90
follows p. 354.

In his early years in New York, Romare Bearden (1911–1988) was a part of the artistic and intellectual community known as the "Harlem Renaissance." Like many other twentieth-century painters, he created works in a variety of styles and media. At different times Bearden employed Social Realism, Abstract Expressionism, and **collage** (paper and other materials, including paints assembled on a flat surface). Bearden frequently chose collage to express his creative and social imagination. He employed flat, bold colors in strong artistic statements to give visual form to his commitment to social institutions and the rituals of society. *Family* (colorplate 90) is a collage created very late in his career. It depicts three generations involved in a family setting that communicates warmth and stability. The family occupies the foreground; there is a suggestion of three-dimensional space in the dwelling and mountains beyond. Nonetheless, the collage seems almost two-dimensional.

In some cases the arts have begun to overlap. Painting, collage, photography, motion pictures, sculpture, and industrial design are combined in various ways, creating hybrid art. Sculpture moves and sometimes makes sounds and projects images, blurring the distinction between art and technology. All these developments vie with each other for attention and acceptance. Because of the proliferation of styles, only some of the most prominent will be treated here.

Abstract Expressionism

Abstract Expressionism, some of which is called "action painting," is related to the Surrealism and Expressionism of the early twentieth century and to the Abstractionism of Mondrian, Kandinsky, and others. It is free and spontaneous, emphasizing color. It has energetic and emotionally suggestive lines, and dynamic spatial qualities that lead to the creation of very large canvases. Even the method of color application is an important part of the expressive character of these works. Jackson Pollock, Willem de Kooning, and Mark Rothko are among the principal protagonists of this style.

Pollock

Colorplate 91
follows p. 354.

With his technique of **action painting,** Jackson Pollock (1912–1956) placed his canvases on the floor and brought his whole body into action while he splashed and dripped colors in swirling configurations. Without any set pattern or design, the paint was applied according to his feelings at that moment. In *Number 1, 1948* (colorplate 91), the splashed and spilled lines appear to have been created in an intense and unrehearsed frenzy of action. However, the structure seems organized. The emotionally charged colors are combined rationally, and the design is developed through the rhythm of the painter's bodily movements. The lines of color encourage us to explore visually the swirling paths of line and color woven into the surface. Nothing is static; there is both physical and emotional movement.

de Kooning

Willem de Kooning (1904–) uses violent strokes of color that seem to have been angrily applied to the canvas. His *Woman, I* (colorplate 92) appears closely connected to the Expressionism of van Gogh and Rouault. Through use of slashing lines and heavy coloring, he expressed the vulgarity of his subject in an almost completely abstract manner. He seems to have focused on the raw, chaotic emotions rather than on the appearance of the woman. He has gone well beyond physical realism in the treatment of this subject.

Colorplate 92 follows p. 354.

Rothko

Mark Rothko (1903–1970) was moving away from Abstract Expressionism when he painted *Number 19* (colorplate 93) in 1958. In his search for expression, he abandoned all reference to objects, and color became both content and form. The work is completely without forms from nature. Patches of color are superimposed one upon another with no hard edges. Colors spread quietly from one form to another because their values are closely related. There is little spatial consciousness, but the colors do set up a gentle, rhythmic movement of abstract forms and gradations of hues that evoke an almost mystical expression.

Colorplate 93 follows p. 354.

Pop Art

The sources of **Pop Art** lie in popular culture, which itself results from the combined effects of mass communication, advertising, mass production, the leveling of social strata, and fashion. In earlier times, high fashion was for the wealthy elite. However, with more money, more leisure, and mechanization, fashion is available to a worldwide market. Advertising has led to the opinion that everyone has the right to be fashionable if they wish. Fashion uses visual ideas at a prodigious rate, and there is a constant search for novelties and gimmicks to further intrigue the public and make what people currently have obsolete. Almost all the objects we use or wear are mass produced. Pop artists have seized on this reality of contemporary life to cultivate audiences for their work.

Pop Art emphasizes mass-produced objects and symbols of the mass media. It is opposed to the so-called fine arts and is almost the opposite of Abstract or Expressionist art, presenting the commonplace, mass-produced visual experiences of society in a blatantly realistic manner. Posters, soup

Figure 14.2 Robert Rauschenberg, *Quote,* 1964. Oil and silk screen ink on canvas, 92 × 72 in. (Courtesy Leo Castelli Gallery, NY)

cans, comic strips, and banal objects of everyday existence become the subject matter for the artists' efforts. These items are usually depicted with photographic realism, often in exaggerated sizes and arbitrary colors. In this art, because of exaggerated size or repeated images, there is an intensity that makes us conscious, often for the first time, of what we see around us every day.

Rauschenberg

Robert Rauschenberg (1925–) is one of the artists whose works precipitated the Pop Art movement. His work links Abstract Expressionism and Pop Art. He attaches real objects or groups of objects, sometimes covered with paint, to his canvases in a modified collage technique. In one of his early works, he exhibited a real bed that was made up and covered with paint. In *Quote* (fig. 14.2), painted in 1964, he created a review of passing events and symbols that affected Americans at a particular moment. Using silk-screen technique, he juxtaposed such images as the well-known photo of President Kennedy, parachute jumping, traffic signs, and other common objects. He also used color, the association of dissimilar images, unusual placement of images, and incongruous spatial relationships to intensify the painting's expressive quality.

Warhol

Andy Warhol (1930–1987), another of the pioneers of Pop Art, used multiple images of mass-produced items as symbols to characterize our culture. His *Green Coca-Cola Bottles* (colorplate 88) proclaims the skills of the world of advertising, which has more respect for the container than for its contents. His subjects in other works range from multiple images of Marilyn Monroe to Brillo boxes and Campbell's soup cans—all symbols of American pop culture.

Indiana

Another Pop artist, Robert Indiana (1928–), uses word images and symbols of commercialism. *The American Dream, I* (colorplate 94) shows a painting of stenciled signs with such words as *tilt* and *take all* to suggest an obsession with pinball machines and to comment on the American dream of winning. Like the works of Warhol, there is nothing personal about Indiana's work; it calls attention to entertainment and commercialism.

Colorplate 94 follows p. 354.

Lichtenstein

Roy Lichtenstein (1923–) shocked the public with his giant comic book illustrations. In an era when the comics were an integral part of American culture, he exalted such comic book heroes as Steve Canyon. His technique even includes the dots which are part of the cheap color-printing process. In his *Drowning Girl* (fig. 14.3), the exaggerated teardrops and the verbal message suggest the melodrama of the scene.

Oldenburg

One can hardly discuss Pop Art without reference to Claes Oldenburg (1929–) who was more a maker of objects than a painter. Influenced by Warhol, he created giant hamburgers and fur-lined cups. He distorted the reality of almost every object he portrayed, taking them out of context, changing their forms from hard to soft, and usually exaggerating their size. *The Toilet* (fig. 14.4) is constructed from metal, wood, foam rubber, vinyl, and plastic tubing. The work satirizes the efficient mechanized culture of today.

Johns

The *Target with Four Faces* (fig. 14.5) by Jasper Johns (1930–) is dominated by a familiar object, a target, over which are superimposed, in bas-relief, four truncated plaster masks. This truncation of the faces, together with the target, depersonalizes humanity; the result is a collective image that suggests a macabre social statement.

Figure 14.3 Roy Lichtenstein, *Drowning Girl,* 1963. Oil and synthetic polymer paint on canvas, 67 5/8 × 66 3/4 in. (The Museum of Modern Art, Philip Johnson Fund and gift of Mr. and Mrs. Bagley Wright. Photo © 1996 Museum of Modern Art)

Op Art

Optical art, or **Op Art** as it is generally called, is a term usually applied to those two- and three-dimensional works that explore optical responses generated by color and line. Although abstract, it is essentially formal and exact. Op Art grew out of the ideas developed in the Bauhaus School of Design in the 1930s. Nonobjective patterns of line, shape, and color act as stimuli to the eye and mind of the viewer. Whatever the expressive result, it provokes a new subjective experience in which illusion, afterimages, and visual movement are real in the mind of the observer but do not exist objectively in the artwork. Op Art does not lend itself to intellectual exploration or

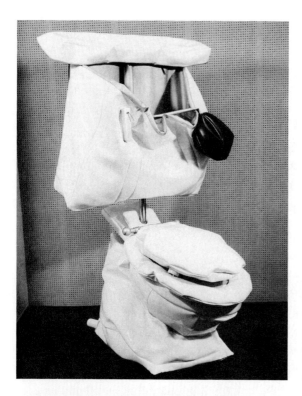

Figure 14.4 Claes Oldenburg, *The Toilet,* 1966. (Soft model) Vinyl filled with kapok, wood painted with liquitex, 50 1/2 × 30 7/8 in. (Collection of the Whitney Museum of American Art, NY)

Figure 14.5 Jasper Johns, *Target with Four Faces,* 1955. Encaustic and collage on canvas with plaster casts, 33 5/8 × 26 × 3 in. (The Museum of Modern Art, NY. Gift of Mr. and Mrs. Robert C. Scull. Photo © 1996 Museum of Modern Art)

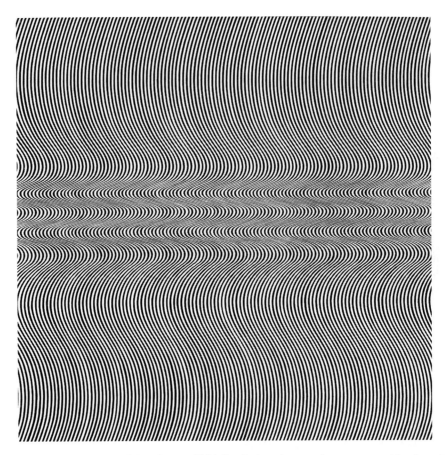

Figure 14.6 Bridget Riley, *Current,* 1964. Synthetic polymer paint on composition board, 58 3/8 × 58 7/8 in. (The Museum of Modern Art, NY. Philip Johnson Fund. Photo © 1996 Museum of Modern Art)

explanation. Its impact is usually limited to the unique and immediate experience it provides.

Agam

Colorplate 95 follows p. 354.

Double Metamorphosis II (colorplate 95) by Agam (Yaacov Gipstein) (1928–) is a structure made of long wooden pieces, and the facets of each strip of wood are painted differently. The strips are organized so the visual pattern changes as the viewer moves from one point to another in the room.

Riley

A second example of Op Art is a work by Bridget Riley (1931–). *Current* (fig. 14.6) consists of black-and-white undulating stripes and a formal progression of line. The work depends on optical illusion to suggest movement.

More recently, Op artists have used light shows to intensify visual experience by adding both movement and artificial lighting in a similar manner to rock music performers intensifying the experience of sound by electronic amplification and movement.

Photo-Realism

Critics distinguish between Realism and Photo-Realism by whether the artist paints from photographs. Many Photo-Realists actually project photographs on the canvas and replicate them with oils. *Study for Differing Views: Dog, 1981* (colorplate 96) by James Valerio (1938–) presents an urban apartment occupied by what may be two alienated people. The interior lighting derives from the television set, which consumes the attention of the woman, and the exterior lighting from the fast-fading twilight. Although valid statements may be made about the vivid colors of the painting, the artist's technique, and the elevated exterior view, the feature that immediately captures the viewer's imagination is the superrealism of Valerio's painting.

*Colorplate 96
follows p. 354.*

Kinetic Art

An example of Kinetic Art by Alexander Calder was discussed in the previous chapter (colorplate 99). Other artists have created machines that move or create a variety of sounds, and may or may not relate to anything else. Columbia Records produced an album, *Chronophagie,* devoted to sound-creating sculpture with selected instruments, created by the brothers François and Bernard Baschet. Jean Tinguely (1925–) created one of the more sensational mechanized sculptures called *Homage to New York.* Its many parts clanged, rattled, and screeched. It was programmed to self-destruct, which it did in a cloud of smoke, supervised by the New York Fire Department and witnessed by a large audience. It was a humorous as well as a prophetic utterance.

SCULPTURE

Minimal Art, or "primary structures" as it is often called, grew out of the work of the Constructivists and is in some ways related to Cubism. It is usually three-dimensional and consists of either a single unit or a series of identically shaped primary forms, not necessarily of the same size. It reduces objects to basic shapes without ornament or an attempt to improve the geometry or volume of the form. This kind of sculpture often seems to penetrate the space we occupy. The work intrigues the spectator by evoking responses to spaces, volumes, and enclosures.

Figure 14.7 David Smith, *Cubi X*, 1963. Stainless steel, 10 ft. 1 3/8 in. × 6 ft. 6 3/4 in. × 2 ft. steel base 2 7/8 × 25 × 23 in. (The Museum of Modern Art, NY. Robert O. Lord Fund. Photo © 1996 Museum of Modern Art)

Smith

David Smith (1906–1965) is in some ways a Minimalist, but his *Cubi X* (fig. 14.7) is more firmly rooted in Constructivism. It is over ten feet tall, and its small base emphasizes the balance among various geometric forms. The burnished surfaces mitigate the feeling created by the intractable nature of stainless steel.

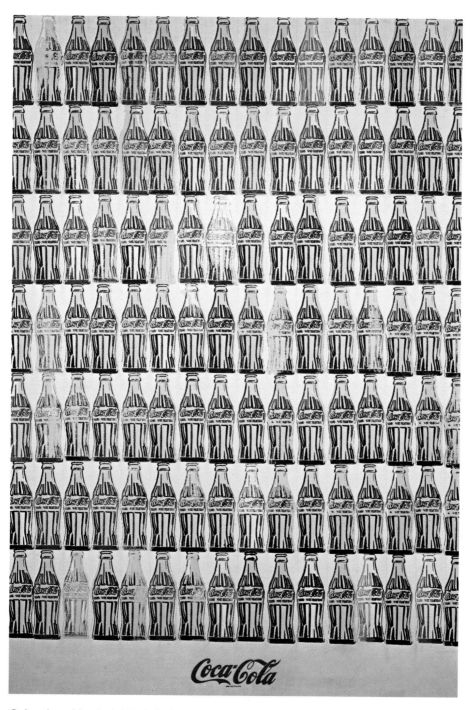

Colorplate 88 Andy Warhol, *Green Coca-Cola Bottles,* 1962. Oil on canvas,
6 ft. 10 1/2 × 4 ft. 9 in. Collection of Whitney Museum of Art. Purchase with funds from
the friends of the Whitney Museum of American Art. Acq. #68.25. *(See p. 343, 349)*

Colorplate 89 Jacob Lawrence, *Vaudeville,* 1951. Tempera on fiberboard with pencil, 29 7/8 × 19 15/16 in. Hirshhorn Museum and Sculpture Garden, Smithsonian Institution. Gift of Joseph H. Hirshhorn, 1966. (Photo by Lee Stalsworth. Reproduced by permission of the artist and Francine Seders Gallery.) *(See p. 344)*

Colorplate 90 Romare Bearden, *Family*, 1988. Collage on wood, 28 × 20 in. National Museum of American Art, Washington, D.C./Art Resource, NY. Courtesy Estate of Romare Bearden. *(See p. 346)*

Colorplate 91 Jackson Pollock, *Number 1, 1948,* 1948. Oil on enamel on unprimed canvas,
5 ft. 8 in. × 8 ft. 8 in. The Museum of Modern Art, NY. Purchase. Photograph © 1996 The
Museum of Modern Art, NY. *(See p. 346)*

Colorplate 92 Willem de Kooning, *Woman, 1,* 1950. Oil on canvas, 6 ft. 3 7/8 in. × 4 ft. 10 in. The Museum of Modern Art, NY. Purchase. Photograph © 1996 The Museum of Modern Art, NY. *(See p. 347)*

Colorplate 93 Mark Rothko, *Number 19,* 1958. Oil on canvas, 7 ft. 11 1/4 in. × 7 ft. 6 1/4 in. The Museum of Modern Art, NY. Given anonymously. Photograph © 1996 The Museum of Modern Art, NY. *(See p. 347)*

Colorplate 94 Robert Indiana, *The American Dream, I,* 1961. Oil on canvas, 6 ft. × 5 ft. 1/8 in. The Museum of Modern Art, NY. Larry Aldrich Foundation Fund. Photograph © 1996 The Museum of Modern Art, NY. *(See p. 349)*

Colorplate 95 Agam (Yaacov Gipstein), *Double Metamorphosis II,* 1964. Oil on corrugated aluminum, in eleven parts, 8 ft. 10 in. × 13 ft. 2 1/4 in. The Museum of Modern Art, NY. Gift of Mr. and Mrs. George M. Jaffin. Photograph © 1996 The Museum of Modern Art, NY.
(See p. 352)

Colorplate 96 James Valerio, *Study for Differing Views: Dog, 1981,* 1981. Oil on canvas, 8 ft. 8 in. × 7 ft. 8 in. (Frumkin/Adams Gallery, NY) *(See p. 353)*

Colorplate 97 Niki de Saint Phalle, *Black Venus,*
1965–1967. Painted polyester, 9 ft. 2 in.
Collection of the Whitney Museum of American
Art. Gift of the Howard and Jean Lipman
Foundation, Inc. 68.73. (Photography by Sandak,
Inc./G. K. Hall, M. A.) *(See p. 356)*

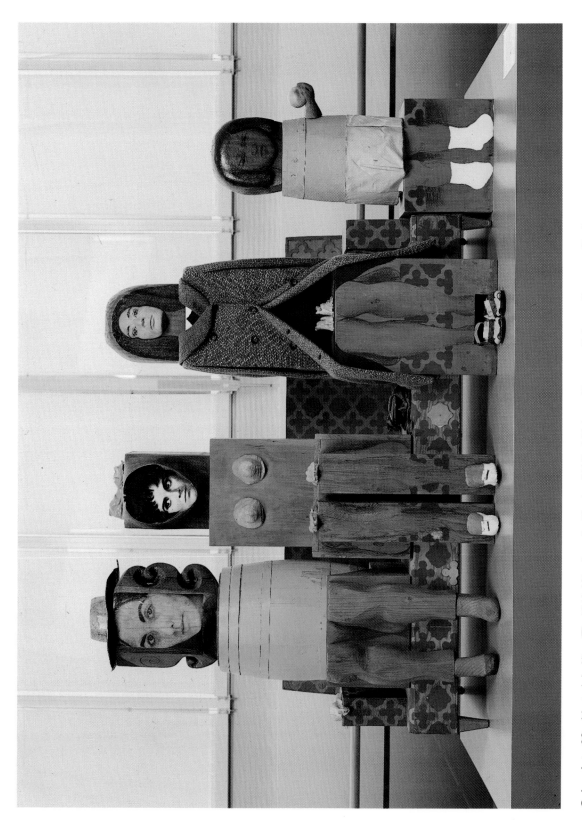

Colorplate 98 Marisol, *La Vista (The Visit)*. Mixed media, life-size. Wallraf-Richarz Museum, Cologne, Germany. (Stadt. Köln/Verwaltung der Museen) (See p. 356)

Colorplate 99 Alexander Calder, untitled mobile. Aluminum and steel, 29 ft. 10 1/2 in. x 6 ft. 4 in. Located inside the central courtyard of the National Gallery of Art, east building, 1978. Washington, D.C., I. M. Pei, architect in charge. (Courtesy of Robert Lautman) *(See p. 320, 360)*

Colorplate 100 Graham Sutherland, *Christ in Glory,* 1962. Tapestry, 74 × 38 ft. Coventry Cathedral, Coventry, England. (© Woodmansterne Ltd.) *(See p. 364)*

Figure 14.8 Barbara Hepworth, Memorial to Dag Hammarskjöld, *Single Form,* 1964. Bronze with granite base, 21 ft. high. United Nations, NY, through a grant by the Jacob and Hilda Blaustein Foundation. (Courtesy United Nations Photo Library)

Hepworth

Barbara Hepworth (1903–1975) was one of Britain's finest twentieth-century sculptors. Like so much art, her work does not fit neatly into any of the specific subgroups of her artistic age. Her focus on primitive, almost organic shapes relates in some way to the Minimalists, but more directly to the work of her compatriot, Henry Moore. Her memorial to Dag Hammarskjöld, *Single Form* (fig. 14.8), stands before the United Nations Building in New York and may be her best-known work. Its dependence on simple shapes is representative of her style. What appears at first glance to be a curved monolithic figure in fact consists of several pieces, each of which has at least two straight sides. The pieces are joined securely to create the larger shape, which is interrupted only by the circular hole toward the top.

de Saint Phalle

One of the most active contemporary experimental artists is Niki de Saint Phalle (1930–). Born in Paris, she grew up in New York and then returned to Europe, where much of her work is displayed. In her productive career she has been involved with assemblages, "shooting art" (in which people shoot at containers full of paint before a canvas), **happenings** (staged or spontaneous multimedia events which were unrepeatable), and other movements. She has more recently created Nanas, brightly colored, decoratively adorned female figures in whimsical poses.

When the word *Venus* is mentioned in an artistic context, the likely association would be either to the Greek *Venus de Milo* or the Renaissance painting by Botticelli, *Birth of Venus* (colorplate 23). Both of these are idealized nude figures, contrasting sharply with de Saint Phalle's *Black Venus* (colorplate 97). This work is a painted polyester figure with exaggerated features. The glossy paint of the figure, the bold, simple colors of the swimsuit, and the beachball contribute to its playful aura. The primitive quality of the human form and the absence of anatomical detail are reminiscent of the *Venus of Willendorf* (see fig. 3.1).

Colorplate 23 follows p. 146.

Colorplate 97 follows p. 354.

Marisol

By incorporating human shapes and representations of human body parts in unusual sculptural settings, Marisol (1930–) plays games with the viewer's perceptions of reality. Her mixed-media sculptures are close enough to human figures that they are identifiable, yet far enough away to awaken strange responses. In *La Vista* (colorplate 98), four human figures are portrayed by using realistically painted representations, found objects, and painted and carved wood for the bodies.

Colorplate 98 follows p. 354.

Smithson

Typical of the works of many artists in the vanguard of their profession, those of Robert Smithson (1938–1973) are difficult to categorize. Throughout his artistic career his works were characterized by exploration. In Robert Hobbs's book on the works of Smithson, the author divides a thirteen-year period of Smithson's career into nine categories. By its very location and character, *Spiral Jetty* (fig. 14.9) is **environmental art.** In spite of its monumental scale, it illustrates Smithson's interest in Minimalism by using 6,650 tons of material to create a simple spiral figure in the Great Salt Lake in Utah. It also relates to prehistoric monumental earthen works (e.g. the Serpent Mound in Ohio and the earth drawings on the Nazca Desert in Peru).

Christo

Permanence has been one of the criteria that aestheticians have used to apply to art. It is this principle that Christo Javachef (1935–) consistently defies as he creates wrappings for anything from castles to coastlines on three continents. These works impinge on the environment and are never

Figure 14.9 Robert Smithson, *Spiral Jetty,* 1970. Rock and earth, 1500 ft. long. Great Salt Lake, Utah. (Gianfranco Gorgoni)

Figure 14.10 Christo, *Running Fence,* 1976. Nylon fabric and posts, 18 ft. × 24 1/2 mi. San Francisco Museum of Modern Art. Gift of the Modern Art Council

confined by museum walls. Consequently, dismantling them after a fixed period of time is part of the creative process. *Running Fence* (fig. 14.10) was a nylon fabric "fence" 18 feet high that extended 24 1/2 miles from Bodega Bay on the west to beyond US Highway 101 near Petaluma, California. It stood complete for only two weeks, and approximately one month later all traces of it were removed. *Running Fence* piqued the imaginations of thousands of people, who traveled to the site to witness this unique object. Works such as this defy all artistic traditions and aesthetic dogmas.

The works of such artists as Smithson and Christo encourage people to see the environment in a new way. By dramatically moving outside ordinary experience, they challenge our notions of beauty and art.

The Arts Today (1945 to the Present)   357

Figure 14.11
Elizabeth Catlett, *Singing Head,* 1980. Black Mexican marble, 16 × 9 1/2 × 12 in. (National Museum of American Art, Washington, D.C./Art Resource, NY)

Catlett

Elizabeth Catlett (1915–) focused most of her professional efforts on African-American subjects and issues. After growing up in the United States, she moved to Mexico, where she and her husband, the Mexican artist Francisco Mora, have both taught for many years. She is one of Mexico's most respected artists, specializing in sculpture and graphic arts. *Singing Head* (fig. 14.11), with its restrained curving lines and gentle abstraction, is characteristic of her style. Half of the human face is convex, and the other half is concave; an abrupt line separates the two halves. The highly polished black marble promotes the play of light on the changing surfaces.

Bourgeois

Another American artist, born in France, is Louise Bourgeois (1911–). In her early years, she worked with her family in the tapestry industry and, after

Figure 14.12 Louise Bourgeois, *Needle,* 1992. Steel, flax, mirror and wood, 9 ft. 1 in. × 8 ft. 4 3/4 in. × 4 ft. 8 in. Cologne, Germany. (Galerie Karsten Greve)

attending art school in Paris, began painting. Sculpture and print-making preceded her most recent artistic efforts, many of which she refers to as "cells." These cells are miniature environments that juxtapose objects with seemingly incongruous qualities (a boulder and plate glass). Although she does not call *Needle* (fig. 14.12) a cell, it brings together steel, flax, wood, and a mirror in a similar manner.

ARCHITECTURE

Architecture after World War II continued in the vein of functionalism that marked the best and most exciting prewar buildings. With an emphasis on technology, architects searched for practical solutions for specific problems or needs. In recent years, they have considered environmental compatibility and land use, as well as aesthetic quality. Efficiency of operation has included such features as climate control, solar energy, and ease of entry and exit. While designing efficient buildings, architects have demonstrated creativity

Figure 14.13 Wallace K. Harrison, Architect in Charge, headquarters of the United Nations (*right*) and General Assembly Building (*background*), 1950. New York. (Courtesy United Nations Photo Library)

and individuality. Moreover, in recent years they have used the talents of sculptors and painters to enhance the function of buildings and relate them to human activities.

One exciting solution to the problem of function and aesthetics is the East Building of the National Gallery of Art in Washington, D.C., designed by I. M. Pei (1917–) and completed in 1978. It was designed to achieve harmony with the other buildings along Pennsylvania Avenue. Moreover, Pei (whose recent pyramidal additions to the Louvre have been met with mixed reactions) oriented the structure so the dome of the Capitol is visible from almost any window or corner. The central courtyard (colorplate 99) is filled with geometric forms: triangles and rectangles confront one in the stairwell, exhibit space, ceiling, walls, and floor. Calder's last monumental kinetic sculpture is suspended from an eighty-foot high ceiling. A huge tapestry by Joan Miró hangs on a nearby wall.

Colorplate 99 follows p. 354.

Of all buildings, skyscrapers continue to be the symbols of twentieth-century economic life and a unique American contribution to architecture. The congestion in the city of New York made it necessary to build vertically in order to create more floor space on a small piece of ground. The United Nations Building (fig. 14.13) shows the use of steel-cage construction in a

Figure 14.14 Wallace K. Harrison, Architect in Charge, main lobby of the General Assembly Building, United Nations 1950. New York. (Courtesy United Nations Photo Library)

skyscraper. The horizontal bands of windows run completely across the face of the building, one band for each of the thirty-nine stories. The arrangement of the well-lighted, airy offices and suites makes this a functional building for the transaction of business and government in the important branches of the United Nations. From the exterior, it appears almost abstract in design. The General Assembly building of the United Nations is shown in the background. The main lobby of the General Assembly Building (fig. 14.14) includes cantilevered balconies in free organic forms, a sharp contrast to the geometric design of the exterior of the Headquarters Building. The sculpture *Zeus* in the foreground of our photo is a gift of the Greek government.

As engineering technology has been refined, the heights of skyscrapers have increased. The building of a skyscraper is both an engineering and an architectural feat. The Columbia Seafirst Center (fig. 14.15) in Seattle, Washington, designed by Chris Simons, is the tallest building (by number of stories) west of the Mississippi, with six parking levels below ground and seventy-six floors above ground. Its exterior combines black granite quarried in South Dakota and gray-tinted glass, giving the building a dark appearance. Although it is a unit, it gives the appearance of interlocking concave and convex forms, offering dramatic contrast to the predominantly rectangular buildings surrounding it.

The Arts Today (1945 to the Present)   361

Figure 14.15 Chris Simons, Columbia Seafirst Center, 1983–84. Seattle, Washington.

The Crystal Cathedral in Garden Grove, California (figs. 14.16, 14.17) emphasizes the recent tendency to do more than merely enclose a space with a steel and glass cage. This edifice grew out of the desire of the pastor of a large congregation to accommodate the "drive-in" portion of his flock and house another large portion of his people in an enclosed space. The enclosed space, however, had to retain the "openness" of the drive-in theater where the congregation had first met.

Figure 14.16 Johnson/Burgee, Architects, exterior of Crystal Cathedral, 1980. Metal pipes and glass, 415 × 207 × 128 ft. at apex. Garden Grove, California. (Gordon H. Schenck, Jr.)

The structure is essentially a frame of steel pipes covered with more than ten thousand specially fabricated glass panes that give a feeling of light and the out-of-doors to both the interior and exterior views. The Crystal Cathedral weds contemporary religious purpose to twentieth-century architectural techniques: the beauty of the interior for the benefit of TV broadcasting, the use of structural steel frame and glass, and the solution to acoustical problems both within and outside the building by the most recent electronic systems.

Much of the success of buildings is influenced by their interior design and furnishings. The cathedral at Coventry, England, was constructed

Figure 14.17 Johnson/Burgee, Architects, interior of Crystal Cathedral, 1980. Garden Grove, California. (Gordon H. Schenck, Jr.)

adjacent to the ruins of a Gothic cathedral destroyed by bombs in World War II. The building incorporates beautiful objects created by numerous international artists and artisans to enhance the liturgical life within. Among these objects are modern German and Swedish stained-glass windows, a baptismal font made from a huge boulder from Israel, Danish mosaics, and a giant tapestry of Christ made in France from a design by the English artist, Graham Sutherland. The tapestry *Christ in Glory* (colorplate 100) is situated behind the altar and depicts the dominating figure of Christ triumphant, surrounded by four gospel symbols. This configuration was traditionally placed in the

Colorplate 100 follows p. 354.

Figure 14.18 Fay Jones, Architect, Thorncrown Chapel, 1980. Eureka Springs, Arkansas. (Photo by Wayne Sorce)

tympanum above the main portal of cathedrals. The four symbols (man, eagle, lion, and ox) are strikingly modern, while the figure of Christ is more traditional. Between his feet is a human figure, and below that is a small panel representing the crucified Christ. The enormity of the tapestry and its vivid colors dominate the interior.

This is a time of great stylistic diversity in American architecture. Two of America's most outstanding architects currently are Fay Jones (1921–) and Frank Gehry (1929–). The Thorncrown Chapel (fig. 14.18), dedicated in 1980, is one of several chapels designed by Jones for his home state of Arkansas. Even in the design stage, the chapel was to be constructed with minimal impact on the environment. This restricted the choice of materials and construction techniques. As a consequence, the materials chosen were those that could be hand carried to the site by two men. The primary materials for the chapel are 2 × 4 and 2 × 6 lumber of varying lengths, glass, and stone.

Figure 14.19 Frank Gehry, Architect, Frederick R. Weisman Art Museum, 1990. Minneapolis, Minnesota. (© Don F. Wong)

The use of stone is restricted to the floor. Glass is used for the walls, allowing the sylvan countryside to be brought into the worship space. The superstructure, which is of wood, creates repeated patterns that are simple yet visually compelling. Thorncrown Chapel's design incorporates an interesting reverse-Gothic structural principal. Unlike Gothic cathedrals, the weight of which was contained by flying buttresses that pushed inward against the walls, Thorncrown Chapel depends on an efficient interior timber framework to control the weight of the building. The interior appointments and architectural details of the building, including light fixtures, door hardware, and pulpits, are all generated from the same artistic impulse as the larger building, creating a unified and restful atmosphere.

The Frederick R. Weisman Art Museum (fig.14.19), designed in 1990 by Frank Gehry, is located on the campus of the University of Minnesota in Minneapolis. Instead of following the earlier twentieth-century adage "Form follows function," Gehry champions the creation of buildings as aesthetic objects. The museum seems to be an array of randomly placed, faceted steel shapes whose surfaces reflect the changing effects of light. In this construct of varied geometric shapes, there appears to be a stylistic connection with analytical cubism. These shapes belie the more straightforward interior design, which houses the varied collection of the museum. Like many new buildings, it has received some humorous nicknames, but its surfaces and shapes continue to attract the admiration of many. It presents a welcome contrast to the budget-driven academic boxes so common to American campuses.

These examples by no means exhaust the innovations in architecture since World War II. They do, however, demonstrate that architects have responded to their time. They have kept art alive and vital by incorporating new materials and new techniques that meet today's functional demands and also express contemporary culture.

MUSIC

Among the technological factors that have exerted influence on recent music is the universal availability of electronic media. It has made the dissemination—and even the creation—of music one of the biggest industries in the world. The editing power of recording technology has given the vast audience of listeners impeccable standards of performance against which they are inclined to judge all performances.

Improvisation is also an important factor. Many composers have provided scores that require improvisatory performance, using new systems of notation. In much popular music, for example, every performance is unique because spontaneous improvisation is an essential part of that style.

Popular Music

Strong rhythm dominates popular musical styles, but it is countered to some degree by a freedom that results from its improvisatory character. This foundation of predictable meter stems naturally from the dance, with which popular music is often closely associated. The freedom of melody within an established meter has intrigued composers and choreographers for centuries and continues to do so today. Dance troupes perform regularly to a wide variety of popular music. One recent successful example is Alvin Ailey's "Cry" (fig. 14.20), which is set to jazz, blues, and soul music.

The unique tone qualities of popular vocalists and instrumentalists are critical to the style. The effects achieved in jazz and popular music with such traditional instruments as trumpet, trombone, and saxophone are emulated worldwide and have been exploited by composers of all kinds. In recent years, there has been an enormous expansion of timbres employed in popular music as electronic synthesizers have become standard.

Jazz performers and composers have been associated with a variety of styles since the 1940s. They include Count Basie, Duke Ellington, Thad Jones, Mel Lewis, Woody Herman, and Stan Kenton (big bands); Charlie

Figure 14.20 Judith Jamison in "Cry." (© Jack Vartoogian)

Parker, Dizzy Gillespie, and Thelonius Monk (bebop); Miles Davis, John Lewis, and Dave Brubeck (cool jazz); Chick Corea, Herbie Hancock, Joe Zawinul, and John McLaughlin (electric fusion jazz); and Anthony Braxton and Gunther Schuller (third stream jazz). Other prominent jazz musicians include McCoy Tyner (piano); Wayne Shorter, Phil Woods, and Branford Marsallis (saxaphones); Maynard Ferguson and Arturo Sandoval (trumpet); Charlie Mingus and Jaco Pastorius (bass); and Elvin Jones and Tony Williams (drums). Prominent women in jazz include Toshiko Akiyoshi (band leader/composer); Carla Bley (composer); Betty Carter, Ella Fitzgerald, Carmen McRae, and Flora Purim (singers); and Jane Ira Bloom (saxaophones).

When Bill Haley and the Comets introduced the world to "Rock Around the Clock," few people realized what a vigorous movement was being launched. Since that time, rock music has continued unabated, growing to one of the biggest industries in the world of music. (It would be incorrect to consider rock an outgrowth of jazz.) After the great success of the early king of rock, Elvis Presley, English musicians dominated popular music (in this case, rock and roll). It started, of course, with that country's first international rock stars, the Beatles, who have been followed by a long list of rock composers and performers who have maintained rock as one of the dominant forces of popular music.

Since its beginnings, rock has characteristically expressed defiance of traditional mores in dress, vocabulary, and music. Another characteristic has been the loud volume made possible through electronic amplification, which adds immeasurably to its compelling character. Performances are characterized by the combination of light, sound, movement, and words into a single emotional event.

In the 1960s, the Beatles represented a phase of rock marked by its interest in philosophical and social concerns, particularly those of Eastern religions. Another English group, the Rolling Stones, represented a more violent, emotional phase of rock that eventually led to a style known as "acid rock" in which the drug culture and the social revolt of youth were emphasized. Such groups as the Grateful Dead and Jefferson Airplane also represented this style. The naming of rock groups seems to be related to the earlier art movements of Dada and Surrealism.

During the 1970s and 1980s, rock began to embrace jazz, African music, electronic music, and blues in one way or another. Chuck Mangione and groups such as Blood, Sweat, and Tears combined more-or-less traditional musical training with elements of jazz, while staying generally within the rock tradition. During this period there was a resurgence of interest in the big band, with Don Ellis as one of its leading proponents.

Music was used to accompany film from its early days. Performed live by instruments ranging from solo piano or organ to full orchestra, music developed a number of stock formulas appropriate to certain dramatic situations. When sound was added to film, music played an increasingly important role. It was carefully shaped by composers to enhance the visual images and spoken word. When combined with a wide array of other sound effects, the aural component of film became one of its most important ingredients.

Music of the widest variety is used in film: folk and popular music, classical adaptations, and original scores. As with the ballet, there is much transitional music in film, interspersed with more complete musical passages. In recent years, much of this music has moved from the film to cassette tapes and compact discs, where it acquires a commercial life of its own. Among the composers who wrote primarily for the concert stage but also wrote for films were Aaron Copland, Dmitri Shostakovich, Arthur Honegger, Jean Sibelius, and Serge Prokofiev.

More recently, Rap singers have burgeoned on the popular scene, reciting rhymed, sometimes violent, and often vulgar protest verse to percussive accompaniments. The energetic chanted form springs from a subculture of America's inner cities. At the same time, the explosion of TV channels and radio stations has created such an appetite for new groups that numerous individuals and groups of sharply contrasting abilities are constantly emerging.

During the 1980s, punk rock, hard rock, fusion, and reggae were especially popular. Madonna may have been the most successful pop-rock artist of the decade. Michael Jackson was also a super star rock vocalist, and Jimi Hendricks was probably Rock's greatest guitarist, while Branford Marsalis, Eric Clapton, and Bob Marley (with roots respectively in jazz, blues, and reggae) enjoyed success as well. Guns and Roses became America's most popular hard rock band. Other groups included Tower of Power, Aerosmith, Led Zeppelin, U2, R.E.M., and a curious group known as 10,000 Maniacs.

Music in the Concert Hall

The term *classical music* usually refers to the long tradition of notated art music, but the term is of dubious value. Substitutions for that term, such as *serious music* or *concert music* are equally objectionable.

The general trends of notated art music in the first half of the twentieth century have been further exploited in the second half of the century. The twelve-tone procedure of Arnold Schoenberg became a tool of many composers, but in recent decades it has been increasingly abandoned. Webern's pointillistic style was a forerunner of composing with electronic sounds. The development of the synthesizer and computer as tools for achieving new tone colors and rhythmic complexities is one of the most novel and influential trends of this period. The improvisatory techniques of jazz and the rhythmic freedom of popular music also are reflected in concert music. A new type of music known as **aleatoric,** chance, or indeterminate music goes beyond improvisation. This style of musical composition is only partially dictated by the notation of the composer. The composer merely suggests certain patterns of sound, if any, in a notation that varies from the traditional to that completely lacking in definite pitch or rhythm. The performer uses these general instructions as a basis for improvisation. In some instances, only the duration of the improvisatory section is indicated.

Music for the stage has been significantly influenced by popular music. In this tradition, a long succession of musical plays dates back to the early decades of the twentieth century. These involved many gifted composers, lyricists, and performers. In the second half of this century, the influence of rock is evident in the stage works *Tommy* and *Jesus Christ, Superstar.* Recent theatrical successes that owe some of their musical character to the popular idiom include *The Phantom of the Opera, Les Misérables* and *Miss Saigon.*

In recent decades, music for the church has included jazz anthems and a variety of other popular styles. In addition, Bernstein's *Mass,* composed for the opening of the Kennedy Center in Washington, D.C., includes popular music in several styles.

Developments in electronic music accelerated after World War II. In the beginning, most electronic music consisted of experimental exercises, with tonal materials gathered from various sources. Composers of electronic music first recorded and then manipulated all manner of sounds. The development

Figure 14.21
Computer music workstation. (Courtesy of Yamaha Corporation of America)

of the synthesizer (fig. 14.21) allowed composers to use sounds generated by electrical equipment. Today, composers routinely combine electronic sounds with traditional instruments.

Karlheinz Stockhausen (1928–), a German musician and pupil of Messiaen, has been one of the leading composers in this field. His work has centered around the electronic studio of the Cologne radio station and the Darmstadt Center for Contemporary Music. In *Gesang der Jünglinge* and *Kontakte,* Stockhausen combined natural and electronically generated sounds. Edgar Varèse (1883–1965) exploited tone color using the synthesizer in *Deserts* and *Poème Electronique.*

At the same time some composers, such as the Italian, Luigi Dallapiccola (1904–1975), continued to employ serialism, but with considerable freedom. Among his many works, the opera *Il Prigioniero (The Prisoner)* combines the twelve-tone technique with the lyrical tradition of Italian opera. Dallapiccola never abandoned his close ties to traditional Italian lyricism despite his loyalty to the principles of Schoenberg and twelve-tone composition.

A number of composers, however, extended serialism to include duration, intensity, timbre, texture, and even silence to produce what became known as "total serialism." Such music lacks themes and thematic development, and the unifying element of serialism is recognizable only to someone who has devoted much study to such works. Stockhausen used total serialism in *Zeitmass,* in which all the elements of music are controlled by detailed markings of every note for its five woodwind instruments. Milton Babbitt (1916–),

The Arts Today (1945 to the Present)   371

an American composer, has also worked with electronic composition and total serialism. His *Ensembles for Synthesizer* is in this style.

Aleatoric music, which incorporates chance improvisation, is in stark contrast to these completely controlled techniques of Stockhausen's *Zeitmass*. His *Klavierstück XI (Piano Piece XI),* written in 1956, includes aleatoric features. It consists of nineteen fragments of notation printed on a large piece of cardboard. The performer plays any of these nineteen patterns that he or she happens to see, and may play it and any succeeding ones that catch the eye, treating them in accordance with the composer's suggested directions. Any segment may be repeated and all need not be played. The piece ends when the performer has repeated any segment three times.

The American composer John Cage (1912–1992) advocated musical aesthetics so revolutionary that, driven to the ultimate, his works became non-music. He "composed" a work entitled *Imaginary Landscape* that calls for twelve radio receivers tuned by chance to different radio frequencies. The resulting sounds are the musical composition. In a sense, this performance is an aural "happening" paralleling the visual "happenings" of the avant-garde in the 1960s. Cage went so far as to compose works in which neither the composer nor the performer contributes a sound. In his *Four Minutes and Thirty-three Seconds,* Cage asked the "performer" only to sit before an open piano with a stopwatch and allow the natural sounds of life to become the composition. These developments all suggest a parallel with the arts of painting and sculpture in which new materials, improvisation, and chance play a controlling role.

Multimedia performances integrate music, dance, dramatic movement, light, painting, and sculpture in various combinations. This was, of course, the operatic thesis of Monteverdi, Gluck, and Wagner. The late twentieth century saw many such attempts in classical and popular music. Rock performance depends greatly on movement, light, and costuming. More traditional composers have used some of these elements, mainly in choral composition. An example of multimedia expression in which physical movement and music are combined is *Circles* by Luciano Berio (1925–). This setting of poems by e. e. cummings for voice and percussionists is calculated to have the performers' physical movements give shape to the composition.

In 1959, Gunther Schuller (1925–) composed a multimedia work called *Seven Studies on Themes of Paul Klee.* This is a musical response to some of the "musical" references in Klee's paintings. Klee was an amateur musician and frequently used musical terms and forms in his paintings. Among the paintings that Schuller chose was Klee's *Twittering Machine* (colorplate 81). He made the music "twitter" with a mechanical application of the twelve-tone technique. Schuller's work makes real the aural experience of the mechanical birds that Klee depicted visually.

Colorplate 81 follows p. 322.

Even in the first half of the century, several composers wrote works that showed a rather naive attempt to incorporate ragtime and jazz into their works, notably Debussy in *Golliwog's Cake Walk,* Krenek in his opera *Jonny spielt auf (Johnny Strikes up the Band),* and Milhaud in his ballet *Le Création du monde (The Creation of the World).* Later, Gunther Schuller, with John Lewis, was deeply engaged in establishing the third-stream jazz movement. He founded the Third-Stream Performance Ensembles at the New England Conservatory, where he taught, promoting a cross-fertilization of classic forms with a variety of modern techniques.

Musical theater and ballet achieved spectacular popularity in the second half of this century. Much of the music used in ballet, however, was adapted from the works of earlier composers. Among the contemporary composers who have written for the dance is Aaron Copland, whose successful ballets include *Billy the Kid, Rodeo,* and *Appalachian Spring,* which were written shortly prior to 1945.

Leonard Bernstein (1918–1990), an internationally known American conductor and composer, was equally at home in classical and popular idioms. Among his classical works is *Symphony no.1, Jeremiah.* In the popular style, he composed several stage works, among which are *Wonderful Town* and *West Side Story. Candide,* the libretto of which is based on Voltaire, blends the traditional operatic style with the more popular style of Broadway musicals. It has been widely accepted and performed on both sides of the Atlantic. Bernstein's *Mass,* written for the opening of the John F. Kennedy Center in Washington, D.C., incorporates jazz and the popular idiom with one of the oldest forms of church music.

There have been a number of composers who have experimented with new techniques since World War II but avoided becoming advocates of any one school of composition by not adopting any one of them exclusively. Olivier Messiaen (1908–1992) was a French composer of unique abilities and techniques. His greatest compositions and influence as a teacher came after the middle of the century. Among those works that display his interest in tone color is the *Catalogue des Oiseaux (Catalog of the Birds),* in which Messiaen's lifelong interest in nature and particularly in the songs and calls of birds is exploited to the utmost. This long work for piano is based on actual bird songs and calls notated by Messiaen during countless field observations of birds in their natural habitats. *Chronochromie (Time-color)* and *Mode de Valeurs et d'Intensité (Mode of Durations and Volume)* show Messiaen's exploitation of rhythmic complexity. His deeply religious sense and highly developed literary interests give his music a very personal flavor. Messiaen's religious intensity was reflected in numerous works for organ and church performance. Among his most successful students at the Paris Conservatory were such important young composers as Stockhausen, Boulez, and Nono.

The American composer Elliott Carter (1908–) used a highly contrapuntal style that gave way in the 1950s to a serialism of intervals and rhythms that characterize his later works. Among his many compositions, his string quartets have achieved the widest audience.

Gyorgi Ligeti (1923–), a Hungarian who fled to Germany in 1956, has worked closely with an electronic studio in Cologne and with the International Courses in New Music in Darmstadt. His works cover the gamut of compositional genres, vocal and instrumental. He has employed electronic devices, serialism, chance, and experiments in tone color, but has maintained a personal style throughout. His *Wind Quintet* and the vocal work for sixteen solo voices, *Lux Aeterna,* both indicate his mastery of vocal and instrumental colors.

Thea Musgrave (1928–) was born in Scotland, where she began her composition studies. Later, she studied with Nadia Boulanger, as did so many of her contemporaries. Musgrave's style has moved from the traditional diatonic to serial technique. Her output is huge, including works in almost all major forms. Among her recent works is an opera, *Mary, Queen of Scots,* written for the 1979 Edinburgh Festival. Most recently her importance includes her work as a teacher of composition.

Krzysztof Penderecki (1933–) of Poland is one of the most widely heard composers of the post–World War II period. One of a large number of Polish composers who have ventured into the most advanced styles and idioms of the time, his works embrace all genres, and his orchestral and choral compositions have won international acclaim. Since its premiere in 1984, the *Polish Requiem* has been repeatedly performed. The Biblical text of the *St. Luke Passion* contrasts strikingly with the contemporary subject matter of *Threnody in Memory of the Victims of Hiroshima.* This latter work, while scored for traditional instruments—fifty-two string instruments—reflects Penderecki's concern with sound groups and instrumental coloration. Much of the score (ex. 14.1) does not indicate definite pitch, and there is no traditional indication of rhythmic pulse or meter. These are indicated rather by blocks of time. The figures 15″, 11″, 4″, 6″, and so forth indicate the number of seconds that a particular sound is to be played. (The symbols are explained in a preface to the score.) The figure ▲ requires the highest pitch possible on the specified instrument, and the only traditional notational symbols are those indicating dynamic change. The work is obviously not built on melodic or harmonic patterns, motifs, or themes but on blocks of tone colors achieved by all sorts of manipulations by the performers—striking on the wood of the instruments, playing behind the bridge, slow **vibrato** with wide pitch differences, and playing on the tailpiece of the instrument. The overall effect is one of striking tonal combinations through which Penderecki transmits his deeply felt reaction to the Hiroshima holocaust (ex. 14.1).

Example 14.1 *Threnody in Memory of the Victims of Hiroshima* by Krzysztof Penderecki. Copyright © 1961 by Deshon Music, Inc., New York, by assignment. Reprinted by permission of Deshon Music, Inc., a division of Belwin Mills Publishing Corporation, Rockville Centre, NY.

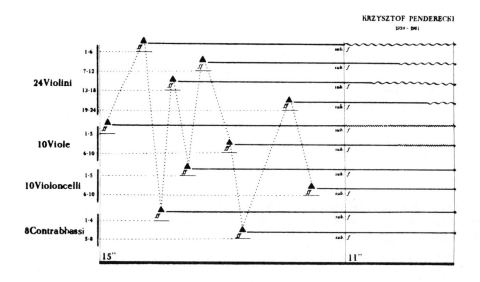

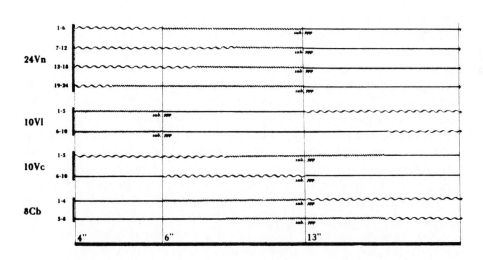

Peter Maxwell Davies (1934–) is an English composer whose compositional techniques reflect an interest in styles that range from medieval polyphony to serial and improvisatory styles. A number of his works deal with sacred themes including a cycle of carols and instrumental sonatas based on the plainsong melody and text *O Magnum Mysterium.*

Taking its name from the visual arts, one of the movements in music that has received much attention in recent decades is **minimalist music,** in which the repetition of brief patterns within slowly changing textures and dynamics creates a trancelike atmosphere. Among the composers writing in this style are Steve Reich (1936–), Philip Glass (1937–), and John Adams (1947–). Reich is well known for *The Desert Music* (1984); Glass for his opera *Einstein on the Beach* (1975) and the sound track for the movie *Koyaanisqatsi* (1983). The John Adams opera *Nixon in China* was premiered in 1987 and *Harmonielehre* in 1985.

Harmonielehre is a forty minute orchestral composition in three movements. Adams pays homage in its title to Arnold Schoenberg's 1910 treatise on tonal harmony. This work is not strictly minimalist, but might more appropriately be referred to as neo-Romantic with some minimalist content. It is a tonal work that utilizes block chords and frequently lyrical episodes.

The music of the Estonian composer, Arvo Pärt (1935–), shows the influence of minimalism but at the same time reflects a strong kinship to Medieval music. A recent composition, completed in the spring of 1994, is *Litanie, Prayers of St. John Chrysostom for Each Hour of the Day and Night.* It is scored for orchestra, mixed chorus, and solo quartet. As the title suggests, *Litanie* comprises twenty-four prayers based on the text of a fourth-century priest. Each of the movements is a brief petition beginning with the words, "O Lord." The first twelve prayers, set in E minor, are in a large arch form; the second twelve, in C minor, build gradually to a climax and a final "Amen." At the midpoint, the tympani begins a heartbeat pattern that marks the passage of time. An earlier composition by Pärt that uses drums to mark the passage of time is *When Sarah was Ninety Years Old,* in which tuned drums repeat insistent, almost hypnotic short patterns.

Summary

The rapidity of change in so many aspects of life has been even greater since the end of World War II than in the first half of the twentieth century. The impact of this accelerated change has led to widespread experimentation in art and music. The sophistication of technology has led to tremendous advances in communication and in the psychology and techniques of the mass media. Technology has also led to the development of new synthetic materials for architecture and the visual arts, and new techniques for sound creation, sound amplification, and recording in music. The forces that have affected the arts have not only been numerous but have also come within a short time span. They have had a powerful impact on artistic creativity and have provided artists with new and sometimes exotic subject matter.

Another important influence on music is the tremendous buying power of the public—not only of the economic elite but of the huge middle class, especially youth. The majority of society is an indifferent and passive population, content to be consumers and spectators. Many artists and composers, especially composers of popular music, have focused their efforts on manipulating this segment of society. The effect is seen most clearly in popular music, which has become an enormous business with literally billions of dollars in yearly sales.

There has been a tendency toward improvisation in all the arts since World War II. While the visual arts have been influenced to some degree by the element of chance in the arrangements of their materials, music has been affected more directly. Post–World War II composers have experimented extensively with aleatoric music, in which some or all elements of music are determined by the chance happenings of sounds. New sounds, some produced by electronic sound generators and computers, as well as new sounds produced by industry, have given composers a wide range of tonal possibilities with which to work.

There are many paradoxes in twentieth-century art. One lies in the strict and systematic discipline of materials and technique advocated on the one hand and the aleatoric combination of materials and elements on the other. Another paradox is the apparent denial of emotion in art, especially in the early part of the century, and a move toward an outpouring of emotion following World War II. The latter is most apparent in popular art and music, in which a complete freedom of emotional expression has become the accepted mode.

Although time is needed to make valid judgments about what in art is most worthy, nothing is as permanent as change. Artists of every medium have tried to reflect the dramatic changes of our time. If the second half of the twentieth century is to be correctly understood, it will be through the continued search for artistic metaphors that express life in the world today.

Suggested Readings

In addition to the specific sources that follow, the general readings listed on pages 388 and 389 contain valuable information about the topics of this chapter.

Gridley, Mark C. *Jazz Styles: History and Analysis.* 4th ed. Englewood, NJ: Prentice-Hall, 1990.

Hobbs, Robert. *Robert Smithson, Sculpture.* Ithaca: Cornell Univ. Press, 1981.

Jencks, Charles. *Post-Modernism: The New Classicism in Art and Architecture.* New York: Rizzoli, 1987.

Johnson, Ellen H., ed. *American Artists on Art from 1940–1980.* New York: Harper & Row, 1982.

Lippard, Lucy R. *Pop Art.* New York: Thames Hudson, 1985.

Lucie-Smith, Edward. *Late Modern: The Visual Arts Since 1945.* Oxford: Oxford University Press, 1975.

Machlis, Joseph. *Introduction to Contemporary Music.* 2d ed. New York: W. W. Norton, 1979.

Salzman, Eric. *Twentieth-Century Music: An Introduction.* 3d ed. Englewood Cliffs, NJ: Prentice-Hall, 1988.

Singerman, Howard, ed. *Individualism: A Selected History of Contemporary Art, 1945–1986.* New York: Abbeville Press, 1986.

Southern, Eileen. *The Music of Black Americans.* 2d ed. New York: W. W. Norton, 1983.

Spies, Werner. *The Running Fence Project.* New York: Abrams, 1977.

Stangos, Nikos, and Tony Richardson, eds. *Concepts of Modern Art.* Rev. ed. New York: Harper & Row, 1994.

Tirro, Frank. *Jazz: A History.* 2d ed. New York: W. W. Norton, 1993.

Watkins, Glen. *Soundings: Music in the Twentieth Century.* New York: Schirmer, 1987.

Glossary

Absolute music　Music that has no extramusical implications.

Abstract art　Art that is not concerned with realistic representation of nature.

Abstract Expressionism　A style of painting that combines personal expression with abstract forms.

A cappella　Unaccompanied choral singing. Music written for voices alone.

Accidental　A symbol used to raise or lower a pitch, usually by one half step (sharp = S; flat = H ; natural = L)

Acropolis　A hill town or fortified hill, usually associated with Greek temples.

Action painting　A technique in which painters use their entire bodies to achieve rhythm and line, usually on a large canvas.

Aerial perspective　In painting, a method of representing the effects of atmospheric conditions on the color and detail of distant objects.

Aesthetics　The study of the nature of the beautiful.

Aleatory　A type of musical composition in which the performer is given liberty in choosing pitches, rhythms, durations, and so forth. Chance improvisation.

Ambulatory　An aisle or walkway around the apse, or cloister, of a church or monastery.

Answer　In fugal writing, a passage in imitation of the subject.

Antiphonal　Music in which alternating choirs perform in separate locations, such as the opposite sides of a cathedral chancel.

Apse　A semicircular part of a church that projects from its main axis.

Arcade　A row of covered arches supported by piers or columns.

Arched vault　See *Vault*.

Architrave　In architecture, the horizontal member that rests on the columns in post and lintel structures.

Aria　An extended vocal solo, usually with instrumental accompaniment, as in operas, oratorios, and cantatas.

Atonality　Absence of fixed tonality.

Augmentation　The doubling of the note values of a musical motive or theme.

Aulos　An ancient wind instrument of Greece.

Baptistry　A building used for baptism, usually circular in shape.

Bar　The vertical line separating the measures in written musical notation. The term is often used as a synonym for *measure*.

Baroque　The style period that followed the Renaissance, encompassing roughly the dates 1600–1725. The period is characterized by a vigorous spirit of ornamentation, action, and elaborate design.

Barrel vault　A semicylindrical vault joining two parallel walls.

Basilica　A rectangular hall flanked by aisles.

Basso continuo　Literally, continuous bass. An important aspect of Baroque compositional style in which a bass instrument, most frequently a viola da gamba, cello, or bassoon, is joined by a keyboard instrument to provide an accompaniment to the other voices. The *basso continuo* music is indicated by a single bass line and numbers that specify the harmonies to be played by the keyboard instrument.

Basso ostinato　A melodic figure in the bass line, repeated consistently throughout a section of a composition or a complete work.

379

Bay   The architectural space defined by pillars or columns, usually spanned by arches.

Blaue Reiter, Der   A school of painting centered in Munich beginning around 1910. It was related to Expressionism. Kandinsky and Marc were among its founders. The composer Arnold Schoenberg was associated with them.

Buttress   A masonry support built against a wall to resist the outward thrust of the wall and roof. See *flying buttress*.

Cadence   The point of rest in a melody or harmonic progression that marks the end of a phrase or section.

Cadenza   A highly ornamental passage that culminates in a cadence played by the soloist near the end of a movement in a concerto.

Canon   A contrapuntal device in which the melody of one voice is imitated exactly by one or more other voices. The term also refers to an entire composition using this device. See *round*.

Cantata   Literally "sung," but more often refers to a multimovement composition for one or more voices with some instrumental accompaniment. They are often sacred, although numerous secular cantatas exist. Two common types are solo cantatas and choral cantatas. These works, of greatly varying length, may include recitatives, arias, and ensembles of varying sizes.

Cantilever   A method of construction in which beams project beyond their supports and are balanced by weights on the attached ends.

Cantus firmus   A melody, either composed or taken from another source, on which certain polyphonic works are constructed.

Canzona alla francese   An instrumental composition derived from the sixteenth-century French chanson.

Capital   The top part of a column, wider than the upright section and usually decorated.

Cella   In Greek temples, the main chamber. The location of the statue of the god to which the temple is dedicated.

Chaconne   See *passacaglia*.

Chamber music   Music written for small ensembles, such as duos, trios, and quartets. The term usually refers to instrumental music but may include vocal music as well.

Chancel   The area of a Christian church around the high altar, usually reserved for the clergy.

Chanson   French word for song. Also, a sixteenth-century French vocal form similar to the madrigal.

Chant, plainchant   Early monophonic music in free rhythm associated with the Christian church. See *Gregorian chant*.

Chiaroscuro   A union of two Italian words whose meanings refer to bright and obscure; hence, the term applies to the treatment of light and shade in painting or drawing. It frequently is used to describe the light effects found in paintings of Rembrandt.

Choir   The portion of a church between the altar and the nave reserved for the lower clergy and singers.

Chorale   Traditionally, a hymn tune of the German Protestant church.

Chord   A pitch complex of two or more simultaneously sounded tones. The study of harmony deals with chordal functions.

Chromaticism   The melodic or harmonic use of tones not in the seven-tone diatonic scale of a composition.

Clavier   A term loosely used to designate a keyboard instrument, such as the clavichord or harpsichord.

Clef   The sign used at the beginning of the staff to designate the pitch of one note; hence, the terms C clef, G clef, F clef.

Clerestory (also spelled clearstory)   The part of a church above the aisles, pierced by windows.

Cloister   A rectangular courtyard along the side of a medieval church that provides a sheltered walkway. Sometimes a residence for people in religious orders.

Cluster   An effect in modern music achieved by striking a number of adjacent keys of the piano or organ or by having several instruments play tones within close proximity of one another.

Coda   The section of a composition that brings it to a conclusion. Codas vary in length.

Collage   A composition in the visual arts created by attaching bits of paper, paint, and/or other materials to a flat surface.

Colonnade   A row of columns supporting beams or lintels.

Color (1) Visually, the experience of reflected light that we identify with the names red, yellow, blue, and so forth. (2) Aurally, the tone quality of individual instruments or voices or a combination of instruments or voices. Synonymous with *timbre*. (3) In isorhythmic music of the Middle Ages, a repeated pattern of pitches, not necessarily of the same length as the rhythmic element, the talea. (Pronounced có-lore).

Column An upright support, usually cylindrical, for a roof or the upper part of a building. Those associated with Greek architecture bear the names Doric, Ionic, and Corinthian.

Complementary colors The hues that are opposite each other on a color wheel, such as green and red, blue and orange.

Conceptual Art A theory that tangible art objects are imperfect manifestations of true art, which is found only in the imagination or mind (i.e., the concept is the artistic entity).

Concertato An Italian term designating the interaction among unequal sound sources.

Concertino See *principale.*

Concerto An orchestral genre practiced since the Baroque period that employs unequal sound sources. The solo concerto reached its greatest development in the Classic and Romantic periods. See also *concerto grosso.*

Concerto grosso An ensemble composition written for two groups of unequal size; most widely written during the Baroque period.

Conjunct motion In music, notes that proceed by whole and half steps in a melody.

Consonance Traditionally, a combination of tones that are pleasing or restful in contrast to dissonance.

Contrapposto In human sculpture, a slight displacement of hips and straightening of one leg to show the weight of the figure resting on that leg.

Contrary motion In contrapuntal compositions, the movement of two voices in opposite directions, one ascending and one descending.

Corinthian An ornate Greek architectural order with a decorated base, slender, fluted column, elaborately ornamented capital, and an entablature. See *order.*

Cornice Part of the entablature. A crowning moulded architectural feature that may project somewhat.

Counterpoint The setting of one melodic line against one or more other lines.

Countersubject A secondary theme in a fugue.

Cubism An early twentieth-century style of painting, and to a lesser degree sculpture, that used geometric shapes as underlying primary forms. In contrast to Impressionism, which it succeeded, the primary concern of Cubism was with form rather than color.

Descriptive music Music that is devoid of any literary program, but is associated in its title with people, objects, or events.

Design The structure or organization of the various components of a work of art.

Development The section of a sonata-allegro form in which the thematic material is varied rhythmically, melodically, harmonically, dynamically, and in other ways.

Diminution Reducing the note values of a musical motive or theme to smaller time values.

Disjunct motion In music, notes that proceed by steps larger than a whole step in a melody.

Dissonance A combination of tones that, because of their tension, seeks resolution to a restful consonance.

Dodecaphonic A method of composing in which the twelve tones of the chromatic scale are used in some prearranged form throughout the composition.

Dome A hemispherical vault supported on columns or walls.

Dominant In tonal music, the fifth degree of the diatonic scale or key. In modal music, one of the two main tones around which the other tones move.

Dorian See *modes.*

Doric The simplest of the three Greek architectural orders. It has no base, a fluted column, an unadorned capital, and an entablature. See *order.*

Dynamics The gradations of sound volume in a composition.

Entablature The portion above the column and below the roof in Greek architecture.

Entasis   A slight convex projection, somewhat below the middle of columns.

Environmental art   Art, usually on a monumental scale, in the natural world. It modifies or alters nature, forcing viewers to see the environment in new ways.

Equal temperament   The tuning of the octave in twelve equal parts.

Ethos   Those characteristics that define a culture.

Exposition   The first section of the sonata-allegro form in which the thematic material is exposed or stated.

Expressionism   A style of art in which the artist's expression of emotions is the principal concern.

Facade   The front or main entrance of a building.

Fauvism   Derived from the French word *fauve,* meaning wild beast. It was used in a derogatory way to describe those Post-Impressionist painters who used garish and unreal colors in a wild manner.

Figured bass   A system of musical shorthand employed in the Baroque period written as a bass line with numerical figures and other symbols placed beneath. Playing from the figured bass, performers can complete the harmonic intent of the composer.

Final   In modal music, the note on which the modal melody rests.

Flying buttress   A half arch used to counteract the outward thrust of the vault, and to transfer the thrust to piers outside the walls.

Foreshortening   The application of linear perspective to human and other forms to help achieve a dramatic illusion of three-dimensional space.

Form   The arrangement of materials and elements into a recognizable object.

Fresco   The technique of painting on wet plaster.

Frieze   The decorated horizontal band of the entablature in architecture.

Fugue   A style of contrapuntal composition based on one or more short themes called subjects and on related connective materials.

Genre painting   A style of painting that represents common people in common pursuits.

It is most frequently associated with painting in the Low Countries during the Renaissance.

Gregorian chant   That kind of chant named after Pope Gregory I. See *chant, plainchant.*

Groined vault   A type of vault created by the intersection of two barrel vaults.

Half step   The smallest interval used in the division of the octave in the equal-tempered scale. Also called a halftone.

Happenings   Multimedia events, staged or spontaneous, which were essentially unrepeatable and impermanent. Some were considered by many to be quite outrageous.

Harmony   The simultaneous sounding of tones, as in chords.

Homophony   Music in which a dominant melodic line is supported by chordal accompaniment.

Hue   A synonym for *color.*

Humanism   A word with varied meanings. In this book it describes the broadest study of the intellectual and artistic efforts of humankind.

Imitation   A device of polyphonic texture in which one voice restates the melody of another voice. The imitation can be strict (exact) or free (similar).

Impressionism   A nineteenth-century French style of painting that tried to capture the painter's immediate impressions, usually of the outdoors. In music, a term associated with the music of Debussy and Ravel.

Intaglio   A graphic technique in which the cutaway parts retain ink for printing, as in engraving.

Interval   The distance between two pitches.

Intonation   The accuracy of singing or playing on pitch.

Inversion   Melodic inversion requires every ascending interval to be replaced by an equal descending one, and every descending interval by an equal ascending one. Chordal inversion implies that some pitch other than the root of the chord is in the bass.

Ionian   See *modes.*

Ionic   A Greek architectural order with a plain base, a fluted column, a voluted capital, and an entablature. See *order.*

Isorhythm   A repetitive device used in medieval music. See *talea* and *color*.

Jazz   An improvisatory style of American popular music that originated with African Americans. It has been adopted worldwide.

Key   The tonal center of a composition. The key note is the first note of the scale on which the composition is based. The term *key* is also used for the levers or elements that are manipulated by the fingers of an instrumentalist, such as the keys of the flute or the black and white keys of the piano.

Keystone   The central stone in a round arch that locks the stones of the arch together.

Kinetic Art   Visual art that depends on the movement of its various parts for its artistic message.

Lauda   Nonliturgical religious music practiced in Medieval and Renaissance Italy.

Leitmotif   A compositional technique made famous by Wagner in which musical fragments are associated with specific persons, ideas, or events, forming the building blocks for larger works.

Libretto   The text of an opera, oratorio, or cantata. Plural: libretti.

Lied/Lieder   The German word for song. Generally used to refer to the German song literature of the late eighteenth, nineteenth, and twentieth centuries accompanied by piano.

Line   In the visual arts, an elongated mark or boundary that aids in articulating form.

Linear perspective   A method of representing the size of objects as they recede into space by the use of lines that imply a vanishing point.

Lintel   A beam over two posts or columns.

Liturgy   The formalized program of worship in the church, consisting of musical and nonmusical parts.

Lydian   See *modes*.

Lyra   An ancient stringed instrument native to Greece.

Madrigal   The most common form of secular vocal music in the sixteenth and early seventeenth centuries.

Major scale   A pattern of steps and half steps within the octave in the following ascending order—two whole steps, a half step, three whole steps, and a half step. Defined another way, a scale of eight tones in which the third and fourth tones and the seventh and eighth ones are separated by half steps, while all the others are separated by whole steps.

Mannerism   A term widely used to describe the arts in the late Renaissance. It refers to any artistic style that relies on formulas and expressive distortions of established norms. In manneristic music of the late Renaissance, dramatic, unprepared dissonances were one of its main features.

Mass   The central liturgical service of the Catholic church, parts of which are often set to music.

Measure   A small rhythmic unit in a composition set off by bar lines that includes the number of beats indicated in the meter signature.

Medium   The technique or material used by an artist to create a work of art.

Melisma   In music with text, the assignment of many notes to one syllable, as found in plainchant.

Melody   A series of pitches that conveys a sense of beginning and ending.

Meter   The organization of accented and unaccented pulses.

Meter signature   The symbol (most frequently numerical) written on the staff at the beginning of a composition indicating its meter. The top number identifies the number of a certain kind of notes in a measure, and the bottom number identifies the kind of note. For example, 3/4 time or meter signifies that there are the equivalent of three quarter notes in each measure.

Metope   In Doric friezes, the panels between triglyphs, usually square and often decorated with sculpture.

Minimal Art   A late twentieth-century style of art which employs severely limited resources.

Minimalist music   A late twentieth-century musical style in which brief patterns, textures, and other musical fragments are repeated for an extended period of time with trancelike persistence.

Minnesinger   Composer-poets of medieval Germany.

Minor scale   A scale pattern that may take any of three forms—harmonic, melodic, and natural. The distinguishing feature of all minor scales is the half step between the second and third notes of the scale.

Minuet   An early popular dance form in triple meter that became part of the suite and the symphony. See kinetic art.

Mixolydian   See *modes*.

Mobile   A kind of sculpture that uses movement to achieve relationships among its various components. See *kinetic art*.

Modality   The application of the system of modes to melodies and harmonies. See *modes*.

Modes   The system of tonal organization that predates the modern major and minor. Dorian, Phrygian, Lydian, and Mixolydian are the names of some of the most common modes. Scales built on each of these modes carry the same names.

Modulation   Changing from one key to another in the course of a composition. For example, the change from the tonic key to the dominant in the exposition of the sonata-allegro form.

Monochromatic   A color arrangement that uses only one hue with varying degrees of saturation and value.

Monody   Through the sixteenth century, music consisting of a single melodic line. After the sixteenth century, music consisting of a melody and a relatively simple harmonic accompaniment.

Monophony   A musical texture consisting of a single unaccompanied line of melody.

Mosaic   A design composed of small units of stone, glass, or porcelain set in mortar.

Motet   A polyphonic vocal composition with sacred text that emerged in the Middle Ages and was especially popular in the Renaissance.

Motive   The smallest unit of musical form. The term *motif* is also used.

Mural   A painting on a wall. Murals may be painted with any kind of paint or technique and are usually very large.

Nave   The central portion or aisle of a church.

Neumes   An early system of medieval notational symbols that indicates musical pitches.

Non-objective art   A post-Cubist movement that attempted to record direct feelings on canvas by exploring relationships among colors and shapes without reference to the world of objects.

Note   The symbol of musical writing that directs the performer to produce a sound of specific pitch and duration.

Office hours   Also known as Divine Office. The fixed arrangement of sung and spoken services of the Catholic church, apart from the Mass. They include psalms, canticles, lessons, and so forth. The seventh hour of the office is perhaps the best known. It takes place at twilight, and is called Vespers.

Oinochoe   One of the principal shapes of Greek vases that were for wine storage.

Op Art   A style of painting that features optical illusions and other devices that call attention to the way the eye sees.

Opera   A staged dramatic musical production performed by singers and instrumentalists with support from lighting, scenery, costumes and often, dance. Its origins were rooted in Florentine Italy in the early seventeenth century.

Opera seria   The predominant form of opera in the seventeenth and eighteenth centuries. Usually to mythological texts, it employed a succession of recitatives and arias rather than continuous dramatic unfoldment.

Opus   Latin word for work. A numbering scheme introduced in the early nineteenth century that indicates the order of publication and the general order of composition of a composer's works.

Order   An architectural term relating to several Greek styles. The orders most often include a base, a column, a capital, and an entablature. See *Corinthian, Doric,* and *Ionic*.

Ordinary   The texts that are common to all celebrations of the Mass (i.e. Kyrie; Gloria; Credo; Sanctus; Agnus Dei; and Ite, missa est)

Organum   An early form of counterpoint.

Ornamentation   Decorative notes added to a musical line either by the composer through symbols or by the performer through improvisation.

Parallel motion   Two melodic lines moving at the same intervals.

Passacaglia A Baroque instrumental form based on a repeated musical phrase four to eight measures in length, and often found in the bass. Very similar to the chaconne.

Pediment A triangular space formed by the gable of a two-pitched roof in classical architecture.

Pentatonic A division of the octave into five tones. Normally, the pattern consists of a whole step, a step and a half, a whole step, a whole step, and a step and a half.

Phrase A musical idea corresponding to a sentence in prose. A phrase consists of one or more motives and ends in a cadence.

Phrygian See *Modes*.

Pier An architectural support, usually masonry.

Pitch The highness or lowness of a musical sound. More accurately, the number of vibrations or cycles per second.

Plainchant See *chant, plainchant*.

Polychromatic A color scheme involving many hues.

Polyphony A texture in which two or more melodic lines are interwoven.

Polytonality The simultaneous use of two or more keys or tonal centers in a composition.

Pop Art A style of art that uses commercial and popular images as subject matter.

Portico A porch, the roof of which is supported by columns or piers.

Post and lintel A system of construction in which vertical supports carry horizontal beams.

Post-Impressionism A transitional movement in the 1880s connecting Impressionism and Cubism in the visual arts.

Primary colors The hues that can be mixed to produce all other hues. The primary colors are red, yellow, and blue.

Principale The smaller group in the *concerto grosso*—the concertino.

Program music Music written to a descriptive text or program. A type of descriptive music.

Proper Those texts in the Mass that are only appropriate for particular occasions, such as funerals, Saint's days, and Christmas.

Ragtime A nineteenth-century musical style associated primarily with the piano and characterized by syncopation, duple march rhythms, and two or more layers of rhythmic activity.

Recapitulation A synonymous term for restatement. The third section of the sonata-allegro form, in which the themes of the statement or exposition are repeated.

Recitative A type of solo vocal performance in which words are sung with a minimum of melodic interest and usually based on speech rhythms, inflections, and syntax. That which is accompanied by the orchestra is called *recitativo accompagnato*. That which is accompanied by the basso continuo only is called *recitativo secco* (*secco* is the Italian word for dry).

Relief sculpture Sculpture in which three-dimensional forms emerge from a flat background.

Rest Musical symbols indicating various periods of silence in a musical score.

Retrogression Reversing the sequence of notes in a theme or melody.

Rhythm The temporal element in music; that which moves the music through time.

Ricercare A sixteenth- and seventeenth-century instrumental form of improvisatory character that evolved into the fugue.

Ripieno The larger ensemble in the *concerto grosso*.

Rococo A style of art and music that is delicate and decorative, which occupies a position between the end of the Baroque era and the beginning of the Classic era.

Rondo The statement and restatement of a principal theme alternating with one or more contrasting themes, e.g., A B A C A.

Round A canon for voices that is repeated as often as desired.

Saturation That aspect of color that relates to the purity of the hue.

Scale The arrangement of pitches of the octave in ascending or descending order. See *major* and *minor*.

Score The notated parts of an instrumental or vocal composition in a composite form from which the work can be conducted or studied.

Sequence   A compositional technique in which a melodic figure is repeated successively at different pitch levels.

Serialism   A method of composition by which the composer extends the technique of twelve-tone composition to other areas, such as rhythm, dynamics, timbre, and duration.

Signature   The symbols set on the staff at the beginning of a piece of music to designate the tonality or key (key signature) and the metric organization (meter signature).

Solo concerto   See *Concerto.*

Sonata   In eighteenth- and nineteenth-century practice, an instrumental composition, usually of three or four movements.

Sonata-allegro form   A movement in an instrumental composition of the Classical period and following, built up of three parts: exposition, development, and recapitulation. One or two themes are presented in the exposition, the themes are treated in a variety of ways in the development, and the original thematic materials are revisited in the recapitulation.

Song form   A simple formal structure; ABA. Sometimes called ternary form.

Steel cage   A construction method in which steel supports in a post-and-lintel system are a self-supporting framework.

Stretto   A section of a fugal or canonic composition in which two or more subject entries overlap.

Style   All the characteristics of an art that make an art object identifiable.

Stylobate   The platform or step on which Greek columns are placed.

Subject   A theme, particularly that of the fugue.

Suite   An instrumental composition especially in the Baroque period, featuring several successive movements, such as Allemande, Courante, Sarabande, and Gigue.

Surrealism   A style of art that attempts to portray the imagery of the subconscious mind.

Swing   A jazz style made popular in the 1930s by big bands.

Symphony   A sonata for orchestra; sometimes used to refer to the orchestra, as in symphony orchestra.

Syncopation   The displacement of the accent from a strong beat to a weak beat or to a weak part of a beat.

Talea   In isorhythmic music of the Middle Ages, a repeated pattern of rhythms, not necessarily of the same length as the melodic element, the color.

Tempera   A kind of paint, often based on pigments suspended in egg yolk, sizing, and water.

Tempo   The speed of performance of a piece of music suggested either by a metronomic rate (i.e., the number of beats per minute) or by a more general term, such as *adagio, andante,* and *presto.*

Tessitura   The range in which most of the notes fall in vocal music.

Texture   In the visual arts, the surface character of an object or its representation by paint or other material. In music, the use of one or the other techniques of monophony, polyphony, or homophony.

Theme   Generally used to describe the tune or melodic subject of a musical work. Can be used, however, to describe a rhythmic or harmonic pattern out of which a composition is built.

Through-composed   Music in which new material is continuously presented.

Thrust   The lateral pressure of an arch or vault.

Timbre   See *color.*

Tonality   The organization of a part or the whole of a composition around a home tone.

Tone   The result of vibrations of a resonating body, received by the ear and processed by the auditory system. Musically, tones have the properties of pitch, intensity, duration, and timbre.

Tone color   See *color.*

Tonic   The first or key note of a scale, e.g., the note C in the C major scale.

Tracery   Decorative stone or iron work supporting stained glass windows.

Transept   The crossing arms projecting from the central axis of a cruciform church.

Triad   A three-tone chord reducible to notes a third apart (for example, C-E-G and F-A-C).

Triglyph   In the Greek Doric frieze, one of two types of alternating panels. Triglyphs, with three vertical flutings, alternate with metopes, usually consisting of figures.

Trio   A composition for three performers. Also, the second section of a minuet or scherzo in the Classic concerto or sonata.

Troubadours   Composer-poets of the twelfth and thirteenth centuries in southern France.

Trouvères   Composer-poets of the late twelfth and thirteenth centuries in northern France.

Twelve-tone system   Music consistently constructed on a pattern of the twelve chromatic tones selected prior to composition.

Tutti   A term applied to passages in which all performers play, in contrast to solo passages.

Tympanum   The surface above a door and below an arch, usually filled with sculptured figures, especially in Medieval and Gothic architecture.

Value   The measure of darkness or lightness of a color.

Variation form   Any instrumental composition in which a theme is stated and followed by any number of subsequent variations.

Vault   A method of covering an area with a roof or ceiling, based on the principle of the arch. See *Groined vault, Barrel vault.*

Vibrato   A device of performance used by singers and instrumentalists, especially string players, to achieve expressive quality by rapidly deviating from the prescribed pitch and returning to it.

Voice   A term applied to vocal and instrumental parts in music, especially in polyphonic music (e.g., music in three voices).

Whole-tone scale   A six-tone octave scale in which all successive tones are a whole step apart.

General Readings

Adams, Laurie Schneider. *A History of Western Art.* Dubuque, IA: Brown & Benchmark, 1994.

Arnold, Denis, ed. *The New Oxford Companion to Music.* 2 vols. New York: Oxford Press, 1983.

Beardon, Romare, and Harry Henderson. *A History of African-American Art.* New York: Pantheon, 1993.

Bowers, Jane, and Judith Tick, eds. *Women Making Music: The Western Art Tradition, 1150–1950.* Urbana, IL: University of Illinois Press, 1986.

Cohen, Aaron I., ed. *International Encyclopedia of Women Composers.* 2d ed. 2 vols. New York: Books and Music, 1987.

Dallin, Leon. *Listener's Guide to Musical Understanding.* 8th ed. Dubuque, IA.: Brown & Benchmark, 1994.

De la Croix, Horst, and Richard G. Tansey. *Gardner's Art through the Ages.* 9th ed. New York: Harcourt Brace Jovanovich, 1990.

Ferris, Jean. *America's Musical Landscape.* Dubuque, IA: Brown & Benchmark, 1990.

Ferris, Jean. *Music: The Art of Listening.* 4th ed. Dubuque, IA: Brown & Benchmark, 1995.

Fleming, William. *Art and Ideas.* 8th ed. New York: Holt, Rinehart & Winston, 1991.

Fleming, William. *Concerts of Arts: Their Interplay and Modes of Relation.* Gainsville: University of Florida Press, 1990.

Green, Mildred Denby. *Black Women Composers: A Genesis.* Boston: Twayne Pub., 1983.

Grout, D. J., and Claude V. Palisca. *A History of Western Music.* 4th ed. New York: W. W. Norton, 1988.

Harris, Ann Sutherland. *Women Artists: 1550–1950.* New York: Knopf, 1977.

Hartt, Frederick. *Art, a History of Painting, Sculpture, and Architecture.* 2 vols. Englewood Cliffs, NJ: Prentice-Hall, 1985.

Heller, Nancy G. *Women Artists: An Illustrated History.* Rev. ed. New York: Abbeville Press, 1987.

Hitchcock, H. Wiley, and Stanley Sadie, eds. *The New Grove Dictionary of American Music.* 4 vols. London: Macmillan Pub. Co., 1986.

Janson, H. W. *History of Art.* 5th ed. Englewood Cliffs, NJ: Prentice-Hall, 1994.

Kostof, Spiro. *A History of Architecture: Settings and Rituals.* New York: Oxford University Press, 1985.

Lamm, Robert C., and Neal M. Cross. *Humanities in Western Culture.* Dubuque, IA: Brown & Benchmark, 1993.

Machlis, Joseph. *The Enjoyment of Music.* 6th ed. New York: W. W. Norton, 1990.

Perry, Regina A. *Free within Ourselves: African-American Artists in the Collection of the National Museum of American Art.* Washington, D.C.: National Museum of American Art, 1992.

Pevsner, Nikolaus. *An Outline of European Architecture*. Baltimore: Penguin Books, 1950.

Sadie, Stanley, ed. *The New Grove Dictionary of Music and Musicians*. 20 vols. London: Macmillan Pub. Co., 1980.

Stangos, Nikos, and Herbert Read. *The Thames and Hudson Dictionary of Arts and Artists*. Rev. ed. London: Thames and Hudson, 1988.

Stolba, K Marie. *The Development of Western Music: A History*. 2d ed. Dubuque, IA: Brown & Benchmark, 1993.

Tischler, Alic. *Fifteen Black American Composers: A Bibliography of Their Works*. Detroit: Information Coordinators, 1981.

Wold, Milo, Gary Martin, James Miller, and Edmund Cykler. *An Outline History of Western Music*. 8th ed. Dubuque, IA: Brown & Benchmark, 1994.

Index

···━●━···

A

The Abduction from the Seraglio (Mozart), 236
Absolute music, *379*
Abstract art, 310, 346–47, *379*
Abstract Expressionism, 346–47, *379*
Academic Festival Overture, Opus 80 (Brahms), 264
A cappella, *379*
Accidental, *379*
Acrobats and Bull, 42
Acropolis (colorplate 10), 43, 48, *379*
Action painting, 346–47, *379*
Adams, John
  The Death of Klinghoffer, 343
  Harmonielebre, 376
  Nixon in China, 376
Adoration of the Magi (Botticelli), (colorplate 20), 132, 137–38
Adoration of the Magi (da Vinci), 138–39
Aerial perspective, 13, *379*
Aerosmith, 370
Aesthetics, *379*
  aesthetic response to arts, 10–12
Agam (Yaacov Gipstein), *Double Metamorphosis II* (colorplate 95), 352
Age of Pericles, 43

The Agnew Clinic (Eakins), (colorplate 58), 271
Ailey, Alvin, *Cry,* 367, 368
Akiyoshi, Toshiko, 368
Alceste (Gluck), 229
Aleatory, 27, 370, 372, *379*
Alleluia (Perotin), 120–22
The Altar of Zeus, 53, 55
Alto Rhapsodie, Opus 53 (Brahms), 265
Ambulatory, 86, *379*
The American Dream (Indiana), (colorplate 94), 349
American Gothic (Wood), (colorplate 2), 16
An American in Paris (Gershwin), 334
Amiens Cathedral, 116
Ancient era. *See* Egypt; Greece; Rome
Annunciation (Fra Angelico), (colorplate 22), 132, 135–36
The Annunciation (Martini), (colorplate 18), 118
Annunciation, Nativity, and Shepherds (Pisano), 117
Answer, 204, *379*
Anthemius of Tralles, 77
Antiphonal, 198, *379*
Aphrodite (Venus de Medici) (Lysippus), 53, 54
Apostles, Portal of Le Beau Dieu, 116
Apotheosis of St. Ignatius (Pozzo), 183

Appalachian Spring (Copland), 373
Apse, 86, *379*
Arabesque Ouverte Sur La Jambe Droite (Open Arabesque on the Right Leg) (Degas), 294
Ara Pacis Frieze (Altar of Peace), 73
Arcade, *379*
Archaic Age, Greece, 43
Architecture
  Baroque period, 186–93
  Byzantine, 75–76
  Egypt (ancient), 36–37
  Gothic period, 106–13
  Greece (ancient), 43, 46–49
  Medieval period, 82–84, 85–87
  Modernism, 321–27
  post-World War II, 359–67
  Renaissance, 149–53
  revivalist, 250–51
  Rococo period, 216
  Romanesque period, 88–91
  Romantic period, 250–51
  Rome (ancient), 65–69
Architrave, 46, *379*
Arena Chapel, 117, 118
Aria, 195, *379*
Armstrong, Louis (Satchmo), 337
Arp, Jean (Hans), *Human Concretion,* 319, 320
Art Nouveau, 305

Arts
  aesthetic response,
      10–12
  approach to study of, 6, 8
  emotions prpoduced
      through, 10–11
  functions of, 4–5
  historical periods of, 5–6
  sociocultural aspects of,
      1–4
*Assumption of the Blessed
  Virgin*
  (Riemenschneider),
  148, 150
*The Assumption of the
  Virgin* (Rubens),
  (colorplate 38), 181
Atonality, 27, 327, 329, *379*
Augmentation, 204, *379*
Augustus of Prima Porta,
  71, 72–73
Aulos, 59, *379*
Ave Maria (Desprez), 156
The Avenger (Barlach), 316

B

Babbitt, Milton, 371–72
  *Ensembles for
      Synthesizer,* 372
Bach, Johann Sebastian,
      173, 175, 204–9
  *Christ lag in
      Todesbanden (Christ
      Lay in the Bonds of
      Death),* 194, 195,
      207–9
  Inventions, 209
  Klavierübung, 209
  Mass in B Minor, 173
  *Passacaglia and Fugue
      in C Minor,* 196,
      205–7
  *Passion According to St.
      Matthew,* 2, 157, 205
  *Weihnachtsoratorium
      (Christmas Oratorio),*
      201

*The Well-Tempered
  Clavier,* 205
Balakirev, Mily, 282
Ballet music, 373
*Banks of the Seine,
  Vétheuil* (Monet),
  (colorplate 62),
  289–90
Baptistry, *379*
Bar, 20, *379*
Barlach, Ernst, *The
  Avenger,* 316
Baroque, use of term, 170,
  379
Baroque period, 170–211
  architecture in, 186–93
  Christianity in, 170,
      171–72
  music in, 173, 194–211
  ornamentalism of, 174
  painting in, 172, 173,
      175–82
  Protestantism in, 171,
      172
  sciences in, 170–71
  sculpture in, 182–85
Barrel vault, 65, 66, *379*
Barry, Charles, 250, 251
Bartók, Béla, 332–33
  Concerto for Orchestra,
      332
Baschet, François and
      Bernard,
      Chronophagie, 353
Basie, Count, 367
Basilica, 74–75, *379*
Basso continuo, 194, *379*
Basso ostinato, 208, *379*
The Bath (Cassatt),
  (colorplate 67), 291
Bauhaus School, 306, 326
Bay, 89, *380*
Bearden, Romare, *Family,*
  (colorplate 90), 346
Beatles, 368, 369
Beethoven, Ludwig von,
      244, 254–57
  Eroica, 11
  Fidelio, 256

*String Quartet no. 16,
  op. 135,* 257
*Symphony no. 3 in E-
  flat Major,* 255–56
Beiderbecke, Bix, 337
The Bells of Cythera
  (Couperin), 217
Bengali Woman
  (Hoffman), 319
Bennet, John, *Thyrsis?
  Sleepest Thou?,*
  159–60
Benoist, Marie-Guillemine,
      247
  Portrait of a Negress
      (colorplate 51), 247
Berg, Alban, 329–30
  Violin Concerto, 330
Berio, Luciano, *Circles,* 372
Berkeley City Club
  (Morgan), 327
Berlioz, Hector, 273–76
  Symphonie fantastique,
      11, 273–76
Bernini, Giovanni Lorenzo,
      175, 182, 184
  David, 182, 184
  Ecstasy of St. Theresa,
      182, 185
  Plaza of St. Peter's,
      190–91
Bernstein, Leonard
  Candide, 373
  Mass, 370, 373
  Symphony no. 1, 373
  West Side Story, 373
  Wonderful Town, 373
Bill Haley and the Comets,
  "Rock Around the
  Clock," 368
Billy the Kid (Copland), 373
Bingen, Hildegard von, *A
  Feather on the
  Breath of God,* 125
Biomorphic forms, 312
The Birth of Venus
  (Botticelli),
  (colorplate 23),
  136–37, 356

Bizet, Georges, *Carmen,* 266

Black Venus (de Saint Phalle), (colorplate 97), 356

Blau Reiter, Der, 306, *380*

Bley, Carla, 368

Blood, Sweat, and Tears, 369

Bloom, Jane Ira, 368

Blues, 336

The Blue Window (Matisse), (colorplate 73), 305

Blume, Peter, 311–12
  The Eternal City (colorplate 83), 311–12

Boris Godunov (Mussorgsky), 283

Borodin, Alexander, 282

Borromini, Francesco, *Sant' Agnese,* 189

Botticelli, Sandro, 133, 136–38
  Adoration of the Magi (colorplate 20), 132, 137–38
  The Birth of Venus (colorplate 23), 136–37

Boucher, François, *Madame de Pompadour* (colorplate 43), 214, 224

Boulanger, Lili
  La Tempête, 298
  Les Sirènes, 298

Bourgeois, Louise, 358–59
  Needle, 359

Brahms, Johannes, 264–65
  Academic Festival Overture, Opus 80, 264
  Alto Rhapsodie, Opus 53, 265
  Ein Deutsches Requiem, Opus 45, 265

Hungarian Dances, 264
Symphony no. 1 in C Minor, Opus 68, 265
Variations on a Theme by Haydn, Opus 56a, 264

Bramante, 153

Brancusi, Constantin, 317
  Mlle. Pogany, 317, 318

Braxton, Anthony, 368

Britten, Benjamin, *War Requiem,* 343

Broadway musicals, 338, 370

Brubeck, Dave, 368

Brueghel, Pieter
  The Wedding Dance (colorplate 31), 145
  Winter, Return of the Hunters (colorplate 30), 145

Burial at Ornans (Courbet), (colorplate 55), 270–71

Buttress, *380*

Byrd, William, *Carmen's Whistle,* 157

By the Seashore (Renoir), (colorplate 65), 290

Byzantine period
  architecture of, 75–76
  mosaics of, 76–77

C

Cadence, 99, *380*

Cadenza, *380*

Cage, John
  Four Minutes and Thirty-Three Seconds, 372
  Imaginary Landscape, 372

Calder, Alexander, 320, 353
  kinetic art, 320
  untitled mobile (colorplate 99), 320

Call of Death (Kollwitz), 306–7

Camerata, 197, 198

Candide (Bernstein), 373

Canon, 24, *380*

Canova, Antonio, *Pauline Borghese as Venus,* 225, 226

Cantata, 198–99, *380*

Cantilever, 322–23, *380*

Cantus firmus, 120, *380*

Canzona alla francese, 158, 161, *380*

Capital, 46, *380*

The Card Players (Cézanne), (colorplate 70), 292–93

Carillon, 87

Carmen (Bizet), 266

Carmen's Whistle (Byrd), 157

Carnaval (Schumann), 262

Carter, Betty, 368

Carter, Elliott, 374

Cassatt, Mary, *The Bath* (colorplate 67), 291

Catalogue des Oiseaux (Catalog of the Birds) (Messiaen), 373

Cathedrals. *See* Churches

Catlett, Elizabeth, *Singing Head,* 358

Cave paintings, at Lascaux (colorplate 8), 34–36

Cella, 48, *380*

Central Park in the Dark in the Good Old Summertime (Ives), 334

Cézanne, Paul, 292–93
  The Card Players (colorplate 70), 292–93
  Chestnut Trees at Jas de Bouffan in Winter (colorplate 71), 293

Chaconne, 205

Chagall, Marc, 312
    Green Violinist, 312, 313
    I and the Village
        (colorplate 85), 312
Chamber music, *380*
Champillion, Jean François,
    37
Chancel, 85, *380*
Chanson, 158, 161, *380*
Chant, 95, *380*
    Gregorian chant, 95–99
Charpentier, Constance
    Marie, *Portrait of a*
    Young Woman,
    Called Mlle. Charlotte
    du Val d'Ognes
    (colorplate 45), 224
Chartres Cathedral, 114
Chestnut Trees at Jas de
    Bouffan in Winter
    (Cézanne),
    (colorplate 71), 293
Chiaroscuro, 176, *380*
Choir (chancel), 85, *380*
Chopin, Frédéric, 262
    Etude in C Minor,
    Op. 10, no. 12
    (Revolutionary
    Etude), 264
Chorale, 157, *380*
Chord, 27, *380*
Chorus, 59
Christ Entering Jerusalem
    (Duccio), (colorplate
    4), 13
Christianity
    in Baroque period, 170,
        171–72
    cross in art, 75, 85
    early, artistic influences
        for, 74
    early, art of, 74–76
    early, music of, 77–78
    in Gothic period, 103–6
    in Medieval period,
        81–82, 85–88
    in Renaissance, 131, 133
    in Romanesque period,
        88, 92–97

Christ in Glory
    (Sutherland),
    (colorplate 100), 364
Christ lag in Todesbanden
    (Christ Lay in the
    Bonds of Death),
    (Bach), 194, 195,
    207–9
Christ Mocked by Soldiers
    (Rouault), (colorplate
    75), 306
Christo, *Running Fence,*
    357
Chromaticism, 196, *380*
Chronochromie (Time-
    color) (Messiaen),
    373
Chronophagie (Baschet and
    Baschet), 353
Churches
    Byzantine, 75–76
    Christian (early), 74–75
    Gothic period, 105–13,
        114, 116–17
    Medieval period, 85–88
    post-World War II,
        362–66
    Romanesque, 88–92
Circle of Mothers (Kollwitz),
    306
Circles (Berio), 372
Clapton, Eric, 370
Clarinet Quintet in A
    Major (Mozart),
    233–38
Clavier, *380*
Clef, *380*
Clerestory, 111, *380*
Clock Symphony (Haydn),
    230–33
Cloister, *380*
Cluny Abbey, 82–84
Cluster, 27, *380*
Coda, 237, *380*
Collage, 346, 348, *380*
Colonnade, 48, *380*
Color, 14–15, 124, *381*
Colosseum, 68
Columbia Seafirst Center
    (Simons), 361, 362

Column, *381*
    Greece (ancient), 46–48
Complementary colors,
    381
Composition in White,
    Black, and Red
    (Mondrian),
    (colorplate 80), 310
Conceptual art, 344, *381*
Concertato, 200, *381*
Concertino, 200
Concerto, 200–203, 332,
    381
Concerto fatto per la notte
    de Natale (Concerto
    Composed for
    Christmas Eve)
    (Corelli), 201
Concerto for Orchestra
    (Bartók), 332
Concerto grosso, 200, 201,
    202, *381*
Confessions (Rousseau),
    243
Conjunct motion, 23, *381*
Consonance, 27, *381*
Contrapposto, 146, *381*
Contrary motion, *381*
Copland, Aaron, 369
    Appalachian Spring, 373
    Billy the Kid, 373
    Rodeo, 373
Corea, Chick, 368
Corelli, Arcangelo, 175, 201
    Concerto fatto per la
    notte de Natale
    (Concerto Composed
    for Christmas Eve),
    201
Corinthian, 48, *381*
Cornice, 46, *381*
Coronation of King Louis
    XV, 174
Corot, Jean Baptiste
    Camille, 250
    A View Near Volterra
        (colorplate 54), 250
Così fan tutte (Mozart), 236
Counterpoint, 119, *381*
Countersubject, 204, *381*

Couperin, François
  The Bells of Cythera, 217
  La Galante, 217
Courbet, Gustave, 270–71
  Burial at Ornans
    (colorplate 55),
    270–71
Courtly love, 105
*Cow's Skull with Calico
  Roses* (O'Keeffe),
  (colorplate 87), 315
Creation (Michelangelo),
  (colorplate 27),
  141–42
Crete, painting of, 42
Cross
  early Christian, 75
  Medieval period, 85
Crucifixion (of Santa Maria
    del Antiqua),
    (colorplate 14), 93
Crusades, 104–5
Cry (Ailey), 367, 368
Crystal Cathedral, 362–65
Crystal Palace, 251
Cubism, *381*
  painting, 307–10
  sculpture, 316–18
Cubi X (Smith), 354
Cui, César, 282
Current (Riley), 352
Cyclades, sculpture of,
  42–43

D

Dali, Salvador, *The
  Persistence of
  Memory* (colorplate
  82), 311
Dallapiccola, Luigi, *Il
  Prigioniero (The
  Prisoner),* 371
Dante and Virgil in Hell
  (Delacroix),
  (colorplate 50), 247
Daphnis et Chloe (Ravel),
  298

Daumier, Honoré, 271
  *The Third-Class
    Carriage* (colorplate
    56), 271
David (Bernini), 182, 184
David (Donatello), 146
David (Michelangelo),
  147–48, 182
David, Jean Louis, 247
  Oath of the Horatii
    (colorplate 44), 223
Davies, Peter Maxwell, *O
    Magnum Mysterium,*
    376
Davis, Miles, 368
The Dead Christ
  (Mantegna), 133
De Architectura (Vitruvius),
  65
The Death of General Wolfe
  (West), (colorplate
  47), 225
The Death of Klinghoffer
  (Adams), 343
Death of the Virgin (stained
  glass), (colorplate
  17), 114
Debussy, Claude, 295–97
  Golliwog's Cake Walk,
    373
  *Prelude to the Afternoon
    of a Faun,* 297
Degas, Edgar, 294–95
  *Arabesque Ouverte Sur
    La Jambe Droite
    (Open Arabesque on
    the Right Leg),* 294
de Kooning, Willem,
  Woman, I (colorplate
  92), 347
Delacroix, Eugène, 244,
  246–47
  Dante and Virgil in Hell
    (colorplate 50), 247
  *Liberty Leading the
    People* (colorplate
    49), 246
Der Blaue Reiter, 306

Descent from the Cross
  (Rembrandt),
  (colorplate 36), 178
Descriptive music, 272,
  277–79, *381*
The Desert Music (Reich),
  376
Deserts (Varèse), 371
Design, *381*
Desprez, Josquin, 155–56
Development, 228, 231,
  381
Dichterliebe (Poet's Love)
  (Schumann), 262–63
*Die Meistersinger von
  Nürnberg (The
  Mastersingers of
  Nuremberg)*
  (Wagner), 277
Diminution, 204, *381*
Disjunct motion, 23, *381*
Dissonance, 27, 332, *381*
Dr. Tulp's Anatomy Lesson
  (Rembrandt),
  (colorplate 34), 176,
  271
Dodecaphonic, 27, *381*
Dome, 65, *381*
Dominant, 96, *381*
Donatello, Donato de
  Niccolò, 145–46
  David, 146
Don Giovanni (Mozart),
  236
Dorian mode, 96
Doric, 47–48, *381*
Dorsey, Tommy and
  Jimmy, 337
Double Cube Room
  (colorplate 41), 193
Double Metamorphosis II
  (Agam), (colorplate
  95), 352
Drowning Girl
  (Lichtenstein), 349
Duccio di Buoninsegna,
  *Christ Entering
  Jerusalem* (colorplate
  4), 13

Duchamp, Marcel, *Nude Descending a Staircase, No. 2* (colorplate 3), 16
Dürer, Albrecht, 143
    Knight, Death, and the Devil, 143–44
Dvořák, *New World Symphony,* 253
Dynamics, 19, 27–28, *381*

E

Eakins, Thomas, 271
    The Agnew Clinic (colorplate 58), 271
    Max Schmitt in a Single Scull (colorplate 57), 271
Ecstasy of St. Theresa (Bernini), 182, 185
Egypt (ancient), 36–41
    architecture of, 36–37
    music, 41
    painting of, 38
    religion of, 36
    sculpture, 40
Eiffel Tower, 251
Ein Deutsches Requiem, Opus 45 (Brahms), 265
Ein kleine Nachtmusik (Mozart), 2, 30, 31
Einstein on the Beach (Glass), 376
Electronic music, 370–71
El Greco, 164, 172
    Laocoön (colorplate 32), 172
Ellington, Duke, 337, 367
Ellis, Don, 369
Embarkation for the Island of Cythera (Watteau), (colorplate 42), 214
Emotions, produced through the arts, 10–11

Empress Theodora and Retinue (colorplate 13), 76
Ensembles for Synthesizer (Babbitt), 372
Entablature, 46, *381*
Entasis, 48, *382*
Environmental art, 356–57, *382*
Equal temperament, *382*
Erlkönig (Schubert), 29, 253, 258–61
Eroica (Beethoven), 11
The Eternal City (Blume), (colorplate 83), 311–12
Ethos, 59, *382*
Etude in C Minor, Op. 10, no. 12 (Revolutionary Etude) (Chopin), 264
Evenings in the Orchestra (Berlioz), 273
Expectation (Klimt), (colorplate 74), 305
Experimental artists, 303
Experimental music, 373–76
Exposition, 228, 231, *382*
Expressionism, 305–7
    music, 329
    painting, 305, 307
    sculpture, 316

F

Facade, 89, 109, *382*
Falconet, Étienne Maurice, *Punishment of Cupid,* 215
Falstaff (Verdi), 265
Family (Bearden), (colorplate 90), 346
Family Group (Moore), 317, 318
Fantasia on a Theme by Thomas Tallis (Williams), 331

Fantasia on Greensleeves (Williams), 331
Farnese Palace, 152
Faust (Gounod), 266
Fauvism, 305, *382*
Feast at the Home of Nakht (colorplate 9), 41
A Feather on the Breath of God (von Bingen), 125
Ferguson, Maynard, 368
Feudalism, 82–84
Fidelio (Beethoven), 256
Figured bass, 195, *382*
Final, 96, *382*
Fitzgerald, Ella, 368
Five Orchestral Pieces (Webern), 331
Flying buttress, 106, 111, *382*
Foreshortening, 133, *382*
Form, 16, *382*
Form follows function concept, 303–4, 322
Four Minutes and Thirty-three Seconds (Cage), 372
Fra Angelico, 135–36
    Annunciation (colorplate 22), 132
Frederick R. Weisman Art Museum (Gehry), 366–67
Fresco, 42, 118, 141, *382*
Frieze, *382*
    Greece (ancient), 49, 50–51
Froberger, J. J., 175
    Suite in E Minor, 200
Fugue, 204, *382*

G

Gabrieli, Giovanni, 164, 175, 198
    Symphoniae sacrae (Sacred Symphonies), 198

Garnier, Jean-Louis-Charles, 251
Gauguin, Paul, *Mahana No Atua (Day of the Gods)* (colorplate 68), 292
Gehry, Frank, 365, 366–67
    Frederick R. Weisman Art Museum, 366–67
Genre painting, 145, *382*
Géricault, Théodore, 246
    The Raft of the Medusa (colorplate 48), 246, 272
Gershwin, George
    An American in Paris, 334
    Girl Crazy, 334
    Of Thee I Sing, 334
    Piano Concerto in F, 334
    Porgy and Bess, 334
    Rhapsody in Blue, 334, 337
Gesang der Jünglinge (Stockhausen), 28, 371
Giacometti, Alberto, *Man Walking,* 319, 321
Gillespie, Dizzy, 368
Ginevra dé Benci (da Vinci), (colorplate 24), 139
Giorgione, Giorgio
    Pastoral Concert, 289
    Sleeping Venus (colorplate 1), 16
Giotto, 118–19
    Lamentation of Christ (colorplate 19), 118
Gipstein, Yaacov. *See* Agam
Girl Before a Mirror (Picasso), (colorplate 78), 308
Girl Crazy (Gershwin), 334
Giulio Cesare (Julius Caesar) (Handel), 210

Glass, Philip
    Einstein on the Beach, 376
    Koyaanisqatsi, 376
Glinka, Mikhail, *A Life for the Czar,* 282
Gluck
    Alceste, 229
    Orfeo, 229
Golliwog's Cake Walk (Debussy), 373
Goncharova, Natalya
    Linen (colorplate 79), 310
    Rayonist Manifesto, 310
Goodman, Benny, 337
Gothic, use of term, 106
Gothic period
    architecture in, 106–13
    Christianity in, 103–6
    Crusades, 104–5
    music in, 119–25
    painting in, 117–19
    scholasticism in, 103–4
    sculpture in, 115–17
    stained glass in, 113–15
Gounod, Charles, *Faust,* 266
Goya, Francisco, 248
    The Third of May (colorplate 52), 11, 248
Gozzoli, Benozzo, *Journey of the Magi* (colorplate 21), 132, 135
Grateful Dead, 369
The Great Constructors (Léger), 344, 345
Great Sphinx at Giza, 37, 38
Greece (ancient), 43–46
    architecture of, 43, 46–49
    historical ages of, 43–44
    Minoan period, 42–43
    music, 58–60
    painting, 56–58
    religion of, 44–45

sculpture, 50–55
    spread of culture, 53
Green Coca-Cola Bottles (Warhol), (colorplate 88), 343, 349
Green Violinist (Chagall), 312, 313
Gregorian chant, 95–99, *382*
Groined vault, 65, *382*
Gropius, Walter, 326
Grünewald, Mathias, *The Small Crucifixion* (colorplate 29), 143
Guernica (Picasso), 3, 308–9
Guido of Arezzo, 119
The Gulf Stream (Homer), (colorplate 60), 272
Guns and Roses, 370

H

Hagia Sophia, 75, 77
Half step, *382*
Hancock, Herbie, 368
Handel, George Frederic, 175, 209–11
    Giulio Cesare (Julius Caesar), 210
    Messiah, 173, 196, 210, 211
    Water Music Suite, 210
    Xerxes, 210
Handy, W. C.
    "Memphis Blues," 336
    "St. Louis Blues," 336
Happenings, 356, *382*
Hardwick Hall, 153, 154
Harmonielebre (Adams), 376
Harmony, 27, *382*
Hayden, Palmer, 314
    When Tricky Sam Shot Father Lamb, 314
Haydn, Franz Joseph, 229–33
    Clock Symphony, 230–33
Hearst Castle (Morgan), 327

Hendricks, Jimi, 370
Hepworth, Barbara, *Single Form,* 355
Herman, Woody, 367
Hermes with the Infant Dionysus (Praxiteles), 52
Hieroglyphics, 37
Hoffman, Malvina, *Bengali Woman,* 319
Homage to New York (Tinguely), 353
Home Industry (Kollwitz), 306
Homer, Winslow, 272
  The Gulf Stream (colorplate 60), 272
Homophony, 24, 26, 119, *382*
Honegger, Arthur, 369
House of Vetti, 69, 70
Houses of Parliament (London), 250, 251
Hue, 14, *382*
Human Concretion (Arp), 319, 320
Humanism, 4, 130–31, 134, 155, *382*
Hungarian Dances (Brahms), 264
Hydraulis, 73
Hymns, 77–78
A Hymn to the Sun, 59

I

I and the Village (Chagall), (colorplate 85), 312
Il Cimento dell´Armonica e dell´ Invenzione (The Contest between Harmony and Invention) (Vivaldi), 202–3
Il Gesù, 188
Il Prigioniero (The Prisoner) (Luigi), 371

Imaginary Landscape (Cage), 372
Imitation, *382*
Impressionism, *382*
  characteristics of, 287–88
  in music, 295–98
  in painting, 288–93
  Post-Impressionism, 288
  in sculpture, 294–95
Indiana, Robert, *The American Dream* (colorplate 94), 349
Ingres, Jean Auguste Dominique, 224
  The Odalisque with the Slave (colorplate 46), 224
Innsbruck, ich muss dich lassen (Innsbruck, I Must Leave Thee), 157
Innsbruck Lied, 157
Intaglio, 143, *382*
Interior of the Pantheon (Panini), (colorplate 11), 223
Intervals, 23, *382*
Intonation, *382*
Inventions (Bach), 209
Inversion, 204, *382*
Ionic, 48, *382*
Isaac, Heinrich, *Missa Carminum,* 157
Isodorus of Miletos, 77
Isorhythm, 124, *383*
Ives, Charles
  Central Park in the Dark in the Good Old Summertime, 334
  The Unanswered Question, 335

J

Jackson, Michael, 370
James, Harry, 337
Jazz, 334, 336, 367–68, *383*

Jefferson Airplane, 369
Jesuits, 172
Jesus Christ, Superstar, 370
Johns, Jasper, *Target with Four Faces,* 349, 351
Johnson Wax Building (Wright), 324, 325
Jones, Elvin, 368
Jones, Fay, Thorncrown Chapel, 365–66
Jones, Inigo, 193
Jones, Thad, 367
Jonny spielt auf (Johnny Strikes Up the Band) (Krenek), 373
Joplin, Scott
  "Maple Leaf Rag," 336
  "Pineapple Rag," 336
Joseph and Potiphar's Wife (dé Rossi), 148, 149
Journey of the Magi (Gozzoli), (colorplate 21), 132, 135

K

Kandinsky, Wassily, *Painting Number 198* (colorplate 76), 306
Kaufmann House (Wright), 323, 324
Kenton, Stan, 367
Key, *383*
Keystone, *383*
Kindertotenlieder (Songs for the Death of Children) (Mahler), 265
Kinetic art, 320, 353, *383*
  mobiles, 320
King's College Chapel (colorplate 16), 113, 114
The Kiss (Rodin), 295, 296
Klavierstück XI (Piano Piece XI) (Stockhausen), 372

Klavierübung (Bach), 209

Klee, Paul, *Twittering Machine* (colorplate 81), 310, 320, 372

Klimt, Gustav, *Expectation* (colorplate 74), 305

Kneeling Woman (Lehmbruck), 316, 317

Knight, Death, and the Devil (Dürer), 143–44

Kollwitz, Käthe, 306–7
    Call of Death, 306–7
    Circle of Mothers, 306
    Home Industry, 306
    Peasants' War, 306

Komm, Gott Schöpfer, heiliger Geist (Come, O Creator Spirit) (Walter), 157

Kontakte (Stockhausen), 371

Koyaanisqatsi (Glass), 376

Krenek, *Jonny spielt auf (Johnny Strikes Up the Band),* 373

Kyrie fons bonitatis, 97–99

L

La Boheme (Puccini), 266

La Campanella (The Bell) (Liszt), 278

La Galante (Couperin), 217

La Madeleine, tympanum of, 92, 94

Lamentation of Christ (Giotto), (colorplate 19), 118–19

Laocoön (El Greco), (colorplate 32), 172

Laocoön and His Two Sons, 55, 57

Las Meninas (Maids of Honor) (Velásquez), (colorplate 39), 181

Last Judgment (Michelangelo), (colorplate 26), 141

The Last Supper (da Vinci), (colorplate 25), 139–40, 175

Last Supper (Tintoretto), (colorplate 33), 175, 197

La Tempête (Boulanger), 298

Lauda, 125, *383*

Laurentian Library, stairwells of, 186

La Vista (Marisol), (colorplate 98), 356

Lawrence, Jacob, *Vaudeville* (colorplate 89), 344

Leaning Tower of Pisa, 87

Le Création du monde (The Creation of the World) (Milhaud), 373

Le Déjuener sur l'Herbe (Luncheon on the Grass) (Manet), (colorplate 61), 289

Led Zeppelin, 370

Léger, Fernand, *The Great Constructors,* 344, 345

Lehmbruck, Wilhelm, *Kneeling Woman,* 316, 317

Leitmotif, 265, 277, 278, *383*

Le Moulin de la Galette (Renoir), (colorplate 66), 291

Le Sacre du printemps (The Rite of Spring) (Stravinsky), 331

Les Demoiselles d'Avignon (Picasso), (colorplate 77), 307–8

Les Misérables, 370

Les Preludes (Liszt), 278

Les Sirènes (Boulanger), 298

Le Travail du Peintre (The Work of the Painter) (Eluard), 304

Lewis, John, 368, 373

Lewis, Mel, 367

Liberty Leading the People (Delacroix), (colorplate 49), 246

Libretto, 236, 284, *383*

Lichtenstein, Roy, *Drowning Girl,* 349

Lied/Lieder, 158, 161–62, 257–61, 262–63, *383*

A Life for the Czar (Glinka), 282

Life of Christ (Giotto), 118

Ligeti, Gyorgi
    Lux Aeterna, 374
    Wind Quintet, 374

Line, 12–13, *383*

Linear perspective, 13, *383*

Linen (Goncharova), (colorplate 79), 310

Lintel, 37, 66, *383, 385*

Liszt, Franz
    La Campanella (The Bell), 278
    Les Preludes, 278
    Piano Concerto no. 1 in E-flat, 278

Litanie, Prayers of St. John Chrysostom for Each Hour of the Day and Night (Pärt), 376

Liturgy, 85, *383*

L'Oiseau de feu (The Firebird) (Stravinsky), 331

Lombardo, Guy, 337

Louvre, 191

Lux Aeterna (Ligeti), 374

Lydian mode, 96

Lyra, 57, 59, *383*

Lyric Age, Greece, 43

Lysippus, *Aphrodite (Venus de Medici),* 53, 54

M

Machaut, Guillaume de,
        Messa de Notre Dame
        (Kyrie), 122–24
Madame de Pompadour
        (Boucher),
        (colorplate 43), 214,
        224
Madonna, 369–70
Madrigal, 158, 159–60, *383*
The Magic Flute (Mozart),
        236
*Mahana No Atua (Day of
        the Gods)* (Gauguin),
        (colorplate 68), 292
Mahler, Gustav, 264, 265
        *Kindertotenlieder (Songs
        for the Death of
        Children),* 265
        *Symphony no. 4 in G
        Major,* 265
Major, 27, *383*
Manet, Edouard, *Le
        Déjuener sur l'Herbe
        (Luncheon on the
        Grass)* (colorplate
        61), 289
Mannerism, 163–64, *383*
Mantegna, *The Dead Christ,*
        133, 134
Man Walking (Giacometti),
        319, 321
"Maple Leaf Rag" (Joplin),
        336
Marisol, *La Vista*
        (colorplate 98), 356
Marley, Bob, 370
Marriage of Figaro
        (Mozart), 236–38
Marsalis, Branford, 368, 370
Martini, Simone, *The
        Annunciation*
        (colorplate 18), 118
Mary, Queen of Scots
        (Musgrave), 374
Mass, 95, *383*
Mass (Bernstein), 370, 373

Mass in B Minor (Bach),
        173
Matisse, Henri, 305
        The Blue Window
        (colorplate 73), 305
Ma Vlast (My Fatherland)
        (Smetana), 282
*Max Schmitt in a Single
        Scull* (Eakins),
        (colorplate 57), 271
McLaughlin, John, 368
McRae, Carmen, 368
Measure, 20, *383*
Medici, Lorenzo de, 132
Medici, Piero de, 132
Medieval period, 81–88
        characteristics of, 81–85
        Christian influence on
                art, 81–82, 85–88
        feudalism, 82–84
        music in, 88
        religion in, 81–82
        time span of, 81
        See also Gothic period;
                Romanesque period
Medium, 12, *383*
Melismas, 97
Melody, 22–23, *383*
"Memphis Blues" (Handy),
        336
Mendelssohn, Felix, 262
        *A Midsummer Night's
        Dream,* 263
Mendelssohn-Hensel,
        Fanny, 262
Messa de Notre Dame
        (Kyrie) (Machaut),
        122–24
Messiaen, Oliver
        *Catalogue des Oiseaux
        (Catalog of the
        Birds),* 373
        *Chronochromie (Time-
        color),* 373
        *Mode de Valeurs et
        d'Intensitè (Mode of
        Durations and
        Volume),* 373
Messiah (Handel), 173, 196,
        210, 211

Meter, 20–22, *383*
Meter signature, 20, *383*
Metope, 49, *383*
Michelangelo, 133, 140–42,
        145
        Creation (colorplate 27),
                141–42
        David, 147–48, 182
        and Farnese Palace, 152
        Last Judgment
                (colorplate 26), 141
        and St. Peter's, 153
        stairway of the
                Laurentian Library,
                186
*A Midsummer Night's
        Dream*
        (Mendelssohn), 263
Milhaud, Darius, *Le
        Création du monde
        (The Creation of the
        World),* 373
Miller, Glenn, 337
Mingus, Charles, 368
Minimalism
        Minimal Art, 353–56,
                383
        music, 376, *383*
Minnesinger, 124–25, *384*
Minor, 27, *384*
Minuet, 228, 231, *384*
Miró, Joan, *Person
        Throwing a Stone at
        a Bird* (colorplate
        84), 312
Missa Carminum (Isaac),
        157
Miss Saigon, 370
Mixolydian mode, 96
Mlle. Pogany (Brancusi),
        317, 318
Mobile, 320, *384*
Modality, 27, *384*
*Mode de Valeurs et
        d'Intensitè (Mode of
        Durations and
        Volume)* (Messiaen),
        373

Modernism
    in architecture, 321–27
    artists of, 303, 304
    characteristics of, 302–4,
        321–22
    form follows function
        concept, 303–4, 322
    kinetic art, 320
    in music, 327–38
    in painting, 304–15
    principles of, 303–4
    in sculpture, 315–20
Modes, 96, *384*
Modulation, *384*
Mona Lisa (da Vinci), 17,
    139
Monasteries, Medieval,
    82–84
Monastery Church of Melk,
    190–91
Mondrian, Piet,
    *Composition in
    White, Black, and
    Red* (colorplate 80),
    310
Monet, Claude
    *Banks of the Seine,
    Vétheuil* (colorplate
    62), 289–90
    *Rouen Cathedral, West
    Facade* (colorplate
    63), 248, 290
Monk, Thelonius, 368
Monochromaticism, 15,
    384
Monody, 125, *384*
Monophony, 24, *384*
Monteverdi, Claudio, 164,
    175, 197
    Orfeo, 197
Monticello, 151
Moore, Henry, 316–17
    Family Group, 317, 318
Morgan, Julia, 326–27
    Berkeley City Club, 327
    Hearst Castle, 327
Morisot, Berthe, *Young
    Girl by the Window*
    (colorplate 64), 290

Mosaic, *384*
    Byzantine, 75–76
Motet, 154, *384*
Motive, 22, *384*
Mozart, Wolfgang
    Amadeus, 229,
        233–38
    *The Abduction from the
    Seraglio,* 236
    *Clarinet Quintet in A
    Major,* 233–35
    Cosí fan tutte, 236
    Don Giovanni, 236
    Ein kleine Nachtmusik,
        2, 30, 31
    The Magic Flute, 236
    The Marriage of Figaro,
        236–38
    *Symphony No. 40 in G
    Minor,* 235
Multimedia performances,
    372
Mural, 312–13, *384*
    Greece (ancient), 56
Musgrave, Thea, *Mary,
    Queen of Scots,* 374
Music
    aleatoric music, 370, 372
    ballet music, 373
    Baroque period, 173,
        194–211
    blues, 336
    Broadway musicals, 338,
        370
    compared to visual arts,
        31
    concerto, 200–203, 332,
        381
    descriptive music, 272,
        277–79
    dynamics in, 19, 27–28
    Egypt (ancient), 41
    electronic music, 370–71
    experimental music,
        373–76
    expressive content in,
        29
    Gothic period, 119–25
    Greece (ancient), 58–60

    harmony in, 27
    Impressionism, 295–98
    instrumental music,
        199–211, 229
    jazz, 334, 336–37,
        367–68
    Medieval period, 88
    melody in, 22–23
    minimalist music, 376,
        383
    Modernism, 327–38
    multimedia
        performances, 372
    Nationalism, 280–84,
        331
    Neoclassical period,
        225–38
    opera, 195, 197, 229,
        236–38, 265–66,
        277–78, *384*
    organizational principles
        in, 29
    piano compositions,
        254, 256–57, 263–64,
        278
    pitch in, 22
    popular music, 334–38,
        367–70
    post-World War II,
        367–76
    program music, 272,
        273–76, *385*
    Protestant, 154, 156–57
    ragtime, 336, *385*
    Renaissance, 133,
        153–63
    rhythm in, 19–22
    rock music, 368–70
    Rococo period, 217
    Romanesque period,
        94–99
    Romantic period,
        251–66
    Rome (ancient), 73–74
    sacred music of early
        Christians, 77–78
    sacred music of Gothic
        period, 120–24, 125

sacred music of
    Medieval era, 94–99
sacred music of
    Protestantism, 154,
    156–57, 173, 198–99
sacred music of
    Renaissance, 154–57
secular music of
    Renaissance, 157–63
suite, 199–200, *386*
swing, 337, *386*
symphony, 230–33, 235,
    256–57, *386*
texture in, 24–26
tone color (timbre) in,
    28, *386*
vocal music, 195–99,
    254, 257–61, 263
Mussorgsky, Modest, 282
    Boris Godunov, 283
Mycenae, art objects of, 43

N

National Gallery of Art,
    East Building (Pei),
    (colorplate 99), 360
Nationalism, 243
    characteristics of,
        280–81
    in music, 280–84, 331
    in painting, 280
Nave, 89, *384*
Needle (Bourgeois), 359
Neoclassical period
    classic ideals in, 222–23
    music in, 225–38
    painting in, 223–25
    sculpture in, 225
Neumes, 97, *384*
New World Symphony
    (Dvořák), 253
The Night Watch
    (Rembrandt),
    (colorplate 35), 177,
    178

*Nike of Samothrace
    (Winged Victory),* 55,
    56
Nixon in China (Adams),
    376
Non-objective art, *384*
Note, *384*
Notre Dame, 108
Notre Dame la Grande at
    Poitiers, 89, 90
*Nude Descending a
    Staircase, No. 2*
    (Duchamp),
    (colorplate 3), 16
Number 1, 1948 (Pollock),
    (colorplate 91), 346
Number 19 (Rothko),
    (colorplate 93), 347

O

Oath of the Horatii (David),
    (colorplate 44), 223
Obelisk, Egyptian, 37
*The Odalisque with the
    Slave* (Ingres),
    (colorplate 46), 224
Office hours, 99, *384*
Of Thee I Sing (Gershwin),
    334
Oinochoe, 57, *384*
O'Keeffe, Georgia, *Cow's
    Skull with Calico
    Roses* (colorplate 87),
    315
Oldenburg, Claes, *The
    Toilet,* 349, 351
Old St. Peter's, 75, 76
O Magnum Mysterium
    (Davies), 376
Op Art, 350–53, *384*
Opera, 195, 197, 229,
    236–38, 265–66,
    277–78, *384*
Opera seria, 210, *384*
Opus, *384*
Orchestra, 254
Order, *384*

Ordinary, 95–96, 97, 99,
    384
Orfeo (Gluck), 229
Orfeo (Monteverdi), 197
Organum, 120, *384*
Or la truix, 125
Ornamentation, 200, *384*
Otello (Verdi), 265

P

Painting
    Abstract Expressionism,
        346–47, *379*
    action painting, 346–47,
        379
    Art Nouveau, 305
    Baroque period, 172,
        173, 175–82
    collage, 346, 348
    conceptual art, 344, *381*
    Cubism, 307–10, *381*
    Der Blaue Reiter, 306,
        380
    Egypt (ancient), 38
    expressionism, 305–7,
        382
    Fauvism, 305, *382*
    Gothic period, 117–19
    Greece (ancient), 56–58
    Impressionism, 288–93,
        382
    Kinetic Art, 353, *383*
    Minoan, 42
    Modernism, 304–15
    murals, 312–13
    Nationalism, 280
    Neoclassical period,
        223–25
    Op Art, 350–53, *384*
    Photo-Realism, 344, 353
    Pop Art, 347–49, *385*
    Post-Impressionism,
        288, 292–93, *385*
    post-World War II,
        344–53
    Realism in, 270–72
    Renaissance, 133–45

Rococo period, 213–14
Romanesque period, 92–94
Romantic period, 245–50
Surrealism, 310–15, *386*
Painting Number 198 (Kandinsky), (colorplate 76), 306
Pair Statue of Mycerinus and His Queen, 40
Paleolithic period, art of, 34–36
Palestrina, Giovanni Pierluigi, 156
Veni sponsa Christi, 156, 194, 195
Palladio, Andrea, Villa Rotonda, 151–52
Panini, *Interior of the Pantheon* (colorplate 11), 223
Pantheon, 66–67, 151
Parallel motion, *384*
Paris Opera, 251, 252
Parker, Charlie, 367–68
Pärt, Arvo
Litanie, Prayers of St. John Chrysostom for Each Hour of the Day and Night, 376
When Sarah was Ninety Years Old, 376
Parthenon, 43, 44, 48–50, 90, 130
Passacaglia, 205, *385*
Passacaglia and Fugue in C Minor (Bach), 196, 205–7
Passion According to St. Matthew (Bach), 2, 157, 205
Pastoral Concert (Giorgione), 289
Pastorius, Jaco, 368
Patronage
Church as patron, 94–95, 132–33

Renaissance, 132–33
Romantic era, 244–45
Pauline Borghese as Venus (Canova), 225, 226
Peasants' War (Kollwitz), 306
Pediment, 47, *385*
Peeters, Clara, 182
Set Table (colorplate 40), 182
Pei, I. M., National Gallery of Art, East Building (colorplate 99), 360
Penderecki, Krzysztof
Polish Requiem, 374
St. Luke Passion, 374
Threnody for the Victims of Hiroshima, 3, 29, 343, 374–75
Pentatonic, *385*
Perotin, *Alleluia*, 120–22
The Persistence of Memory (Dali), (colorplate 82), 311
Person Throwing a Stone at a Bird (Miró), (colorplate 84), 312
Petrouchka (Stravinsky), 331, 332
The Phantom of the Opera, 370
Photo-Realism, 344, 353
Phrase, 22, *385*
Phrygian mode, 96, 99
Piano compositions, 254, 256–57, 263–64, 278
Piano Concerto in F (Gershwin), 334
Piano Concerto no. 1 in E-flat (Liszt), 278
Picasso, Pablo
Girl Before a Mirror (colorplate 78), 308
Guernica, 3, 308–9
Les Demoiselles d'Avignon (colorplate 77), 307–8

Pictures at an Exhibition (Ravel), 298
Pier, 89, *385*
"Pineapple Rag" (Joplin), 336
Pisano, Giovanni, *Annunciation, Nativity, and Shepherds*, 117
Pitch, 22, *385*
Poème Electronique (Varèse), 371
Polish Requiem (Penderecki), 374
Pollock, Jackson, *Number 1, 1948* (colorplate 91), 346
Polychromaticism, 15, *385*
Polyphony, 24, 25, 119, *385*
Polytonality, 327, *385*
Pont du Gard, 68–69
Pop Art, 347–49, *385*
Popular music, 334–38, 367–70
Porch of the Maidens-Erechtheum, 51, 55
Porgy and Bess (Gershwin), 334
Porta, Giacomo della, 188
Portico, 66, *385*
Portrait of a Negress (Benoist), (colorplate 51), 247
Portrait of a Young Woman, called Mlle. Charlotte du Val d'Ognes (Charpentier), (colorplate 45), 224
Post and lintel, 37, 66, *385*
Post-Impressionism, 288, *385*
painting of, 292
Post-Modernism, use of term, 344
Pozzo, Fra Andrea, 182
Apotheosis of St. Ignatius, 183

Praxiteles, *Hermes with the Infant Dionysus,* 52
Prelude to the Afternoon of a Faun (Debussy), 297
Presley, Elvis, 368
Primary colors, 14–15, *385*
Principale, *385*
Program music, 272, 273–76, *385*
Prokofiev, Serge, 369
Proper, 95–96, 99, *385*
Protestantism
  in Baroque period, 171, 172
  music of, 154, 156–57, 173, 198–99
  Reformation, 131
  in Renaissance, 131, 143, 145
Psalms, 77–78
Puccini, Giacomo, 264, 266
  La Boheme, 266
Pugin, A. Welby, 250, 251
Punishment of Cupid (Falconet), 215
Purim, Flora, 368
Pyramids, 36–37
  Pyramids of Giza, 37

Q

Quadrivium, 103–4
Quote (Rauschenberg), 342, 348

R

The Raft of the Medusa (Géricault), (colorplate 48), 246, 272
Ragtime, 336, *385*
Rain, Steam, and Speed: The Great Western Railway (Turner), (colorplate 53), 249–50

Rape of the Daughters of Leucippus (Rubens), (colorplate 37), 181
Raphael, Sanzio, 133
  School of Athens (colorplate 6), 13, 16, 142
  Sistine Madonna (colorplate 7), 16, 18, 31, 135, 143
Rap music, 369
Rauschenberg, Robert, *Quote,* 342, 348
Ravel, Maurice, 298
  Daphnis et Chloe, 298
  Pictures at an Exhibition, 298
Rayonist Manifesto (Goncharova), 310
Realism, 243, 266, 270–80
  characteristics of, 270
  in music, 272–79
  and Nationalism, 281, 282
  in painting, 270–72
Recapitulation, 228, *385*
Recitative, 195, 237, *385*
Reich, Steve, *The Desert Music,* 376
Reims Cathedral, 109–11
  Rose Window (colorplate 15), 110
Relief sculpture, *385*
  Greece (ancient), 45
Religion
  Egypt (ancient), 36
  Greece (ancient), 44–45
  Rome (ancient), 64
  See also Christianity; Protestantism; Sacred music
R.E.M., 370
Rembrandt van Rijn, 172, 175, 176–80
  Descent from the Cross (colorplate 36), 178
  Dr. Tulp's Anatomy Lesson (colorplate 34), 176, 271

The Night Watch (colorplate 35), 177, 178
  Supper at Emmaus, 171, 178–79
The Remnants of an Army (Thompson), (colorplate 59), 272
Renaissance
  architecture in, 149–53
  characteristics of, 130–34
  Christianity in, 131, 133
  Greek influences, 130, 149, 151–53, 196
  humanism in, 130–31, 134, 155
  mannerism in, 163–64
  music in, 133
  painting in, 133–45
  patronage during, 132–33
  Protestantism in, 131, 143, 145
  sacred music in, 153–57
  sculpture in, 145–48
  secular music in, 157–63
Renoir, Pierre-Auguste, 290–91
  By the Seashore (colorplate 65), 290
  Le Moulin de la Galette (colorplate 66), 291
Requiem (Verdi), 266
Rests, 19, *385*
Retrogression, 204, *385*
Rhapsody in Blue (Gershwin), 334, 337
Rhythm, 19–22, *385*
Ricercare, 158, *385*
Riemenschneider, Tilman, 148
  Assumption of the Blessed Virgin, 148, 150
Riley, Bridget, *Current,* 352
Rimsky-Korsakov, Nikolai, 282
Ripieno, 200, *385*

Ritornelli, 197
Rivera, Diego, 312–13
   "Detroit Industry"
      (colorplate 86), 313
"Rock Around the Clock"
   (Bill Haley and the
   Comets), 368
Rock music, 368–70
Rococo, use of term, 212,
   385
Rococo period, 211–17
   architecture in, 216
   characteristics of,
      211–13
   music in, 217
   painting in, 213–14
   sculpture in, 215
   time span of, 212
Rodeo (Copland), 373
Rodin, Auguste, 295, 296
   The Kiss, 295
Rolling Stones, 369
Romanesque, use of term,
   88
Romanesque period, 88–99
   architecture in, 88–91
   artistic influences for, 88
   Christianity in, 88, 92–97
   music in, 94–99
   painting in, 92–94
   sculpture in, 91–92
   time period of, 88
Romantic, use of term, 242
Romantic period
   architecture in, 250–51
   characteristics of,
      242–45
   combining of arts in,
      244
   life of artist in, 244
   music in, 251–66
   and Nationalism, 280
   painting in, 245–50
   and patronage, 244–45
Rome (ancient), 63–78
   architecture of, 65–69
   Christian art, 74–76
   Christian music, 77–78

Greece influence, 63–64,
   66–67, 69–70, 73
music, 73–74
religion of, 64
rise of, 63
sculpture, 69–73
Rondo, 228, 262, 279, 385
Rossi, Properzia dé, Joseph
   and Potiphar's Wife,
   148, 149
Rothko, Mark, Number 19
   (colorplate 93), 347
Rouault, Georges, 306
   Christ Mocked by
      Soldiers (colorplate
      75), 306
Rouen Cathedral, West
   Facade (Monet),
   (colorplate 63), 248,
   290
Round, 24, 385
Rousseau, Jean Jacques,
   243
Rubens, Peter Paul, 172,
   173, 175, 180–81
   The Assumption of the
      Virgin (colorplate
      38), 181
   Rape of the Daughters of
      Leucippus (colorplate
      37), 181
Rubinstein, Anton, 282
Ruisdael, Wheatfields
   (colorplate 5), 13, 16
Running Fence (Cristo),
   357

S

Sacred music
   of early Christians,
      77–78
   of Gothic period,
      120–24, 125
   of Medieval period,
      94–99

of Protestantism, 154,
   156–57, 173, 198–99
of Renaissance, 157–63
"St. Louis Blues" (Handy),
   336
St. Luke Passion
   (Penderecki), 374
St. Paul's Cathedral, 192–93
St. Peter's, 133, 153
   old, 75, 76
   plaza of, 190–91
Saint Phalle, Niki de,
   355–56
   Black Venus (colorplate
      97), 356
St. Trophime, portal of, 92,
   93
Salisbury Cathedral, 112
Salon of Marie Antoinette,
   216
San Ambrogio, 89–91
Sandoval, Arturo, 368
Sant' Agnese (Borromini),
   189
San Vitale, church of
   (colorplate 12), 76
Saturation, 15, 385
Scale, 385
Scarlatti, Domenico, 175, 199
Schloss Augustusburg
   castle, stairwell at,
   186, 187
Schoenberg, Arnold,
   328–29, 370
   Serenade, op. 24, 329
Scholasticism, 103
School of Athens (Raphael),
   (colorplate 6), 13, 142
Schubert, Franz, 257–61
   Erlkönig, 29, 253,
      258–61
   Symphony in C Major
      (The Great), 261
   Unfinished, 261
Schuller, Anthony, 368
Schuller, Gunther, 373
   Seven Studies on Themes
      of Paul Klee, 372
Schumann, Clara, 262

Schumann, Robert, 262–63
    Carnaval, 262
    *Dichterliebe (Poet's
        Love),* 262–63
Schütz, Heinrich, 175,
    198–99
Score, 19, *385*
Sculpture
    Baroque period, 182–85
    Cubism, 316–18, *381*
    Cycladic, 42
    Egypt (ancient), 40
    environmental art,
        356–57, *382*
    Expressionism, 316, *382*
    Gothic period, 115–17
    Greece (ancient), 50–55
    Impressionism, 294–95,
        382
    Minimalist, 353–56
    Modernism, 315–20
    Neoclassical period, 225
    post-World War II,
        353–59
    Renaissance, 145–48
    Rococo period, 215
    Romanesque period,
        91–92
    Rome (ancient), 69–73
    Surrealism, 319, *386*
Secco, 237
Secondary colors, 14–15
Second Council of Nicaea,
    85
Sensationalist artists, 303
Sequence, *386*
Serenade (Schoenberg),
    329
Serialism, 327, 330–31,
    371–72, *386*
Set Table (Peeters),
    (colorplate 40), 182
Seurat, Georges Pierre,
    *Sunday Afternoon on
    the Island of La
    Grande Jatte*
    (colorplate 69), 292

*Seven Studies on Themes of
    Paul Klee* (Schuller),
    372
Shorter, Wayne, 368
Shostakovich, Dmitri, 369
Sibelius, Jean, 369
Siena Cathedral, 117, 118
Signature, *386*
Simons, Chris, Columbia
    Seafirst Center, 361,
    362
Singing Head (Catlett), 358
Single Form (Hepworth),
    355
Sistine Chapel, 141–42
Sistine Madonna (Raphael),
    (colorplate 7), 16, 18,
    31, 135, 143
Skolion of Seikilos, 59
Skyscrapers, 360–61
Sleeping Venus
    (Giorgione),
    (colorplate 1), 16
The Small Crucifixion
    (Grünewald),
    (colorplate 29), 143
Smetana, Bedřich, 281–82
    *Ma Vlast (My
        Fatherland),* 282
    Vltava (The Moldau),
        282
Smiling Angel, 111
Smith, David, *Cubi X,* 354
Smithson, Robert, *Spiral
    Jetty,* 356, 357
Social Contract (Rousseau),
    243
Sociocultural aspects, of
    arts, 1–4
Solo concerto, 200
Sonata, 227–29, *386*
Sonata-allegro form, 228,
    229, 231, *386*
Song form, 228, *386*
Space, 13–14
Spem in alium (Tallis), 157
Sphinxes, 37
Spiral Jetty (Smithson), 356,
    357

Stained glass
    development of, 114
    Gothic period, 113–15
The Starry Night (van
    Gogh), (colorplate
    72), 11, 293
Statue of Athena, 48
Steel cage, 322–23, *386*
Step Pyramid of Saqqara,
    36
Stockhausen, Karlheinz
    Gesang der Jünglinge,
        28, 371
    *Klavierstück XI (Piano
        Piece XI),* 372
    Kontakte, 371
    Zeitmass, 371, 372
Strauss, Richard, 278–79
    Till Eulenspiegel, 279
Stravinsky, Igor
    *Le Sacre du printemps
        (The Rite of Spring),*
        331–32
    *L'Oiseau de feu (The
        Firebird),* 331
    Petrouchka, 331, 332
Stretto, 204, *386*
*String Quartet no. 16, op.
    135* (Beethoven),
    255–56
Strophic song, 258
*Study for Differing Views:
    Dog, 1981* (Valerio),
    (colorplate 96), 353
Style, 2, *386*
    in visual arts, 16
Stylobate, 46, *386*
Subject, 204
Suger, Abbot, 107–8
Suite, 199–200, *386*
Suite in E Minor
    (Froberger), 200
*Sunday Afternoon on the
    Island of La Grande
    Jatte* (Seurat),
    (colorplate 69), 292
Supper at Emmaus
    (Rembrandt), 171,
    178–79

Surrealism, *386*
    painting, 310–15
    sculpture, 319
Sutherland, Graham, *Christ in Glory* (colorplate 100), 364
Swing, 337, *386*
Symphoniae sacrae (Sacred Symphonies) (Gabrieli), 198
Symphonic cantata, 265
Symphonie fantastique (Berlioz), 11, 273–76
Symphony, 230–33, 235, 256–57, *386*
Symphony in C Major (The Great) (Schubert), 261
Symphony no. 1 (Bernstein), 373
Symphony no. 1 in C Minor, Opus 68 (Brahms), 265
Symphony no. 3 in E-flat Major (Beethoven), 255–56
Symphony no. 4 in F Minor (Tchaikovsky), 283
Symphony no. 4 in G Major (Mahler), 265
Symphony no. 40 in G Minor (Mozart), 235
Syncopation, 336, *386*

T

Talea, 124, *386*
Tallis, Thomas, *Spem in alium,* 157
Target with Four Faces (Johns), 349, 352
Tchaikovsky, Piotr Ilyitch, 282, 283
    Symphony no. 4 in F Minor, 283
Tempera, *386*
Temple at Karnak, 37, 39
Temple at Luxor, 37

Temple at Pergamum, 53
Temple of Amon, 38
Temples, Greece (ancient), 46–50
Tempo, 20, *386*
10,000 Maniacs, 370
Tessitura, *386*
Texture, 24–26, *386*
Theme, *386*
Theotocopoulos, Domenicos. *See* El Greco
The Third-Class Carriage (Daumier), (colorplate 56), 271
The Third of May (Goya), (colorplate 52), 11, 248
Third-Stream Performance Ensembles, 373
Thompson, Elizabeth, 272
    The Remnants of an Army (colorplate 59), 272
Thorncrown Chapel (Jones), 365–66
The Three Fates, 49, 50
Threnody for the Victims of Hiroshima (Penderecki), 3, 29, 343, 374–75
Through-composed, *386*
Thrust, *386*
Thyrsis? Sleepest Thou? (Bennet), 159–60
Till Eulenspiegel (Strauss), 279
Tinguely, Jean, *Homage to New York,* 353
Tintoretto, Jacopo, 164, 175
    Last Supper (colorplate 33), 175, 197
Titian, Tiziani Vecelli, 142
    Venus and Adonis (colorplate 28), 142
The Toilet (Oldenburg), 349, 351

Tommy, 370
Tonality, 27, *386*
Tone, 22, *386*
Tone color (timbre), 28, 253
Tonic, *386*
Tower of Power, 370
Tracery, *386*
Transept, *386*
Triad, *386*
Triglyph, 49, *387*
Trio, 231, 237–38, *387*
Trivium, 103–4
Troubadours, 105, 124–25, *387*
Trouvères, 105, 124–25, *387*
Turner, J. M. W., 248–50
    Rain, Steam, and Speed: The Great Western Railway (colorplate 53), 249–50
Tutti, 200, *387*
Twelve-tone system, 329–30, *387*
Twentieth century, post-World War II
    architecture in, 359–67
    characteristics of era, 342–43
    music in, 367–76
    painting in, 344–53
    sculpture in, 353–59
    See also Modernism
Twittering Machine (Klee), (colorplate 81), 310, 320, 372
Tympanum, 92, *387*
Tyner, McCoy, 368

U

U2, 370
The Unanswered Question (Ives), 335
Unfinished (Schubert), 261
United Nations, 360–61

V

Valerio, James, *Study for Differing Views: Dog, 1981* (colorplate 96), 353
Value, 15, *387*
van Gogh, Vincent, 293
    The Starry Night (colorplate 72), 11, 293
Varèse, Edgar
    Deserts, 371
    Poème Electronique, 371
Variation form, 228, *387*
Variations on a Theme by Haydn, Opus 56a (Brahms), 264
Vaudeville (Lawrence), (colorplate 89), 344
Vault, 65, *387*
Velásquez, Diego, 175, 181
    Las Meninas (Maids of Honor) (colorplate 39), 181
Veni sponsa Christi (Palestrina), 156, 194, 195
Ventadorn, Bernart de, 124
Venus and Adonis (Titian), (colorplate 28), 142
Venus of Willendorf, 34–35, 43, 356
Verdi, Giuseppe, 264–66
    Falstaff, 265
    Otello, 265
    Requiem, 266
Vibrato, *387*
A View Near Volterra (Corot), (colorplate 54), 250
Vignola, Giacomo da, 188
Villa Rotonda (Palladio), 151–52
Vinci, Leonardo da, 3, 133, 138–40, 145
    Adoration of the Magi, 138–39

Ginevra de´ Benci (colorplate 24), 139
The Last Supper (colorplate 25), 139–40, 175
Mona Lisa, 17, 139
Violin Concerto (Berg), 330
Visual arts
    color in, 14–15
    compared to music, 31
    expressive content in, 16
    form in, 16
    line in, 12–13
    medium in, 12
    organizational principles in, 15–17
    space in, 13–14
    style in, 16
Vivaldi, Antonio, 175, 201–4
    Il Cimento dell´ Armonica e dell´ Invenzione (The Contest Between Harmony and Invention), 202–3
Vltava (The Moldau) (Smetana), 282
Vocal music, 195–99, 254, 257–61
Voice, 24, *387*

W

Wagner, Richard, 277–78
    Die Meistersinger von Nürnberg (The Mastersingers of Nuremberg), 277
Walter, Johann, *Komm, Gott Schöpfer, heiliger Geist (Come, O Creator Spirit),* 157
Warhol, Andy, *Green Coca-Cola Bottles* (colorplate 88), 343, 349

War Requiem (Britten), 343
Water Music Suite (Handel), 210
Watteau, Antoine, *Embarkation for the Island of Cythera* (colorplate 42), 214
Watzek House (Wright), 324, 325
Webern, Anton, 330–31
    Five Orchestral Pieces, 331
The Wedding Dance (Brueghel), (colorplate 31), 145
Weihnachtsoratorium (Christmas Oratorio) (Bach), 201
Wells Cathedral, 112–13
The Well-Tempered Clavier (Bach), 205
West, Benjamin, 224–25
    The Death of General Wolfe (colorplate 47), 225
West Side Story (Bernstein), 373
Wheatfields (Ruisdael), (colorplate 5), 13, 16
When Sarah was Ninety Years Old (Pärt), 376
When Tricky Sam Shot Father Lamb (Hayden), 314
Whistler, James, 291
Whiteman, Paul, 337
Whole-tone scale, 297, *387*
Williams, Tony, 368
Williams, Vaughan
    Fantasia on a Theme by Thomas Tallis, 331
    Fantasia on Greensleeves, 331
Wilton House, 193
Wind Quintet (Ligeti), 374
Winged Victory (Nike of Samothrace), 55, 56

Winter, Return of the Hunters (Brueghel), (colorplate 30), 145
Woman, I (de Kooning), (colorplate 92), 347
Wonderful Town (Bernstein), 373
Wood, Grant, *American Gothic* (colorplate 2), 16
Woods, Phil, 368
Wren, Christopher, 191–93
   St. Paul's Cathedral, 192–93

Wright, Frank Lloyd, 323–26
   Johnson Wax Building, 324, 325
   Kaufmann House, 323, 324
   Watzek House, 324, 325

X

Xerxes (Handel), 210

Y

Young Girl by the Window (Morisot), (colorplate 64), 290

Z

Zawinul, Joe, 368
Zeitmass (Stockhausen), 371, 372